THERE AND BACK AGAIN

A CHILD OF THE SIXTIES RETURNS TO HIS CATHOLIC ROOTS

JOE SHANNON

DEDICATION
IN THE SPIRIT OF LUKE 11:9

TO ALL WHO ASK, MAY YOU RECEIVE
TO ALL WHO SEEK, MAY YOU FIND
TO ALL WHO KNOCK, MAY THE DOOR BE OPENED
AND TO YOU, FELLOW PILGRIMS,
COME WHAT MAY, CARRY ON. . .

JOE

TABLE OF CONTENTS

ACKNOWLEDGMENTS

I hardly know where to begin as it's been over a decade since I first purchased a stack of legal pads and thought to myself, "Well, guess I may as well start at the beginning." Three wonderful, talented folks spent hours helping me with the editing. First, Devra Torres, who I'd been introduced to at Christ the King Parish in Ann Arbor and who has since relocated to the East Coast. Next, Mary Shannon Via (my cousin), and self-proclaimed queen of all things punctuation/grammar, who sniffed out many of those blemishes ... "Damn those dangling participles." Finally, Gary Senick, a Detroit boy still livin' in da hood, who spent hours with me at and after the school day ended at Fordson; I especially valued his insights as we were largely cut from the same piece of cloth: age, music likes etc.

There have been a number of readers, some who read portions and others the entire book. I'm afraid I can't remember you all (remind me if you see this), but I tried to get a mix of folks who knew me well, and indeed were eye-witnesses to some of the events. I also wanted to hear from both men and women; you'll excuse me if I think the sexes sometimes bring different perspectives to the table, and I wished to hear both. I received tons of valuable input, including constructive criticism and affirmation concerning certain topics I was anxious about including. Nobody said, "You shouldn't do this." And, I made sure the readers I asked were folks who would tell me what I needed to hear, not what I wanted to hear. So in this regard I'd like to especially thank Al Kresta (host of "Kresta in the Afternoon" on Ave Maria radio), Tom Roy (old neighbor and talented artist as you can see for yourself–he did front/back covers), apologist Dave Armstrong, and Beth Patton. Thanks so much, and you other readers, thanks to you also.

And so, let the journey begin.

THERE AND BACK AGAIN: A CHILD OF THE SIXTIES RETURNS TO HIS CATHOLIC ROOTS

INTRODUCTION

Some of you may recognize the title of this book, *There and Back Again,* which is the subtitle of J.R.R. Tolkien's fantasy novel *The Hobbit.* The most loveable of hobbits, Bilbo Baggins, gave this same title to the memoir of his wondrous adventures outside of his beloved Shire. Well, nobody is going to mistake me for a hobbit. Perhaps someone might mistake me for the skin-changer Beorn in Tolkien's tale, who at some times is a large bearded man and at others is an enormous black bear. My daughter would say that I'm more of a teddy bear. Although any similarity between my tale and Bilbo's is both slight and coincidental, I would argue that there's a bit of Mr. Baggins in most of us.

This *There and Back Again* is largely a tale of my having "left" the Catholic Church for some thirty-five years and my subsequent return, not before taking first one path and then another. These paths included southeastern Michigan, which is where I grew up; California, where I went to catch the tail end of the counterculture revolution that took place in the 1960/70s; Florida, where the Jesus Movement stirred deep, buried longings in me; and some thirty-plus years of wandering in and out of a number of Evangelical, Pentecostal and Protestant churches. Included in these wanderings is the story of my eleven years as a pastor.

In 1985, I resigned (retired) as pastor, returned to school, and earned a teaching degree. Currently, I have put notch number twenty-eight on my teaching sidearm. And, yeah, I have kids (three adult children, two boys and a girl). To them, I say, "Your ol' man's thinkin', not about retirement, but about a career change." When I left the pastorate, I told myself that I'd be back one day. When that day comes, it could quite possibly be as "Father/Friar Joe"! Bit of a long shot I know.

About fifteen years ago, my marriage of twenty years ended after my wife filed for divorce. At that stage, having recently turned fifty, the next few years turned into Midlife Crisis Meets Dark Night of the Soul. At that stage, having recently turned fifty, the this "stroll" on the outskirts of Mordor, if you'll allow me a bit of Middle Earth imagery, I hardly knew what to think, to say, or to believe. I'd been rocked by an uppercut from Godzilla (or maybe it was a Balrog, to keep to the Tolkien theme). All of my grand plans (Career Pastor and "Until-Death-Do-Us-Part" marriage) had "fallen into shadow." If I was ever going to make it to another round and not end up as more human refuse littering the edge of the highway, I would have to face this opponent head-on. My wonderful aunt, Angie Derderian, put it to me boldly during these dark days: "Joey, you're a Shannon. You'll survive." So, for the last fifteen years, I've put pen to paper, trying to make some sense of it all. Mind you, I haven't been doing this 24/7. There have been long gaps in the writing process, interspersed with a flurry here and there. Mostly, I've just been putting myself in the zone when the mood strikes and recounting my life as best I can.

By now, have you guessed that I'm nostalgic? I suppose that I'm somewhat like Bilbo. I've been fashioning my memoirs, but with a twofold purpose in mind. First, I wanted to try and figure out what happened in my life. I hoped that writing my story would shed light on events that I find more comfortable to avert my gaze from than to look at hard. Second, I wanted to address the numerous and, I suspect, unending queries as to why I would even think of, let alone actually return to, the Catholic fold after all this time. Incidentally, my timing never was very good. These are not exactly the best of times to identify oneself as Catholic, but I'm okay with that. My return surprised me more than it did anybody else. However, I did see it coming. This was no hasty overnight decision; actually, it was years in the making. There are a good many spokes on the wheel that brought me home to the Church of my youth.

I do not regret my decision to return to the Catholic Church. However, I'd be less than honest if I said that all of my Catholic issues have been resolved. So, when people ask, I can't really give a nice, clear, convenient, adequate, quick response to the questions about my return to Catholicism. (Well, I can, but I don't usually care to…) Hence, this book; incidentally, I don't spend a lot of time on "Catholic issues" until Part 4.

Think of this book as a couple of old buds sitting in a quiet corner of an Irish pub: "Here's the answer to your question(s). Oh, and you're pickin' up the tab. Hah!" More often than not, the fifteen plus years that it took me to write this book found me engaged in fierce spiritual battles. On a good many occasions, it felt as though I'd come out on the losing end. I've trudged through the muck and mire of a good many spiritual lows and wrestled the Seven Deadlies (sins) in both their physical and spiritual manifestations, all with varied success. A goodly portion of this book was written during extended periods of anger and depression and of having thoughts that were both suicidal and homicidal. Therefore, I'm concerned that these periods can't help but affect the tone of my story and amount to one very unedifying book. I'm also acutely aware that if we Christians will be held responsible for every word that we speak, how much more will we be held responsible for every word that we put to print? The fact that my children will read this book gives me great pause. Friends, family, enemies, former students – what will they think? So, why bother? Who cares? So what! Overall, I've tried to be both honest and charitable in my life and in my dealings with people. I'm more disappointed in myself than in anyone or anything on those occasions I missed the mark. My journey has taken me down some dark roads. I've not said everything in this book. There are still some skeletons that are dangling deep in my closet, skeletons best left to Jesus, to my confessor, and to me. If you are familiar with some of the events in this tale, you may want to put an entirely different spin on them. That's okay. That's your story; this one's mine.

"So, why are you doin' this, Joe?" ask my pals in the Irish pub.

"Because I think I'm supposed to," I answer.

There are a long list of things I've done that I thought I was "supposed to do," as in "God was leading me to do such and such." It turns out that on some of these occasions, I was deceived.

The world, the flesh, and the Devil are our adversaries, and one or more of them will best us at times. I pray that this is not one of those times. If you read no more than this introduction, then please leave with this thought uppermost in your mind: I (we) look through a glass darkly (1 Cor. 12:13). For the past few years, mine has been downright murky. Still, at the end of the day, as for Joe Shannon's household, we, like Joshua, will follow the Lord!

Fans of Tolkien's trilogy *The Lord of the Rings* will recall the hobbit protagonist Frodo giving some sage advice to his friend and traveling companion Sam at the onset of their journey. This was advice that Frodo's uncle, the aforementioned Bilbo Baggins, shared with him years earlier: "It's a dangerous business, Frodo, going out of your door. You step into the Road, and if you don't keep your feet, there is no knowing where you might be swept off to." The days that followed my graduation from high school (St. Agatha, Redford, MI, Class of 1970) were my stepping out the door onto the "Road." In my heart, I'd begun to drift away from the Catholic Church a few years earlier. The spirituality that I experienced during my years in high school consisted largely of habit and what was expected. There was little substance beyond the facade. However, I never did entirely turn my back on her (the Church).

Rather than go with chapters, I've divided this book into five sections (eras): The Early Years – Growing Up in the Shadow of Detroit (1952-70), The Florida Years (1971-73), The Shalom Years (1973-85), Get Back Joe Joe (1986-2006)… and the Fordson Years (2007-2018 and counting). My departure from and return to the Catholic Church will not be addressed directly until Part Four, but these events are always simmering on the back burner until the heat is turned up, c. 2003. The theological issues that I had to confront as I seriously considered coming back to Catholicism (and still grapple with, in some cases) will not be gone into at great length. There are many capable writers out there who have plowed that field. When the time comes, I'll share some personal reflections and insights, and I'll refer you to some thinkers and writers whom I found beneficial in sorting out some key theological issues. For further reflection on these matters, please see Appendix 8: *Catholic Issues*.

I hope that you enjoy the journey (mine as well as your own). We're not likely to see any trolls, elves, or dragons in my *There and Back Again*; then again, we might. Grab your walking stick and knapsack – we're off! "The road goes ever on," wrote Tolkien.   Above all, I wish you Shalom.

Joe Shannon, January 2018

PROLOGUE

"History," I began, "has the potential to reveal where I've come from, where I've been, and where I may be headed." This mantra, part of the introduction to the course on World Civilizations that I'm teaching at Clara B. Ford High School (a Dearborn public school on the grounds of Vista Maria, a live-in treatment facility for adolescent females that is located on the outskirts of Detroit), always struck me as rather profound. The mantra is certainly a necessary component to self-understanding as well as to the matter at hand. However, my declaration is met with both indifference and a dash of mild curiosity by my first-period class. The twelve girls in my class, who range in age from thirteen to eighteen, are sizing up yet another adult, a rather large and imposing one with whom they'll have to cope for at least one semester at this "quaint" lock-down facility. I have served as the instructor of English and Social Studies at CBF for sixteen years. Therefore, I know it is likely that I'll connect with only a handful of students. On any given day, only a couple of students (again, keep in mind that the classes at CBF are small by today's standards) will focus on the lesson. Other challenges make up for the small teacher/student ratio. Students are seldom placed in a class by the levels of age, grade, and ability. Some students have fairly proficient writing skills, can construct a basic essay response or compose a one-act play, and so on, while several others will have no clue as to what constitutes a sentence. Some won't know what a noun is. In any event, most students quickly will find some diversion. Some will be reading something they shouldn't, horoscopes from today's newspaper or juicy articles from *Cosmopolitan* on which they've somehow gotten their hands. Others feign taking notes while writing a letter to their judge, therapist, boyfriend, or girlfriend. Some will be fighting to stay awake due to the drowsy side effects of medication. Others complain that they got little to no sleep last night due to unit disruptions: fights, fire drills, truancy attempts, a roommate who cried or sang until 4 a.m., and other excuses. Some days, the environment in the classroom fuels agitation and distraction, such as the classroom being too hot or too cold. Then there are the interruptions by the staff of Vista Maria, such as yanking first one kid and then another for med-runs, family therapy, or inappropriate dress. Also, there is a constant flow of employees and visitors in the hallways; many of these people seem oblivious to the fact that classes are in session. Their chatter and laughter make it impossible to leave the classroom door ajar. One girl is preoccupied with consuming her late breakfast - a pop tart. Still, the other teachers and I press on, keeping in mind that, as trying as conditions at Vista Maria/CBF can be, many of these young ladies are in a far more safe, clean, and nurturing environment than they seldom (or ever) have experienced thus far. Teachers wishing to preserve their sanity (provided they had some to begin with) must take care not to get mired in the muck of the mentality of "So, just live with it," the slow, subtle acceptance of shortcomings in education and treatment here as the norm.

Previously (2001-2015) teachers were working under the banner "No Child Left Behind," one of those catchy little phrases that some politicians and educators like to rally around. I would affirm that, indeed, every effort should be made not to leave any student behind, but regrettably it's not happening. Nor is one likely to get a one hundred percent return in the realm of education. On some days, I feel like the farmer in the Parable of the Sower (Mt 13:3-9), who's seed (in my case, lessons) fell on differing types of soil and yielded a crop accordingly. Small successes are to be preferred to none. If so, my efforts (and those of countless other teachers) will not have been in vain. Like the sower, we seldom witness the mature fruits of our labor. (This is especially true at CBF, where students come and go as quickly as things happen in Dorothy's Munchkin Land in the movie version of *The Wizard of Oz*. To be fair, though, some students do stay a year or more.) For ten-plus years, I've also been teaching a modified version of an introductory class on Shakespeare. Many students genuinely appear to enjoy these timeless tales; *Macbeth, Hamlet,* and *King Lear* have been my staples. Perhaps the students enjoy them because these tragedies so mirror their own lives; such is the power of the Bard.

The bell has rung. One group of students has shuffled out. Momentarily, a new group will straggle in. Shouts from the hall-monitoring staff cut through the sounds of slamming locker doors and laughing students. "Move along ... no P-C-in (personal contact) ... get to class ... take off that jacket ... give me that note...." The staff barks out these directives like some pissed-off drill sergeant. Then, louder and bolder, a command rises above the clucking and clattering: "CLEAR THE AREA!" Clear the area, aka CTA, means that a crisis situation has developed, usually a potential fight or a student/resident unwilling to comply with a directive. Students know that those three words are a signal for them to leave that area immediately, usually to go to some prearranged site, such as a vacant classroom or a hallway, until the staff can secure control or prevent an imminent or already escalating situation. Typically, teachers only take part in these affairs, which may include a restraint, as a last resort; I've been in a few humdingers. These situations can last from several minutes to an hour. The one this morning has left me with an empty classroom. Truth be told, I wouldn't be disappointed if this one lasted awhile.

I stand, stretch, and stare northwest out the window towards Rouge Park. Today, my mind is flooded with personal events of the last few years, primarily my divorce. In 2002, my wife of nineteen years filed for divorce. Shortly after our twentieth anniversary, she got what she wanted. My signature remains conspicuously absent from the divorce document; I refused to sign it. There was no question that our marriage had been in a terrible state for years - beyond salvaging, most would argue - but I went into it for better or for worse, till death do us part. Basically, the court said to me, "We understand your unwillingness to sign this document, but we don't need your signature. You're divorced." If I continue to dwell on this, like one of the Shakespearean characters to whom I'll soon introduce my students, King Lear, I too "shall go mad!"

Beyond the tree line that fills the western horizon rests the land of my youth - Redford Township. Immediately, powerful images of a largely pleasant childhood kick aside the more recent dark pages of my life, for the moment, anyway. A slow smile smoothes out the lines of my aging face as, in my mind's eye, I'm back in the township on Gaylord Street once again...

PART ONE

Redford Township, which is on the western border of Detroit, was a great place to grow up in the 1950s and 60s. Adjacent to a major Midwestern industrial city, it still retained a bit of a rural feel. This was especially true of my street, Gaylord, where our home was located between Grand River Avenue and Seven Mile Road. On Gaylord, new homes were scattered among large wooded lots and dwellings that we kids were convinced had been constructed by pioneers. Gaylord, which has only recently been blacktopped, also had a creek running through it. A gravel street in the township meant monthly visits from the road-grader, a monster machine that loomed like some mammoth Tonka toy on steroids. The road-grader was guaranteed to provide a welcome diversion to youngsters like me, who pedaled up behind it. We crisscrossed one or more of the tightly packed ridges that were yet to be leveled. As we did, the whirr of old, unpopular baseball cards, which we kids had stuck cleverly between the spokes of the wheels of our bikes to give them that throaty sound, was all but drowned out by the grinding scrape of the road-grader's massive blade, which smoothed out the wear and tear of the previous weeks' traffic. There, peering down from his throne, hat cocked to one side, sat the operator of that mighty machine. A Lucky Strike cigarette dangled precariously from his mouth as he smiled and threw us a careless wave. Following in his footsteps might have been my first career choice. However, that ambition would later take a back seat after I'd finished several of the popular books that feature the Hardy Boys. Now, I would be a detective.

On any given day, especially during the warmer months, the clanging of bells signaled the approach of various fruit-and vegetable-peddlers; the milkman for Twin Pines Dairy; and our favorite, the Good

Humor Man, who had ice cream in his truck. I can still hear the click of those heavy, latched doors on the side and rear panels of the Good Humor Man's truck as he reached in through the foggy mist of dry ice that engulfed his arm, only to reappear magically grasping our orders: Eskimo Pies, Chocolate Eclairs, Fudgesicles, and Orange Crèmesicles. During the winter months, the trucks belonging to Nick Bos, the florist from down the street, made wonderful moving targets for the snowball gauntlet provided by us kids.

In my neighborhood, families were large and kids were everywhere. There were ball diamonds aplenty at nearby schools. Having a decent bat and ball helped to land you a spot in a pick-up game. Usually, the younger guys got positioned in right field and batted last but, hey, at least you were in the game. These pick-up games were just the right venues to hone your skills for the big leagues – Little League, with its breakdown of Minors B and A, and then the Majors. It seemed like every boy in the neighborhood was on a team. Hours before game time, we'd don our uniforms, proudly displaying our colors for all to admire while racing around on our bikes. Neighbors were close. Since most families had only one vehicle, we learned to rely on each other in case of emergencies, or simply to borrow an occasional egg or some milk and to get rides to church, school, and the grocery store. Speaking of stores, we had the good fortune of living in close proximity (five minutes or less of bike-riding time) to half a dozen party stores; usually of the mom-and-pop variety. It was a daily ritual to saunter out to one of these stores (or sometimes to several, on those rare occasions when your pocket jingled with loose change). We would stock up on candy, purchase some pretzel sticks and a cold Faygo or Nesbitt's soda (called "pop" in Detroit), and peruse the stock of baseball and horror-film cards for new arrivals. It's amazing that we have any of our teeth left, especially in a pre-fluoride period. Our teeth and gums were forced to do battle with countless gooey confectionery concoctions as addictive as any nicotine-laced Pall Malls. These included Black Jacks, Mary Janes, Bit-O-Honey, jawbreakers, Bazooka bubble gum (with the corny little comic strip wrapped around the gum), licorice rope, wax lips and fangs, and little wax bottles with awful-tasting green or yellow syrup inside. If it was Saturday, often a trip to see a movie at the Redford or Irving Theatres was in the works. Beforehand, one took care to load up on boxed candy to smuggle into the theatre to avoid long lines and the price-gouging at concession counters. Milk Duds, Lemon Drops, Boston Baked Beans, Red Hots, and those wonderful rubbery treats, Juicy Fruits, and their demented little brothers Jujubes (I lost a couple of fillings to those rascals) composed our arsenal for double-feature matinees. Any neighborhood party store worth its salt (or, rather, its candy) also must have a wide and current selection of comic books: *Superman* and *Batman*, of course, but also *Aquaman*, *The Green Lantern*, *The Flash*, *Hawkeye*, *Doctor Strange*, and *Sgt. Fury and His Howling Commandos*. Stanley's Drug Store at Grand River and Beech Daly Road had as good a selection as any.

Home computers were not yet on anyone's radar screen, and slot-car tracks and pinball arcades were still a few years off. Still, there was plenty to do. There was a Boys Club near Seven Mile and Beech Daly, with a couple of burger joints, Bates Hamburgers and Top Hat, nearby to satisfy those hunger and thirst pangs. We also had a lot of rainy-day diversions. We made our way merrily through hula hoops, Silly Putty, Wham-O slingshots, cap guns, pea-shooters, ladyfinger firecrackers, B-B guns, yo-yos, trading cards, pick-up-sticks, Slinkies, boomerangs, balsawood planes with adjustable wings and a small metal bit on the nose to give weight to them, and rockets powered by water compression. Games were simple: Hide-and-Go-Seek; Frozen Tag; Kickball; 500 (a game in which fielders accumulated points by successfully fielding grounders, line-drives, and fly balls, thereby earning the right to be the next batter); Pickle; Mother May I; and a neighborhood favorite, Fence-Walking. There was rarely a shortage of participants, as kids hurried through dinner to get back into the action. Then, when the street lights came on, recognizable shouts from neighborhood mothers and fathers summoned their respective broods back to their roosts, or at least to the safety of back yards and a little Flashlight Tag.

Living between two major thoroughfares (Grand River and Seven

Mile) gave us quick access to the city and its delights. Seven-Grand was our mall. Hardly more than a strip-mall by today's standards, it was pretty impressive back in the day. Seven-Grand had Federals Department Store; Winkleman's (a women's clothing store); S. S. Kresge and Cunningham's drug stores, each with soda fountains; Sims Brothers (which carried men's and boys' apparel), all sprinkled in among half a dozen other stores. Edgewater Amusement Park, located near Seven Mile and Telegraph Road, had a legendary ride, the Wild Mouse. I already have mentioned the Redford and Irving Theatres; further east was the Great Lakes Theatre, another great source for movies. The Irving Theatre on Fenkell aka Five Mile was in "beautiful" downtown Brightmoor (a tough neighborhood even back then), a community on the western edge of town from which both sides of my family, Shannons and Evans, hail. They lived in the Smith Projects, on Evergreen between Outer Drive and Schoolcraft Road.

Deeper in the city were two prime sporting venues, Olympia Stadium (on Grand River) and Briggs (later Tiger) Stadium on Trumbull Street and Michigan Avenue. Scores of young Township fans of the Detroit Tigers baseball team would head over to Seven-Grand, catch the Grand River Express bus to Trumbull (a trip of twenty to thirty minutes), and hike a mile south to the ball park. There, we would spend a thrilling afternoon basking in the sun, deep in the center-field bleachers (cheap seats). In one hand, we would clutch a ball-glove in the event that Willie Horton or the visiting Harmon Killebrew of the Minnesota Twins might launch a rare home run into the seats in straightaway center. The other hand intermittently held a game program, a box of Cracker Jacks, or a hot dog lathered in mustard on a steamed bun. Bus fare, tickets for the game, soft drinks, and snacks – all for just a few bucks! A double-header could last well into twilight, when the stadium lights, gigantic headlights that added a whole new feel to the game, burst forth like so many mini-suns.

Further up Grand River, Olympia Stadium played host to the Detroit Red Wings hockey team, which at that time featured the production line of Ted Lindsay, Sid Abel, and Gordie Howe. On some

5

Saturdays, the rink would be covered and a ring put up. This would herald a "Big-Time Wrestling" event. Tonight's feature card includes a grudge match between Bobo Brazil and Killer Kowalski; "Leaping" Larry Chene versus Ernie "the Cat" Ladd; a midget tag-team match; and a title bout pitting the reigning champ, the Sheik, against local favorite Dick the Bruiser. Will the Sheik get his "camel clutch" locked on before the Bruiser can clobber him with a ringside chair or anything else that he can lay his hands on? The scenario for the earlier, "warm-up-the-crowd" bouts was pretty predictable. Some no-name wrestler, who looked like he signed on the dotted line the night before (just prior to slipping off a bar stool at the Lindell Athletic Club), was pitted against one of a dozen colorful characters like "Wild Bull" Curry. The out-of-shape rookie, we knew, would somehow manage to mount a successful offense against the cagey, heavily favored veteran, only to have victory denied at the last moment. The rookie would be left stunned, half-conscious, in the center of the ring, or sprawled out on the disgusted patrons in the second row. These people had the misfortune of buffeting the rookie's reentry into Earth's atmosphere following his ejection from the ring. What a way to make a livin'!

The Shannons on Gaylord Street – my dad, Harold; my mom, Gloria; my older sister, Susan; my three younger brothers, Dan, Jeff, and Ken; and me – had one of the first TVs in the neighborhood. Choices were limited to half-a-dozen channels, but why did programs back then seem so much better? One simply can't claim that we were just kids and that television was largely a new novelty. No, it's more than that; legions of seniors and Baby Boomers would nod their assent. We Shannon kids munched our Alphabets, Rice Krispies, and Sugar Pops cereals to those great Saturday morning cartoons like *Heckle and Jeckle* and *Felix the Cat; Deputy Dawg* was my favorite. Later, we got into several local kids' shows: *Lunch with Soupy* (featuring Soupy Sales, a comedian who later became known nationally); Johnny Ginger's *Curtain Time Theatre; Milky the Clown* (which was sponsored by Twin Pines Dairy); and *Captain Jolly*. Dad liked Westerns like *Wagon Train* and *Cheyenne*, the latter with big, handsome Clint Walker. Mom enjoyed variety shows and *Ben Casey* – that is, when she had the luxury of relaxing in front of the TV, which was difficult with five kids, a constant barrage of visitors, the occasional boarder, and … well, you get the picture. Additional "boob-tube" fare included *The Twilight Zone, The Real McCoys, The Adventures of Ozzie and Harriet, The Honeymooners, My Three Sons, The Patty Duke Show, Leave It to Beaver,* and *The Many Loves of Dobie Gillis.* Two of my "role models," the smart-aleck kid Eddie Haskell and the cool beatnik Maynard G. Krebs, were characters in the latter two programs. On Saturdays, when foul weather was on the day's menu and the local matinees at nearby theatres had already been seen, the TV wasn't a bad second option. On one local program, we'd catch some out-of-shape wrestler in a gladiator outfit hosting *Hercules* and other "sword-and-sandals" flicks with actors like Gordon Scott and Steve Reeves. With lions roaring in the background, this gladiator would strut around a cardboard-looking version of the cellar of the Roman Coliseum while brandishing a whip. A real treat would be for him to host a *Tarzan* picture featuring our favorite, Johnny Weismuller. Saturday nights meant *Shock Theatre:* Prior to the start of some drive-in-reject horror film, a white, glaring skull would appear, set against a solid black backdrop. While some haunting music of a most unsettling nature played, the announcer intoned the title of the show in a sepulchral manner. This was more unnerving than the picture itself! A few years later, the lighthearted *Morgus Presents* filled the void when the run of *Shock Theatre* came to an end; it became one of my favorites. A demented scientist, Morgus the Magnificent, hosted late-night, sci-fi films like *The Day the Earth Stood Still.* The nutty Morgus was joined by his co-host and sole friend Eric, a talking skull. If one's homework was completed satisfactorily, Sunday evenings began with *The Wonderful World of Disney*, followed by *The Ed Sullivan Show*, and, finally, *The ABC Sunday Night Movie,* which we were rarely allowed to finish, as it was a school night.

·   ·   ·   ·

Heading west out of Redford held adventures of other sorts. The imposing grandeur of the historic Botsford Inn and, just beyond it, the

Grand River Drive-In Theatre, which had an A&W drive-in restaurant nearby, attracted a lot of Township dwellers. A forty-five minute cruise out old Grand River in Dad's red-and-white '56 Chevy Bel-Air culminated in a day's visit to Kensington Beach or Walled Lake Amusement Park. Later, we'd add Camp Dearborn to the list. Located west of Milford, Michigan, Camp Dearborn was founded by Orville Hubbard, a long-term, controversial mayor of the City of Dearborn. You should have seen the look on the faces of the Camp's employees as they checked in the Shannons for a week of camping in D-Row of Tent Village. We kids had our clothes and toiletries packed neatly into some handy long-necked sturdy beer cases that we'd pilfered from Shannon's Lounge, a bar that was owned by my dad's brother Bob. It looked like we were setting up a "speakeasy" right there in the middle of Orville Hubbard's camp. No doubt Pops had a few cases of Stroh's and/or Carling's packed tightly beneath our "suitcases." After an amused look, not unlike what you might give the Beverly Hillbillies or the Little Rascals had they pulled up, the Camp's employees let us in for some city-folk campin'. We kids, along with an army of cousins, friends, and new temporary neighbors from rows of tents as far as the eye could see, had a ball. Although our parents had earned a well deserved break, I think that they were glad to get back home, especially with Labor Day and kids marching back to school on the horizon.

Heading west out on Seven Mile or Eight Mile Roads, past numerous fruit and vegetable stands in season, brought you to Northville. Sometimes, these jaunts included a trip to the cider mill. Occasionally, Dad liked to take in the "trotters" at the Northville Downs racetrack. During the winter months, a couple of decent sledding hills loomed nearby, which we'd use after we'd grown tired of the "monster" slopes at Lola Valley Park, which was in the neighborhood. Yep, Redford was a great place to plant a crop of Baby Boomers.

We Shannons were Irish Catholic and proud of it. My dad's oldest brother, Bob, who owned Shannon's Lounge, also lived in the township, over on Kinloch Street near Redford Union High School. Bob and his wife Mary had six kids, whose ages were in close proximity to ours. It seemed that there was a Catholic Church every mile and in every direction (back then, Redford Township had at least five of these churches). The Kinloch Shannons attended Our Lady of Loretto at Beech Daly and Six Mile Road. We attended St. Agatha at Beech Daly and Pembroke Streets. Dad had another brother whom we affectionately called DJ. His family settled in the suburb of Southfield, just north of Eight Mile. There were lots of Shannons in "the hood."

My sister Susan and I were the only kids in our family to graduate from St. Agatha – classes of 1968 and 1970, respectively. My three younger brothers would transfer over to public school at Redford Union. I suspect that the financial strain of private parochial education had gotten to be too much for my parents.

On Sunday mornings, our Mass of preference at St. Agatha's was the one at 8:30. Harold and Gloria saw to it that we were properly groomed and attired; tied neckties and shined shoes were *de rigueur* for us boys, at least in the early years. First Holy Communion, Confirmation, regular confessions, meatless Fridays, nightly bedside prayers, Grace before dinner, Stations of the Cross on Good Friday, Advent wreaths, and Midnight Mass on Christmas Eve all formed a part of our Catholic family tradition. Sometimes, my dad and I would venture out to Dun Scotus (a monastic house in Southfield, Michigan), for the Sacrament of Confession on Saturday evenings. Pops used to like to sit quietly in the sanctuary listening to the Franciscan Brothers chant and sing.

When I was in grade school, the reforms of Vatican II swept through the Church. The most significant developments that impacted us youngsters were the change in the liturgy from Latin to English and the gradual change to the habits worn by the nuns, which went from medieval-looking to a more contemporary, but still conservative, look. What connection, if any, the latter had with the Vatican reforms in the 60s I couldn't say; perhaps it was simply a reflection of the cultural "changing times" and a desire on the part of certain religious to appear a little earthier.

During seventh and eighth grades, I served as the reader of the

Scriptures and the leader of the responses and the hymns at weekday student Masses. I had a decent voice. Elvis, Lou Christie, Del Shannon, and Dion – I could nail them all. It was quite a thrill to be up front at the lower level of the altar, with the shiny metallic microphone, sturdy wooden lectern, Mass readings, and songbook all in order. The statue of the Church's patron, the martyr St. Agatha, loomed behind me, sword pointed menacingly at her breast. Her statue bid worshipers to recall the price that one might be called upon to offer in taking up the Cross of Christ. Lector responsibilities kept me in the good graces of the nuns whose patience I sorely tried. I don't recall many (if any) of my classmates wanting in on the "Mass Reader" action; St. Agatha's was stuck with me.

Typically, the role of celebrant at these weekday morning Masses was delegated to one or more assistant priests. On one occasion, Father John T. Reid, the founder and pastor of St. Agatha's, was the celebrant. We grade-schoolers viewed this man with a mixture of awe, terror, and mystery. On one particular day, I must have been in Frankie Valli-falsetto mode. I was not a fan of the Four Seasons, but their song "Sherry" was one of those "try-to-hit-it" songs (the high notes, that is). During a sung response, a hymn, or some other part of the liturgy, I let the high notes ring. After that, I stepped back from the microphone and turned up to look at the altar, prompted by an awkward silence. Why wasn't Father Reid continuing with the liturgy? He was renowned for his speedy liturgies and prayers. His rosaries during Forty Hours Devotion are in the *Guinness Book of Records* for the pace with which he rattled them off (just kidding). There he stood, stiff as one of the sculptured characters on the Stations of the Cross, his eyes fixed on me. The church's enormous crucifix was a silent observer in the unfolding drama. Father Reid's fixed glance was not particularly threatening; rather, it was more puzzled. In any event, it was still unnerving. His eyes fluttered. Clearing his throat, Father Reid seemed to collect himself and finally resumed the liturgy. Slightly shaken, I beat a hasty retreat as the last note of the recessional hymn died out. I avoided Father Reid for some time after that. Heck, as far as I knew, he may have actually liked my performance or just found it amusing. More likely, he was trying to probe the heart's intent and discern if indeed blasphemy had been committed; no sense in taking chances.

Years later, my take on Father Reid was that his bark was worse than his bite. He was Old School. From where I stood, or rather, sat, he got the job done, handling a parish serving northwest Redford Township that included a school from first through twelfth grades. We kids could be a rowdy bunch (a Little Rascals/Three Stooges/Bowery Boys stew), especially my class, the Class of '70. We needed a firm hand (sometimes, backhand) to keep us on the "straight and narrow." The changes and challenges in the wake of Vatican II must have been daunting indeed for the priests, nuns, and laity of their generation. Anyway, may Father Reid rest in peace and glory, even if, in later years, he did yank at my sideburns, declaring, "Don't come in here Monday without those being raised above the earlobes!" No muttonchops in his school c. '67. Eventually, my classmates and I wore down Father Reid and the other administrators on the issues of hair, uniforms, and a host of others. The times, as Bob Dylan sang, were indeed "a-changin'." It just took a little longer, for better or for worse, to make inroads at St. Agatha.

St. Agatha was split into an elementary school (grades one through eight) and a high school; both were in the same location in adjacent buildings. The high school sat alongside the south side of Pembroke, with Pierson Junior High on the north. I transferred to St. Agatha at the start of second grade after going to kindergarten and first grade at Volney Smith, a public school. Three significant events, two largely personal, are as clear in my mind as if they happened last week. The first was a run-in with my fifth grade teacher, Mrs. M. She could not be described as an attractive woman by any stretch of the imagination. Ancient (she had seen a lot of years), short, stocky, and gruff of voice was Mrs. M. She also had hairs protruding where they had no business being. In my young mind, Mrs. M. would have made a good nun or a good wife for Quasimodo, the hunchbacked bell-ringer of Notre Dame. She was as gentle as a lamb one moment, as dark and terrible as a Black

Forest troll the next. One day, following recess, we kids had just settled into our seats when Mrs. M. proceeded to parade me and another male student to the front of the class. Both of us were made to stand at attention, backs against the chalkboard. It was clear that something was up. Mrs. M. was livid. The students remained hushed, tense; they sensed a coming storm. Then Mrs. M. broke loose like some long-imprisoned Balrog deep within Moria's mines in J.R.R. Tolkien's book *The Fellowship of the Ring*. There had been some scuffle on the playground that resulted in a couple of bloodied noses and some torn trousers – kid stuff. I had been singled out, along with my accomplice, as the alleged perpetrators of the assault. By now, he stood weak-kneed next to me, trembling like a leaf. "What's more," Mrs. M. said, "This hasn't been the first incident." She meant to "nip it in the bud" right now! For several minutes, Mrs. M. thundered forth her opinion of playground bullies. These tirades were interspersed with slaps and good old-fashioned shakings, complete with my head bouncing off of the chalkboard like some wayward pinball. She'd lost it. My classmates sat frozen, speechless, waiting for this nightmare to subside. There was no inquiry, no chance to offer some verbal defense. Mrs. M. had tried and convicted me, and my execution seemed imminent.

Shortly after the onset of Mrs. M's hysterical tongue-lashing, I had a thought. It dawned on me that her objective was to bring me to tears and perhaps have me wet my pants to humiliate me in front of the class. She failed. According to one old classmate, Mrs. M. also earned several bruising kicks to the shins before coming to her senses. I can't say that I recall this part of it, but it may indeed have been the case. Whenever I run into one of my old classmates and we get to reminiscing, this episode inevitably comes up. It must have made quite an impression on the class. I would have loved to have been the invisible listener around my classmates' supper tables that evening as mom and dad posed the question, "So, honey, how'd school go today?" I don't recall having told my parents (or an attorney or the ACLU), as I likely would have gotten another whooping, innocent or not. Actually, that particular day, I was innocent. Remember when your parents would spank you and find out later that the "crime" was committed by one of your siblings? Parents always would fall back on the "Well, that was for all the times I didn't catch ya" line. After that one incident, I don't recall any more problems with Mrs. M.

Roughly a year later, one of our classmates, Christopher Smidak, was struck and killed by an automobile while walking to school. In a different way, this seemed as traumatic as when President Kennedy was assassinated. This kid, I knew; I sat next to him at lunch, in class, and at daily Mass. Now he was dead. Suddenly, the mortality that has us all in its sights was no longer some will-o-the-wisp reserved for next of kin and elderly neighbors. At the funeral Mass for my classmate, I'll never forget the look on his mother's face.

The third and most significant event (actually issue) of those pre-high school years wasn't being with my first girlfriend, Michele C.; she might dispute this claim. It also wasn't sitting behind the National League All-Star outfield of Roberto Clemente, Willie Mays, and Hank Aaron or even the Beatles coming to Detroit. It was my feet. To begin with, they were huge. This proved more of a burden to my parents, since extra-sized shoes were expensive. However, it also was a burden to me, since the styles of these shoes were quite limited. Who wants to wear wingtips or Hush Puppies when your friends are strutting around in pointed shoes with Cuban heels (greaser gear), Beatle boots, and penny-loafers? The real issue was of a more serious nature: Severe heel pain, particularly in the left foot, which was brought on by too much Tarzan-like activity as a youngster. Around 1964 or 1965, the pain would make even the short distance to a nearby closet unbearable, especially first thing in the morning. On some days, I'd crawl from my bed to the closet. Generally, the pain would typically begin to ease after several minutes. Unless my feet had endured a pounding during the day, my discomfort was hardly noticeable. For some months, I avoided telling my parents, certain that they'd blame it on the heavy cleats we kids loved to wear on the heels of our shoes. Eventually, I had to tell them. A trip to a specialist at the Fisher Building in midtown Detroit revealed the source of the pain – my left heel had a tiny shattered bone. It was uncertain if even surgery could fix it, and it may be something I'd just have to live with including the possibility of spending my adult years confined to a wheelchair. Since my right foot had a hairline fracture, we went with a walking cast on that foot ushering in a wait and see approach. Future sports involvement, if any, would be tenuous. Prior to this, I'd been as roughhousing and athletic a kid as any. Sports were important to me; especially baseball. This aspect of my life had come to a grinding halt, and it couldn't have happened at a worse time. I'd looked forward to advancing to Pony League (following Little League) and football in the seventh and eighth grades. Now this vine-swingin'; backyard-hockey playin'; shed-, garage-, and tree-fort jumpin' off of; barefoot-creek-hoppin'; happy-go-lucky kid became increasingly insecure and withdrawn. Television and the refrigerator were my new best friends. Then the weight came.

Hitting your teen years as a chubby kid (think Pugsley on *The Addams Family* television show) is just plain awful. Immediately, you are directed to the husky section of the young men's clothing departments at Sims and J. C. Penney's. You avoid beaches and pool parties so that you don't have to offer some lame excuse as to why you can't take off your shirt. In gym, you struggle to reach ten push-ups when the guy on either side of you is already sounding off twenty-five. As I recall, the only benefit to being overweight came later, in high school. After all of us had gotten our driver's licenses. I always got the task of driving into the Grand River Drive-In. Two or three buddies would cram themselves into the trunk. Hopefully, they wouldn't suffocate or cramp up until I pulled into some dark row in the rear where they could jump out safely. However, as the lone driver, one did have to remain cool and stoic as you endured one or two stares from the receptionist in the ticket booth. First, they seemed to say, "What kinda weird guy are you, goin' alone to a drive-in movie?" Then there was that knowing smirk as they glanced at the rear of your vehicle, which practically rested on the blacktop entrance while the front end rode abnormally high. Apparently, these receptionists didn't care one way or another. I don't recall ever having gotten busted, but I had heard about others who weren't so lucky.

The "battle of the bulge" would dog me all through high school. In spite of my lingering feet issues, I did manage to earn a letter in Varsity baseball. Since I couldn't participate in more than one sport (my feet wouldn't have taken the stress), I drifted further and further away from the "jock" scene. I never participated in Varsity Club or bought a Varsity sweater. Once, after getting "the raspberries" over my lack of school spirit, I temporarily fixed my Varsity letter to my mid-length leather jacket, the attire popular with "Greasers" and "Continentals" (the latter a mixture of "Greaser" and "Soul") at that time. This didn't go over too well.

I have mentioned my three significant events but, come to think of it, there is one more. Not the birth of my parents' baby, Kenneth, although I guess that was pretty important. In 1963, my dad's brother Bob opened Shannon's Lounge at the southwest corner of Gaylord and Seven Mile (called Gay Seven because of the location). Shannon's was right down the street from us. Dad liked to tip a few cold ones after work; plasterers' work builds quite a thirst. Shannon's Lounge was so close that we kids could just about holler to him, "Dad, dinner'll be ready at six." Sometimes, when Dad's plastering gig was slow, he'd tend bar down at Shannon's: white shirt and bow tie, friendly smile, and a bit of Irish humor. As a young teenager, I spent a good many hours down there, usually performing odd jobs like cleaning up the parking lot. At other times, I might pedal to or from a nearby favorite "beer-and-wine" (aka "party") store and, if I noticed Dad's beat-up workingman's pickup with the bean-bag ashtray and the cheap transistor radio squeezed into a corner of the dashboard that both further identified the rig as Pop's, I'd stop in and hit him up for a buck and a Coke. It was always a good time when he was sitting at Shannon's after a hard day's work. Dad would be talking with his buds and with the locals like old Scotty, a guy who looked like he was ninety-nine, with pure white hair and a massive goiter protruding from the side of his neck. You also could count on running into a few relatives at Shannon's.

During summers and on an occasional Saturday, I would labor for

Pops (building scaffolding, mixing "mud"). In addition to being paid well, working for my dad often meant a stop at Shannon's and an endless supply of Coke, warm toasted cashews, a ground round, and a handful of red quarters (I knew where they were stashed behind the bar, specially-marked quarters for the bartender and barmaid to use when regulars weren't feeding the jukebox). The play-list on this jukebox, mostly the Frank Sinatra, Dean Martin, and Tijuana Brass type of fare, was slim pickings for my taste; however, Dion's "Ruby Baby," Roy Orbison's "Oh! Pretty Woman," and a Stones' tune or two ate up a good many of my quarters. Seated high atop a bar-stool, small table strategically situated between the jukebox and the pool-table action – this was a great way for a twelve-year-old to end the work day, to be sure.

I guess that it's a small thing, but it impressed me that my dad always insisted on paying his complete tab, even though he was the younger brother of the owner and a sometime employee of the bar. "Joey, how many Cokes did you have?" he'd inquire, as he dug out that weathered wallet from his rear pocket. On several occasions, I recall bumping along on my red-and-white Schwinn down Gaylord to Shannon's, one hand clutching the handlebars of my bike, the other holding tight to Dad's sack lunch, which he'd forgotten on the counter after heading out to tend bar. "Gee, why doesn't he just grill a burger?" I'd wonder. Dad wasn't that way. He looked up to his older brother(s), and there would be no taking advantage of the situation. However, we kids still made out, especially every March 18th following the St. Paddy's Day Celebration at Shannon's. Platters of leftover lunch meat and snacks made their way down the street north to our house. This was followed by what must have resembled the reception that a mother robin receives when she alights on her nest, where her open-mouthed, squawking fledglings are waiting impatiently for a portion of the juicy worm that is dangling precariously from her beak. Likewise, we eagerly awaited this smorgasbord of deli delights, a welcome diversion from our usual lunch fare of bologna or peanut butter and jelly sandwiches.

I've mentioned that I turned to television and food to help to fill the void left by the curtailment of my involvement in sports. Add music to the mix. The Rock 'n' Roll Pneumonia (not to mention the Boogie-Woogie Flu) had crept in years earlier and had refused to leave. I had a sister who was two years older and numerous aunts, uncles, and cousins in close proximity to my age who sometimes boarded with us. This meant an introduction to R&B and rock 'n' roll, among other things, at an early age. In addition to being loyal viewers of *American Bandstand,* we had one of those record players with twin speakers that you could disconnect and spread several feet apart on both sides for a fuller sound. Our record player came complete with a little spindle-like gadget that you could mount on the stem of the turntable, holding and discharging a half-dozen 45s. We'd have neighborhood kids over for our own little "hops," complete with Limbo and Twist contests. We danced to "It's Pony Time" by Chubby Checker, "Mashed Potato Time" by Dee Dee Sharp, and "The Bristol Stomp" by the Dovells. At the Seven-Grand shopping center nearby, you could pick up the latest 45s, along with one of those compact little cases that could hold up to twenty-five or more records, at either Federals or S.S. Kresge. I still have four of these cases, jammed full. The first record that I'd received as a gift (my tenth birthday I think), was Elvis's "Return to Sender." My first out-of-pocket purchase was Chris Montez's "Let's Dance." No, it was Tommy Roe's "Shelia." Wait, it was the Tornados' "Telstar."

My godfather from Cleveland and his wife, who my sister and I affectionately referred to as Uncle Moe and Aunt Eleanor, gave me my first transistor radio, a hand-held orange and white beauty with a single earplug attachment and two feet of speaker wire to accommodate late-night clandestine listening. Upstairs, with the lights out and my transistor resting on the edge of my pillow, I'd fall asleep listening to local deejays such as Joel Sebastian and my favorite, Lee Allan and his wild horn. The only exception would be *Hockey Night in Canada*, when the Wings skated against the fierce Montreal or Toronto clubs. More often than not, I'd be tuned into those great soul-searching melodies like "Tie Me Kangaroo Down, Sport" by Rolf Harris, "Alley Oop" by the Hollywood Argyles, and something about a one-eyed, one-horn, flying purple-people eater ("Purple People Eater" by Sheb Wooley). These lulled me to sleep, interspersed with tearjerkers like "Patches" by Clarence Carter and "Last Kiss" by J. Frank Wilson, and, of course, a dose of teenage love via "Hey, Paula" by Paul & Paula or "Johnny Angel" by Shelley Fabares. I had a huge crush on Shelley, a young actress who appeared on the TV series *The Donna Reed Show*. When I sang along privately, it was "Joey Angel."

Like every other kid in America, I sat transfixed before the tube, impatiently sitting through Ed Sullivan's corny guests and acts that always seemed to include some guy spinning multiple dinner plates on pool cue-like sticks before one or more came crashing down, a comedian for the adults, some cute animal act, and then, finally..."Ladies and gentlemen, the BEATLES!": Instant pandemonium – The British were back and were taking captives in droves. Who'd have thought a song about wanting to hold someone's hand could ignite such a firestorm? George was my favorite Beatle - loved his guitar chops.

The A.M. radio with which my siblings and I grew up was the only game in town for the better part of the sixties. It exposed its listeners to a wide variety of musical genres, all loosely labeled under the rock 'n' roll banner. A thirty-minute playlist might include James Brown's "Can't Stand It," the Dave Clark Five's "Bits and Pieces," Bobbie Gentry's "Ode to Billy Joe," and the Beach Boys' "Shut Down" - Soul, British Pop, Country, and Surf Rock. You could like it or lump it. I loved it. Contrast that approach with most formats of the last few decades that rarely stretch out beyond a lone style, sound, or genre. The F.M. long-play takeover towards the end of the sixties continued to offer a musical buffet, albeit with a "hip" bent to it. A radio show (indeed, some rock concerts) would mix and match strange musical bedfellows. Audiences would be exposed to a musical menagerie of styles. One moment, you'd hear the hard-driving tune "Magic Carpet Ride" by Steppenwolf and, the next, the haunting ballad "The Hurdy-Gurdy Man" by Donovan. I suspect that it was much the same in other large urban areas where teens were glued to their radios for a good part of the day. Detroit kids knew their music and I was one of them.

I made a half-hearted attempt to do the garage-band, lead-singer thing, but the insecurities about my weight hindered that pursuit as effectively as the issues about my feet had ended sports. The world only needed one Chubby Checker. My singing responsibilities at weekday Masses allowed me the protection of standing behind a large podium; you couldn't belt out "Land of a Thousand Dances" with one of those on stage. With such powerful incentives to slim down, you'd think that I'd have risen to the challenge. As most of us know (or learn), an addiction to food, coupled with one of the Seven Deadlies - gluttony, and other addictions (vices, crutches, call them what you will) often needs some radical intervention with which to come to grips. My "miracle diet" was five or six years down the road.

Music remained a refuge during high school. I'd race home to catch the TV show *Where the Action Is* with its regulars Paul Revere and the Raiders, a rock/R&B band that wore American Revolution outfits. Other afternoon fare included the teen dance shows *Club 1270* from the ABC studio in Southfield and *Swingin' Time* from CKLW in Windsor, Ontario, right across the Detroit River. These programs featured local artists like Mitch Ryder and the Detroit Wheels and the Opposing Forces; the latter featuring vocalist Ken Hasper who you will meet later. In the evening, there was *Shindig* and *Hullabaloo*, programs aimed at teenagers that showcased national and international recording stars like the Animals, the Byrds, Petula Clark, Darlene Love, Sam Cooke, Lesley Gore, James Brown, and Herman's Hermits.

I'm certain that my parents and siblings thought me odder than usual during this phase. While they sat huddled around the TV watching *My Favorite Martian* in the family room that my father had added onto the rear of the house several years earlier, I sat alone, lights out, rocking back and forth in our tiny living room, "Within You Without You" from the Beatles' *Sergeant Pepper* album playing as loud as I dare. You had to pass by the living room to use the bathroom. On these occasions, my dad would pause, listen for a moment to the foreign sound of George Harrison's sitar, shake his head, and head back to the family room to wait for *Bonanza*. Musically, Pops was Old School; Perry Como's "Catch a Falling Star" was more to his taste. He'd tolerated "who put the bomp in the bomp bah bomp bah bomp," but Bob Dylan screeching "Johnny's in the basement mixin' up the medicine" and the like was too much. "What the hell are you listenin' to?" he'd holler. Welcome to the Generation Gap. Now I say the same thing to my kids.

My Top 40 A.M. leanings were about to head in a new direction. I was about to discover the freeform world of F.M. radio. My introduction to the counterculture came through my older cousin, Mike Shannon. I'd always looked up to Mike, a fellow dweller of the township. Mike had a rep that helped me to get out of a few scrapes. In a word, he was cool. From the '63 Stingray Corvette in which Mike would cruise Telegraph Road, Wilson Pickett jumping out of the stereo, to the sharp Continental clothes he wore, complete with thick-and-thin socks and brown-on-yellow shoes from Florsheim Shoes, he was BAD! Mike looked like a white Jackie Wilson with an attitude; he was Agent Double-O-Soul (to borrow the title of the song by Edwin Starr).Well, at least that's how he was when I saw him last. Some time thereafter, Mike split for the West Coast c.'69. Eight months later, I saw him pull into a local McDonald's. Mike was perched behind the wheel of a VW micro-mini (a hippie bus). He had engulfed his head in hair like a character out of *Zap Comix*. Mike had Joe Cocker on the eight-track and some peculiar tobacco-like aroma emanating from within his bus. I did a triple take.

The gang of lads with whom I played cards also switched from the A.M. to F.M. format, which was growing in popularity at the time; WABX was the hippest station in town. The deejays played underground rock and an occasional jazz tune. This station had a tremendous effect on us. What I began to view as corny school dances fell like dominoes to the almost mystical lure of places like the Raven Gallery, the Crow's Nest West, and the Grande Ballroom; the latter, one of the first major rock clubs in the country, featured international acts like the Yardbirds, the Who, and Cream, as well as local heroes like SRC aka Scot Richard Case, the Amboy Dukes, and the MC5.

I can't say precisely what prompted my growing disinterest in Catholic spirituality, nor can I put a finger on the day, month, or year when it started to happen. There are likely a number of spokes to that wheel. I never abandoned the faith; it just sort of took a backseat to current interests. I was comfortable confining my "faith walk" to one hour on Sundays. My attendance at weekday student Masses was discontinued sometime during high school. Why? I couldn't say. The Who's rock opera"Tommy" was much cooler than anything by the Singing Nun. The disbanding of Cream and the bid by the Detroit Tigers for the '68 World Series took precedence. Socially, I'd have to decide if I would remain a part of the high-school status quo or cast my lot with the slowly emerging counterculture presence. Hippies at St. Agatha! The horror of it! I'm sure that I didn't understand how or if Jesus wanted to be a part of every area of my life, and that ultimately He knows what's in my best eternal interest. Then, it was tough to trust certain areas of my life to His direction, just as it is now. The priests, nuns, and teachers who tried to come off as hip and still spiritual didn't convince me. Had I been properly catechized, some might wonder? Was my growing disinterest in Catholicism just adolescent growing pains? Is it the Prodigal Son story yet again? Perhaps I came under the sway of the anti-establishment mantra "Turn on, tune in, drop out." Too few mature Catholic role models and peer-support groups with a spiritual component? Was it all of the above?

It strikes me as futile to sit around and blame this, that, and the other for one's shortcomings. Still, as I suggested to you and to my World Civilizations class, thoughtful and prayerful reflection on one's past can bear good fruit, including understanding, the healing of relationships, and, ultimately a closer, more genuine walk with the Savior. Furthermore, this book is an exercise to understand (historically) what prompted me to stray from my Catholic roots, only to find myself back thirty-five years later. What it is not is some vain attempt to make myself feel better by making others feel worse. If it sounds rather like I'm wielding a sword at times, it comes to mind that such blades usually cut both ways. Indeed, on Judgment Day, at whom shall I (or we) point a finger before the all-knowing mind of the Creator?

Regretfully, my high-school years ended on a sour note. I had taken an after-school job as a stock-boy and cashier at the Uniroyal Tires store, which was in the Kmart at Eight Mile and Beech Daly Roads. The possibility of a promotion to Accessories Manager following my graduation was not far-fetched. This, in turn, could lead to a management position at a Uniroyal store in several years. At the time, I didn't see myself as college material, nor did anyone else. However, I did possess some leadership qualities. I recall one good sister/nun (we called her Little Caesar on account of her short stature and emperor-like demeanor) cornering me in the hall and screeching out, in a somewhat controlled outburst, "Joe Shannon! You have real leadership ability, but you're leading people the wrong WAY!" At any rate, since I wasn't exactly an honor student and, barring getting a low lottery number and a Vietnam War tour prize, my career choice seemed solid; more on that in a moment.

Just prior to graduation, I went on the annual Senior Boys' retreat at St. Paul's Seminary near Schoolcraft and Outer Drive in Detroit. The weekend would leave a bad taste in my mouth for years to come. The motivation behind the retreat seemed like a last-shot bid to recruit potential seminarians before all of the males in my senior class launched out on divergent paths following our quickly approaching graduation. There was nothing wrong with that. It was the "means to an end" that didn't sit well with me. I should point out that most of the weekend was viewed through the lens of the cherry sloe-gin and the THC (marijuana in tablet form, more or less) that I'd smuggled in for myself and any takers. Still, I don't think that my perception was entirely distorted. I recall hearing very little about God "calling" one to priestly orders. Instead, one or more "hip" current seminarians, some with cigarettes in hand, told us how cool seminary life was; sprinkled in were a few off-color jokes. The last carrot dangled before us was that the seminary could be our ticket out of Vietnam (if the draft lottery went bad). I grant that this was something to think about, but what seemed conspicuously absent in this charade of "fishing" for candidates was, or should have been, some inner conviction of the Holy Spirit to serve the Body of Christ in this capacity. (As I said, perhaps the Spirit was speaking in spite of a misguided approach, and I may have been too "wrecked" to hear it.) I've since learned that God uses all manner of signposts to guide His people, including, but not restricted to Scripture, the lives of the saints, adversity, one's spouse or children, nature, and, at least on one occasion, Balaam's ass (Num 22:28).

Mr. Cool Seminarian seemed to discern that I wasn't "buying it" and that I exerted some influence on my classmates. By the end of high school, I'd gotten three nicknames. The first two were "Mooner," which I picked up in seventh or eighth grade (and that's all I'll say about that one), and "Rocker," because I couldn't sit still and was always humming some rock ditty. The third was "The General," because the school authorities – especially the principal, Sister Gilmary, and Father Reid, aka "Skeeter" (I'm not sure how he came by that nickname, which likely was bestowed on him by some former upperclassmen) – were convinced that I orchestrated much of the mischief that transpired before, during, and after school. I didn't – well, not as much as they suspected. Anyway, this young seminarian at St. Paul's decided to make an example of me. He had me get on the floor for some group-ritual/exercise thing, which I went along with initially. I assumed that it was going to be one of those trust deals where you close your eyes and expose the other retreat members to a bit of teamwork-building exercises. I was wrong. At his command (and this may have been prearranged), my classmates, friends, and chaperones attempted to strip me of my clothes. How far they intended to go I couldn't say. I lashed out like a cornered bear, kicking, punching, and cursing until someone in authority called a halt. I jumped up and, after letting the seminarian and anyone else I suspected was in on the prank know what a bunch of cowardly "faggots" they were, stalked back to my room to hibernate and to plot my revenge.

This disastrous weekend (for me, at least) left me sadly disappointed at what potentially could have been a spiritually awakening experience. On the contrary, it became just another nudge in the direction of a spiritually counterfeit smorgasbord lurking around the bend. Graduation came and went. The next day, deciding that it was time to make my own way, I moved out of my folks' house in the Township to a house on Oakfield Street in Detroit. The real darkness was looming overhead, waiting to engulf me.

. . . .

When you're the first person out of high school to get your own pad, you get downright popular. It wasn't much – a rental property on the west side of Detroit near Seven Mile and Southfield Roads. The house was in a part of town that was in the throes of what the media called "white flight," or was it fright? Either way, neighborhoods were changing overnight, due, in part, to the fallout from the riots a couple of summers before. Two high-school buds, Bill Rundel and Ron Allgeyer, and Tony Itria, an east-sider who I worked with at the Southfield Kmart location, shared the place with me; the rental agreement and the utilities were in my name. We caused a bit of a stir on move-in day as well as after it. It seems that our mostly elderly neighbors had not anticipated a crisis of this nature: a hippie horde settling among them. I guess that the black-light effect on the row of mounted shotguns on the living-room wall (we liked to hunt) raised some eyebrows. This is before we'd installed garage-sale drapes. There was no doubt that the White Panther garb favored by one of my housemates further fueled the fear that revolutionaries had established a beachhead in the tidy, still-respectable neighborhood. The late hours that my roommates and I worked meant that we were coming and going at all hours. Sometimes, we'd come in at 3 a.m., laden with a sack of groceries. This kind of thing led Ma and Pa Kettle across the street to assume the worst: DRUG DEALERS! Lots of our buddies were into the then-current BSA and Triumph motorcycle craze. "Oh, no, they're bikers too!" we could hear our neighbors saying.

I don't think that I ever was cut out for the communal thing; at least not for the version that some of my associates and our hangers-on seemed to be into. My idea of the end of a long day in automotive-accessories retail was not walking into a house full of people (most of whom I'd never seen before) and finding my albums strewn all over the floor and my bed disheveled. Nor was it seeing someone snorting a brown powdery substance off the kitchen table next to a dirty, empty plate of what looked to be all that was left of my mother's homemade spaghetti, which I'd anticipated enjoying for the last several hours. Tomorrow, I was scheduled for a twelve-hour shift. This would not do. Recently, I'd gotten the promotion for which I'd been hoping during my senior year

(Accessories Manager for Uniroyal Tires at the Kmart in Clawson, a nearby suburb). This, coupled with an anonymous call that I'd received, which said that the police were going to "hit" the house soon (how do you verify that?), made moving out seem like a smart move. The house was usually "clean," but all that it would take would be one forgotten roach or a tab of mescaline between the couch cushions. If the anonymous call was the neighbors' attempt to try and put a scare into us, it worked; well, sort of. Now that I had the gig in Clawson, I'd get a place there. Besides, the Oakfield Street crowd wasn't likely to drive over to the east side to party every night.

A new life-chapter unfolded abruptly before me. I was eighteen. Unlike Alice Cooper's soon-to-be-released hit song "Eighteen," wherein he laments the plight of eighteen-year-olds who "just don't know what [they] want," I not only knew, I was on my way. A new apartment and a job promotion; both would be short-lived.

It was likely a combination of things, not the least of which seems pathetically silly in retrospect: I dreaded that my promotion meant that there would be no flying the "freak flag" high; not even at half-mast. No earring, no outlandish hippie garb, and none of that all-important badge that most separated us from the "straights" – long hair. At Uniroyal, hair must be something of which Ward and June Cleaver (the parents in the television series *Leave It to Beaver*) would approve. While I was stocking shelves and unloading trucks, no one had cared; now I was in management. I absolutely loathed looking like a "narc" (someone who squealed about drug use), a weekend hippie, or, worst of all, a redneck. The more that I looked at cases of STP Oil Treatment, anti-freeze, custom wheel-rims, and eight-track tape players, the more apprehensive that I grew regarding my career choice ... and I'd only been at it a month! I couldn't shake the feeling. The "revolution" was goin' down and what was I doing? Standing at the cash register explaining the difference between AC and Champion spark plugs to a middle-aged woman whose husband had sent her on an errand for something with which she was quite unaccustomed. My interest in work evaporated overnight and my job performance mirrored my attitude. I developed an acute case of Maynard

G. Krebs Syndrome. I don't recall if I was sacked or left voluntarily but, after two months, my plan for lifelong success and financial security ground to a halt. Now what? Go to college? Vietnam was still a possibility if the war escalated. Some of the old gang – Tom Roa, Jim Maltesta, and Tim Sutherland – had planned to go out to southern California for a bit of a Holiday Adventure/Check-Out-the-Scene deal. In August of 1970, I decided to thumb out, hook up with the gang, and see what was happening firsthand.

I set out, a bulky, green, Army duffle bag resting by my side. Also by my side was Pat Daly, a fellow from the township whom I didn't know all that well but who seemed easygoing. It would be nice to have some company on what we expected to be a three-day journey, a hitchhiking adventure to be sure. Our launch pad was the On-Ramp at I-94 and Telegraph. On the first leg of the trip, we never waited more than ten minutes for a ride; consequently, we made excellent time. One ride in particular stands out: A young lady in a Volkswagen Beetle picked us up outside of Des Moines, Iowa, and took us all the way to Salt Lake City, Utah. We must have looked pretty harmless to her. She also must have been out-on-her-feet (or, should I say, seat) tired. Following introductions and half an hour of casual chitchat, she was apparently satisfied enough to turn over the wheel to us. With a "Wake me if ya need me," she curled up in the rear seat and was out in no time. No offense to you "Cornhuskers," but Nebraska is a good state to drive through at night unless endless miles of cornrows appeal to you.

At this pace, Pat and I would make our California destination ahead of schedule. However, the land of Joseph Smith, Mormons[1], and salt flats cast a less-than-friendly look on two scruffy hippie types heading west. Spending six hours on one corner under the August midday sun in Salt Lake City almost proved our undoing. Finally, a truck pulled over. While my partner jumped in, I looked back at the city like some Old Testament

---

[1]   Church of Jesus Christ of Latter-Day Saints (aka Mormons), founded in New York State by Joseph Smith.

prophet and cursed it for its inhospitable treatment of strangers. However, Utah is one scenic state: The landscape was breathtaking. Having just driven through Iowa and Nebraska no doubt enhanced its appeal to the eyes.

A young guy, who was being harassed in some redneck town in Nevada where we'd had the pleasure of being dropped off, asked if he could join us. We felt a bit sorry for this guy, whose name escapes me now. However, I can't forget seeing the mixture of terror and pleading written across his face. My buddy Pat and I said, "Sure," to his request, agreeing that there was safety in numbers. The downside was that, if we were having trouble scoring rides for the two of us, then now we could wind up as buzzard food out here.

Those of you who have stood along the highway, thumb outstretched, know the sweet little "rush" that comes when a vehicle pulls over and motions for you to hop in. When three of you are in hostile territory (Redneck USA) and the traffic is sparse, well, when that U-Haul swung over, it was like Christmas morning. The rear door was rigged to prevent it from closing. Inside the truck were half a dozen other pilgrims who were headed west. They greeted us with curious but friendly nods. The captain of our ship was a kindhearted soul who felt that it was his duty to pick up every hitchhiker between Reno and Frisco. He had one pilgrim ridin' shotgun up front and, by the trek's end, a baker's dozen in the rear. In spite of it getting a bit crowded in the U-Haul, everyone took it in stride, helped by a bit of fresh air. We were grateful not to be growing alongside the tumbleweeds common to this stretch. Soon, the snacks, drinks, and rolled cigarettes made their way around. I contributed a can of Campbell's Bean-with-Bacon soup to the hobo buffet. First one, then another shared some tale of the road, like jumpin' trains, as well as advice and places to avoid. There was much to learn.

Finally, Pat and I made it to San Francisco. Somehow, we packed Fisherman's Wharf, Golden Gate Park, and the Haight-Ashbury district into thirty-six hours. I thought that being from Detroit meant that I possessed a good deal of street smarts, but I wasn't ready for all of this. It probably was good that I was just passin' through. I loved riding the trolleys. Doing so was a must since, as a kid, I'd seen them in those Rice-a-Roni commercials on TV. While riding on one of the trolleys, I had my first encounter with a transvestite – plop, right next to me. I couldn't figure if this person was a he, a she, or what, so I just laid low, said nothing, and acted like everything was business as usual.

When Pat and I got to the Haight, I'm not sure what I expected. Scott McKenzie on the corner singing about "flowers in your hair" (I had none) in his hit song "San Francisco"? Hippie chicks in long flowing skirts, braless, and reeking of patchouli oil, peering warmly at me over their rose-colored granny glasses? The Jefferson Airplane and the Grateful Dead jamming in Golden Gate Park? Perhaps if we'd have arrived three years earlier.... Now, the streets were largely vacant. There were a handful of panhandlers, hustlers of various kinds, who plied their wares as well as a bunch of Hare Krishnas up the street making a racket. There were no Merry Pranksters or Diggers to be found. Oh, well, perhaps they'd all taken the advice in the song by the blues band Canned Heat and gone "up the country." San Francisco was a beautiful city, but the hookup date with Tom, Jim, and Tim from Detroit (Saturday noon) was approaching fast for Pat and me. We were scheduled to meet these guys in Huntington Beach, California. A quick glance at our map told us that the route to Los Angeles seemed to be a no-brainer: South U.S. 1 along the coast. Yeah, this seemed good to us and to the hundreds of others on the road who were headed in the same direction.

"We could be stranded here for days" was not some exaggerated lament. One apparently popular spot near a truck-stop ramp on southbound U.S. 1 had twenty-two people perched like starlings on a fence, and not just with their thumbs out. A combination of competition and desperation bred innovation. Several held signs like "$ for Gas," "Poet," "Fortune Teller," and "Trying to Get to My Mother's Funeral." There were people with pets, guitars, and children; now, there was us. Initially, this whole hitchhiking thing was cool. I'd only spent ten bucks thus far. I'd also met many kindhearted souls who, in addition to sharing their mode of transportation, offered snacks, drinks and conversation. This was especially true of the older folks who picked us up, the ones who had older teenagers themselves. These folks hoped that their own kids might meet with good fortune, were they ever on such an adventure. Ever since Salt Lake City, though, our journey had become "kind of a drag," in the words of the Buckinghams in their song of the same name; yep, ever since Salt Lake City (barring the fun ride in the U-Haul). After separating ourselves from the pack and putting on our best boyish, innocent, Midwestern smiles, Pat and I were rewarded with a ride.

The last leg of our journey was largely uneventful, except for two things. First, we decided to crash for the night near Monterey, due to the lateness of the hour and our being road-weary. The next day, Friday, we hoped to reach Huntington Beach. We'd taken refuge in a culvert a quarter mile off the freeway. There were no visible signs of life anywhere. Pat and I had a late-night hobo meal over a crackling fire. While we ate, we looked at the brilliant stars that illuminated the sky. I had visions of the L.A. scene dancing in my head. Suddenly, I said, "Huh, what's that?" I turned to a nearby thicket. No doubt the sound was made by some raccoon out on a nocturnal foraging expedition. I slid my hand down my leg and over the inside lip of my boot until my fingertip met the hilt of a Bowie knife. Bear? Minutes later, a muffled human cough came unmistakably from the same dense thicket. Were we being watched? Months earlier, I'd read about some crazed "Sickle Killer" who stalked the streets of Sacramento. Was this same Grim Reaper on the run? By a horrible twist of fate, was he digging in for the night nearby? Worse, was he eyeing us and waiting for the moment when our heavy eyelids submitted to the laws of fatigue, giving him the opportunity to pounce on us like some crazed-with-hunger panther and cleave our throats? "Maybe that's Bigfoot," I thought. I know how the mind plays tricks. One's imagination can see a python curled menacingly above until the moonlight escaping from behind the clouds reveals a large gnarled vine glued to a tree limb. True enough, but I hadn't conjured up a human cough. Now, my Bowie knife with its handle resting outside of my boot was at the ready, and I whispered a warning to my companion to be alert. What was to be a restful night turned into anything but. My eyes and ears strained for any sound, for any sign out of the ordinary. There is a horrible scene from the film

Easy Rider where the two bikers (Peter Fonda and Dennis Hopper), accompanied by an attorney (Jack Nicholson), are set upon and beaten with bats by a group of redneck thugs. It ran like a never-ending reel in my mind's eye. This was California, not the South. Ah, yes, but ... only a few hours earlier, thirst had driven us to a lonely out-of-the-way market near a gas station where our ride was filling up. Running over to the nearby store, I stopped short before bounding up the wooden-plank steps. There, next to the door, was a crude sign in big, bold letters: "No Niggers, Indians, or Hippies." This had to be some joke, but perhaps not. No doubt the gas station has cold drinks.

Let's go back to the creature in the thicket. Exhaustion finally won out. The early-rising birds didn't need to chirp twice to roust us. I sprang up quickly. A glance over at Pat assured me that his head still appeared attached. We'd lived to see another day. Forward.

We passed through dozens of towns and small cities, including Pismo Beach. Hitchhikers are always on the lookout for the ideal spot to position themselves for the most advantageous place from which to secure a ride. (Freeway on-ramps before drivers begin to accelerate are the usual *modus operandi* for hitchhikers.) Traffic was light and there were no competitors yet, so our prospects seemed fairly good. As the minutes evolve into hours, hitchhikers begin to take note of the most minute, mundane aspects of their surroundings. As Pat and I repositioned ourselves to escape the noonday sun, scrawled letters on the back of a "Yield" sign caught my attention. Amid a host of names and dates, there was a message from months earlier that was a stark reminder of just how desperate our situation could become: "God give the people of Pismo Beach sight; been here six hours. Signed, Rick from Virginia Beach, Virginia." Six hours! That guy must have been a leper or a double for Charles Manson. It turned out that my companion and I had better success than our fellow pilgrim from the eastern seaboard: we made L.A. late Friday night. Our noon rendezvous at Huntington Beach was all but assured.

Our last "ride" into the city dropped Pat and I off across from a city park and left us with this sage advice: "Sleep under the trees so the police helicopter searchlights can't spot you." (It was illegal to crash in city parks.) This made sense. In the wee hours of our first night in L.A., we found just such a spot and polished off the last of our provisions –crackers and grape jam. Our minds turned briefly to tomorrow's plans before sleep overcame us.

"What odd sound is that?" I wondered. There was a strange "whoomp"– like sound coming from behind a grassy knoll nearby. I hoped that there wasn't another psycho killer lurking in the shrubs. Thankfully, nothing emerged. Dawn had crept upon us unaware and sunlight began to trickle through the huge oak under which we had taken refuge. I still lay in a bit of a restless stupor listening to the strange "whoomps." An odd, prickly, foot-fallen-asleep feeling was covering the lower half of my body. As full consciousness won out over road weariness, a new horror greeted my now fully opened eyes. The lower torso of my body was engulfed by legions of ants, hence the prickly feeling. Fortunately, they weren't the fire-ant, biting variety. It seems that I'd gotten a bit of grape jelly on me during my late-night snack. When I leapt to my feet to rid myself of my uninvited bed-mates, I heard a husky voice ring out from beyond the knoll: "Hey, what the hell ya doin'? Get outta there!" Now what? The guy didn't look like a cop or a park attendant. Instead, it looked like Robin Hood and His Merry Men had come from Sherwood Forest. Wasn't there an episode like this of *The Beverly Hillbillies*? Of all the places in L.A. to choose to crash, we had to select a cozy spot right behind an archery range. The local medieval buffs held their Saturday morning archery-practice on this range – hence the thumping sound, as their arrows buried themselves in straw targets. Fortunately Pat and I had had the good fortune to be shielded by an ancient oak. Since these fellas seemed like decent shots, we didn't need to be told twice to beat it out of there.

In August, it's hot in L.A... On Saturdays, everybody and their brother heads to the beach. Huntington was one of the favorites. It has a carnival-like atmosphere, head- and surf-shops, burger stands, and a huge pier that juts out into the Pacific. When he heard that this was our first visit to the area, our "chauffeur" pointed out a few landmarks and some other points of interest. "You're just minutes from the beach," he remarked casually. It was eleven a.m. and Pat and I exchanged grins at the success of making our destination in a timely fashion. All the while, we looked forward to seeing the familiar, friendly faces of our buddies.

"Oh, my God, look at all these people. We'll never find them!" I said. Several weeks ago, when my pals and I laid out this venture back in Detroit, we agreed to meet at noon on the first Saturday of August. We thought that this would be easy enough, like hookin' up with friends at Camp Dearborn. However, at Huntington Beach, there were throngs of people as far as the eye could see. The beach was as wide as a football field from the parking lot down to where the waves crashed on the shore. North to south, it just faded like some vanishing point in a painting or on train tracks. "A hundred thousand people, easy," I ventured, "How will we ever find them?" Actually, Tom, Jim, and Tim found Pat and me at 12:30 p.m.; not bad.

The five of us decided to stay in Huntington Beach and to get an apartment there. Our crash pad, which was two blocks off of the beach, accommodated us comfortably. We were within spittin distance of a club – The Golden Bear (Kind of a Detroit Grande Ballroom type venue), that catered to the resurging Blues scene crowd, featuring bands like John Mayal's Bluesbreakers and Elvin Bishop. I had no specific agenda other than just checking out the scene, and what a scene it was! You've heard California jokingly referred to as "The Land of Fruits and Nuts"? Huntington Beach was the entire fruit-and-nut salad bar: people in every flavor imaginable. There were beautiful young women everywhere. I suspected that many of them were searching for fame and fortune in nearby Hollywood. It seemed like every guy on the beach except me had that lean, tan, bleached-blond surfer thing going on. On the bright side, I guess that this had helped my friends to spot me in this sea of Coppertone humanity. I had a nice tan from the neck up and elbows down, the fruit of three days hitching in the summer sun. The rest of me was snake-belly white, revealing a guy who worked indoors and was hesitant to go shirtless at the beach. The good news was that my hair was finally starting to grow out and the excess pounds clinging to my once-athletic body had begun to retreat. No doubt this was thanks to my new hobo diet and frugal approach to spending, as I had no idea how long I'd be doing the California thing.

After a week, the wonder of it all began to subside. Uneasiness about the whole scene was growing like some English ivy up the side of a stone cottage. The vibes just weren't right. Thousands of kids like us had descended on California; Frisco, Big Sur, and Huntington Beach were three of the most popular destinations. These kids were looking for something – adventure, a party, the so-called freedom that life on the road offers. However, when your cash flow dries up, along with the spirit of the Summer of Love from three years earlier, things can get ugly. People go into the "survival-of-the-fittest" mode. I needed something more laid-back.

In addition to the throngs of sun-worshipers, the south California beaches appealed to an astonishing assortment of peddlers. These people were selling every imaginable commodity; legal and illegal. In addition, there were various cult and evangelistic Christian groups working the beach. They were well in tune with the fact that scores of homeless, penniless, naïve, and friendless youths were looking for something with which to identify and to become a part of. Many of the members of these groups had good intentions, but others reminded me of vultures circling around weak prey on which they hoped to feed. The two-block stroll to the pier from our apartment often resulted in my buddies and I getting an armload of literature (tracts) to check out once we settled at "our" designated patch of beach turf for a day of hanging out. These tracts and fliers centered on subjects like The Children of God (aka The Family International, a religious movement created in the 60s that promoted salvation, the apocalypse, and using spirituality to fight "the System"), meetings of Eckankar (a religious group that uses spiritual exercises to experience the light and sound of God), free health clinics, this and that yogi, the newest enlightened master in town conducting seminars on how to find the "god" in you, and warnings about bad acid circulating the beach. Various Christian groups offered places to "crash," to find a decent meal, and to help you to find work. In addition, they offered Bible studies that were aimed at rebellious, disenchanted youth.

The previous tenants of our apartment had left behind several telltale signs of a potential pilgrim on the road to Nirvana. One wall was graced by a prominent poster of Meher Baba, an eastern mystic who was all the rage out here. To me, he just looked like another dark-complexioned Indian dude with long hair and a set of deep, black, haunted eyes. Two books, Khalil (aka Kahlil) Gibran's *The Prophet* and Baba Ram Dass' *Be Here Now Be Now Here*, were left on a tired old coffee table. Two pages from the latter did a bit of a number on my head, shaping my spiritual mindset for the next year. Ultimately, they became the focus of a key spiritual battle down the road. On a left-hand page of *Be Here Now Be Now Here*, a well known passage from the Gospels was written in beautiful Old English script. The passage is the one in which Jesus declared, "I am the Way, the Truth, and the Life. No one comes to the Father but through me" (Jn 14:6). The page on the right beckoned the reader to ponder the following thought: "Was Jesus saying that He (Jesus) was the sole, exclusive way, or that His way was the way? The latter view was the `true' meaning behind Jesus' statement." Jesus' *way* was peace and love. Above all, Jesus was a revolutionary who could have strolled into these modern-day temples filled with corrupt Pharisee-like priests and ministers, denounced their hypocritical ways, and overturned the collection tables. Of course, He would have done all of this while wearing flowing hair and a beard and being garbed in a simple tunic and sandals. Like a largemouth bass tying into a shiny lure, I bought this hook, line, and sinker. The uniqueness of Jesus' ministry, death, and resurrection escaped me; it had been neatly smoke-screened. I'd not yet met C.S. Lewis and been challenged by his "Lord, Liar, Lunatic" premise concerning the uniqueness of Jesus. At this point in my life, Jesus was just another in the pantheon of so-called ascended masters (avatars). Indeed, I thought that there were many paths to the spiritual mountaintop. My favorite t-shirt, which had the warm, smiling face of Jesus on the front and marijuana plants on the back, proclaimed my new state of awareness. All that I needed was to master the blues harmonica and I would indeed be able to return to the Motor City as a Renaissance Hippie.

Although we had just settled into our apartment, the group of guys from Detroit with whom I was rooming announced that they would be heading home soon. For me, the prospect of staying out in southern California without friends from home and with funds growing thin was not pleasant. These facts, along with my new-found, all-embracing spiritual awareness, led me to the discernment that perhaps everything out here on the west coast was not so good. I thought, "I'm outta here...." I'd done California. After about a month, Tom, Jim, Tim, Pat, and I left for home.

. . . .

What now? I was back in Michigan from California and somewhat disillusioned with the whole hippie thing. Along with two buddies from high school, Tom Engel and Gary Beach, I ended up at a trailer park – Mother Hefler's Motel and Trailer Park, I think – in Dearborn Heights, a western suburb of Detroit. Mother Hefler's was near Warren Avenue and Telegraph Road. What a dive! You see places like this occasionally in northern Michigan, usually along some secondary road in a rural area: junkyards plunked down in the middle of some serene setting with rusting automobiles from a bygone era, rotting boat-hulks and trailers from *Yogi Bear* cartoons with flattened tires and faded license plates strewn about like industrial-waste weeds. Our new digs were not in a forgotten, obscure corner of some up-North rural Michigan county; this was a major intersection at the north end of Dearborn Heights. The World's Ugliest Trailer contest was underway and our place was in the finals.

Our trailer was short and quite compact by today's standards. Fortunately, Tom, Gary, and I worked different shifts and were seldom there at the same time. Our trailer was not unlike, a bit longer perhaps, than one you may recall Jethro Bodine, in a *Beverly Hillbillies* episode, using as a portable bachelor pad; didn't work out too well as you may recall, especially when you park it on a beach, tides and all. It had been a long time since our trailer had seen good times. The exterior needed a paint job pronto, now it was a fading, sickly, World War II jeep green. It was hot as blazes in the front and cold as Dante's lower region towards the rear. We suspected that the place was haunted. Radios and water-taps would go on at all hours as if by some unseen hand. We'd heard, but never could verify, that someone had been electrocuted years earlier when a falling radio brought this poor soul's bubble bath to an abrupt end. I don't recall having had a bathtub there (too small – only room for a small shower), but details didn't matter. We weren't trying to solve a crime or to conduct séances; the place just had a weird vibe to it. Furthermore, when you're 6'4" and 220 pounds like I was, the trailer could be downright claustrophobic. The trailer park itself seemed to attract a real criminal element; there were a lot of shady characters slinking around as well as some drug dealing. Come to think of it, this kind of fit our description as well....

This period would be one of the darkest of my life. I had no career prospects. I was back at Uniroyal Tires in Southfield, but not as Accessories Manager. Now I was just a glorified stock-boy/cashier with the rep that I'd had my shot and blown it. I turned to the amphetamine "speed" to get me through the workday and to hashish and downers (reds, we called them) to crash at night. I disliked both coffee and beer (legal speed and downers, as I liked to refer to them), and it was much easier to pop a few bennies in the morning and the flip-side downers at night. Well, all of this can get rather expensive. A means to remedy that was buy drugs in bulk and to deal some on the side. That way, you could meet your costs and maybe even turn a little profit. What a slippery slope that financial plan can quickly turn into! We kept ounces of hash in a jar of instant coffee that was set inconspicuously on a kitchen shelf. After we cut up the hash into grams, it looked like cubes of soup broth bullion; we would then wrap the hash in tinfoil and situate them in the coffee jar so they could not be detected with the eye. But where sin abounds, grace much more....There were a couple of good things about this location: regular gas wars at nearby Telegraph and Warren Avenue and a decent fish-and-chips place within walking distance to help curb those late-night attacks of "the munchies," cravings for food and drink of an intense, almost maddening nature. Also, it was at this Trailer Park from Hell that I first met Lee Brubaker.

On that day, Tommy Roa, my old high school buddy and brief

roommate out in California who had just returned from an extended stay in Florida, dropped in unannounced. (No doubt he was hoping to catch a free buzz). Accompanying him was a rather dramatic-looking young man who introduced himself simply as Brother Lee. This gentleman had broad-shoulders, golden-bronze skin, and bleached-blond hair that went over his collar. He quietly took a seat while the rest of us exchanged greetings over a hash-pipe. I'm the worst at remembering names: if I misname you or peg you with a nickname, you're stuck. Why I can recall the latter easily enough is a mystery to me. Our quiet guest, whose real name had momentarily escaped me, had a magnificent lumberjack-like beard. "Hey, Moses," I asked him, "Can I get you something to eat or drink? Wanna get in on this bowl of hash?" I meant no disrespect by calling him "Moses." While he declined my hospitality, he took on his new name good-naturedly. "Moses" continued to endure this layover until the conclusion of his ride's visit. It turned out that "Moses," a Florida boy originally from Vero Beach, was en route to see friends in Ontario. My buddy Tommy, whom he met while working in the citrus groves in Florida, had offered to take him as far as Windsor. Oh, yeah, "Moses" carried a Bible – a big black one, not one of those small, inconspicuous pocket-versions. I never would have guessed that I'd meet "Moses" again on his own turf.

My buddies and I soon bid farewell to the trailer park from a cheap horror-movie set and ended up back in Redford Township. We found a nice apartment above a party store on Grand River and Woodworth Street. By now the three of us (Tom Engel, Gary Beach, and yours truly) made pretty good roommates. We knew how much space each other required, knew one another's likes and dislikes and work/sleep schedules, and kept our partying to a minimum. My appetite for all things "spiritual," which was planted months earlier on the beaches of California, continued to grow. I received nourishment from visits to various Detroit-area head-shops and bookstores that stocked books and magazines catering to my new interests, especially the Mayflower Bookstore, an esoteric shop in the northern suburb of Ferndale. Among my interests were *The Egyptian Book of the Dead*, the works of Edgar Cayce, astral projection, UFOs, and, if humor were on the menu, Gilbert Shelton's underground-comic series *The Fabulous Furry Freak Brothers*.

The inside of the door of our apartment was outlined with a paisley cross that glowed when a black light was turned on. A picture of "the laughing Jesus" smiled out at you from the center. On either side of Jesus were pictures representing the good and wicked thieves (revolutionaries) at the Crucifixion. The good thief was symbolized by one of my spiritual heroes, George Harrison. His triple-LP set, *All Things Must Pass*, had been released recently and was receiving considerable play on my stereo. The wicked thief was John Lennon, whom I adored musically but whom I suspected of hovering near bankruptcy spiritually. On the wall of the living room was a large black-and-white poster of Janis Joplin. Her head was thrown back, and she was belting out some bluesy ballad into a tightly gripped microphone. Another large black-light poster asked if anything other than one's own mind actually exists. There also was a Playmate calendar and a glossy print of singer/songwriter Leon Russell bangin' on his keyboard. In addition, we had an assortment of candles and incense burners as well as ashtrays and beanbags. In the center of our living room was our stereo system - the Hippie Altar...sorry, no lava lamp. Yes, coming to this apartment from the trailer park was like the Clampetts moving to Beverly Hills.

One evening my roommates Tom Engel and Gary Beach and I hosted a "trips" party, styled somewhat after the Merry Pranksters. The party store beneath us came in especially handy on these occasions, supplying cigarettes, rolling papers, munchies, and Boone's Farm wine. Since I looked to be in my mid-twenties, the proprietors of the store always sold alcohol to me without carding; actually, I was nineteen. Michigan had not yet lowered the drinking age to eighteen, a brief, ill-conceived experiment that took place in the mid 1970s. When one was "trippin'," venturing out to deal with the world (especially the police, should you get pulled over) was not a good game plan. On the occasion of this particular party, a half-dozen of us were kicking back, listening to the album *In Search of the Lost Chord* by the Moody Blues. In the apartment, candles were aglow, and a strong smell of weed wrestled with jasmine incense for dominance. Just as my friends and I were waiting for the windowpane acid that we'd dropped earlier to kick in, a kitchen mishap briefly distracted us. As some of you know, pot-smokers are often afflicted by the munchies. In order to get a jump on this condition while we still were able, my buddies and I had put on spaghetti noodles to boil while a tangy sauce simmered on a rear burner. A few of us stood around the stove, eyes fixed on the kettle as the noodles began to writhe and bubble in a boiling mass. Nobody lifted a finger or said anything. We just continued to stare intently as the noodles began to boil over; hissing, sputtering ... we remained hypnotized for several minutes. Finally, the water was gone. The few remaining noodles in the pot started to convulse like worms on hot pavement in July. I reached over and shut off the burner. We looked at each other and simultaneously let out a "Wow, far out!" Like I said, we were waiting to "get off." Having the party store near at hand and Hefty's Coney Island across the street dispelled any concerns about immediate future malnourishment. However, the good vibes were about to come to a screeching halt.

The conversation had turned to the topic of the possibility of traveling into other dimensions. In one of my "how-to" occult books, I had read that, if you concentrated long and hard enough on a given object or spot, you could access a door to another dimension. I know that this sounds goofy but, when you're nineteen, "peaking" on acid, and increasingly coming under the dominion of the Dark Side ... well, you get the picture. We agreed that our point of focus would be the poster of Janis Joplin that was hanging on the wall. We turned off the Moody Blues and began to glare silently at the poster of Janis. Flickering candles lent a haunting feel to the proceedings, which went on for what seemed like several minutes. Suddenly, the image of Janis began to age, slowly at first, then rapidly. Finally, like some portrait of Dorian Gray in Oscar Wilde's novel *The Picture of Dorian Gray*, all that remained was Janis' screaming skull, with strands of silvery white hair clinging in patches like cobwebs as she belted out a heart-wrenching tune of love gone badly. Then, utter blackness ... aha, was the door to some hidden dimension ready to swing open? Who or what was that figure in the distance? Some object was traveling straight towards us at an ever-increasing speed. It appeared to be a head with no discernible body, not unlike the Wizard of Oz as he first appeared to Dorothy and her companions. However, this was no Wizard of Oz: it was Lucifer. A slight, sinister grin spread across his handsome face. Then I heard him speak, as if by telepathy, for his lips moved not: "I got Janis, and I'm going to get you, too." Janis had died recently. The statement that I heard is in no way a pronouncement on her eternal destiny; the devil is, after all, the father of lies. Just as quickly, everything returned to the blackness of the pit as in Edgar Allen Poe's tale *The Pit and the Pendulum*. In the blink of an eye, there was Janis, once again as originally depicted, at the peak of her career.

You're probably thinking that this is an easy one to figure out. Atmosphere, imagination, and hallucinogens can have people seeing all sorts of wild and bizarre sights and sounds. However, did I neglect to mention that all of us at the party saw the same image and received the same communication? After our "experiment" was over, my fellow tripsters jumped to their feet. Without so much as flashing the peace sign, they beat it out of there as if our unwelcome guest might reappear at any moment.

It was the middle of the night. Alone and not expecting to "come down" for hours, I clutched the St. Joseph edition of the Catholic Bible to my chest like some Spartan shield and bid any evil spirit(s) be gone. No doubt I slept with the light on. This wouldn't be the first or last time that I'd awaken with my Bible snuggled up alongside me like some child's teddy bear. Reflecting on the incident afterwards, I concluded that the moral of the story was a warning to stay away from hard liquor and heroin, both of which contributed to Janis' demise, or so we'd heard.

The episode also inspired me with a bit of sick humor for future "trip parties." In homage to two of my favorite boyhood television shows, *Shock Theatre* and *Morgus Presents*, I purchased a lifelike skull that glowed in the dark. (Both programs featured skulls and are described earlier in this document.) At my parties, I would carefully place the glowing skull under the couch where I could reach it easily. I would switch off the lights unexpectedly, at just the right moment. In the initial darkness, before the eyes of the party-goers could adjust, I would locate the glowing skull. Slowly, I would sweep it around before the horrified gaze of my mystified guests. The skull seemed to move on its own. Of course, one also had to have the appropriate music to ensure maximum "freak out," something like Pink Floyd's trippy record *Ummagumma*, which included the song "Careful with That Ax, Eugene," or an album of Hollywood haunted-house sound effects, such as rattling chains, moaning voices, and the like. No doubt a few minds were blown.... This was a great way to liven up a party. It also was a good way to end one quickly if you were ready to "crash" and people were slow to take the hint. I could only get away with this prank a few times, but my reputation as a somewhat eccentric wizard wannabe took root. Go figure.

Big changes were about to be set in motion. They began with two township police officers banging on my door in the middle of the night. One of my shaken roommates, Gary, awakened to inform me that I had visitors – the police! My other roommate, Tom, who had just gotten off of the night shift at the Great Scott supermarket nearby, was busily rolling joints at the kitchen table. When the cops came, he was either unable or too rattled to put "Operation Super Flush" into action. (We'd rigged our toilet to an industrial-strength level in order to accommodate large quantities of you-know-what that needed immediate disposal.) Tom stuffed his stash into a Trix cereal box, deciding to take the risk rather than to watch his handiwork go swirling down to the netherworld.

The two police officers asked me if I knew where my car was. "Sure, it's right down there," I replied casually. Stepping out onto the balcony, I said nothing as I pointed to the empty spot where my 1965 Ford Mercury Caliente, a cool little baby-blue convertible, slept at night.

"Your vehicle is about a mile from here," said one of the officers. He added, "It was on fire. The fire department just put out the fire ... looks like your car is totaled."

Apparently, my lack of concern and bewilderment aroused suspicion. Later, I explained to an investigator, "It was the middle of the night, I was exhausted, and what's done is done." I concluded with, "Hopefully, insurance will cover it, so why get all bent out of shape?"

On the night of the incident, the police traced the license plate of the Caliente to my parents' address while trying to track down the owner of the vehicle. (Since I moved so much, I continued to use my parents' address for years on important documents such as auto registration). My folks knew that I had a recent run-in in Toledo, Ohio, that included a brief stay in their exotic jail, which was over a hundred years old and would have made a suitable movie set for Poe's *The House of Usher*. I was jailed for transporting illegal fireworks (dangerous explosives). The guys who sold the fireworks to me, some unsavory characters down in Lucas County, had misled me. At a future date, I'd be called to testify against them. Now, in the middle of the night, my mom and dad were told that their son's car was discovered in flames with no sign of an occupant; my poor parents. Well, I'll let you draw your own conclusions, but hereafter the township police began to keep a close eye on our pad. That gets old really quickly.

After graduation from high school, our crowd frequented the Eastown Theatre, an eastside rock club that was located near Harper Avenue and Van Dyke Street. After the closing of the Grande Ballroom, the Eastown became the place to hear popular acts like Procol Harum, King Crimson, Traffic, and the Allman Brothers. Three concerts there were especially memorable, all for different reasons. First was a show by Derek and the Dominos, a group led by guitarist Eric Clapton, who had been in the Yardbirds, Cream, and Blind Faith before forming this outfit. Derek and the Dominos may have been the most incredible onslaught of musical rock sound ever to make its way deep into the innermost recesses of the ear and beyond. Regrettably, I'd missed Cream and Blind Faith on their visits to Detroit. I vowed not to make the same mistake thrice. When Clapton and company launched into their version of Jimi Hendrix's "Little Wing," well, it just didn't get any better.

The second was a show by Mountain, which featured another guitar hero, Leslie West. This particular concert included an unknown opening act (at least to my crowd and me), Mylon. We'd come to the show anxious to hear cuts from Mountain's new release *Nantucket Sleighride* and planned to use the opening act as an opportunity to ensure that a proper hash buzz was on tap by the time Leslie West and company hit the stage. What? Who's this! A guy came onstage, clothed in leather from head to toe like some skinny Jim Morrison. He had a cross on his back that blazed forth like neon whenever he turned his back to the audience and the spotlight hit it just right. Out of the mouth of this guy, who had a bit of a southern twang, came rockin' bluesy gospel sounds. He was singing something about "Sunday School Blues." The audience, skeptical at first, was soon won over. This guy, who turned out to be Mylon LeFevre, rocked! Of course, it helps if you have a crackerjack, tight band with three Supremes-like chicks singing backup and a southern-rock, soulful sound on which to build your message. Mylon tore it up. There was no escaping what was behind their out-front, in-your-face lyrics. There was no subtle "try to be cool, sneak the message in so we don't offend people," approach.

What was most astonishing is that Mylon got called back for more encores than Mountain. The audience was on its feet, clapping and singing to "Old Gospel Ship" as though we'd all misread the Eastown marquee: "Mountain, Tomorrow Night … Tonight Only: Mylon."

Mountain's set was impressive, but something was happening to me. I couldn't shake what I'd heard earlier. Mountain performed one of their favorite tunes of mine, "Travelin' in the Dark," which is about a bunch of whalers hooked into a big one with a little love gone sour in-between. Well, when Mountain played this song tonight, it had a whole different meaning for me. It was about me! I was travelin' in the dark (spiritually) and couldn't see a thing. Earlier, I'd been singing enthusiastically with Mylon and the crowd about a trip that I was going to take on that Gospel ship. Was I?

Usually, I was pretty careful about what albums and/or eight-tracks I bought with my frugal income. The day after the concert, I went in search of Mylon's *We Believe* album. I often played it when feeling down; I still have it.

My third memorable show, and one of the Eastown's last, turned out to be as bad as the previous one was good. This was a concert by Black Sabbath and Fleetwood Mac. I went to hear the Peter Green version of the

Mac (Green is an amazing English blues/rock guitarist who had left the "Mac" about this time and would spend the next decade battling mental illness). I was accompanied by three weekend-hippie chicks from the suburbs – Southfield. Like its predecessor, the Grande, the Eastown was not a safe, cozy venue. First of all, getting in and out of the Eastown's neighborhood was an adventure in itself. You would have to work your way through a gauntlet of panhandlers, junkies, pimps, and dealers as well as freaks looking for a free or cheap ticket to the show. Conditions inside the Eastown were despicable. Only desperation would drive a person to venture into one of the restrooms, which would have made the third level of Dante's Inferno seem like a five-star spa. Consequently, you didn't go down to the Eastown in your finest hippie attire. You were going to be packed in like sardines, sitting on a floor with beer, pop, coffee, and who knows what else on it. Burn holes were a common hazard: a "joint" would make its way merrily along, clinging to some roach clip, with its original owner long since forgotten. Nobody was going to see you anyway, so stick with your old Levis, t-shirt, and tennis shoes or moccasins. In part, the night of the Sabbath/Mac show led to the fire marshal shutting down the Eastown soon after. The theatre was closed for numerous violations, including greatly exceeding the number of patrons allowed.

Early in the evening of the concert, I made the mistake of dropping a tab of acid and providing the three teenybopper hipsters who were with me with half a "hit" each for their first "trip." This ushered in one blunder on top of another. Somehow, the girls and I snaked our way onto the main floor and secured a piece of "turf." Once settled in, that was it - moving was out of the question. Bad vibes hung heavily in the air. This, of course, was the perfect setting for Sabbath's "gentle" ballad "Iron Man."

The set by Fleetwood Mac, who were the opening act, was cool. My major concern for the upcoming Sabbath set was that a cramp might strike my 6'4" body, which then was in the full lotus position. That never happened; I just went numb. This reminded me of when I was a kid playing backyard hockey: Although my feet were freezing, I ignored it the best that I could rather than leave the game. That prickly feeling came for 10-15 minutes, and then nothing … you're numb. I knew that if I was

44

"getting off" on the acid, the girls certainly must be. As Sabbath violated our sense of hearing, one of the girls started to lose it; a panic attack, perhaps. She started yelling, "I gotta go. Ya gotta get me outta here!" In spite of attempts by her friends and me to calm her down, she grew louder and more insistent. The other concertgoers sandwiched up against us grew increasingly annoyed at her outbursts.

"Here's another fine mess I've gotten myself into," I thought. When you're getting "off" on acid, it's often all that you can do to keep your own head together; now, I had these three female hippie wannabes in their cute crushed-velvet bell-bottoms in my charge. During a lull in the show, we made our move and somehow worked our way to the front entrance. Finally, we were out into the night air. We still had a three-block walk to my car and the worst of the pre-show gauntlet of lowlifes, who were standing out in the street, with which to contend. They were in foul moods because they hadn't been able to "crash" the concert. We had no alternative but to traverse this group of exiles from a bad movie, who eyed us like so many buzzards. With one girl clutching each arm and the third close behind, we pressed forward, ignoring the threatening taunts and obscene comments. A girl screamed: It was the third member of our party. Several men had grabbed her and thrown her up against a wall. There were no police, bouncers, or sympathetic Good Samaritans. We were alone. One man frisked down the girl for anything of value while another pinned her arms to the wall. A third began to unbutton her blouse.

I wish I could say that I waded into these guys like Bruce Lee. I did wade into them, like some guy freaking out on acid. The reckless boldness with which I threw them off of her must have stunned them. I'm sure that these men wondered if I was armed, crazy, or both. I called them every foul name that I could conjure up and threatened them with what I'd do to them and their "muthas." Had they been so inclined, these guys could have had their way with us. Perhaps, God in His mercy still had a guardian angel assigned to this wayward son of the Church. Who knows? We got away from the men and ran to my car. I was so enraged over the attempted assault that, after I dropped off the girls (a relief, to be sure), I went to my pad and fetched a 16-gauge semiautomatic shotgun. I fairly giggled as I anticipated the look on the faces of those lowlifes when they recognized who it was with a shotgun aimed at their crotches. By that time, I was so stoned that I couldn't find my way back to the Eastown. Thank God!

. . . .

Word reached me that a certain sergeant wanted to bring me in for questioning about the "barbecued-car" incident. Provided that I had a hand in it, this could lead to felony fraud charges for the money that I'd collected from the insurance company. I'd since purchased a hot 1967 Nova SS (very unhippie-like; no Beetle or Econoline van for me). Tommy Roa, the fella who had stopped in unexpectedly at the trailer with "Moses" several months earlier, informed us that he'd soon be heading back to Florida - a hippie "snowbird," to be sure. His description of the environment (ocean and tropics) and the laid-back atmosphere grabbed my attention. The township police were turning up the heat, so it was time for a change of scenery.

In a couple of days, I unloaded my beloved Nova, stored my personals at my folks' place, bid "Later" to my roommates, and headed south with Tommy and our new buddy Steve Matsos from Livonia. The three of us went down I-75 in a pea-soup green 1963 Ford Falcon. Our "chariot" had a hole in the rear floorboard. During a freak snowstorm in central Ohio, we discovered to our chagrin that the only windshield wiper that worked was the one on the passenger side. But, not to worry: just get behind an eighteen-wheeler and stick close and/or have the person "riding shotgun" guide you. Yikes!

I'd made up my mind to travel south clean. Scenes from the film *Easy Rider* still lingered in my mind's eye. I would not risk getting "popped" in some redneck, one-horse town in Tennessee or Georgia. I-75 had not yet been completed, so we'd have to ditch the freeway for a stretch of several hundred miles. When I got settled in Florida, I'd have my "stash" mailed down or "cop" what I could locally.

"Hey Redford Township police, 'catch me if you can,'" to borrow a phrase from an old Dave Clark Five tune. "Rocker has left the building, er state."

Harold Shannon - Salem High School
Salem, Ohio, 1943

Gloria Evans - Redford High School
Detroit, Michigan, 1949

St. Agatha Church, Redford Township, MI (1948 - closed 2005)

"Rub a dub dub, lil 1 yr. old Joey's in the tub."

Joe Shannon in tub.

Joey, ridin' the Redford
Township range.

Shannon Home on Gaylord.

Joe's 4th Grade Class
St. Agatha Catholic School

Joseph Shannon
St. Agatha High School
Redford Township, MI 1970

Little Joe - "Stick 'em up!"

So named as it sat on the corner of
Gaylord and Seven Mile Road.

Reece M. Shannon

Ryder J. Shannon

Cory J. Shannon & Samantha Mulhall

Hayley A. Shannon

Jesse E. Shannon

Cory J. Shannon

Joseph R.D. Shannon & Barbara Auxier

Kenneth Shannon

Jeffery Shannon

Daniel Shannon

Joseph R.D. Shannon 1952---

Susan Shannon

Harold Shannon   and   Gloria Evans

Joseph Shannon & Mabel Bastien   John Evans & Alice Potter

SHANNON

PART TWO

Talk about a fish out of water (or, in this case, a mammal in water). From the cold, gray gloom of early November 1971 in Detroit's shadow, my friends and I took a twenty-plus hour drive south. This was something of an adventure: We piloted the Ford three-on-the-tree Falcon, which had an unquenchable thirst for Wolf's Head 30-weight oil, down I-75. She didn't look like much, but she was true. She brought us safely to an area that the Florida Tourist Bureau marketed as "Where the Tropics Begin." Our one luxury on the trip was a Panasonic eight-track tape player and half a dozen tapes.

While growing up in southeast Michigan in the 1950s and 1960s, the communities of Redford, Livonia, and Southfield were still developing into full-blown "burbs." Our neighborhood in Redford still had enough creeks, woods, and meadows, along with the nearby Rouge River watershed and parks like Lola Valley and Bell Creek, to sustain a fair amount of wildlife. After hitting the nearby candy store for supplies, I liked nothing better than to spend the day pedaling my twenty-six-inch red-and-white Schwinn bike down to the Rouge in search of muskrats, turtles, and snakes. We kids grew up watching *Michigan Outdoors*, a local television program hosted by Mort Neff, which helped fuel our interest and appreciation for the outdoors. We thrilled to the cry of pheasants crowing in nearby woods and dreamed of living on a farm. I can hear farmers chuckling at that youthful romantic notion of farm life. However, nothing prepared me for the setting to which I awakened, somewhat stiffly, in Florida.

I spent my first night sleeping on Wabasso Beach, which is now a Disney resort site just north of Vero Beach. Fortunately, my partners Tom Roa and Steve Matsos knew something of tides. We'd bed down just over a slight bluff, which kept us hidden from view. This bluff was a stone's throw away from where the surf crashed on the beach. Otherwise, City Boy Joe might have awakened to a seaweed-saltwater bath.

Orchid Island, a stretch of land along A1A between Sebastian to the north and Vero Beach to the south, was like suddenly finding oneself dropped into a Tarzan flick or some Lost World epic. Okay, I know it's not the Amazon Basin or the Serengeti, but please keep in mind that twenty-four hours earlier I'd been sitting in Bates' Hamburgers at Seven Mile and Beech Daly in Redford.

In a few days, Tommy, Steve, and I settled into an efficiency apartment (one of six, divided into three sets of two). It was on a winding dirt road that ran adjacent to the Inter-Coastal Waterway (Indian River) that separated this strip of Florida from the mainland. The road was aptly named Jungle Trail. It was a largely secluded setting. I, at least, was not interested in drawing any attention to ourselves, though we continually managed to do just that. I quickly discovered that this area, indeed much of Florida, was seriously redneck, including many of the local, long-haired, hippie wannabes. A hundred paces to the left of our porch sat the apartment's dock, which jutted some twenty feet out into the river. It looked like the setting for that 50s drive-in thriller *The Creature from the Black Lagoon*. If you made a hard right off of our front porch, you'd be reaching quickly for your machete. The thick, impenetrable vegetation and numerous palmetto shrubs looked every bit as formidable as those I'd viewed in countless lost safari flicks. The cluster of cottage-like apartments stood like a small outpost in the midst of an old citrus grove, which was losing the fight to the island's reclamation of its natural vegetation. In season, beautiful crimson orchids abounded; hence, the name Orchid Island. Banana, avocado, and stately royal-palm trees further enhanced the tropical vibe. The Atlantic Ocean was a five-minute jog along a nearby trail that wound through an abandoned grapefruit grove. This was interspersed with magnificent trees with wonderfully gnarled dangling vines that Bomba the Jungle Boy would have put to good use.

The ocean appeared unjaded and mysterious. It was more alive than when I had experienced it briefly during my earlier sojourn to the California coast. The Atlantic lapping the Florida coast had a different vibe to it; I relished this vibe and felt intoxicated by it. In part, I suppose this was true because the West Coast beaches that I frequented (Huntington, in particular) often were shared with a hundred thousand fellow inhabitants of Planet Earth. By the time my friends and I hit the California beaches (noonish), they had been picked clean of any treasures, shells, and such that the sea had spit up the night before. The beaches serving Los Angeles were an endless clutter of humanity woven into a colorful fabric. This fabric primarily was made up of young hippies, surfers, and aspiring Hollywood actor-types. The smell of French fries, Coppertone, and pot swirling in the sea-salt air launched an all-out offensive assault on one's olfactory senses. The pounding, rhythmic sound of the surf mingled with the distant, distorted screech of a lifeguard's megaphone, followed closely by staccato whistle blasts and a warning to swimmers to stay out of the surfer zone. Behind you, the strings of an acoustic guitar gently paid homage to the Beatles' song "Norwegian Wood." Hoards of panhandlers, cult groups pushing their respective gurus, and street entertainers acting as though they were performing under the big top comprised the gauntlet to and from our off-beach pad. Not so at Wabasso -"our" beach, as we liked to refer to it. This was the Atlantic. Coney Island was 1200 miles north and Miami was 75 miles south. Many are the days in which I strolled on Wabasso Beach with not a soul in sight, a quarter mile in either direction. Your sole company might be a couple of pelicans, fifty yards off shore. They would glide several feet above the turquoise sea, on the lookout for today's seafood special. Occasionally, these birds would swoop down like senior citizens darting in and out of the salad bar at Big Boy's restaurant. I especially enjoyed getting down to the beach between tides, while an array of fascinating objects still lingered like little treasures scattered in the moist sand. They would be on display for a brief period, until a distant relative of the wave that put them there came to reclaim them for her strongbox beneath the sea. There were wonderful, fascinating objects: shells of every size, shape, and color; Portuguese man-of-wars, looking like some shriveled-up purple balloons, with their dark blue, delicate ribbons stretched like spider webs in the sand; prehistoric-looking horseshoe crabs; driftwood; and other debris. On occasion, I would see a dead fish of a species unbeknownst to my experience with bluegills, bass, and catfish. This was the kind of sea fodder that fascinates someone, especially youngsters and older folks new to the environment. Basking in the sun, surrounded by a host of worshiping fiddler crabs, I felt like a kid, half expecting to see gold doubloons washed ashore.

Even the ten-minute walk to and from the beach was an adventure. In an amusing way, it rekindled those childhood memories when, like Daniel Boone, we kids explored the woods, meadows, and creeks near Gaylord Street in Redford just before civilization swept through. As Joni Mitchell declared in her song "Big Yellow Taxi," "They paved Paradise and put up a parking lot...." Okay, so there weren't lions, tigers, and bears on Orchid Island, but there were armadillos, spiders, and snakes. The latter two were of a size and species I'd only seen previously – and from a safe distance – at the Detroit, Belle Isle, or Toledo Zoos.

On the trail leading to the beach, several members of our merry band of self-imposed exiles had encountered what had to be the same snake, basking in the mid-morning Florida sun. Perhaps a blue indigo, it was dark purple, almost black. By my Michigander standards, which were based on my experience with garter snakes, this creature was enormous. On one occasion, I assumed initially that a branch had fallen from a tree until it slithered hurriedly into the dark vegetation crowding the narrow path. Another time, I nearly stepped on the thing while jogging along the path (which likely would have done it a great deal more harm than me). Unlike that vine-swingin', Jane-lovin', elephant-ridin', croc-wrestlin' hero of Saturday afternoon jungle flicks, Tarzan, I wanted no part of a snake whose head and tail escaped my view. I may have exaggerated its length, but I could make out its girth clearly: this snake was the size of my forearm. I was no Marlin Perkins. No python was going to suffocate me! I bolted outta there like I was chasin' the Good Humor truck down Gaylord Street.

As days turned into weeks and we grew more comfortable in our surroundings, Tommy, Steve, and I liked nothing better than running around all day clad in little more than the standard-issue hippie loincloth – faded cut-off Levis. Unshaven and wearing seashell necklaces and earrings while carrying spears and fishing tackle, we no doubt resembled the mutinous crew in Robert Louis Stevenson's classic book *Treasure Island.* (I love the film version with Wallace Beery as Long John Silver.) Beach days often meant little, if any, contact with the locals. Occasionally a lone tourist or local senior seashell collector would happen upon this castaway/hippie/pirate band. After determining that we were largely a harmless breed, s/he would have a picture snapped with these sea-dogs to show the folks back home in Baltimore what s/he had survived in a harrowing encounter on Skull Island. Oh, brother!

Strolling under the canopy along Jungle Trail on the side of the Inter-Coastal likewise provided unexpected, sometimes nerve-rattling encounters. This was especially true for someone like me, whose previous wilderness adventures were limited to Michigan's bucolic Proud Lake and Kensington Metro Parks. When my friends and I had settled initially into our quaint little jungle paradise, I would take an occasional dip in nearby Indian River. However, I soon thought better of it. The water, a dark, brackish mixture of salt and fresh, was not nearly as refreshing to swim in as the ocean or as the nearby pool hidden back in the groves that we'd dubbed the Sulfur Pond. From the safety of our dock, I spent a fair amount of time scrutinizing the denizens of the peculiar ecosystem with which an unwary swimmer would share the water. These included small sharks, puffer fish that looked like something out of a *National Geographic* special, and crabs the size of a man's hand as well as rays and jellyfish. While I hadn't seen any alligators, one or two were rumored to be slinking around Indian River. Yep, I'd think twice before again diving into those foreboding waters.

During one of my lazy afternoon strolls along the river, there was a commotion in the water near the shore. I heard a noise about twenty yards ahead under some overhanging branches. I was all attention. Slowly edging forward, I was ready to beat a hasty retreat should this be the alleged alligator, waiting for some two-legged snack to venture too close to the river's edge. I didn't want to end up like one of those poor wildebeest you see on those nature shows, wild-eyed with panic after having been embraced in the vise-like jaws of a crocodile on the Nile River. "Hey, what's this?" I thought. There seemed to be some massive, walrus-like beast sunning itself on the surface. "Damn, a hippopotamus!" I shouted. I thought that the hippo must have escaped from one of those mom-and-pop jungle-critter tourist traps that litter Florida. Wouldn't you know it? By the time that I raced back to the Jungle Shack Inn and summoned witnesses to come and see for themselves, the locals who'd been alarmed by my shouts nearly collapsed from hysterics. It seems that I'd just encountered a Florida manatee. "Never heard of one," I sniffed to the locals.

Just across Indian River was the small community of Wabasso, which you got to via a recently completed bridge that brought you out to U.S. 1. Wabasso was home to the Indian River Fruit Company. Here, Tommy, Steve, and I found work in the citrus groves, primarily picking grapefruit. What a sorry group of pickers we were, with the possible exception of Tommy, who had a year's worth of experience under his belt, er, sack. We followed his lead and struggled to pick up the technique. In addition, we strove to learn proper grove etiquette, especially when dealing with the boss man and the locals, who were primarily African American. The latter just couldn't seem to fathom why these white boys would leave "them high payin', union, auto-factory gigs up North." My friends and I rarely put in more than half-a-day's work. We earned just enough to keep a collective roof over our heads, to pay our commissary tab, and to provide some bare necessities. Now, a big night out meant a stop at McDonald's in Vero, a pack of Kools to share among us, and a bottle of Boone's Farm wine. Visitors from back home sometimes worked with us in the groves. However, few of them could endure it for more than a week. I'd had a bit of a run-in with one of the local fruit-pickers. One day he came strollin' by my set (a group of trees, usually four to six, which you were assigned to pick). In one hand, he was carrying a skinned animal, which I learned later was a raccoon. In the other hand, he carried a long, bloody knife. The fruit-picker had one of those double-meaning, stupid grins on his mug that, if put into words, might say, "Gonna be some good eatin' up here tonight, and, boy, don't give me no trouble or I'll skin yo' ass too." It took me a while to get the hang of fruit-picking. However, as my proficiency improved, and I'd work a set of trees where a snake had been spotted, which no one else would. Due to this, the locals grew less suspicious of this white boy from the big city. In fact, several of them warmed up to me, which came in very handy one evening. On this Saturday night, my buddy Dale Campbell, another guy from back home who had recently joined our merry band and who looked like an anorexic version of Ted Nugent, and I sauntered into a watering-hole in Wabasso, a tired-looking blue cinder-block place on the only avenue in town. The bar's patrons seemed to turn as one and greet us with a silent, uniform look of astonishment. We may have been the first, not to mention the only, white dudes to step foot in there. Fortunately, my fruit-pickin' pals were at the bar and momentarily gave us a hearty welcome. The laughter, the clinking of glasses and the crash of balls on a pool table signaled that calm winds had returned.

· · · ·

No doubt you've heard of one version or another of the grapefruit diet. The grapefruit is one of a long list of miracle foods (sometimes in pill form) that is guaranteed to peel away that excess flesh like the skin off of an onion. Well, friends, I'm here to tell you the grapefruit diet works! But, and a big butt it is/was, you not only have to eat 'em, you have to pick 'em! There's no workout in my memory book that can rival the "fruit-picker workout." My friends and I were laboring under the Florida sun and filling bin after bin with grapefruits. Sometimes, we toted a sack that reached fifty-plus pounds up and down a ladder, moving fast to avoid red fire-ants. I don't recall seeing too many chunky veteran fruit pickers.

As the months rolled by, the pounds peeled off. By the end of my first picking season, I'd shed forty pounds. It also should be noted that, in addition to my current, physically demanding career, junk food had all but disappeared from my diet. When not dangling precariously from a ladder with a sack full of grapefruit, I spent a great many hours body-surfing. I rode the waves at nearby Wabasso Beach; which is a rigorous workout in itself. How many portly surfers do you know? Kawabunga! The upshot of this was that, over a six-month period, a rather dramatic physical transformation had transpired. I'd arrived in Florida looking like some husky hippie biker, a character right out of *The Fabulous Furry Freak Brothers* comics. After several months spent working in the citrus groves, body-surfing for endless hours, eating less junk food, and smoking fewer cigarettes, I looked and felt better than I had since my sixth-grade heel-pain dilemma transformed me into the Pillsbury Dough Boy Look-alike. In body, at least, I felt newly energized. Spiritually, I was starving. That, too, was about to change.   Months earlier, while living in Detroit and during my brief sojourn to the west coast, I'd developed an interest in all things "spiritual." I was interested especially in eastern mysticism and the occult, a world of strange, foreign ideas that I'd heard of but never pursued with any serious devotee passion. I'd dabbled a bit but lacked the discipline to pursue it in earnest. Now, in the relatively quaint, nature-saturated environment of Florida, surrounded by friends who ran the gamut from like-minded curiosity to "Could care less," I set sail determined to seek out the meaning of life. Did God exist? What is it that I should do with my life? Zero prospects loomed on both the skilled trades and academic horizons. I needed direction.

The laid-back, tropical, ocean-side environment in which I was living lent itself to a "getting-back-to-nature" vibe; "naturally stoned," as it were. It had been a while since I'd paused to take serious note of the grandeur of creation. Indeed, nighttime at our secluded seashore, which was devoid of even light pollution, could be magical, even apocalyptic. Storms far out at sea would make themselves known by distant flashes, which were followed momentarily by deep, low rumbles. This made it seem as though opposing naval fleets were slugging it out for supremacy of the east Florida coast. There were crystal-clear nights, when "shooting stars" streaked across the sky as if to announce that God and the Celestial Host were going head to head at intergalactic pinball. On other nights, a glorious moon cast enough "lesser light" to dare one to take a nocturnal swim. "Sharks didn't come in this close"; ah, the bliss of ignorance. On some nights, phosphorescent particles glittered like cold sparkler-lights as a fish or a wave disturbed the water. A shower of sparks danced briefly above gentle waves. On nights like these, especially when I was alone, my mind seemed bent on confronting issues that increasingly brought uneasiness to my laid-back lifestyle. "God, are you there? Do you care?"

Daylight hours brought no mental rest regarding the God Issue. One moment, I would be innocently peeling a hand picked banana from behind our tropical pad and the next examining an intricate, diamond-studded, lace-patterned spider-web that was glistening in the morning dew. This web was hung precariously amid orchid vines that threatened to smother our lair. It was a thing of such symmetry, constructed to ensnare and, ultimately, to kill. I saw easy-moving, armored armadillos foraging in the tropical underbrush. At every turn, creation raised the God Issue. Later, I'd discover that this is precisely what the Apostle Paul was referring to in the first chapter of his Letter to the Romans: the invisible God has been made known to the Gentiles by this creation–nature. Fueled by drugs, rebelliousness, and a lack of direction, my spiritual inquiry had been clouded by a host of "what if's" and "so what's." Back in Detroit, my inquiry appeared to take the shape of the Grim Reaper closing in. Now it was time to sort things out. I couldn't hang in Florida playing Huck Finn and picking grapefruit for the next ten years. Besides, this communal thing was okay for the time being, but....

The nature vibe that I was experiencing in Florida was so intoxicating that I was content with being "naturally stoned," for the most part. In time, as George Harrison had crooned, "All things must pass." Drugs (primarily hash and psychedelics like acid and mescaline) worked their way back into the equation. My friends and I argued that weed and hash mellow you out, but with booze you lose: Boozers get violent and play the fool. Had not God sanctioned the use of the "holy herb"? Back then, this was a popular

59

slogan imprinted on t-shirts. Typically, the image depicted a hemp plant accompanied by a verse from Genesis announcing all plant life to be God's handiwork and, therefore, to be declared good. (Hmm, would this include poison ivy?) Now, a lesser authority than the Divine was usurping His authority. This slogan also appeared on bumper stickers. However, you had to be an imbecile to plaster one on your rear bumper unless you liked attention from the police.

I began to have reservations about the use of hallucinogens, so-called mind-expanding drugs. I thought of them as something of which God, if indeed He existed, would not approve. What about bad trips (bummers)? I knew people who had "flipped out," or at least had heard about them. I decided to put this notion to a test. "Copping" from the local hipsters was too risky. They struck me largely as a bunch of redneck surfers who knew little about what was "happening." They preferred the down-home southern rock of Black Oak Arkansas and Mason Proffit to sophisticated English bands like the Moody Blues and Traffic. These Florida hipsters had never read, let alone heard of, Bob Dylan's book *Tarantula* and did not know about Ken Kesey's Merry Pranksters. In short, these people were come-lately hippie wannabes. The merchandise at the lone Vero Beach "head shop" looked like the same hippie garbage (black lights, posters, and tapestries) that you'd find at Kmart. The only hippies with whom I made any effort to connect were cut from the same "pilgrim" cloth, as I was – on-the-road spiritual seekers who found it prudent to travel "clean," like my friends and me. The images of the South from *Easy Rider* dangled like the sword of Damocles over rural, central, east-coast Florida, which, though magnificent, was a Merle Haggard-lovin', George Wallace-lovin', grits-lovin' place. Anyway, the locals didn't have what I wanted. It now occurs to me that, a few years earlier, the first hippies on the Detroit scene – the Wayne State University, Plum Street (the city's version of Haight-Ashbury), and Ann Arbor crowds –no doubt felt about me the way that I now felt about the locals in east-coast Florida. Deep down, I knew that I'd come late to the dance (or movement), but I'd done my damndest to catch up. I had left my stash, a quarter ounce of hash and a dozen tabs of acid, with a trusted buddy back home. Once I'd secured a mailing address, he promised to mail the rest of my stash to me – for a gram of hash of course.

Located on a quiet street a block off of U.S. 1, the Wabasso Post Office was a quaint facility about the size of a small party store. Here, my friends and I rented a small post-office box. The office was "womaned" by a couple of employees who reminded me of Aunt Bea from *The Andy Griffith Show* on television; they were warm and friendly, something that we hippies weren't accustomed to from the locals. "My, those folks back home must have a lot to say," an "Aunt Bea" remarked innocently as she handed me a letter that was too bulky for our cheapest P.O. Box, one of the smallest size. "Yes, they do," I smiled back. Like a kid on Christmas morning who can't wait to try out his new bike, I raced back to my pad on Jungle Trail to see what Santa had sent.

Up to this point, I'd steered clear of "hard" drugs such as heroin. Back in "the D," I'd seen "the needle and the damage done," in the words of singer/songwriter Neil Young, firsthand. Months earlier, speed and downers had taken a toll on my health. Lately, though, the natural buzz of living free and easy on Orchid Isle (well, not exactly free) with just an occasional joint or bowl of hash had been liberating. I was fit in body, and my mind appeared to be making its way out of a dense fog. The pace of life here was much more to my liking than on the west coast, where the frantic, paranoia-saturated, rip-off, cultic, narcissistic mass of lost humanity that washed up on the Southern California coast (have I forgotten anything?) created the downer vibe of the previous summer. Let us not forget the demon-possessed apartment in Redford, with its make-a-good-Alice Cooper-album-cover vibe. Now, I "sat" on some powerful acid.

The fear of getting "popped" might have been moved to a rear burner, but it was still on the stove. The local law enforcement and the few neighbors with whom we rubbed shoulders on occasion regarded us as more of a curiosity than a threat. Echoing Gomer Pyle, they might have declared, "Hippies from the big city. Shazam!" As long as we didn't bother them, our neighbors appeared content to leave us to our own devices. I know that I was leading up to my psychedelic showdown with God. First, though, I want to mention a few run-ins with the local fuzz. While reminiscing with the old Wabasso gang about these encounters elicits plenty of yuks, they were nerve-rattling at the time. Certainly, they were no laughing matters.

The first encounter was innocent enough. Back in Redford, it hardly would have raised a blip on the screen. On this night, three out-of-state longhairs were crusin' the "mean streets" of Vero Beach (Vero Gulch, as one of my buddies liked to refer to it). We decided to hit Big Daddy's Liquor Store and pick up some wine to take the edge off of the hash that we planned to fire up back at the pad (Vero is a fifteen-minute drive south of Wabasso down U.S. 1 or A1A). Since I looked the oldest, I went in to make the purchase, just like I used to do back home; I rarely was asked for ID. Moments later, I was saddled back into my "shotgun" position with two bottles of cheap wine, Boone's Farm and Spanada, positioned carefully between my feet. No sooner had Tommy put the mighty Falcon into second gear when we were surrounded by what must have been the entire Vero police force (three squad cars), their lights flashin'. You would have thought that Bonnie and Clyde had just knocked over the liquor store. You old "heads" out there will recall that heart-in-your-throat sensation when those flashing lights first appeared in your rear-view mirror. My mind raced with questions like, "Are there any roaches in the ashtray? Did I ever find that hit of speed that fell behind the rear seat? Where are those Zig-Zags (rolling papers)? I better slip them under the terrycloth seat covers." I exclaimed nervously to Tommy and Steve, "At least we ain't holdin' any dope." Actually, I suspect that the locals were a tad bored, and we were the only action on a slow, uneventful shift on a weekday evening. "The registration's in the glove box," Tommy muttered. Popping it open, a bunch of bent-in-half palms, which likely were left in there from Palm Sunday[2] past, burst out like a jack in the box. A picture of the Blessed Mother rested atop the registration. Slowly, and with a delicateness reserved for such items, I positioned them, shrine-like, on the lid of the glove box, where they would be in full view of the officers' scrutiny. It never even entered my mind that these cops might be less than impressed with Catholic "magic" charms. However, they were the only cards that we held. Momentarily, the beam of a flashlight swept from one to the other of us until it fell on the Blessed Virgin Mary. I imagined that one of the cops hollered something like this at one of his fellow officers: "Hey, Buford, looks like we got us some church-goin' boys that got on the wrong track

---

[2]   The Sunday before Easter which introduces Holy Week. Liturgies for this special day often include the blessing of and procession with palms, marking Jesus' triumphal entry into Jerusalem followed by His Passion, Death, and Resurrection.

tonight." I seem to recall handing them some line about the drinking age being 18 in Michigan (which it might have been). Actually, little was said. After the cops made us pour out the wine, they told us to get out of town. The apologies and "Yes, Officer Krupke" were barely off of our lips when we pulled over at another liquor store, this one halfway between Vero and Wabasso. This was in Gifford, a small, off-the-map, dirt-poor; predominately black community where police and most white folk didn't tread after dark. But, hey, we're from Dee-troit!

On another occasion, seven or eight of us were enjoying a spectacular day at "our" beach. As was often the case, we had the place to ourselves, pretty much. Public access to the beach was a quarter-mile north of where the trail from our pad came out across A1A onto the area that we frequented most often. By this time, we'd all gone full-throttle into the back-to-nature thing. A couple of young ladies from back home who'd temporarily joined our gypsy band took it upon themselves to do a little more serious sunbathing and shed their tops. Not to be outdone, we fellas hit the surf in our birthday suits. When you think about it, how dumb can you get? You're trollin' out there with your most vulnerable body part exposed and all of them critters swimmin' around, just waitin' to make a eunuch (castrated man) out of ya. We were enjoying a grand old time when, out of nowhere, sharp whistle blasts pierced the air. "What are lifeguards doin' 'round here?" I wondered aloud. As far as I could tell, we were the only ones around. More whistle blows, then "Uh oh." Coming from over the sandy, palmetto-patched knoll that separated the beach from A1A by some fifty yards were two honest-to-God, good-ol-boy, Indian River County sheriff deputies. Whistles in mouths, they waved us in. There was no escape. Moments later, all of us were assembled in a small group. The girls had been able to cover themselves quickly, but we fellas had to stand there awkwardly, trying to shield our privates while enduring the type of disgusted glares that Fred Rutherford would give his son Lumpy after he'd done something particularly stupid on the *Leave It to Beaver* television program.

"Just what in the Hayal do y'all thank yer a doin'?" asked one of the deputies. I thought, "This is it. That jail cell that our *Easy Rider* heroes Hopper and Fonda ended up in at that hick, redneck town is about to be our new zip code." One member of our party began to launch into a philosophical, back-to-Eden, God-awareness defense of letting it all hang out, but I cut him off, apologized, and said that this wouldn't happen again. My apology seemed to satisfy the deputies and, so, after a stern warning, they left us to ourselves. No doubt we retreated to the security of our Jungle Trail abode, where we could calm our nerves with a bowl of hash and a bottle of Boone's Farm and could celebrate our latest escape.

Our third Encounter of the Close Kind with the local keepers of the peace was as bizarre as it was nerve-rattling. At certain times of the year, swarming, annoying insects would create a real nuisance. Our landlord, a friendly, heavy-set fellow just shy of forty, forewarned us that bug-sprayers would be out to launch defensive measures against the coming horde and that we might be inconvenienced for several hours. We didn't give it much thought until several days later. By this time, we'd gotten to know some of the locals who lived in adjoining apartments. We'd also befriended a couple of "old salts" from Boston who had sailed a trimaran (a multi-hulled boat) clear down the east coast. They had come up the Sebastian Inlet to escape the ocean for a spell and ended up mooring off our dock for a month. Folks from back home continued to trickle down. The upshot of this was that, on any given night, a fair amount of those "hippies on Jungle Trail," as we were referred to, wandered in and out to catch a buzz, to grab a bite, to socialize, and to listen to music. On this particular night, a dense cloud of marijuana smoke hung in the air with no breeze to chase it out into the jasmine-scented night air. It's dark on Jungle Trail. The single amber porch light barely illuminated the entrance to our apartment. A knock on our screen door revealed the shadowy outlines of two figures lurking outside. The door creaked open, followed by an uncomfortable silence; even the faint strains of Ten Years After's song "I'd Love to Change the World" seemed to go limp. I'd been sitting on the floor like some novice yogi, head down, eyes nearly closed, nodding in time to the music. Now, I peered towards the screen door to welcome our new guests, whom I thought had come to party with us. Eyes still at floor level, I noticed two pairs of shiny black boots. As I went up their legs I saw green pants with black stripes and, finally, revolvers! "Damn, y'all got some big-ass bugs down here," I muttered, wondering why the hell these insect exterminators would come out at midnight.

My friends and I couldn't have been more surprised if Bigfoot himself had just walked in. Nobody said a word. My eyes locked on a baggie full of Bugler tobacco. Rather than toting a big can of tobacco to the groves and the beach, we used baggies. Consequently, I thought that the baggie in question was filled with pot. My heart was playing "Wipeout" louder than the original record by the Surfaris! I wrestled with the overpowering impulse to grab the baggie and flush the contents. Like the nervous murderer in Poe's short story "The Tell Tale Heart," I knew that they knew. How could they not? A cloud of cannabis smoke the size of Texas still lingered in the air. Plus, there was the smell and the red, sleepy eyes of everyone in the apartment. After what seemed like minutes, the "bug exterminators," who actually were Indian River County sheriffs, told us about the reason for their unexpected visit. Earlier that evening, a woman's purse had been snatched from the Laundromat adjacent to a convenience store that was popular with the locals, with migrant fruit-pickers, and with travelers on U.S. 1. Two of our party ("them hippies") had been up there about that time. This was true enough, but we were not thieves. Tommy and Dale, the two potential suspects, had to take a harrowing late-night ride. Think about it: Dale and Tommy were stoned, were out in the middle of nowhere, and were in the back seat of a car belonging to a sheriff from Indian River County. Soon, Tom and Dale were to be confronted by the support cast from the future *Deliverance* movie. Oh, my! Unfortunate as this course of events was, my friends and I needed to get these officers out of here before they had something bigger than a potential purse-snatching with which to nail us. An hour later, the collective sigh of relief was heard 'round the world when our "brothers" bounced through the door cleared of any wrongdoing. Now it was time to laugh, albeit a bit nervously. How long would our lucky streak run? What would they have thought back home? The headline could have read, "Detroit Hippies Busted by Insect Exterminators." Anyway, I'm thankful that I didn't have to explain why I was flushing legal smoking tobacco down the toilet.

. . . .

The time had come for my acid test. The boys were goin' crusin' and I wanted to be alone. Unfortunately, this is not a good idea when you're tripping on acid. One tab, ironically named Purple "Jesus" (so-called because of a small, cross-like cut on a purple microdot), would do nicely. I had cigarettes, munchies, music, a Bible, and Tolkien's *The Hobbit* to read. I also had the expectation that sometime tonight God was going to reveal the sense – or nonsense – of taking so-called mind expanding drugs.

In my case, I hoped to attain some new spiritual awareness from this experience.

Acid kinda creeps up on ya. The paneling in our apartment was that knotty-pine type that reminded me of so many cottages and cabins in northern Michigan. An hour after dropping the Purple "Jesus" Acid (LSD), I grew intrigued by the dark knots in the paneling. Suddenly, they were transformed into deep, dark eyes that were glaring at me. You've seen the symbol of the Greek comedy/tragedy theatre masks; these were similar. The knotty eyes looked at me with a sinister twinkle from every corner of the room, just as though disembodied spirits somehow had become lodged in the pine panels. They were unable to speak and unable to escape; they just scowled … at me. These tragedy/comedy masks caught in the web of some hellish torment, pressed in. "I don't think they like me," I thought.

Turn up the music. Have a cigarette. Throw cold water on your face. No good. All three rooms of our cottage were paneled in knotty pine. There was no rest for the eye. The masks were everywhere and were closing in like those zombies in the movie *Night of the Living Dead*. Was I to play some role in a Poe-like, "Pit and the Pendulum" - style tale? Heated, crushing, eye-covered walls were bent on forcing me into a pit of nameless terrors! I was feeling claustrophobic. At this moment, a growing panic attack prevented me from recalling that the poor unfortunate wretch in Poe's short story had been "miraculously" delivered moments before the heated iron plates of his dark cell forced him into the abyss.

Nature took charge: I had a sudden urge to escape the demon-like images that were pressing in on me. Come on, feet, don't fail me now! I bolted out the door, out into the ink-black night on Jungle Trail. You'll recall the axiom "Leaping out of the frying pan into the fire." I planned to make for the path, head down to the beach, and get myself together, away from those sinister, angry eyes. By that time, the gang would have returned. Together, we would exorcise those evil orbs back into Gehenna.

The tropical vegetation and animal life of Florida can be intimidating during the day, but at night and on acid? Whoa, Nelly! Fifty yards down the path, I had a change of heart. Images from the *Jungle Jim* TV show with Johnny Weismuller that I had watched as a youngster flashed across my mind's eye. I saw lost, stupid, white men stumbling along foreboding jungle trails, searching vainly for some outpost of civilization. They were cut down by a python lurking in the branches or by a pygmy's poisoned dart. Horror of horrors, these men would be impaled on stakes in a carefully hidden pit meant for an unwary elephant. Here, the Stygian darkness, numerous vines, limbs, and palm fronds pressing in on the obscure path made a hasty retreat difficult. I would have to pick my way along carefully lest I lose the trail altogether. "Don't leave the path," Gandalf had warned Bilbo and the dwarves prior to entering Mirkwood Forest. If they had, they'd be lost beyond rescue, likely falling prey to enormous, sinister, flesh-eating spiders.

"Ah, Jungle Trail!" I breathed a sigh of relief. What to do now? There was no one else around. I couldn't linger out on the meandering roadside with the Indian River mere feet from me. At any moment, some alligator or giant squid-like tentacle from a Jules Verne novel would make me the recipient of its tender affection, dragging me to a watery grave and to a fate worse than death. Dare I go back into the apartment and confront that legion of hellish eyes?

When I returned to my apartment, the evil eyes had not abandoned their post. I grabbed my Bible, recalling how it had helped me to ward off the demonic presence emanating from the Janis Joplin poster at our pad in Redford. Then, the Bible was like a cross in the face of a vampire; no such "luck" this time. Having just finished *The Hobbit*, I dove into Tolkien's first book of the trilogy - *The Fellowship of the Ring*, and rapidly made my way to the place where the hobbits fall under the enchantment of Old Man Willow. I grew so intrigued by the tale that I nearly forgot about the ominous presence locked in the wood paneling. Before you could shout "Tom Bombadil," the screen door burst open. The cavalry had returned. "Hey, Rocker, whatcha' doin'?" one of them asked (Rocker being my nickname from high school you'll recall). "Nothin,' just reading," I replied. What a night. The sinister eyes had turned back to their inanimate state, knots of pine. I don't recall if I told my buds about my "trip." Perhaps it was best left untold. I would let sleeping dogs (and demons) lie.

I concluded that LSD was not the way for me to expand my mind and to attain some sort of God-consciousness (sorry, Timothy Leary). Reasoning that there was no sense in flushing the rest of my stash of acid, I sold it to the locals. My reaction (bad trip) would not necessarily be theirs; plus, I could use the extra "bread." Besides, it impressed them. The locals couldn't get LSD and were willing to pay or trade big "lids" of kick-ass weed for a couple of tabs. Also, our stash of hash was dwindling. Talk about moral relativism.

.　.　.　.

The apartment adjacent to ours was occupied by newlyweds, Clay and Karen VanAntwerp. A friendly couple, they appeared to be cut from one hippie strain or another, at least outwardly. Surprisingly, Clay and Karen always turned down our requests to join us for a bowl. "We get high on Jesus," they'd quip. On weekends, they would invite us to go to "the Tent" with them. The whole idea of having church in a tent was foreign to me. However, I discovered that it barely raised an eyebrow down South when a big tent sprang up overnight on some vacant lot with a huge sign announcing "Holy Ghost Revival with Reverend Such and Such." One such tent caught our eye on the way to work in the citrus groves one morning; this was not "the Tent" our neighbors invited us to visit, but one in nearby, predominately black, Wabasso.

A couple of grove-workers invited my friends and me to evening services at the current, week long tent revival meeting in Wabasso. However, the carload of us that pulled in the roughly cut, weeded lot one evening were prompted more by coincidence – a wine run, and the curious, pulsating sounds of what sounded like a not-too-shabby R&B band. The first thing that I noticed was that we were the only white folks under the big top; everyone else was African American. As one, the "faithful" turned to scrutinize us; even the music skipped a beat. A couple of grove-workers recognized us and rushed over to offer a welcome. In a few minutes we were clapping, swaying, and joining in the worship (I thought that this was kind of a southern version of a Motown Revue down at the Fox Theatre in Detroit). The attention of the crowd focused once again on the platform full of musicians who looked and sounded like Booker T. and the M.G.'s meet the Temptations. After twenty minutes, the crowd of the hundred-plus faithful had been worked into a fever pitch. All of a sudden, out leapt Evangelist Ella Hopkins from the stage-right side of the semi-trailer (the trailer that obviously was used to haul the tent, chairs, and sound equipment). A sign in bright orange letters boldly proclaimed him as "Prince of the East Coast." Evangelist Hopkins was lookin' like James Brown, cape and all. Hopkins' passionate, 30-minute message was interrupted repeatedly by shrill bursts from the Hammond B3 organ and by shouts from the big-kneed gals in shut-yo-mouth bonnets who hollered,

68

"Thank ya, Jesus!" At the conclusion of his sermon, we heard several testimonies from Brother and Sister So and So about how God had given them a miracle in response to their "seed-faith" and giving to the "man of God," the man being Evangelist Hopkins. Then there was a collection, which I thought was conducted rather hurriedly, lest the memory of the "You-can't-out-give God" testimonials would cause potential donors to waver. Following the collection, the evangelist made a startling announcement: God had revealed to him that someone in the congregation had a hearing problem. Most likely, they were deaf, or nearly so, Hopkins stated. He concluded, "If you know of such a person, you might have to communicate to him/her that tonight is their night. God is gonna set them free!" The eyes of my friends and I grew wide as we looked at Merle Maddox, one of our tribe, who was nearly stone deaf. None of us moved or spoke. Again, Reverend Tutti Frutti (I'd dubbed him that because his preaching reminded me of Little Richard) made the plea, but no one accepted the challenge. A nervous tension filled the air.

"Merle, get up there. Let the dude pray for you," my friends and I cajoled. Assuming that Hopkins could only be talking about Merle, we quickly explained to him what was up. When no one else responded to the challenge, our hard-of-hearing comrade, who was not shy or easily intimidated, went forward, receiving the laying-on of hands and a prayer for healing. The faithful grew still and quiet. They were like the crowd at an old-fashioned circus, waiting breathlessly for some pretty young thing to step off of a platform high above their heads and to execute a dazzling display of perilous aerial daredevil moves. After instructing Merle to face the crowd of perspiring, expectant faithful and to lift his hands when he heard his name, the preacher man moved some dozen steps behind Merle. You could hear a pin drop. Then, Reverend Good Golly Miss Molly whispered into the microphone with a barely audible "Merle." Merle's hands shot up. The crowd went wild while we rushed down to embrace our healed comrade. The band put it in overdrive and the congregation danced and shouted well into the night. Finally, we took our leave, ecstatic over our buddy's miraculous healing and a night of free entertainment to boot. The following morning, we discovered that Merle still couldn't hear worth a damn. We were all disappointed and not a little angry. For once, we were stumped. I don't think any of us knew what to make of what had happened last evening at that Tent Revival.

． ． ． ．

The Tent, as it was fondly referred to by regulars, and not to be confused with the one we visited earlier in Wabasso, and the same one our friendly neighbors Clay and Karen relentlessly bid us visit, was not some fly-by-night, week-long, tent-revival affair. It served as the temporary home of Truth and Life Ministries until funds could be raised to build or secure something more permanent. With one look at the crowd of people who made up the "faithful" at the Tent, you knew that it could be quite a spell before this transpired. On a good weekend night, the place fairly burst with a menagerie of "Jesus People." My buddy Tommy hadn't appeared particularly eager to visit the Tent; he'd been there the year before. I've since made some assumptions about that, but assumptions are usually best kept to oneself. However, with little else to do on a Saturday night, the Jungle Trail gang and I headed into Vero for a fast-food fix. After splurging at McDonalds, and with the evening still fresh and not much else to do, and the Tent being nearby, we thought, "What the hell, let's check it out," to which Tommy reluctantly agreed. It was his car after all.

When we pulled in off U.S. 1 somewhere between Vero Beach and Fort Pierce, I immediately noticed forty to fifty people, most of them young. Some of them were standing while others were seated on folding chairs in a semi-circle around a stage. The tent flaps were up to let the breeze through. Up on stage, some skinny preacher was doing what looked to me like a poor imitation of Mick Jagger; I assumed that he was leading some worship songs. The parking area was a grassy field bordering some train tracks. My buddies and I pulled in as far away as possible from the entrance of the tent. We'd have a bowl of hash first before joining the meeting.

I usually rode shotgun, too big for the rear seat of a Ford Falcon. In the middle of getting a buzz on, we suddenly were startled by a man's face peering in the window. "You guys from Michigan?" he inquired. "Brilliant," I thought, "the dude can read license plates." Steve and I slid out of the Falcon to check out the service while our new "friend" hopped in to make the acquaintance of the others. It turned out that this guy was Tim Meyer, the unofficial church "bouncer." Originally from Dearborn, Michigan, Tim had moved down to Vero Beach where his family now lived. Tim currently worked as a commercial fisherman and diver, and like me, he also found it prudent to move out of Michigan for reasons I'll let him explain some other time; can you hum the tune, "I Fought the Law" … and the law won. He would play a significant role in my life in the months and years ahead.

Going into a Pentecostal meeting is one thing, but going in stoned? Oh, boy. We plopped into a couple of chairs in the back row, surveyed the scene, and turned our attention to the preaching of Reverend Ichabod (who was tall and skinny, like Ichabod Crane in *The Legend of Sleepy Hollow*). Two rednecks, who'd obviously been drinking, sat to our right with no one in between. During the service, they muttered something about damn hippies while giving us big, grim, meant-to-intimidate stares. I looked like a biker, but Steve was more than Gomer and Goober could swallow: Steve was wearing a bandana around his neck, a purple tank-top, and elephant bell-bottoms with yellow stripes; to top it off, Steve, who sported a reddish-brown Afro, had a giant dope-pouch strapped to his side like a six-gun. Momentarily, the preacher paused and asked for testimonies. A couple of folks stood up and gave thanks for recent blessings, prayers answered, deliverance from this and that, and occasional interruptions of heartfelt praise. To my surprise, Steve raised his hand and stood up to testify. "What the hell you got to testify about?" I wondered, as he launched into some New Age-soundin' Jesus-spin rhetoric. Well, our redneck neighbors had seen and heard enough. "I thank it's time we kicked some longhaired ass," the one nearest to us slurred as he struggled to get to his feet. "How 'bout you ladies step out into the parkin' lot."

"Kiss my Detroit ass, you … we'll do it right here," I bellowed.

The preacher pleaded for order, "We're in the house of God, blah, blah, blah."

Things were just about to get really interesting when Tim, the dude from the parking lot, materialized in between us and the drunken rednecks and took control of the situation. The reek of booze emanating from Okeechobee, Florida's finest earned them a speedy escort to their old eyesore of a pickup truck, along with a "Come back if and only when you're sober."

•   •   •   •

It might not have been the jungles of Vietnam, but you'd look like you'd been through hell and back after a hard day's work in the groves.

71

You'd leave with sweat-drenched clothes that reeked with the overpowering, pungent odor of sweat and overripe citrus. If you had long hair, you'd look like a Rastafarian by the end of the day. Any uncovered skin, especially your arms, would be covered with scratches from working around and inside of the trees. On one occasion, a hoop earring that I was wearing apparently became entangled in a tree branch. Unbeknownst to me, it ripped right through my earlobe. This went undetected until the end of the shift, when one of the crew noticed that my right lower ear was covered with blood. The bleeding had stopped, so I paid little mind to my injury. I thought that my daily swim after work at Wabasso Beach would cleanse and hasten the healing. All of my other scratches had always magically disappeared the day following a saltwater dip. Indeed, I'd struggled on and off for years with some type of foot fungus, "jungle rot," we called it. After a month of swimming in saltwater, it hit the road just like Jack in the song by Ray Charles and didn't come back "no more, no more, no more, no more." The most annoying things about my latest mishap were losing a cool earring and possibly having to wait a spell before wearing another. I did eventually end up piercing the other ear. However, the tear in my right ear didn't heal. After a week, my right earlobe grew increasingly discolored in spite of daily swims and soaking the infected area in peroxide. Had something like a spray used in the groves infected my ear? In another week, the lower half of my right ear had turned black. My buddies half-jokingly remarked that it looked like leprosy. This wasn't leprosy: it was gangrene. My ear was nasty to look at and didn't smell very pleasant, either. I began to let my long hair drape over my ear to avoid embarrassment and annoying inquiries. As another week rolled by, my anxiety reached near-panic levels. The entire lower part of my right ear was discolored, rotten, and leaking pus. It also stank like road kill that was left too long in the Florida sun. It finally dawned on me that this part of my ear might have to be removed. I had no money and no insurance. If I didn't act soon, I might lose the whole ear!

At about this time, my friends and I decided to pay another visit to the Tent. After all, lots of cute chicks were hangin' there. They also had a decent worship band with kind of a folk-rock, little-bit-of-soul vibe thrown in. The band was good, with the exception of some guy who'd play an accordion that tortured your eardrums. Usually, though, he'd wind up jumping off of the stage to roam around the perimeter of the tent, shouting and carrying on. I used to hope that this guy would trip on one of the tent stakes and break his neck, er, accordion....

My buddies and I had been told (or warned) that "the man" would be at the Tent on Sunday evenings. "The man" was Evangelist Herman Stalvey. We figured that going to the Tent on a Sunday night would provide a cheap diversion to our usual existence out on Jungle Trail, which was to get high, to listen to all six of our eight-track tapes, and then to crash. On this particular night, the mood was like going from a minor-league ballgame to a major-league game, especially as compared to our initial visit and run-in with the front-teeth-missin,' cheap-tattoo-sportin,' Skoal-chewin' rednecks. Tonight, the Tent had a bigger crowd. There was a controlled intensity waiting to be unleashed, like when you're patiently enduring an opening act at a rock concert. Many of you have seen Robert Duvall's brilliant portrayal of a southern evangelist in the film *The Apostle*. Such was Herman Stalvey. He commanded your attention and preached a straightforward in-your-face message from the Good Book like there would be no tomorrow. This was Neil Diamond's Brother Love's Travelin' Salvation Show live and up-close. As with my first visit to the Tent, I was stoned. After finding a safe seat at the rear, I took it all in with a mixture of awe and amusement. This was like nothing for which my Catholic upbringing had prepared me – a three-hour service with a heavy dose of Down South, Holy Ghost, "God's gonna burn your barley field"-hearin', foot-stompin', demon-evictin', and tongues-speakin.' All of this was cool, and I could appreciate the real dedication and sincerity of these "simple" folk. Heck, I loved Jesus, too, but had moved on to something more profound, a New Age thing before it was called New Age. After all, I thought at the time, there were many paths to the mountaintop. Jesus was just one. If your "bag" is Jesus, that's hip.

I almost had to slap myself with what happened next. Apparently, Herman Stalvey had concluded his sermon. He paced back and forth in the area in front of a plywood platform/stage that was covered in cheap, red, indoor/outdoor carpet. He looked over the audience as though he might be trying to recall one last detail, the icing on the cake of his message, perhaps, or a final warning of impending doom. Then Stalvey paused, fixed his eyes on me, and asked me to come down. "God has business with you," he declared.

"Uh oh," I thought, "I'm in for it now. This guy somehow knows I'm wrecked (stoned)." Earlier, Stalvey had pointed out a few other members of this ragtag congregation. He told them words of knowledge and prophecy: things (needs, desires, afflictions and whatnot) that only God, they, and he knew about. Stalvey proclaimed that God was going to work a miracle in their lives. A few were prayed over, and at least one ended up flat on his back as though he had fainted. No one seemed to get too upset about this. "God's just operatin' on so-and-so. Give God the glory!" the preacher cried. Now he wanted me to march down front! What for? No doubt to cast a demon out of me. I went forward with my best Dee-troit swagger, vowing to play out this thing and not to be intimidated. This whole God Issue had been weighing heavily on my mind. Inwardly, I'd been pleading with and even daring God to give me some sign of His reality. All the while, I outwardly played the role of a Moody Blues-listenin', hash-smokin', astral projectin' spiritual heavyweight. Meanwhile, there was Stalvey, who looked and sounded like a mixture of Elvis, Buddy Holly, and Conway Twitty. This dude was country. Later, I found out that he'd grown up in a large family on a farm near Homerville, Georgia, Okefenokee Swamp country. An ex-military man and a supporter of George Wallace, he declared that God called him to reach out to the hippies and to other poor, disenfranchised members of humanity who had been abandoned by mainline churches. Talk about God moving in mysterious ways! Anyway, Stalvey seemed to be for real. If he was in it for the money, he'd sure picked the wrong flock to fleece. The exchange between Stalvey and me went something like this:

Stalvey: "Welcome, brother. Have you ever been here before?"

Me: "Yes, sir, a while back ... on a Saturday night, I think."

Stalvey: "Where ya from?"

Me: "Detroit."

Stalvey: "Well, good to have ya. Brother, the Lord spoke to me about a problem you're having with your ear. Would you let us pray for you? We've never talked before, have we?"

Me: "No, sir."

It wouldn't occur to me until later to consider just how Stalvey knew about my ear. None of us had talked to anyone, and I kept my ear carefully covered, not wanting to gross anyone out, and especially around the ladies. And, truth be told, I was a bit nervous and still buzzin' like a hive of honeybees.

Stalvey: "So, how 'bout it. May we pray for you?"

Me: "Sure."

I thought to myself, "Why not?" These prayers couldn't hurt. Also, I didn't want to embarrass the guy or to hurt his feelings. Stalvey seemed sincere enough. I could tell, though, that he was uncertain about the exact nature of what was wrong with my ear, only that it obviously wasn't a hearing impairment, since we had no trouble communicating. After laying the microphone on the platform behind us, Stalvey placed his hands on my ears while he and the congregation prayed the prayer of faith. Then he shook my hand and bid me Godspeed while the house worship-band tore into a foot-stompin' version of "Jesus on the Mainline." Shortly thereafter, the service drew to a close. There were hugs and pats on the back as well as cries of "Jesus loves you!" and "Come back!" I did my best to appear appreciative. However, after jumping into the old Ford Falcon, I breathed a sigh of relief. All of that attention was a bit much.

I wasn't quite sure what to make of this. A quick glance in the rear-view mirror as we motored home revealed no change to my rotting earlobe. I can't say that I felt anything particular when I was prayed over. "Oh, well," I thought, "No harm done. But how the hell did he know?" Before "crashing" that night, I stood silently before the bathroom mirror, hair back, wondering what was to become of my ear. Could I lose my hearing in that ear as a result of this spreading "bubonic plague"? If it continues to spread, could I lose my entire ear? That night, my mind was clouded with apprehension long after my head hit the pillow. Before I drifted into sleep, something materialized that was hidden deep in my memory from the Catholic days of my childhood. It was one of the most wonderful stories from the Gospels, "The Cleansing of the Ten Lepers." "God," I murmured half-asleep, "if you're real and you did it then, you can do it today. Just like those Tent folks prayed for, please heal my ear."

No doubt my housemates leapt from their beds as though a fire alarm bid them flee. I couldn't stop shouting, "Look, look at my ear!" My morning ritual consisted of splashing cold water on my face and then tying back my hair for a workday in the groves. On this morning, my ritual revealed the lower half of my infected ear to be completely healed. It fairly glowed! There was pink, moist skin with no sign of infection. The split was closed and the tiny ear-pierced hole was still there. This was no scab falling off; my lower ear had rotted clear through. "Praise God!" I cried.

My roommates and I celebrated my good fortune by not going to work. This was not entirely unusual, as just about any reason would do, including waves of three feet or better for body surfing. Ah, but now.... The hash pipe was well stoked and the wine flowed that day as we thanked God for my miracle. I also recalled how some of the healed lepers had neglected to return and thank Jesus. I didn't want to be among that lot.

Going to the Tent, especially on Sunday evenings when "the man," Herman Stalvey, was there, now became a regular ritual for several of us. Typically, the services ended with an altar call – an invitation to come forward and get right with God. This could be a first-time declaration or, in the case of "backsliders," an opportunity for forgiveness and a return to the straight and narrow path. The parable of the Prodigal Son was a favorite sermon at the Tent. The "altar-call" part of the meeting always made me uncomfortable, especially when the preacher might declare something like, "You never know when God's gonna call you home. This could be your last chance. One day that ol' heart a' yers is gonna stop! Will you be ready? You could pull out on that highway yonder and have an ol' 18-wheeler flatten you like a frog on the side a' the road."

Was I ready? My nervousness - betrayed by cotton mouth and by the sweat trickling down the center of my back during these soul-searching probes – suggested perhaps not. I was Catholic, or sort of. I'd stopped attending Mass more than a year ago. I'd come to believe that my spiritual quest had led me to other paths. These were valid paths, I assumed, different than the faith of my fathers, but well grounded nonetheless. I had my shortcomings, but considered myself loyal to my family as well as a good friend. Certainly I considered myself not to be evil, not possessing the hardcore depravity of a Charles Manson or a Lex Luthor (Superman's archenemy). However, don't ask my siblings about that.

"You must be born again," Stalvey thundered, wiping perspiration from his brow while he paced back and forth like a prizefighter who was waiting for the bell's signal to resume the boxing match. Well, there was no denying that I hadn't been following Jesus like these folks. This narrow view – Jesus is the *Only* Way – was a bit over the edge. I considered this view to be both arrogant and a stumbling block. There were many paths, weren't there? The debate raged within me. I'd adopted the view of Cosmic Consciousness: Jesus' way (peace and love) is the Way, but there are a myriad of spiritual masters to guide one in the "way." You'd think that you wouldn't return to a church service that made you so uncomfortable, challenging so much of what you'd come to hold dear: the cause, the movement, the revolution. However, the folks who attended these meetings at the Tent got me to thinking about what I saw and heard. The old-time religious messages, coupled with the undeniable power of the Holy Spirit, were dramatically working in and changing people's lives. "These signs will accompany those who believe: in my name they will drive out demons...." (Mk 16:17).

No doubt much of the professional community that did psychoanalysis would have a field day here at the Tent. I wasn't naive. I know a con when I see one. The world is full of hustlers, frauds, and rip-offs that aren't below using people's emotional and physical pain and fears to pry their last bucks out of their pockets. Heck, these scam artists come in all shapes and sizes; some are even behind pulpits. I didn't get this vibe at the Tent. While there was a great deal that I didn't understand, especially in regard to spiritual gifts like those to which Paul refers in I Corinthians:12, and this business of having a personal relationship with Jesus, I knew that my ear had been healed. I was the one seeking, asking God to reveal Himself to me, and all kinds of wild things were happening.

The regular attendees at the Tent were a virtual smorgasbord of humanity: black, white, young, old, surfers, locals, and out-of-states (snowbirds). Mostly, they were poor to lower middle-class. Most of us hippies developed a real loyalty to our own kind. Our attitude was that if "straights" (all others) didn't mess with you, leave 'em well enough alone. I'd pick up a "freak" thumbin' a ride (and just about anyone else) in a heartbeat and expected them to do the same; this was "the code of the road." (In Graham Nash's song "Teach Your Children," he, David Crosby, and Stephen Stills sang, "You, who are on the road, must have a code that you can live by.") The Tent folks, even those cut from a different cloth, appeared to be genuinely thrilled to see you at service. Not only that, but they made a sincere effort to let you know that you were welcome at various home prayer-meetings, potluck dinners, and seaside baptisms. Furthermore, they would ask, "Do you have a place to stay? Do you need a job?" I was used to most strangers backing off of me. I enjoyed the power trip of intimidating others, especially the forty-plus crowd. I'd "get off" on their looks of disgust, looks based solely on appearance. They would look at me disgustedly until their eyes met mine and they guessed rightly that I was no flower-in-my-hair, Haight Ashbury-variety peacenik. But these "Tent People" had something that the hippies didn't. Hippies love their own, but these folks don't care what package you come in or what baggage you're carrying.

. . . .

Ol' Brother Lee Brubaker, whom I'd met in Detroit the year before, was a regular at the Tent. His bronzed skin, broad shoulders, bleached-blond hair, and full beard reminded one of a modern-day John the Baptist. (Remember that I called Lee "Moses" back in Detroit?) Like Lee, another regular, Brother Al Posada, seemed fearless. At one of my first visits to the Tent, Al, who was born in Colombia, saddled his half-my-size self in the chair next to mine and offered me a Bible. From that day forward, he went out of his way to befriend me. Another fellow whom you've met already was Tim Meyer, the Tent "church bouncer" from Dearborn, Michigan. Tim, whom we called Tim the Fisherman, was made of the same stuff as Lee and Al. Like them, he took a no-holds-barred approach when it came to sharing the Gospel. These three, who were about my age and had similar backgrounds, were not easily intimidated. Tim, an ex-Grande Ballroom freak, knew exactly where we were comin' from; no doubt he felt a connection with us Detroit boys. He promised to come out to Jungle Trail and look in on us.

Tim stopped by, all right. We could hear him coming a mile away, chuggin' down the Inter-Coastal in his boat. When he eventually butted upside our dock, I couldn't help but wonder how he'd gotten his hands on Bogie's boat, *The African Queen*. She was Tim's pride and joy, just like our beloved Falcon was to us. It was quite a treat to go "rivering" with "Captain Bligh," especially with other craft on the river. Vero, which was "Fat City," attracted a lot of boaters, the "Thurston Howell" variety, like Jim Backus's snooty, upper-crust character on the television show *Gilligan's Island*. When these boaters caught sight of us, those anchors jumped into the boat like a defeated marlin and the throttle jammed as far forward as she'd go. It kinda reminded me of one of my favorite childhood flicks, Walt Disney's *Swiss Family Robinson*, and the harrowing encounter that the Robinson family had with a band of scalawags. We were an evangelistic challenge, to be sure.

I suspect that my confession of faith was just a matter of time; heck, I was the one practically begging God to make contact with me. It was brought about by a combination of things: being immersed in nature's splendor; the witnessing of the other young men like Tim, Al, and Lee, who'd been there and done that and concluded that Jesus was the answer; the warmth of folks with whom you had little in common previously and who shared their lives and what little they possessed willingly and joyfully with a nineteen-year-old Yankee hippie with a Detroit attitude; and the fiery, take-no-prisoners sermons from Evangelist Stalvey. My conversion was inevitable, which is not to suggest an absence of mental anguish and that most wonderful yet dangerous of gifts, free will. On a chilly-by-Florida-standards February night in 1972, just a month after my twentieth birthday, I made my way down to the dirt-floor altar of that ragged revival tent, knelt down, and asked Jesus to save me and to forgive me of my sins.[3]

The days immediately following my confession of faith were no picnic. The spiritual warfare unleashed against me seemed uncanny. In a strange way, it buoyed my re-found faith; otherwise, I might have been knocked out in the first round. To continue the analogy, the boxing ring was our little six-cottage outpost on Orchid Island. Some other longhairs had moved into a recently vacated (gee, I hope we didn't have something to do with that) apartment. Anyway, these guys were the hell-raisin', Wet Willie (a southern rock/soul band)-lovin', surf-ridin' local variety. Now, Orchid Island seemed like a mini pop festival on weekends. People I'd never met before were offering me fat joints and gorgeous girls were paying some attention to me (no one ever accused me of being a Don Juan). One day, a guy who looked like one of those dudes from a surfer magazine rattled the screen door and asked if we'd like to try some spaghetti, the kind with "magic" mushrooms. "Hmm, smells good," I thought. Then it came to me: Hold on here. None of this stuff ever happened before. Why now?

If I was serious about picking up my cross and following Jesus, it was clear as crystal that I needed to split this scene and not be slow about it.

---

[3]   In the Protestant Evangelical tradition (and Pentecostal groups like those who met at the "Tent"), that precise moment after a person reaches the age of reason, and makes a personal confession of belief in the risen Lord – Jesus, accepting his sacrifice at Calvary as the only thing capable of washing away one's sins; aka being "born again."

Upon hearing about my dilemma, two brothers in Christ from the Tent, Mark Nicholson and Troy Moody, graciously offered me a berth in their apartment in Vero as a temporary refuge until I got on my feet. It might not sound like a big deal to some, but this was my first big test (trial), to leave the security and comradeship of the Detroit gang and launch deep into the unknown. All of my possessions fit snugly into a single army duffel bag. Unlike Lot's wife, I would not look back (Gn 19:26).

Not too many weeks later, the Michigan Jungle Trail Tribe slowly broke up. Most headed back to Michigan to resume school, jobs, or love interests; several lingered in and around Vero. Merle, who made a confession of faith on the same night that I did, moved into a broken-down, yellow school bus that was resting in a vacant lot off of U.S. 1 in Vero. Later, he tried living in an orange-and-white silk parachute that was situated among the palmettos just off of Wabasso Beach. The parachute looked like something from which Sinbad the Sailor might emerge at any moment. I tried staying there but couldn't deal with the tiny, jaws-mounted-on-wings sand fleas and gnats that could pass through mosquito-netting and drive you mad. They and some vandals from Jerkville led Merle and me to explore new living options soon thereafter.

Meanwhile, I settled somewhat precariously into my new life as a disciple of Jesus, one of Stalvey's bunch. A local police officer referred to me as a "Tent Kid" after I'd come out of the library directly across from the police station. He found it oddly suspicious that I had no shoes on and brought me in for questioning. Citrus groves gave way to various construction jobs that were plentiful; Florida was booming before the oil embargo in 1973. Now, Bible studies and prayer meetings supplemented the weekend revival services. I pitched in when and where I could, including taking the Saturday all-night sleepover prayer-time shift at an old building that was the size of a two-car garage. Located near Rt. 60 and 43rd Street, it served as our humble outreach headquarters.

. . . .

Merle Maddox and I moved back to Wabasso. We found a two-room shack (three rooms, if you include the bathroom) that could have been the twin of the one that Jed Clampett and Granny lived in back in the hills. But, hey, it was dry, cheap, and set back from U.S. 1. Since I had no wheels, this was a great place from which to hitch a ride. While I worked a construction gig at John's Island, my place became a convenient pick-up spot, what with half the labor force passing that way. I was really uneasy and conflicted about working on John's Island. I was helping to tear up "our" beautiful beach and replace it with ugly condos that were made of pink stucco. Due to the nature of my job, I felt like a traitor to the cause (environmental). "Aren't there enough of these condos?" I thought. "There'll be no public beach left between Jacksonville and Miami." In time, Merle left our shack. He had unfinished business up in Michigan to address. It didn't take long to find a new roommate. Johnny Wilkins was as southern a fella as I've ever met. A Vietnam vet of my own age, he and I knew each other from the Tent and worked together briefly on a landscaping crew. Johnny jumped at the idea to stay at the "Wabasso Inn." After he'd moved his waterbed into the living room, there wasn't space for much else but a couch (my bed), a table, and a lamp. We had no TV or radio. Therefore, before turning in, we would spend a considerable amount of time ribbing each other for amusement, especially about our respective geographic DNA composition. Johnny possessed that type of southern drawl that took some getting used to, especially for someone like me, who was used to Midwestern accents. No doubt my jive, fast-talking, Motown, snowbird butchery of the English language put his patience to the test on more than one occasion. Ol' Johnny would think nothing of going out in the middle of the night to hunt turtles, frogs, crabs, and crayfish to supplement our not-too-prosperous larder. He looked a sight, wading out there with a miner's light fixed atop his head; a giggin' spear in one hand and a club in the other; a gunny sack secured to his belt; and a headband securing his long, wild locks. I wouldn't go wading in those snake-infested, who-knows-what-lurks-at-high-noon waters with a twelve-gauge, let alone on a moonless night. Johnny was a little crazy, which probably was why I liked him. He'd been a commando in Nam, sometimes working behind enemy lines. Night giggin' in the swamp was a walk in the park for Johnny. I preferred to get our main course at the Winn-Dixie grocery store in Vero or at a late-night rib place in Gifford - Fagan's Roadside Barbecue. Still, Johnny's swamp-turtle potato soup wasn't that bad. It tasted like chicken.

December of my first year as a Floridian rolled around. I was determined to spend Christmas with my family and, hopefully, to see some of that white stuff – snow. In order to save on money, Ron Allgeyer, a buddy of mine from Redford who'd come down several months earlier to check out the Florida scene, agreed to thumb back with me for the holidays. He had visited months earlier and decided to stick around, having scored a decent construction gig. Evangelist Stalvey was holding a revival up in Cocoa Beach, and Ron agreed to take in a meeting with me on our way north. This would be my first trip home after embarking on my "Jesus journey" some ten months earlier. Uncertain about what challenges might await me in Redford, MI, I felt that I needed what we referred to fondly as a "double dose of the Holy Ghost."

There was nothing particularly unusual about the meeting that night, nothing, that is, until I went forward for prayer. After the laying on of hands, Brother Stalvey warned me that I'd have an encounter with the powers of darkness when I went back home. He concluded by telling me to fear not and to remember that, "...greater is He that is in you than he that is in the world" (1 Jn 4:4). Hmmm, what on earth was that supposed to mean? Anyway, the rides came quick and easy until Ron and I hit colder weather just inside of Tennessee. While Ron didn't say anything and was a good sport when it came to adversity, I couldn't help but think that he was looking at me out of the corner of his eye, just waiting for me to pray us up a ride. I'm sure that I was praying. In addition, I probably was muttering a few curses at the men with Michigan plates who were headed north. The Bible Belt? Gimme a break. At this rate, Ron and I would miss Christmas altogether or freeze to death. Finally, we decided to make our way to Knoxville and grab a flight into Metropolitan Airport in Romulus, Michigan, which was not far from home.

This turned out to be the right move. From Metro, we secured a lift to the corner of Gaylord and Seven Mile, where Shannon's Lounge sat. We opted not to peek in as it was well after dark and I was beat. Ron headed south to his folks' house and I headed north to "Home Sweet Home" at 19782 Gaylord. It was Christmas Eve, 1972, and, yes, tiny flakes danced merrily to the ground. It was magical. My heart raced as I anticipated bursting through the side door to surprise my family, whom I hadn't seen in months and whom I had really missed. I was having one of those Perry Como moments, like the one where he croons, "Oh, there's no place like home for the holidays" in the song "Home for the Holidays." This was especially true when it meant a healthy slab of my mother's date-nut loaf, apple dumplings, and the only fruitcake that I ever enjoyed.

Christmas couldn't have been better. I took the laid-back approach with regard to my new enthusiasm for Christianity. I'd only be home for a week, and this wasn't the time or place to play the "heavy" and put their Irish Catholicism under the spotlight as something inferior to the "real" Christianity that I'd embraced. Besides, if my behavior (speech, sobriety, etc.) didn't convey that some life-transforming event had transpired in my life, then they'd never buy it anyway. Several months earlier, I had written to my dad and let him in on my conversion, minus some of the details that cause parents to lose sleep (my acid test, for one). So he and mom sort of knew that something was up. It also was time to look in on some of the ol' gang.

. . . .

Bill and Gidget Rundel had married just out of high school, had a son, and moved to Brightmoor; the area on the west side of Detroit that you may recall from Part One of this book. They had heard that I was in town and asked - actually pleaded - with me to stop over. Bill was one of the crowd with whom I ran during my senior year in high school. It was upstairs at his folks' house on Indian Street between Seven Mile and Grand River that I'd smoked my first joint while listening to Led Zeppelin's self-titled debut album. Midwesterners know how early it gets dark in the winter months. Even though it was only 7 p.m., the streets of Brightmoor were grim and foreboding when I pulled up alongside the curb on Blackstone near Lyndon Street. I felt compelled to take along a Bible and an eight-track of Mylon's *We Believe*. Bill and Gidget greeted me warmly, and we lost no time reminiscing and catching up. Their baby boy already was down for the night. After an hour, the conversation, while genuine, seemed perfunctory. If Bill and Gidget were having trouble, I'd wait for them to bring it up. Minutes later, Gidget was unable to contain herself any longer. She talked quietly, as though someone might be listening. Gidget whispered, "Rocker, I'm not quite sure how to explain it, but there's an evil presence in this house." Of course, she and Bill were concerned for their own welfare and that of their young son.

Three things happened simultaneously. First, a wave of anxiety washed over me. I desperately wished to bolt for the door. Also, my two friends seemed to undergo a disturbing metamorphosis right before my eyes. Now they leered at me, as though waiting for a signal to leap upon me with tooth and fang. Had they lured me here to kill me? Were they into some Manson Family-like cult? Then there was another occurrence. Gidget, Bill, and I had been fairly sedate most of the evening, sitting in the living room up front. The baby's bedroom was all the way in the rear of the house. Now, to top it all off, their young boy began to shriek and scream as though someone or something was holding his feet to the flame. "It's happening," Gidget sobbed.

Herman Stalvey's words came back to me: "Joe, when you're up in Detroit, you're gonna have a run-in with evil." This was it. I can hear some psychoanalyst explaining all of it right now. But, hey, when you come face to face with the Dark One or one of his minions, you know that you're dealing with something otherworldly. This was no drug-induced flashback or some Houdini-exposed charlatan trickery. This was spiritual warfare. Armed with my Bible, Mylon on the eight-track player, and the discernment to recognize what was going on, faith flooded my heart. I went from room to room pleading the blood of Jesus. I insisted that whoever or whatever was in this home depart it and trouble the family no more. I'd witnessed this practice at the Tent, but as a spectator; now, I was in the ring – a combatant. Just as turning on a light in a room dispels the darkness therein, I felt that the light of Christ in me likewise was dispelling the demonic presence that had plagued Bill and Gidget's home. Like an old classic Dracula film, wherein the vampire is repelled by a crucifix, the powers of darkness fled before me. While there was no physical evidence of this warfare, I sensed that the enemy was in retreat. I breathed a sigh of relief. The whole ordeal was over in five minutes. The baby drifted back to sleep. Bill and Gidget's countenances once again signaled the warmth of old friends. With Mylon still providing the rockin' revival backdrop, I shared with them how Jesus had changed my life. An hour later, tears streaming down her cheeks, Gidget bid me Godspeed, saying, "Whatever evil presence was here, Rocker, I know it's gone."

Before I headed back down South, I had two more important things to do. I'd been without a vehicle for the last year. I walked, hitched, and arranged for rides to work, worship, and fellowship while putting as much cash aside per week as I could. Finally, I had a sizable sum stashed away. When I returned to Vero, I would be seated behind the helm of a brand-new, baby-blue Ford Econoline van, which I bought for $2,500.00. Those were the days. The other task was to see my extended family (primarily cousins) and my old Redford crowd at Shannon's Lounge. Initially, I thought that this might be a golden opportunity to give testimony to my life-transforming experience in Christ at the annual New Year's Eve Bash. I sauntered into the bar at around 11 p.m. and Shannon's was filled with people, wall to wall; although I recognized some of them, most were strangers. Michigan soul-rocker Mitch Ryder was on the jukebox, playing at a dangerous decibel level that caused the jukebox to shake like an overloaded washing machine. Most of the revelers were hell-bent on getting wasted before the countdown that heralded the New Year. My three cousins (Pat, Mike and Tim), who were working the jammed counter at the bar, could spare only a "Hey, good to see ya" and a warm handshake. Then, an altercation at the entrance on Seven Mile erupted into a brawl. Guys and gals were trading punches. That fire quickly subsided, and I was able to settle into a lone vacant seat in a corner that allowed for a panoramic view. I searched through the smoke-fueled haze for any familiar faces. A growing mood of disquiet crept over me. Something wasn't right. Images of my brothers and sisters in Christ down South flashed across the screen of my mind. At this moment, they'd be dancing and singing God's praises at the New Year's Eve "Watch" service; what a great moment for Jesus' return, I used to think. Indeed, it wouldn't be difficult to separate the sheep from the goats on New Year's Eve. As my eyes drifted from one end of the lounge to the other, a bizarre transformation took place. I had a vision, due perhaps to imagination but … definitely not to any drug-induced hallucination. The crowd at Shannon's metamorphosed as one, not into beautiful butterflies or fresh new creations of some fashion. No, they were changing into skeletons, the living dead. The roof opened slowly. At once, I could see from within and without. They were partying in a giant coffin! As the lid began to ease back down, I sensed that Death had come to harvest a crop. There was little that I could do to convince these folks of the imminent, eternal danger threatening them. As with Noah, they would have laughed me right out the door.

I beat it out of Shannon's and resolved to return one day; then, there would be no retreat. I took the experience at face value, not as an all-encompassing indictment against bars, taverns, nightclubs, or even alcohol. Rather, I took my experience to mean that the attitude of "eat, drink and be merry for tomorrow we die" (Lk 12:19) has enslaved many a fool, to the extent that he or she is oblivious to the eternal peril near which s/he lingers so precariously.

· · · ·

After the holidays, I drove my new van back to Florida. Living in Wabasso was awesome – quiet and close to the beach. However, as the months peeled away, I noticed a change in my roommate Johnny. This change was subtle at first, then abruptly obvious. One Saturday, I returned from running a few errands to see Johnny scrubbing off the scripture passage "For the wages of sin is death" that was emblazoned on the side of his white van. Rather than attending fellowship, Johnny had begun to stay back at our pad in order to entertain a young lady with whom he'd taken up. I really liked ol' John, but I decided that it was time to check out. I couldn't afford the place by myself, nor had I the heart to tell him to split. Finally, after expressing my intentions, we shook hands and went our separate ways. I moved back with my two former roommates, Troy and Mark, to Vero Beach. We found a place that we affectionately dubbed Cockroach Junction. A three-bedroom "condo;" Cockroach Junction was cheap housing. It was one of about a dozen units with four or five apartments per unit, a weather-worn, dull-blue place that was wholly unattractive to the eye, especially since the buildings sat next to the well manicured, resort-like, private setting of Dodgertown. The two were separated by a seven-foot-tall chain-link fence. Whatever it was, Cockroach Junction was a roof over one's head. Our "condo" cost sixty dollars a month, plus utilities. Can you believe it?

From time to time, folks from home would continue to drop in. On one occasion, my mother gave me a "heads-up" that my brother Danny and a couple of his friends would be stopping by. Mom said that they would be in a van, which turned out to be an old school bus. The "couple of friends" evolved into a dozen of Redford Township's "finest" young residents, doing their version of Ken Kesey and the Merry Pranksters. The "ship" was piloted by my cousin Pat Shannon. Thankfully, he dropped off just my brother and his buddy Tom Penman at the "Junction" and continued south to Fort Lauderdale with the rest of the Redford Pranksters. Pat arranged to pick up Dan and Tom on his return voyage.

It was great to have family around for a change. Dan and Tom would use my pad to crash. I could arrange for a ride to work so they'd have a vehicle with which to explore the area and hang out at any one of several beaches nearby. I'd explained to Dan and Tom that I often attended a place called the Tent and that half of the residents of Cockroach Junction were "Stalveyites" (Tent People). No doubt their curiosity was aroused. With little else to do in the evening, they accepted my invitation to attend the service on Sunday evening. Inviting folks from back home to the Tent (especially friends and family) always proved a bit nerve-rattling. You hoped that nothing too weird would happen, like hearing Brother or Sister So and So give some bizarre message in tongues or seeing hecklers and drunks of the sort that I'd encountered on my first visit. Above all, you hoped that, if these family members or friends were "called out" (ministered to by one or more of the spiritual gifts mentioned in 1 Cor.:12), then it would be "right on" … edifying. Many of these episodes left me puzzled and wondering about the validity of certain manifestations. However, I always could fall back on my own experience (the healing of my ear) and others that seemed genuine enough to bolster my "babe-in-Christ" faith and the understanding of such matters to which I'd never been exposed as a Catholic. Yet, there were times when I wondered, "Is this the Holy Spirit, or are we just fishin' here?" Well, wouldn't you know it: On this Sunday night, Tom, a tall, gangly, wild-eyed fella with a chronic disheveled look (not unlike my brothers and me), would be called forward for ministry. Like us, Tom was a Catholic from the West Side of Detroit. This was his night. What precisely Evangelist Stalvey said to him our collective memories couldn't say exactly. Whatever this was, it freaked out Tom. "That guy read my mind," he'll tell you to this day.

Like Thomas the Apostle ("Doubting Thomas") in the New Testament, Tom was a skeptic. On the day following his call forward, he and Danny went to a secluded beach near Wabasso. There, Tom wrestled with the events of last night's service and wondered what all of it meant. For Tom, the real issue was, "Does God even exist?" Swimming alone thirty yards off shore, Tom finally concluded that no, God does not exist. However that preacher came to know about his personal life, Tom thought, there was some trick to it, some psychic chicanery that he would figure out in time. At the very moment Tom concluded God didn't exist, he realized suddenly that he had to struggle to stay afloat. He could not make it back to shore. First the sea, then panic had him in their clutches, and unbeknownst to him, had Tom been caught in a riptide? He and Dan, both average swimmers at best with no ocean experience, were no match for what had gotten hold of Tom. Fortunately, Danny, who'd been dozing nearby, was aroused by Tom's frantic cries and managed somehow to get Tom safely to shore. Hmmm, was it just a coincidence that Tom had nearly fallen victim to the ocean's grasp the moment he'd concluded God didn't exist?

There are other dangers that two pale-skinned snowbirds (especially of the Celtic variety) can run into unknowingly at the beach. I warned Dan and Tom that the Florida sun can be a deceptive friend. The ocean-side breezes mask just how deep-fried you may be getting. Most Michigan guys want a bronze-surfer, Coppertone tan to take back home. Also, it is important for a guy not to embarrass himself for one more day on a Florida beach with a complexion that calls to mind the underside of a snake. The upshot was that, following their "life-flash-before-my-eyes episode" at the beach, Danny and Tom walked into Cockroach Junction glowing like a couple of radioactive humanoids from one of those B-movie apocalyptic sci-fi flicks at the drive-in. They were already in pain: their earlobes and the tops of their feet (not to mention the rest of them) were airbrushed candy-apple red. Dan and Tom were in for a long night. My roommates and I could only launch a counter-assault that was feeble at best. Before we turned in, Dan and Tom lathered the now-blistering, "on-fire" portions of their tortured bodies in Noxzema (a poor man's Solarcaine). I turned over my waterbed to them and hit them with the crossfire of two floor fans. Sleep was nigh impossible for Tom and Dan; it came in fits and starts. All that they could do was to lie there and gaze up at the tapestry of the Laughing Jesus, which was illuminated faintly by an outside streetlight that snuck around an ill-fitted blind. The Laughing Jesus tapestry looked down at them; no doubt they appreciated the irony.

· · · ·

I met Colleen, a dark-complexioned beauty, in Florida. Originally from Northville, Michigan, a town west of Redford, she was one of many who were friends of or related to one of our merry band of Michiganders. Like my brother Dan and his buddy Tom, these folks dropped in from time to time, some for an overnight stay, others for a week or more. One evening, Colleen made her first visit to the Tent. She happened to sit next to me. Whenever our bare arms happened to brush against each other, I was thrilled. This was not altogether unusual, given the tenor of those high-octane revival meetings, with their heap of Fringeville humanity tightly hemmed in, swaying to and fro to the rhythm of a fiery sermon or a rock-fueled gospel hymn. It was hard not to look at Colleen. Could it be that she was ordained to be the future Mrs. Shannon – my Eve, as it were? One's mind could not wander long during one of Herman Stalvey's Elijah-like, in-your-face sermons. We soon approached that moment in the service where we veterans, with whom I now numbered myself, waited anxiously, hopefully. We stormed Heaven's Gate with pleas that God would move in our midst, that He would deliver, heal, set the captives free – especially the young woman to my right - in that Holy Ghost-filled tent-revival atmosphere to which we'd become accustomed.   "Young lady, would you please stand up?" Evangelist Stalvey asked Colleen. "Praise God," I thought. "Here we go." I was all attention now – all of us were. Stalvey let his fixed glance rest solely on Colleen and bid her not to come down front, as was his usual custom, but to stand right where she was. Colleen rose cautiously. As she did, she looked like an angel who carried a heavy burden, beautiful yet troubled. After asking if they'd ever met before and determining that they had not, Evangelist Stalvey pointed out to Colleen that she had some serious health issues of a feminine nature. He told Colleen that God was going to operate on her. Before he could continue, Colleen collapsed to her knees, heavy sobs rising slowly from somewhere deep within. Those of us in the Tent knew that this was no obscure, stumble-around-in-the-dark, or ambiguous word of knowledge. I don't recall if I reached out a reassuring hand to Colleen or assisted in praying over her, as was our custom. I do know that she had a serious encounter with God that night, one to an extent that few others have had that I have witnessed. I tried to fight off the memory of what seemed to be Merle's temporary (one night only) restoration-of-hearing miracle that had happened less than a year before. Whatever was happening to Colleen, I hoped that it was the real deal, as it was with my ear.

Several days later, Colleen and a friend from Michigan, Debbie, were going to Texas for whatever. They said that they would be back. Upset and a little dismayed, I thought of little else for several weeks. I asked questions like "Where is she? I thought they'd be back by now. God, what's goin' on?" Then, the news: "Colleen got married!" Whaddya mean she got married? Colleen only had been gone a month. What cruel joke was this? It seems that Colleen had met some older guy in Texas, a self-styled bishop of a group called Sons of the Kingdom (one of many cult groups that sprang up like tares among the wheat of the Jesus Movement). I never saw Colleen again. To this day, I'm not sure what to make of the certainty I'd had that she was the woman with whom God intended me to be. Maybe it was just wishful thinking, but I was so sure. I don't know that I've ever been smitten so quickly by any woman since; love at first sight. I look forward to coming to a deeper understanding of an exceedingly long list of items on that Blessed Day. I suppose that most of them only will be fully understood when I see Him - Jesus, face to face.

. . . .

My buddy Tim (the bouncer and fisherman) had visited Michigan and had come back to Vero. He was not alone one evening soon after, when he pulled in at the Tent. Tim had one messed-up-lookin' dude in tow, an acquaintance from back in Dearborn. A quick appraisal of this fella, Ken Hasper, revealed him to be an imminent ICU case. Ken was wrapped in a blanket and was shaking uncontrollably. Apparently, this guy was seriously ill (later, I found out that he was in the throes of a violent withdrawal from heroin). Once the service got underway, I paid him little notice. Typically, our tent meetings ended with an altar call, and tonight was no exception. Usually, a substantial number of the members of our congregation would end up around the platform where the pulpit was located and the band stood. These members would kneel and humble themselves before God. They would pour out their hearts, repenting of wrongs committed and interceding for some loved one. Some would be moved to kneel alongside one another and intercede (pray) with each other, bearing one another's burdens. At times, they would offer encouragement and a reassuring hand on the shoulder. People would be weeping, laughing, singing, and speaking/praying in tongues. As the Spirit led, the music ministry provided appropriate background music. As this was our opportunity to "do business with God," these closing moments could get rather emotional. Many had very real, desperate needs and had nowhere else to turn. Meanwhile, traffic continued to whisk by on nearby U.S. 1. What a curious sight we must have been to those on the highway bound for who knows where. One of the many things that I admired about these folks was the manner in which they reminded me of so many characters in the Bible: The Samaritan woman at the well, the Prodigal Son, Joshua outside the walls of Jericho, the woman taken in the act of adultery and about to be stoned, blind Bartimaeus, Peter in the Garden of Gethsemane when he lopped off the ear of the servant of the High Priest. These were folks who had no need to put on "airs." If it meant touching the hem of Jesus' garment or ripping off the roof of a house where Jesus was visiting to get your sick friend to Him, they would do it. These folks didn't need to be cajoled out of their seats to go forward and kneel on the hardened earth in a ragged old tent. "God resists the proud but gives grace to the humble" (Jas 4:6). Well, I reckon that's why the Lord moved in such powerful ways in the midst of these people. The mood on the night that Tim brought Ken to the Tent was expectant. There was a lot of energy in the air, the vibe of life and death hanging in the balance. It was Ken's time. Amid the loosely controlled, borderline-chaos mix of altar-call celebrations and continued pockets of earnest prayer here and there, Ken "was suddenly walking and leaping and praising God," just like the lame man who was healed in Acts 3. It happened just like that: the tremors, nausea, and altogether wretched state of cold-turkey withdrawal disappeared like a ship over the horizon, never to return. Like those at the temple that day in Acts 3, we at the Tent "were filled with amazement and astonishment at what had happened to him."

Like so many of these deliverances and healings at the Tent, this was not the end but the beginning. I was thrilled for Ken. Stuff like this made Christianity real and helped to fortify one's faith. The fact that Ken's path and my own would reconnect down the road was not the faintest of blips on my radar screen. The following week, both of us were taken a bit aback. We were at a Sunday evening service, as before. We were seated in the same row, separated by ten chairs and a half-dozen folk. Ken now looked every bit the young man who recently had been snatched from the jaws of death. We found ourselves at that part of the service – following the sermon and prior to the altar call –when the spiritual gifts discussed by the Apostle Paul in his first letter to the Corinthians often would manifest themselves. These gifts especially included tongues, interpretation, prophecy, and words of knowledge. Let me retreat for a moment and mention something else. In the months following my own experience of healing, deliverance, regeneration, being born again, and being baptized in the Holy Spirit[4] (have I forgotten anything?), I was left to ponder, "Well, what now?" I'd bumped around several construction jobs and eventually would pick up a carpenter's union card with the thought of taking on the trade of my spiritual namesake, Joseph. However, I could never shake the thought that I might have a calling to become a minister, after the fashion of these Tent folks and the larger Jesus Movement. However, the how, when, and where had not been revealed. I had wondered if my calling was indeed real, not just my own fancy.

Some months later, I was at one of our services at the Tent. At the end, Evangelist Stalvey told me (prophesied) that I had been called to be a shepherd/teacher of God's people. This was a confirmation, or so I took it, of the burden that I'd carried since the night that I'd been set free. I was not part of the inner circle of the goings-on of the ministry, and I don't know that I ever shared my anxiousness with Pastor Stalvey, specifically in regards to the matter of my calling. Now, in my mind, it was settled. It was a great source of relief to have the issue of my life's calling resolved. Details were slow in coming and the way often was hidden, but I was twenty years young and rarin' to go. Also, most people in the Jesus Movement with whom I was associated then and in the years ahead had adopted a kind of Pre-Tribulation Rapture[5] approach to life that echoed

---

[4]   The modern Pentecostal movement is characterized by belief in the possibility of receiving the same experience and gifts as did the first Christians 'on the day of Pentecost' (Acts 1. 1- 4), commonly referred to as The Baptism in/of the Holy Spirit.

Cross, F.L., and Livingstone, E.A. eds. *The Oxford Dictionary of the Christian Church.* 2nd ed. New York: Oxford University Press, 1993 (Pentecostalism 1062).

[5]   The "secret rapture," an idea rooted in fundamentalist Protestant teaching, holds that Jesus is coming back not once, but twice. On one of these occasions He will come secretly and "snatch" true believers from a world mired in unprecedented turmoil. This event has been labeled the "rapture" from the Latin verb meaning "caught up." There are several variations associated with this event. One popular version, Pre-Tribulation Rapture, holds that believers will be "snatched" up and subsequently will not have to endure earth's darkest hour-The Great Tribulation.

Hal Lindsey's book *The Late Great Planet Earth*. We sensed that we had little time left to realize our ministry before the twinkle of an eye and, then, too late, "Wish we'd all been ready," as Larry Norman sang in his worship song "I Wish We'd All Been Ready."

Meanwhile, back at the Tent, Pastor Stalvey pointed out Ken and me. He said that the two of us would labor together one day, spreading the Gospel to the city of Detroit. A few other details accompanied the message, but that was the gist of it. While the congregation clapped and sang and shouts of "Thank you, Jesus," "Yes, Lord," and "Halleluiah" rained down, Ken and I leaned forward and eyeballed each other before sitting back. While I can't speak for Ken, I know that I thought, "Him? Yeah, right." I'm thrilled that the guy got his act cleaned up, but work with him spreading the Gospel throughout southeast Michigan? If it's supposed to happen, it will. Coupling this with the mentality of "You do the possible and God will do the impossible" fairly summed up our approach to such matters. Meanwhile, Ken headed back North and I resumed a "work, wait, and see" approach in the Sunshine State.

There comes a time when you realize that your parents aren't quite like Ozzie and Harriet Nelson or Ward and June Cleaver and that maybe your dad can't whip every other dad in town. I know that you're thinking, "This guy's twenty years old and just now figurin' that out?" Please grant some leeway to me for a moment. I'd heard tell of the end of "the honeymoon period," a time in most marriages – several months to a year – in which one's spouse becomes different from the person with whom you exchanged vows in the not-so-distant past. Your spouse could take on the nature of some less-than-angelic creature or could lose the countenance of a knight in shining armor. (In time, I would discover this for myself.) Families have "black sheep," villages have "idiots," and local churches, well, let us be charitable and say that they have all of the above. As the weeks turned to months and I waited for the right moment, signal, call, or green light to take the Good News back to the streets of Detroit, I'd come to find out that our little congregation was far from perfect. Oh, I wasn't entirely naive and/or blinded by love like poor Helena in Shakespeare's play *A Midsummer Night's Dream*, but it's inevitable that conflicts are going to arise in time. These conflicts can be theological, as in "once saved, always saved," disputes for example, or cultural, as in "to drink or not to drink alcohol." There are also the ever-present conflicts with personality and ego. I suppose that these issues shouldn't take one entirely by surprise, since several letters in the New Testament are devoted to like matters. In the Christian's struggle with the world, the flesh, and the Devil, one is bound to pick up a few bumps and bruises along the way. The Body of Christ is a family and families have rows. The larger point being that, towards the final months of my twentieth year, I realized that my Christian experience had been somewhat narrow thus far. A number of years of lukewarm, immature Catholicism coupled with eighteen months of hardcore Pentecostal-revival activism would be what I'd carry back to Detroit with me. I had a vision of taking the best from the Tent and combining it with some of the methodology and music from the Jesus Movement at large, with which we rubbed elbows on occasion. With these elements, I wanted to establish a ministry (church) in or around Redford, the city of my youth.

The old Tent on U.S. 1 finally gave way to an old, weather-worn church/schoolhouse, a barn-like structure on the outskirts of Gifford; a predominately black community north of Vero. Our congregation had purchased several acres west of Vero on King's Highway (now 58th Avenue), and plans for a "real" permanent home for our church finally seemed about to be realized. More members of the congregation were "stepping up to the plate" and dedicating themselves to different ministries. In part, these ministries were intended to free up Herman Stalvey, unburdening him from many of the time-consuming responsibilities typically assumed by a pastor so that he could fulfill his calling as an evangelist. There were rumblings and hurt feelings, due greatly to the aforementioned personality conflicts. Sometimes, folks would leave for what they thought might be greener pastures. I kept myself at a distance from these family spats. After all, I sensed that my hour would come any day now. I didn't date. I worked, studied, and spent a good deal of time alone in prayer and meditation. I waited for that light to turn green.

In October 1973, I sensed that the time was right. I put my affairs in order and expressed my intentions to Brother Herman. During a Sunday evening service in mid-November, I was formally ordained by Truth and Life Ministry of Vero Beach, Florida. I received the laying-on of hands and was commissioned to go forth and spread the Good News. The following weekend, I preached my first message, which was about Jesus as the Way, the Truth, and the Life (Jn 14:6); and the dangers of dabbling with the occult and eastern mysticism. I counseled that New Age pagan hippieism was largely a sham and that psychedelic drugs didn't help, either. I concluded by stating that, just as Jesus opened blind eyes two thousand years ago, He still does – curing spiritual blindness, in my case. My final days at Truth and Life Ministry were emotional, as you might expect. After I packed my van, I said my goodbyes to my brothers and sisters in Christ who had taken me in a year earlier and made me a part of their families. After receiving hugs and prayers from them, I was well on my way. Signs for U.S. 1 North turned into signs for I-75 North. Driving at a leisurely pace would give me time to think, to reflect, and to pray. I would not miss another Thanksgiving away from home. I had no idea how all of this would play out, but the conviction to start up a church in the Detroit area was fixed in my mind. I intended to bring a taste of Holy Ghost-and-fire-revivalism back to my family and friends and to the legions of young folks in the hippie movement who had been let down and ripped off, the ones in whom "straight" churches had little interest

Joe Shannon, Steve Matsos, Kenny Pore. Willow, MI c.1973

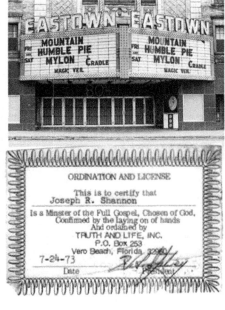

Wabasso Beach, Orchid Island,
FLA c. 1971

Our surfer pad on U.S.1, Wabasso Beach, FLA c. 1971

Merle's Wabasso Beach Pad c. 1972
Merle Madox, Christine Matsos, Steve Matsos, Bob Garcia, Debbie Hildreth

c. early 1970s. Joe and several other Michigan lads lived in these apartments on Jungle Trail (just off A1A) between Sebastian and Vero Beach, Florida (Orchid Island): these pics are c. 2016.

PART 3

THE SHALOM YEARS 1974 – 1985

Kinda hits ya' like an unexpected smack upside the head. Twenty-four hours ago you were living on the east coast of Florida, mild days, soft sea breeze with a hint of salt and jasmine to soothe the senses ... now, turning up the collar to fend off the chill of a stark, gray November in Detroit. Not for a visit, but back ... here to stay and share the Good News. Where to start? What now?

My first night back was a wake-up call to be sure. Tim Meyer – the Fisherman, unofficial church/tent revival bouncer from Vero Beach who originally hailed from Dearborn, had moved back to Michigan some months earlier. We had intended to hook up back in Detroit. Tim was aware of my calling to the ministry and now would be a source of encouragement and support as I sought to find my way and carry out what I'd been called to do – establish a church (outreach), that targeted the counterculture folks the "straight" churches either didn't want or know how to reach. The building Tim and several others were living in looked like something from the set of one of those *Escape from New York* flicks. On the south side of Grand River and east of Livernois, it was one of many stark reminders that the Motor City was indeed burning several years earlier, and while I can't say for certain, the folks living there may have been squatting ... pay rent for this dump? Some were folks with some connection to the nearby *House of Prayer* ministry whose congregation were meeting in a nearby building also on Grand River; a former Black Panther location. *House of Prayer* ministry had also gotten their hands on the old Grande Ballroom, and would for a short time play host to the bourgeoning contemporary Christian music scene featuring groups like the Phil Keaggy Band, and Crystal River from Vero Beach, Florida. Sirens, gunshots, barking curs, dripping water and scurrying rats kept sleep at bay that first night back in Detroit, and with the first faint light of a dull, cold, dreary, Motor City November morning, I bid Tim farewell and said, "I'll be in touch."

It was in Brightmoor, a section of west Detroit, ground zero Fenkell aka Five Mile and Lahser, that I felt the call to establish an outreach. My grandmother – Ma Evans, still lived in this part of town (c.'73), and my folks resided in neighboring Redford Township where I'd grown up. Up and down Fenkell, McNichols, Burt and Lahser Roads I drove, looking for just the right location. A storefront perhaps ... *Brightmoor Tabernacle*, an Assemblies of God Church that also served as the location for the Assembly's *Central Bible College* where I'd later take classes, and *St. Christine Catholic Church* stood as outposts of light along Fenkell, where biker clubs, pawn shops and liquor stores sporadically interrupted the view of familiar side streets and lower income homes in various stages of neglect and decline ... abandoned cars and trash-filled vacant lots added to the ambiance. The old Irving Theater where we kids spent many a Saturday afternoon on the edge of our seats for a double feature of sci-fi horror and suspense flicks ... remember *The Tingler*? ... Was now a Triple X Theater with adjoining adult book store complete with seedy looking men loitering about and a few business types scurrying to get in lest some passerby recognize them. If ever there was a neighborhood in need of a street level church, surely it was the tired, old neglected streets of Brightmoor. I half expected, hoped actually, that God would speak to me like He had to ol' Brother Stalvey back in Vero Beach years ago, who'd pulled off on the shoulder of U.S. 1 between Vero Beach and Fort Pierce to look over a vacant lot he thought would make an ideal location for tent revival meetings; 'cept he had no tent. Moments later a car pulled over behind his and a black man hopped out and approached him declaring, "Brother, the Lord just spoke to me to give you an old tent...." No doubt the both of them drew a few stares from automobiles rushing Fort Lauderdale bound ... what with a black and white man dancing around in an overgrown vacant lot praising God. Well, I heard no voices and of the few buildings I did get out to get a closer look at, no one came out and offered one to me to do the Lord's work. The most promising one was a vacant church on Schoolcraft west of Evergreen – *Pillar of Fire Church*. Kind of a cool name, and even though a "church" building was not exactly what I had in mind, I was open to it. What's more, two blocks west of the church sat the Turf Lounge, currently co-owned by my mother's brother – Harry Evans. Hmm, perhaps a little bit of family competition ... Holy

Spirit and spirits. A Brightmoor location never panned out. However, in a few years, *King's Kids* Christian Motorcycle Club would plant their flag in Brightmoor. They'd have their work cut out for them, and I was pleased to be something of a mentor to club president Jim Wilhelmson. Also, one of the more memorable weddings I officiated was a King's Kids ceremony … like being on the movie set of a Peter Fonda biker flick, different vibe of course. *Teen Challenge* would also open an outreach near old Redford High School on Grand River, so Brightmoor was well covered.

I'd also visited *The Lord's House* in Livonia and the *Fisherman's Net* in Warren, but these and others I checked out didn't seem the right fit; I was still uncertain if I should plant a new outreach or cast my lot (net) with an established ministry. There was one place, however, that suggested some possibilities. It was some place near Tim's old stomping grounds from his high school days in Dearborn. Actually, this place was in Inkster at the corner of Beech Daly and Dartmouth. It was an old, tired looking building, what had once been the neighborhood market with an apartment on top, that had fallen into the hands of some local Jesus "freaks" who had been using it for informal Bible Studies and prayer meetings after they'd outgrown gathering in a nearby home.[6] "We called it *Shalom House*," explains Jack Wyatt, "because the neighborhood needed God's peace … we didn't want to call it *Peace House*, and so we decided on *Shalom House*." Several of the brothers who had taken it upon themselves to oversee the fellowship were moving on to other pursuits including school, jobs and what not, and it appeared that *Shalom's* presence in the neighborhood would be short-lived. There was no formal board, no official leadership with local church affiliation, just young brothers and sisters in Christ (mostly of the counterculture variety) getting together to lift up Jesus and have a laid-back non-threatening place to bring their friends to hear the Good News. Clearly there was a need for someone to step up. The few meetings I looked in on were sparsely attended, seemed to lack clear direction, and musicians and Bible study leaders were not always dependable.

---

[6] During the early seventies, young folks from Trinity Baptist on Beech Daly south of Van Born in Taylor began meeting at the Coombs' home in south Dearborn Heights.

Tim and I had been seeing more of each other as we'd both landed gigs at the Ford foundry near Flat Rock. He moved into *Shalom House* and prodded me on a regular basis to get more involved. I'd hooked back up with Steve Matsos who I'd originally gone to Florida with, and with a couple of buddies, roomed at his vacant girlfriend's mother's house – Arlene Wells – in Willow, a sleepy little one-pony town a few miles from the auto plant, and by the way, I hated it … the job that is. The foundry reminded me of scenes from Tolkien's *The Lord of the Rings* tales wherein Saruman's "factory" (he produced Uruk-hai aka super Orcs), whereas we made automobile "heads" for Ford car engines. It was always loud, dark, dirty and hot. I worked on a head-line and had to wear overalls over street clothes, asbestos gloves, hard hat and breathing mask while doing monotonous heavy lifting … drugs and booze were everywhere … card and dice games … often you'd have to wait an extra five minutes to punch out at the close of your shift because so many guys in front of you had a stack of time cards (their buddies' who'd split earlier) to clock out. No wonder we turned out more scrap than satisfactory finished product. Once a week I'd go to a Swedish sauna to sweat the factory filth out of my skin pores. I'd have thought twice about moving north had I known this was what awaited me. Still, it was a job, and in the meantime I took a more visible role at Shalom and after a few months and with a considerable amount of lobbying on my behalf, Tim and I convinced the few remaining brothers who'd had some level of leadership recognition that God had called me to assume a pastoral leadership role here at Shalom, and with general support, there were a few skeptics, my tenure as pastor began c. January 1974; I was twenty-two.

It was my intention from the get-go to establish a local church, building on the unstable foundation of a loose street ministry that appeared ready to, like the proverbial rudderless ship, run aground. This approach ruffled a few feathers. Folks who were content, anxious about change perhaps, adamant that Shalom should remain as it was, had been, a loose, laid-back sorta' charismatic Jesus People fellowship. "Don't go gettin churchy on us" they'd fuss. Next thing you know we'll be bringing in pews and wearing suits. Not my vision at all, but then the more vocal nay-sayers had never been involved in a church like the "Tent" in Vero Beach. Mighta' been a good thing they weren't now that I think of it … they might have really freaked! Still, I had no desire to pastor a "straight" church;

there were plenty of those around. We needed a place where the lost felt welcome and could witness first hand God's life changing power; where they and their families and friends could grow and serve God in serving each other. I was not interested in competing with local churches, nor did I want to steal their youth base from them. Anyway, our target group would not set foot in a straight church, and with God's help we'd reach a group going largely unevangelized.

· · · ·

I thought the Jesus Movement was predominately Charismatic/Pentecostal[7] (from here on out, I'll use the terms interchangeably). My experience with post-Catholicism Christianity having been largely confined to the southern tent revival circuits, some of which, like *Truth and Life Ministry* of Vero Beach, had accepted the challenge to reach out to "hippies;" many then traveling the South and West like nomads on the hunt ... searching, searching for something to fill the vacuum of the waning Peace Movement. I naively assumed that if you were a Jesus Person (a young c.70s follower of Jesus), odds were you were charismatic. I mean, why not? However, back in Michigan I'd learned 'taint necessarily so. Indeed, some of the folks who'd been hanging around Shalom, including several in something of a leadership role, were not so disposed, but were more theologically aligned on this and other issues according to traditional Baptist dogma. Many of these good folk hold that the spiritual gifts the Apostle Paul comments on in 1 Corinthians Chapter 12, and a "Baptism in/of the Holy Spirit" accompanied by visible outward manifestations such as speaking in tongues, ceased with the death of the last apostle (commonly thought to be John c. the end of the first century), and/or completion of the New Testament canon.

There was yet another issue that reared its head early on, not a matter that theologians typically wrestle with and against one another, but nonetheless, the type of dispute that can lead to a fracture in the congregation and send some scurrying for greener pastures; in this case smokier. There was a small group hanging around Shalom at this time who

---

[7]   Used throughout in the narrow sense, pertaining to those gifts and ministries described in the New Testament including but not limited to: speaking in tongues, prophecy and the baptism of the Holy Spirit.

liked to have a cigarette along with the Bible lesson; during it! In what I call my first exorcise of budding pastoral authority I declared, "I think not. Go out in the parking lot if you must or come and receive prayer for deliverance. No smoking inside, and get these damn ashtrays outa' here." I know a bit rough around the edges; however, our smoking dogma went something like this: smoking might not send you to Hell, but you'll sure smell like you've been there. Oh and please don't mention it, but on special occasions I liked to fire up a cigar, but not during Bible study!

By the time 1975 was rolling into view, *Shalom* had gone through a rebirth of sorts. I appreciated what had transpired before, but was fully determined to press forward with the vision of *Shalom* as a local church. In July of 1974 we incorporated with the State of Michigan as the *Way Truth and Life Ministry* (the name *Shalom* now relegated to our coffee house outreach, though everyone still simply referred to us as *Shalom*), and in 1977 we'd finally receive our tax exempt status.

• • • •

The Beech Daly storefront years (1973-78) were for many old Shalomites, myself included, some of the most memorable. When you put a bunch of "on-fire" Christians in such a setting: on Beech Daly, Robichaud High School a half-mile north, Daly's Drive-In a half-mile south, dope den next door to the South, ghetto, white trash, strung-out, post-hippy humanity struggling to survive on the east Inkster/southwest Dearborn Heights border, well, it's like *The Book of Acts* Part 2. We certainly attracted our fair share of odd folks. Our first official secretary, Toni Orosz, perhaps overwhelmed by the never-ending line of shell-shocked humanity streaming through the door, rolled her eyes one day and lamented, "Why doesn't God ever send any together people here?" We laughed. It did get wearying at times, but deep down we knew it's the ill who need a doctor's care, not those enjoying good health (Mk 2:17).

A preacher once told me, after I'd explained what a tough challenge *Shalom* had with regards to ministering to people on the edge, and not a few who'd gone over it, that his flock were more of a challenge! "What'aya mean?" I fired back, knowing he pastored a "nice" church in Farmington.

He went on, "My people think they're okay and have largely put their spiritual lives on cruise control … at least your people know they need help!" Another pastor from a "straight" church told me many's the minister who'd give their eye-teeth to be involved in the likes of what was happening at Shalom. So, what was happening?

By 1976 we had a fairly established routine: Midweek Bible Study, Sunday evening service (our crowd were not early risers), and Friday night coffee house … weekly home prayer meetings helped to ensure the communal prayer life of the fellowship remained vibrant.

The coffee house was our big draw and started off modest enough. The spark that ignited this fuse was another one of my Tent cohorts from South Florida, a musician who'd come North to see firsthand what was goin' on. Kenny Pore, with a handful of musicians, took the initiative getting the coffee house up and running. Not all of the musicians were Christian, including one fella from the Inkster hood – Black Eddie we called him, to distinguish him from several other Eddies; late twenties, sportin' a fro, dark shades and a gold tooth that twinkled when the stage lights hit it ... who'd wander in, flute in hand, bit of a low glow on having just come from the methadone clinic. He was real laid back. I don't know what became of him, but he was grateful we'd let him sit in and get his music groove on. Our approach to "witnessing" was typically low key on Friday nights. If an unbeliever's heart was touched, a seed(s) planted, it was hoped, encouraged, that they'd come back Sunday evening for the "you must be born again, make up your mind, two roads from which to choose" service complete with an old- fashioned altar call.

We'd painted the exterior of the building, and an artistically gifted old neighbor of mine from Redford Twp. – Tom Roy, designed and painted two big colorful signs: *Shalom Coffee House* and *Way, Truth and Life Ministry* (he also designed two awesome business style cards and Shalom's first official coffee house poster). Dozens of carpet squares adhered to the store's wooden floor made sitting cross-legged for coffee house programs more comfortable. A half-dozen vintage maple wood diner type booths were salvaged from a restaurant in Hazel Park that had a date with the wrecker's ball, we'd rescued and now lined the back wall. There was a small stage with a white parachute overhead. Several nice black "bar" stools for musicians (compliments of Shannon's Lounge in Redford Twp.), a modest sound system (an old Peavy "head" that looked like it was on loan from *Henry Ford Museum*), and for several years folks packed the place (packed as in 100+). It's a wonder the fire marshal never shut us down … guess being in Inkster had a few perks.

Our first official coffee house night (as in promoted with flyers and scheduled artists) ended with quite a bang. Several local musicians from Downriver were on stage. The place was comfortably full … things couldn't have been better. You veterans of spiritual warfare know the routine. Guess we upset someone. One side of the stage led to a small room with a couple of couches, a place to seclude oneself for prayer, guitar tuning and so on before taking the stage Friday nights and before Sunday services. Adjoining this room was another small room, an old pop/beer bottle storage room with a flat, leaky roof, one window looking out into the parking lot and a rear door for private entry. Welcome to my bedroom/study. I'd been sitting at the desk in this room with a clear view to the stage, enjoying the music and basking in the glow of the Holy Spirit. There was pounding at the rear door.

"Joe, you in there?"

"Yeah. What's goin' on?"

"There's some chick in the parking lot that's ill. I think she may have had a seizure or somethin'."

"Does she need an ambulance?"

"No ... seems to have subsided, but she said she'd like prayer."

"Sure, bring her in."

A young, heavy set woman from the neighborhood, seventeen or there abouts, cautiously stepped in and sat on the edge of my bed. I sat directly across from her in the desk chair … closed the door to the adjoining room as the concert was still in full swing just a dozen paces away from us, and now bent forward the better to hear and focus on the matter at hand. After brief introductions, the two of us now alone, I asked her if indeed she'd like prayer. She nodded yes and I gently placed my hands on her shoulders and then all hell broke loose. She went into full blown seizure mode after falling to the floor. I knew nothing about seizures … there was a phone in the room, but I didn't call for an ambulance. Rather, as the music and clapping continued in the background, I knelt beside her and asked Jesus to set her free from this affliction. At the name of Jesus she suddenly metamorphosed into a screaming, snarling creature, face contorted as though she were in great pain, and in a voice that sounded like a cross between Dick the Bruiser and some ancient banshee out on a lonesome bog at midnight, and at dangerous decibel volume, told me to

107

back off or I'd be killed. Her hands outstretched, claw like, as if momentarily she'd rip my eyes from their sockets. The more I prayed the more intense her screams, interrupted by brief periodic seizures of varying intensity that would subside long enough for this inhuman voice to resume its threats: "She's ours … we're Grand Mal, and we'll never leave."

After ten minutes of this and during a brief lull in the encounter, I suddenly realized the music had stopped and chuckled to myself as I heard cars spitting gravel as they peeled out onto Beech Daly … hmm, wonder what they're thinking? I now noticed several people in the adjoining room were praying, their inquisitive, questioning looks met mine. I'm no expert (I certainly wasn't then), but this sure seemed to smack of a close encounter of the demonic kind. Later I'd have time to reflect on, among other things, the whole timing of the incident … did seem a bit coincidental. The successful launch, we're here to stay coffee house outreach of *Shalom*. Had we irritated someone? A half dozen folks, including several of the musicians whose concert had come to a screeching (screaming) halt, remained near at hand as we prayed fully two hours over this young lady, whose seizures had subsided and appeared in no immediate need of medical attention, but the battle with foul, threatening, blasphemous multiple voices continued unabated. Chief amongst them was one that identified itself as 'Gran-Mal.' At first I thought she was screaming 'Grandma, Grandma'. It was guttural, slurred, and hard to understand. Not until later would I realize the epilepsy connection. I know what some of you are thinking. I suppose I would too. As with many things in life, you had to be there. In the early hours of the morning she suddenly relaxed, smiled and whispered, "Its over. I'm free." Good thing. I was exhausted. I'd had encounters with the dark side before, but nothing like this. It wouldn't be the last. Do I think epilepsy is a demonic affliction? No. However on this occasion there was some connection. I'm no expert concerning these matters. I only know, along with half a dozen others who were there and who witnessed first-hand the bizarre manifestations, that this was a real encounter with the dark (demonic) side. See the ninth chapter of the *Gospel of Mark* for a similar story.

For the next several years I had a box seat every Friday night at the *Shalom Coffee House*, enjoying a menagerie of largely local, but occasionally nationally known contemporary Christian music acts (see

Appendix One for complete list). These ran the gamut of folk rockers after the style of Barry McGuire and Judy Collins, to the power trio sound ala *Blue Cheer* and the *James Gang*, and everything in between. The common denominator – lift up Jesus. However, there were more than a few bumps and pot holes along this coffee house outreach highway.

On one occasion, my buddy Kenny Pore, had booked a band from Monroe (The Faunce Brothers), for an upcoming engagement at Shalom; however, he'd be outta' town – no problem. When the band and their entourage (20 plus) arrived for the scheduled show, set up and went into the usual sound checks including rehearsing a couple numbers, something didn't seem quite right. Personally, I didn't have a problem with a good deal of secular rock music as long as it didn't carry overt or even subtle messages that conflicted with the Gospel, but when these guys launched into the Stone's "Honkey Tonk Women" ... and at the conclusion someone hollered out something about where in the set list that number was ... well, it was time to investigate and have a look-see at this play-list. They were all secular tunes! The only one I recognized as having a remote chance of carrying some level of spirituality conducive to what we were about was *Uriah Heep's* – "Stealin,'" and even that was stretching it a bit.

What gives? The upshot was there had been some misunderstanding; they and their music were not Christian. Wait till I get my hands on Kenny, but what now? It didn't seem right to tell them to pack it in ... thanks, but no thanks. Meanwhile doors open in less than an hour and I'm beginning to sweat. I decided to let them go on. They'd gotten to *Shalom* early and were ready to go by 8:00 p.m... During summer months we rarely started before 9:00 what with it still being light and many performers having worked jobs during the day. I snapped up the phone and asked (begged, threatened, bargained) with Ken Hasper to come do a follow up set to the boys from Monroe. He agreed. In the meantime, I stationed myself at the rear entrance (main entry), and with the help of several coffee house workers, we stopped folks on the way in, appraised them of the situation, asked them to please stay ... and, oh yeah, PRAY! God's gonna' take this what looks like a disaster and whip somethin' good up. Wouldn't you know it. Turns out this may have been one of our most fruitful nights. The band and their entourage ended up hanging around after their set (as we'd conspired). They had to. They couldn't tear down their equipment until Ken Hasper finished his set, and they got a musical testimonial earful.

Coincidentally, several of the Monroe crowd had known Ken as a heroin addict, and could now see for themselves the 180 degree turn his life and music had taken. The Holy Spirit touched lives in a powerful way that night. A good many of them, in days and weeks to come, made the decision to embrace Christianity and follow Jesus. Many continue to follow the Master and some are, as we speak, working in outreaches that stretch around the globe.

. . . .

Two memorable musical acts from Spring Arbor, different as night and day, bring a smile to my face. One, a solo act, a young Christian fella from India studying in the States came and shared his personal testimony as he played the sitar. Sitting cross-legged on stage under the billowy white parachute, and of course, I had a couple sticks of incense goin' just to add to the vibe. I loved stuff like that ... a bit of the Merry Prankster still clinging to the flesh I reckon'. God is so big and I/we here at *Shalom* would occasionally throw you a spiritual "knuckleball" just to keep ya' guessin'.

On another occasion, a Spring Arbor based jazz fusion band – *Progressive Razz*, showed up for a gig. It took them 30 minutes to lug in all their equipment (monster Marshall amps, elaborate drum set – so big it had to be set up off stage). "Hey guys, uh, in case you didn't notice, small coffee house, not Cobo Hall." It was a warm evening. We opened every door and window ... most folks hung outside. We had a large backyard, heck, even with their amps on one you could hear them down at Daly's Drive-In. John Waycaster, a solo acoustic folk singer, opened. It was a good night in spite of the miss-communication.

In time, we also gave a good many local and national acts some serious radio exposure. I'm often asked if I had a favorite. You already know the safe answer, but since I don't usually play it safe, yes, I do have a favorite ... well, I'll have to narrow it to two, but keep in mind, I really liked a good number of the artists who graced our stage over the years. If *Shalom* has any legacy, and I'd argue it has a largely favorable one, it's that we gave a number of local musicians an outlet to experiment, hone and deliver their music and message. Same holds for Sunday night services where I liked to share the pulpit with a variety of different styled preachers of the Gospel. Anyway, back to my personal favorite, two actually. First, *Heavenly Day*, later *Sail*, a free spirited, Neil Youngish eclectic group, that never practiced (they joked) until they had an engagement at Shalom (practice being a half hour before concert time). They were a wonderful mix of the spiritual and lighthearted (who else do you know who sings an ode to *White Castle* hamburgers?). One could never be sure who might be sitting in with them ... sometimes Paul Patton, other times Jan Krist; you never knew. Good musicians ... down-to-earth but eyes heavenwards ... the kinda group made to play coffee houses.

My second choice comes from down Interstate 75 a ways, the *John Vass Band*. They had a sound like no one else. It gave me goose bumps. Okay, I may have had a crush on his sister who sang with the group, but I just shook my head when they hit that musical groove; Moody Bluesish. Another group, from Rochester, had a similar vibe – *Morningstar*. John Vass and company only played Shalom a couple times, but wow!

Most Friday shows were taped and in no time we'd accumulated quite a library of reel-to-reel tapes. These were often edited and put on cassettes for personal use and/or as a post-concert "gift" to artists as a sign of our appreciation. Incidentally, from day one we always saw to it that Friday night musicians and Sunday guest speakers always received some type of monetary gift – enough to cover expenses and eat out afterwards; sometimes more as circumstances allowed. After all, most artists we hoped would return, and we wanted their experience here to be as much of a blessing to them as it had been to us. At some point the idea was put on the table to make use of these recordings by turning them into radio shows. The station manager at WMUZ in Detroit was receptive to the idea, and shortly thereafter the *Shalom Coffee House* (an edited tape) began to air once a week at a 9:00 p.m. slot at a cost of $90.00 per program. Big bucks for us, but we thought the program met a legitimate need. There were no regular contemporary Christian music programs on the Detroit airwaves. What a convenient way to let family and friends, strangers and neighbors know, who might not be able or care to venture into *Shalom* on Friday nights for full-throttle street-level music and ministry, but in the secure comfort of their car/home at night give a listen. Also, it was a nice incentive, not that we really needed one, but to be able to tell musicians under consideration for booking that we'd be taping the show and, with their approval, would air them. "Hey, mom, dad, sis, it's me ... on the radio!"

You'll recall the spiritual warfare we ran up against the night of our first official coffee house. I could hardly wait to see/hear what Balrog-like demon rumblings this venture would awaken from some forgotten murky abyss. Expect the unexpected. As you might imagine, we'd told everybody and their brother/sister to tune in for our maiden voyage on the airwaves. The first show would feature Ken Hasper. Ah, 8:59 p.m., and any moment now my velvety smooth vocal chords would spring forth from the nearby stereo announcing that: "You're listening to the sounds of the Shalom Coffee House." A brother from Ecorse, MI, Dave Mehi, who often played bass at Shalom accompanied by his wife Jean on guitar and vocals, [8] assisted me with editing the tapes at a "brother's" – Gene Bowman, from *Trenton Assembly of God* – home studio. We carefully labeled the thirty minute reel-to-reel tape and turned it in well before broadcast time, confident our blood, sweat, tears and prayer would be "soundly" rewarded.

Nine o'clock glowed brightly on the dial. Hey! What's this? Horrors … the tape, our tape, our first big show, a "million" family and friends all over southeast Michigan are holding their breath waiting to hear … well it came on alright … on the WRONG speed! It sounded like I'd popped a handful of downers and now had marbles swimming around my mouth. What gives? Turns out we'd recorded the tape at a slower speed than was the typical standard used for quality purposes. Okay, but why isn't the engineer on top of this? Minutes agonizingly ticked by and still the "downer" DJ and folk singer gurgled out of the speaker like dirty bath water fighting its way through a clogged drain. My fingers frantically worked the old fashioned, pre-touch phone in a 911 panic attack state. Why isn't anyone at the station answering? Panic and embarrassment were just giving way to anger when suddenly, the tape surged forward and now familiar songs and voices danced forth on unseen airwaves. The whole episode took less than five minutes; long minutes indeed. Turns out the engineer preloaded the tape, unaware it had been recorded at the wrong speed, and went to use the toilet just before 9:00 p.m... There's no phone

---

[8]   Joe and Ken Hasper would team up with Dave and Jean Mehi, Kevin Rakozy and Dino Vallone in the first of several incarnations of the *Shalom House Band*. A show for Channel 56 called *Its Your Turn*, and a gig at Detroit's old Grande Ballroom (then in the hands of Detroit's House of Prayer Ministry) are two of their more memorable performances.

or speakers in the Men's room. Good thing he wasn't constipated. In the future, no one needed to remind us to record the shows at the proper speed.

In the reception area at WMUZ, posted on the wall, was a large map of southeast Michigan and Ontario, with various circular configurations that indicated the distance the station's radio signal traveled, affected by, I'd never have guessed, the time of day; the signal traveling further after sunset. No, I don't know why. But when our show hit the airwaves, it traveled to the furthermost reaches of WMUZ's "universe." I was struck by how large an area it was. I no longer flashed back to that night several years earlier, when Evangelist Stalvey announced that Big Joe Shannon and newly delivered from heroin addiction Ken Hasper would take the Gospel to the city of Detroit, with skeptical amusement. Indeed, Detroit and then some.

Even though the radio show was only aired once a week at ninety bucks a pop, it didn't take long, given our limited financial resources, for it to become a financial burden. We weren't really big on fund raisers, extra offerings (seed faith, gimmick pledges) or any arm (wallet & purse) twisting techniques so often resorted to by Christians who've launched into one venture or another by "faith," only to discover later that God may not have been initiating said move. We didn't have a long time to soul search and analyze what motivated our "leap" of faith onto the airwaves. Were they, the shows, bearing any fruit? Is this the flesh – our own ego at work? Maybe it's just a financial storm (trial) to be weathered … blah, blah, blah. Currently we were taking in just enough to cover *Shalom's* basic expenses, rent, overhead, etc. My first year at *Shalom's* helm I'd continued to work at the Ford foundry, but that got to be too much. I quit Ford and for a year took no salary (there wasn't any); third year, fifty bucks a week. You get the picture. I can chuckle now when I look over my annual earnings Social Security statement from the Feds, the pastoral years ('74-'85) were somewhat lean to be sure; wasn't in it for the money anyway.

While working in the yard one afternoon, and mentally wrestling with this whole radio state of affairs … part prayer, part worry, second guessing … then surrender and put it in God's hands … the voice of Evangelist Stalvey a not too distant memory ringing in my ears: "You do the possible and He'll do the impossible." Well, we'd done what we could and kept some Christian integrity in the bargain. My mental "wrestling match" took a reprieve as a small, yellow, late model sports car eased into the gravel parking lot. Hmm, can't belong to a Shalomite.

A young (40ish) good looking, smartly dressed ala Mod Squad fella' jumped out and wandered up. Said he'd often passed by and was curious about us. He followed me inside and we chatted for a while. "What churches should be doin'," he agreed, "Is there anything I can do to help?"

"Anything you can help us with," I chuckled to myself, eyein' his sharp threads, Rolex watch and the image of that sports car dancin' in my head. Before I could answer, he pulled out a checkbook and scribbled an amount that, surprise, surprise, covered the couple radio shows we'd fallen behind on and then some. I thanked him and fought to conceal my excitement. Didn't want to give him the wrong impression ... like the Fonz, I'd be cool about the whole matter. As he slid behind the wheel of his slick ride he handed me a business card, adding he'd be in California on business next week, but call him the first of the month and we'll talk more about this radio show. Wow! By the way, Larry Cheek was a Seventh Day Adventist[9]; well, sort of.

When the first of the month rolled around I didn't need any reminder or encouragement to give him a holler'. That business card was thumb tacked smack dab in the middle of the bulletin board above my desk. He invited me to come up to his office in the new Twin Towers office complex at Ford Road and Southfield. The idea of the radio show sat well with him, so well that he offered to pick up the ninety dollar a week tab indefinitely. He, sometimes with his wife and one or more of his three teenage kids, began dropping in Friday nights, and before you could say, "Ellen White," small groups of Seventh Day Adventist kids became Friday night regulars. The plus side of our Friday night ministry was that it was fairly low key, non-threatening, and low on doctrinal fine points and hair splitting issues

---

[9]   Adventism, which developed in nineteenth-century America, and whose central focus is the Second Coming of Christ to establish his millennial reign. Emphasis is also placed on the Old Testament and Hebrew Law, and indeed, many groups have embraced the Jewish Sabbath and dietary laws. Seventh-Day Adventist are one of the largest and best organized of the Adventist bodies. There continues to be some debate as to whether SDA are a sect, cult, or denomination.

… big on music and lifting up Jesus in a laid-back atmosphere. I'm glad they felt welcome. Our relationship with these young Adventist folks, howbeit temporary, allowed for some additional favorable contacts. A Dr. Weaver, an Adventist and prominent local surgeon, also known for his popular "Five Day Quit Smoking Program," offered, at our request, to present a talk at Shalom; rather graphic and not for the weak stomachs as I recall. When someone from the audience during a question/answer period following the presentation suggested pipe smoking was not so bad, Dr. Weaver, almost as if the question was a "plant," quickly, almost nonchalantly pulled up a slide. "Folks, what you're looking at here is a fella who several months earlier I was forced to remove half his jaw in order to save him. Oh, and you might like to take note of this, he never smoked a cigarette. His poison was a pipe." Silence … a man with half a jaw was not a pretty site. He also wryly pointed out we ought to cut the "coffee" from coffee house, for health reasons. We didn't.

Thanks to Larry Cheek, I was also given an ongoing invitation to personally make use of the Adventist camp – Camp Grayling. Beautiful place; just needed to avoid it if you were looking for peace and quiet when the nearby National Guard were conducting military exercises several weeks during the summer. Also, if you wanted a cup-a-joe and bacon (real) and eggs in the morning, you'd have to head into town … the camp being a caffeine & meat-free zone.

Larry also thought my wardrobe could use some CPR (he wasn't the only one), and invited me over to his home in nearby Dearborn Heights to rummage through his walk-in closet the size of a local Sims Men's Wear Store. "Grab some shirts … what size shoes do you wear? Here, take this wristwatch."

Not quite my style, me still being in a bit of a post-hippy pre-grunge look. I politely passed on most of his disco, Mod Squad, wanna' be hip threads. A couple things however looked like they might come in handy for a wedding or some such affair, as folks expected more outa' their preacher than faded jeans, flannel shirt and tennis shoes that looked like hand-me-downs. Oh yeah, I did, after a minimal amount of arm twisting, give in and take a nice looking wristwatch and sports coat.

Funny that just about this time a rumor started circulating that I was dealing drugs "under" the pulpit … glad the watch wasn't a Rolex. Also, a cousin who suspected that this whole preacher trip was a charade of some sort approached me about runnin' a blind pig out of Shalom's basement, and of course, I'd get a cut on the take. Not too many weeks later, during a packed coffee house, I received a call from the Inkster police. Muggings were on the rise in the neighborhood and we tried to keep a few fellas out in the parking lot especially on Friday nights when we might not wrap up till after midnight. The police asked to meet me out front in five minutes … guess they had a line on a few dudes who might be behind the muggings and thought I might be able to ID 'em.

Well, the cops pulled up right out front … no flashing lights or sirens, but visible and not all together unusual … they often stopped by … curious as to all the activity around the old Kulas' Market and former dope house. I slipped out the back and cut through the parking lot so as to avoid attention … things inside were going smoothly and we always had plenty of able staff. It was dark and chilly so I hopped in the rear of a squad car and discussed with the two officers recent drug traffic in the hood. One officer flipped on the interior light so I could look at some mug shots. Suddenly I glanced over at the front entrance to Shalom, and there, huddled around the front door and windows, a dozen sets of eyes took in the scene out front; Pastor Joe in the back seat of a squad car. The expressions on several faces spoke volumes. So, the rumors were true … busted his ass. Before I could read too much into their mystified looks, my business with the police concluded, I hopped out and bound up the steps with a laugh. The danger of jumping to conclusions might not have been the theme of the following Sunday's sermon, but I no doubt worked it in somewhere.

· · · ·

To say I was a tad unorthodox in my ministerial approach including my appearance would be, well, if you were there you know, and if you weren't you can likely make a fair assumption. "…I have become all things to all…," Paul the Apostle declared (1 Cor 9:22). We took Paul seriously, and/or it may in part be similar to when a snake sheds its skin, it may take a while to wiggle free from the old and embrace the new. Either way, during most of the Seventies, Shalom's evangelism/outreach largely targeted the fading remnants of 60's counterculture, and so our methodology and dress struck some within the at-large Christian community as naive, unbiblical, worldly and counter productive, and of

116

course we neither pioneered nor were alone in this; the Jesus Movement in general faced the same stigma, and our/their response, "You shall know them (Jesus' disciples) by their fruit …."(Lk 6:44), and when hundreds of thousands of young people across the land are embracing the timeless message proclaiming, "Jesus loves you and can set you free," howbeit with a repackaged contempoary look, well, how ya gonna argue with that? Many others however, while themselves not embracing the John the Baptist "look," conceded that God, who often works in mysterious ways, may indeed be using these young folks who didn't often feel comfortable in the more traditional mainline churches to reach a "wayward" generation. "God," we'd suggest, "was more concerned about your heart than your hair." If I were to have run around with a 50's crew cut hairstyle and 3 piece suit, it would appear just as out of place if you planted me thus attired in first century Palestine.

"Wow, preacher with an earring," exclaimed Mike Johnson[10] when we first met. For years I continued to sport a modest earring as it sometimes opened doors for personal testimony as to my ear healing (Pt.2). For now at least (70s/80s), most Shalomites were not uptight about appearance, however, neither was it an anything goes approach; modesty being at least one non-negotiable guiding factor.

I never weary of reading the Gospel narratives and the astonishing amount of diverse situations that confronted Jesus. The oft times unorthodox way, at least by the Scribes and Pharisees reckonings, with which Our Lord resolved issues, be they sickness, demonic, questions concerning the Law, appropriate Sabbath behavior and the like, often to the utter dismay of His critics and even His disciples. Be it the Samaritan woman at the well (Jn 4), blind Bartimeus by the roadside (Mk 10: 46-52), the woman about to be stoned after being discovered in an adulterous act (Jn 8), are just a sampling that reveal Our Lord loves to save, and that He was not content to sit comfortably somewhere, finely attired, waiting for the lost to come find Him. No, He is/was the Good Shepherd who leaves the 99 lost sheep and seeks out that one which has strayed (Jn10). We

---

[10]   Pioneer of Jesus Music (10/11/46 – 2/9/13) who played Shalom c. '80 as a promoter of Compassion International music. His album with Danny Taylor and Randy Matthews was a Nightlight Show staple.

admired and sought to emulate that spirit, and while we may have been a bit rough around the edges, God used us nevertheless. Oh, and music ... don't get me started, but I'm humming Petra's anthem, "God Gave Rock and Roll to You," just now.

Here's a lil Shalom unorthodox episode. A young gal (early 20s) approached me privately to request prayer and a little advice concerning a work issue. Seems some guy (coworker) had been making unwanted advances and was slow to take the hint she wasn't interested. She liked and needed the job, worried that if she approached management with this issue it might somehow be turned around and reflect poorly on her, and/or fall on deaf ears; sexual harassment was not always taken seriously, especially back then. "Okay, let's pray about it," I suggested," keep me posted."

A week passed by and when she strolled into my office the look of frustration etched on her face said it all, well nearly. So, what's to be done? Three days later I showed up at her workplace; we were gonna do lunch. Hand in hand we strolled through the factory purposely intending to pass by the work station of the fella who'd been harassing her. There he sat while we slowed and paused as his eyes first rested on her, then grew large as he gotta load of me. Nothing was said, but he clearly read the situation; he never bothered her again. Clumsy perhaps, not how Jesus would have handled it, maybe, but effective, and in retrospect I'm well acquainted with how these good intentions can sometimes backfire and before you know it your mole has metamorphosed into a mountain. For my part, my spiritual logic had largely been shaped by my mentor Evangelist Stalvey; his guiding principle, "You do the possible and God will do the impossible." Anyway pastoring, with its endless challenges, victories and heartaches, seldom grew boring. Go figure.

· · · ·

Wednesday Bible studies were initially handled by several of us more Scripture savvy brothers who might take several weeks at a stretch and cover an entire book, usually from the New Testament, and/or develop some theme and/or address a current sensitive issue or some hot topic associated with what was happening with the at-large Jesus Movement. In time, God directed two older men (older as in their thirties), Jim Duncan and Jerry Heady, both with Assemblies of God exegesis backgrounds, who, along with their families, felt comfortable in *Shalom's* setting, and who provided us as a young growing congregation with some sound instruction in the Scriptures, and I think they enjoyed having a place where their kids could grow up in a contemporary Christian environment. In time, Jim would carry the bulk of the Bible Study duties and serve as one of our first elders. Good Bible teaching was something we sorely needed and God sent us some capable men, including occasional guest teachers ... anyone remember Steve Patton's study on salt (Mt 5:13)?

Not that we were in a panic concerning our identity during the Beech Daly years, but, given all the cult nonsense going on, it had to be addressed. Being refereed to as those Jesus Freaks at the corner of Beech Daly and Dartmouth didn't cut it. Some of the high school-aged kids' parents had concerns ... was this one of those *Children of God* (a cult who gained widespread notoriety during the seventies for their unethical approach to spreading the Gospel) type places? There was also that gnawing dread that in time, if we weren't careful, we'd evolve into the very thing (straight church) that so many of us had washed our hands of. Still, it seemed reasonable that if we were to continue pursuing our vision to the fullest, we'd need a strategy that would dismiss any cult connection suspicions and maintain our contemporary integrity (whatever that means). I always treasured Paul's advice: "Test everything and retain that which is good" (1 Thes 5:21) ... followed closely by his counsel to Timothy: "...let no man despise thy youth ...."(1 Tm 4:12). During the whole Beech Daly stretch I was, after all, only in my twenties.

As I mentioned, several of Shalom's "go to" guys came from Assembly of God[11] backgrounds. Most of us, however, were not willing to entirely submit to various Assemblies' do's and don'ts concerning such matters as staying out of movie theaters, total abstinence from alcohol, rock music; scruples we weren't as uptight about, well most of us. Another

---

[11]   The Assemblies of God are the largest Pentecostal body. Ardently fundamentalist, its theology is Arminian; there is strong belief in the infallibility of the Bible, the fall and redemption of man, baptism in the Holy Spirit, entire sanctification, a life of holiness and separation from the world, divine healing, the second advent of Jesus and his millennial reign, eternal punishment for the wicked and eternal bliss for believers. They are especially insistent that baptism in the Holy Spirit is evidenced by speaking in tongues, and that all the gifts of the Spirit shall be in operation in the normal New Testament church.

significant impact-er concerning our approach to all things spiritual, included my own and several others' Catholic background. I never jumped on the anti-Catholic bandwagon. I used to remove the Jack Chick and certain Keith Green tracts from our literature tables. Occasionally, people would leave these tracts, which were overly critical of and hostile towards Catholicism, on our tables. There diatribes directed at Catholicism struck me as unfair and unsound. My take on the Catholic Church then and for years afterwards was that it (the C.C.), had in its ranks many who knew and served Jesus as Lord, and sadly, a goodly number who were clueless. I simply took it that the C.C. had over the centuries picked up a lot of excess unnecessary baggage, but if you looked close enough all the essentials were present. I had a good many friends who continued to labor in Catholic parishes and communities; some of them charismatic. I'd always admired the work of Catholic groups like the Capuchins who labored amongst and fed the city's poor. Historically, I recognized the tremendous debt all Christians owed the Catholic Church (the canon of Scripture and the great creeds, the latter formulated to articulate what the Church affirms as that delivered "...once for all handed down to the holy ones" Jude 1:3), and to resist intrusive and destructive heresies. I'm well acquainted with the historical fodder used for bashing the Catholic Church: indulgences, crusades, relics, inquisitions and the like, much of it misunderstood and exaggerated. Furthermore, down the road while as an A P European History teacher, I would have an obligation to demonstrate the Church's innumerable contributions, largely via monastic institutions during the Middle Ages, in the arts, sciences, literature and hospitality, to say nothing of the spiritual light it faithfully preserved in the wake of numerous invasions by peoples, Vikings for instance, who were less than enthusiastic towards the Church and its mission (see Thomas Howards' *How the Catholic Church Built Western Civilization – Suggested Reading*). The C.C. did and continues to have its shortcomings; who among us doesn't? Anyway, the Catholic Church had their work, I had mine, and there was no sense wasting energy bad-mouthing them. Seems I'd read something about "let each esteem others better than themselves" (Phil 2:3). Most of the younger Shalomites were in the 18 – 25 year bracket, children of the Jesus Movement which sprang up alongside the sixties counterculture (Digger, Hippie, Beats) movements. We had no intention of returning to or being part of anything that resembled the "dead" church of our parents. The upshot of all this is that in time, our church, *Shalom*, its by-laws and constitution, took on a strong dose of Assemblies of God, meat and potatoes as it were, blended with a bit of Catholic charismata, the vegetables, and spiced with a sauce that had a strong Jesus Movement kick to it. Sounds pretty good, eh? A hip Assemblies, Catholic Charismatic, Evangelical hybrid ... ah, but would it hold together?

· · · ·

You never knew who or what was gonna' walk through those doors at 3852 Beech Daly in 1977. Dope house tenement right next door to the South ... main drag between Michigan Ave. and Van Born gave us plenty of visibility ... right on the dividing (fault) line between predominately black Inkster and white Dearborn Heights. Yep, we got all kinds, and at all times of the day. Plus, word quickly got out to local churches, who interestingly enough had initially eyed us with a bit of suspicion that this Shalom place would take in prêt-near-anybody, you know, the hard cases. I often wondered why not one local minister ever stopped in to say hello, welcome to the neighborhood, or even inquire, "So, what are you folks about?" Yet in time they'd come pleading with us to take someone (homeless, speed freak, schizophrenic, chain-smokin' insomniac) off their hands. When we'd get loaded up we'd sometimes turn to *Teen Challenge* and *Challenge House*, both of Detroit; sometimes members would open up their own homes to help folks struggling to get back on their feet.

At *Shalom*, the living arrangement rule was sisters up, brothers down (ground floor & basement); however, the only shower was up. With six or more folks living there at a time, well, getting into the bathroom became a prime tool for the Holy Spirit to develop patience in these young Christians. The basement became something of a dormer for brothers. It was the basement of a youngster's nightmares. Dark, several rooms, old water stained masonry; massive outdated boiler ... the place looked like Norman Bate's nursery. One brother, newly led to Christ, was one of those cases wherein he needed to immediately get out of his current living situation (dope house), or he wouldn't make it.[12] I put him in a small room in the basement near the foot of the stairs and across from the boiler grate

---

[12]   See Parable of the Sower, Lk 8:5

(the room had no door), bid him goodnight and all seemed well. An hour later his frantic screams woke me with a start. Seems the boiler had kicked in with that rumbling sound like a cave troll with indigestion, and it being winter, sometimes flames leapt from the grate looking for a means of escape, all the while uttering a hissing, moaning sound like some turn-of-the century steam engine about to expire, in a half-hearted attempt to push heated water up two floors to waiting, tired, old dry radiators. This brother, in his new, unfamiliar, pitch black surroundings … unable to find a light, his bed only feet away from the boiler grate that now looked every bit as menacing as the gates to Mordor, was convinced he'd died and gone to Hell. Ah, another peaceful night at Shalom.

Some folks described us as a lighthouse, a spiritual emergency room and other unmentionables … indeed; we certainly attracted an unusual clientele. Went with the territory I suppose. Bit of a trick sometimes discerning between a lost (really screwed up) soul in need of redemption, and the occasional wolf in sheep's clothing; some subtle, others flashing their wolfish fangs. Two pseudo hippie biker types wandered in one evening and asked to speak to me in private. Back in the prayer room adjacent to the stage they matter-of-factly announced that Satan had sent them here to kill me. I had a bit of a cocky side to me embedded in a solid 6'4" frame. Earlier in the week I'd listened to a testimonial from one of the few radio preachers I enjoyed – Brother Schambach. Apparently during one camp meeting he was being harassed by some witch who threatened to poison him if he didn't immediately pack up his revival tent and hit the road … she even told him how: "I see how all these people bring you cookies, cakes and what not. I'm gonna' make you a pie, and before you know it, you're dead!" [13]

The Satanists, or so they claimed, seeing I was not easily intimidated decided to split but not before warning me to "watch my back." I thought about hurling a little taunt after them something like, "the one angel who's

---

[13]   Ol' Brother Schambach, not one to be easily intimidated, fired back, "Well, be sure to make it lemon meringue, it's my favorite…. You can't harm God's anointed anyway you ol' crone … 'Touch not mine anointed, and do my prophets no harm' (1 Chr 16:22) … 'They shall take up serpents; and if they drink any deadly thing, it shall not harm them…' (Mk 16:18) Halleluiah!"

got my back can put a thousand of your master's to flight," but stifled it and the night quickly swallowed them up. Wouldn't ya' know it. A week later they opened a *Satan House of Worship* two blocks to our north on the east side of Beech Daly ... big sign and all, nightly worship! Hmm, we're only open three nights a week ... we can't have this. My gut told me these guys were just a couple a posers lookin' for trouble and a few laughs, and if they were Satanists, probably the wanna-be, weekend, carney variety, but the situation was annoying. Many of the Jesus People crowd circle we moved in would have suggested handling it by going over and just talking to them ... take 'em some cookies ... tell/show them God's love. A lot of these sometimes well-meaning folks are good at telling you what to go do and say but ask them to tag along and "well, I can't now brother, busy, but I'll keep you in prayer."

Ken Hasper and I drove by the new *Satan House*, pulled in front and agreed together in prayer and cursed it in Jesus' name. A week later it burned down. No, we didn't firebomb it. As I recall, we were out of town ... camp-out or something. Then a short while later I drove by and I couldn't believe it. The house was gone! Just fresh bulldozer tracks where it had once been." It's a fearful thing to fall into the hands of the living God" (Heb 10:31).

Edith was a tall, solidly built black woman who might have once been, and with a serious makeover possibly again, an attractive woman, but you'd have to look hard to arrive at that conclusion. She was fond of wearing cheap red and blond wigs that never quite sat properly affixed to her head ... almost comical. From time to time she'd drop in on a service and was one of several we kept close tabs on. Once she tried to set the place on fire after having been discovered wadding up paper and stuffing it behind a painting, waiting for an opportune time to put a match to it which thankfully she never did. She was way out there. The worst of it was she'd figured out where I slept. From time to time, usually during the warmer months and when a full moon lit the Inkster night sky, like some cat outside your window raising a racket that sends you scrambling for a heavy object ... her hoarse pleas would wake me out of a sound sleep: "Ministah Joseph, Ministah Joseph ... It's me Edith. Ministah Joseph, I love you. Can I come in?"

Best thing to do was ignore it. If she persisted, a call to the Inkster Police and hopefully Marty the Cop would be on duty and would take care of it. Sometimes you just shake your head and try to remember, like 'em or not, Jesus died for them too, and its God's will that all people be saved (1 Tm 2:4). She seemed real resistant to the Gospel. When we left the neighborhood it was the last I'd seen/heard of her.

Another gal, dubbed the "snake" lady, was something of an embarrassment. When you have visitors who are weighing the pros and cons of all things Pentecostal, well, she could undo in five minutes what we'd spent months trying to Biblically articulate and demonstrate. In the words of Barney Fife, we shoulda' "nipped this one in the bud." You could almost count on it, when after months of pleading, praying, encouraging family and friends to come visit ... when and if they should, then get ready for warfare of the looney-tune type. What's peculiar about the "snake" lady was that she never came alone, but always had several teenaged kids in her wake, at least one of them her own; likely why we hesitated to give her the heave ho when she went into her "act" as for all I knew, God would use these crazy antics to reach these kids. Her "M.O." was clear enough. During worship (this would usually be before and/or after a typical service), especially during those more enthusiastic moments when we expected the Holy Spirit to speak to us via gifts of the Spirit including tongues and interpretation, prophecy and words of encouragement and exhortation, she would slowly begin to dance and writhe around like a belly dancer who'd just snorted up some horse tranquilizers; hence the name "snake" lady. The sounds that accompanied this lurid dance would make fresh milk curdle, and I won't dignify it by calling it "counterfeit tongues." Typically, the congregation's eyes would flit from her (and the many others like her who we seemed to attract), to me ... "well Pastor Joe, how ya gonna' handle this one?"... I read in some of the amused, others annoyed looks. We did have a couple fellas, seasoned, discerning and BIG, who I could give a nod to and they'd get the individual out of the area and try and minister to them (kinda' like Tim the Tent Bouncer's role back at the Tent near Vero Beach) ... every street ministry should have a bouncer with the gift of discernment who works out at the local gym.

Barry was a big dude ... could pass for the lead singer, harp player for Canned Heat. He was barefoot, smelled awful ... oh, and claimed to be from Pluto. This cat was out there. Someone said, but we couldn't verify it, that he was a disc jockey from Ann Arbor who'd flipped out on LSD. He seemed harmless enough and we liked a challenge. He certainly didn't seem to fit the always possible "angels unaware" visitor profile (Heb 13:2). Upshot, we'd take him on and see what happened. Turned out he had this annoying, unnerving habit of, while sitting in the back during our Sunday evening services, glaring at me as I delivered my sermon, and making strange hand signals directed towards me as though he were trying to hex me or put the voodo-hoodo on me.

A week later, the church secretary, Toni, who lived in the apartment above Shalom, went with me to run an errand. We couldn't leave our man from Pluto alone at Shalom, so it being nice weather, we decided he could get some air ala a ride in the back of my pickup. We had to run into a supermarket on Warren east of Southfield and left our "client" in the back … who seemed content enough … parked right out front on Warren. We only needed a half-dozen items and good thing too. When we came out, traffic was at a near standstill. Barry was standing up in the bed of the pickup truck, and where he got it I still haven't figured out – a toy cap gun. He was shootin' at cars, hollerin' and carryin' on like he was Marshal Dillon trippin on a few peyote buttons. We were in Detroit, and I could see it all unravel before my eyes … they'd blow him away before … well, no sirens or lights … quick, calm Wyatt Earp down and let's beat it. Man what else could happen? Those were the days, was it "pigs-in-the-parlor"? (Our code for demon possession), or was it just another casualty of the sixties/seventies drug culture. He disappeared just as mysteriously as he had arrived. Always said he was waiting for a UFO to come pick him up.

Speakin' a UFO's, we had another character from the neighborhood, who, while he might not have been a wolf in sheep's clothing in the spiritual sense, was a wolf, actually, more like a jackal; he had an eye for the ladies, teen ladies. He wasn't a drug accident, just a plain nut. He'd saunter up to me with a dumb grin/smirk on his face, always had a huge wad of bubble gum workin' like he was ready to head out to the pitcher's mound, and while he was older than most of us, I thought it peculiar that he was already sportin' a wig, one of those so obvious ones that well, anyway, he used to wink at me and mumble something about who I was in touch with … who I worked for. Said he knew.

"Hey speak English man, whataya getting' at," my patience with this guy wearing thin.

"The signs man … the signs on the building."

"What about 'em?"

"The sun motif man," he winked. "It's a signal. I know you're in touch with aliens man."

Sometimes you just wanted to smack people upside the head. I suspect this guy watched too many episodes of *The Invaders*[14], or flipped out at a local matinee feature of *Invasion of the Body Snatchers*. He was convinced we were in cahoots with aliens, and the two suns on our sign out front (one rising, one setting) were really a secret code ... a signal to interplanetary travelers ... a way station where they could receive aid; help to blend in. And he knew. Said he was aware! Shoulda' introduced him to Barry from Pluto. No doubt they'd a hit it off swell. Sometimes the best thing you could do was, "yeah pal, you're right ... look, please don't let on, and have a nice day ...." Then go down to Daly's for a footlong, fries and a coke. Later pray, "Lord, give me a shepherd's heart ... a heart for the lost." Which reminds me; a shepherd watches and protects the flock. I warned the young ladies about this guy and you can bet if I saw him eyein' one a little too close ... with wolves, sometimes you can't be nice.

There were other encounters that weren't so amusing. Tommy Safin was Jack Wyatt's cousin and looked like a poster boy for the Hell's Angels. He worked for a dairy company and occasionally would drop by with a gallon of ice cream under each arm. When he was sober, he was a sweet, gentle dude, providing you could get past the "outlaw biker" exterior, but that wasn't especially odd at Beech Daly *Shalom*. Problem is, often as not, he'd drop in tanked; and it was Dr. Jekyl and Mr. Hyde now showing at *Shalom House*. One evening, and wouldn't you know it, just before our Coffee House program was set to get underway, Tommy staggered through the front door swearin' like a sailor and looking like Evel Knievel after he'd missed a jump. He was loud and obnoxious, looked to have just come from the bar having drunk up his paycheck, and as folks were beginning to wander in, I decided the prudent thing to do was get him out to the back yard. Fortunately Jack was on hand, and a well-meaning but a bit of an overbearing brother (the only guy who wore a white shirt and tie regularly to *Shalom*), Halleluiah Eddie (Masicotte) we

---

[14]   Popular sci-fi TV show during the sixties. A peculiar, but slight finger deformity, distinguished aliens from the humanity they'd plotted to infest and eventually take over.

called him, assisted me in trying to calm Psycho Tommy the Biker down and keep him (he was a big boy), from reentering the building, and stop foul mouthing people coming from the parking lot who were taken back a bit by the now getting-out-a-hand scene near the rear entrance. We didn't want to call the cops. He was Jack's cousin and that could get real ugly. I stood directly in front of him hoping to prevent him from bolting up the steps and into the building. Jack was on one side, pleading ... trying to talk some sense into Mr. Intoxicated Berserko, Eddie on the other side, Bible opened to his favorite text and lettin' loose with the Word of God, his finger flaying the air for emphasis like some southern revivalist preacher from the film *The Apostle.* Oh, did I mention that Tommy had me by the throat? While Eddie was giving him what for, Tommy would glare at me one moment, and then fix his eyes on a tattoo of the devil on his forearm, then back at me, a wild glaze covering his eyes. Then suddenly, like a scene out of Mary Shelly's *Frankenstein* (Boris Karloff in the role of the monster), he had those tattooed knuckled hands shuttin' off my windpipe. The louder Eddie quoted from the Bible, the tighter the grip. He'd keep glancing at the little dancing devil on his arm as if he somehow got his strength from it ... some demonic power ... he continued to tighten like a Burmese python. Jack's continuing to plead ... Eddie's firin' away this passage, that passage ... a small crowd gathering, and I'm on the verge of blacking out. Lord, I'm gonna' plant my size fourteen where he'll take notice if you don't do somethin' quick ... how's that gonna' look to these young Christians gathered 'round. "The light of the body is the eye" (Lk 11:34), I suddenly recalled. I locked my eyes on his. I couldn't speak because he had me good and throttled ... his snarls and contorted face would have won him the Wolfman role over Lon Chaney Jr... As our eyes remained momentarily fastened on each other, I mentally rebuked him in Jesus' name. Instantly his hands drew back, his face in a painful contortion, he flew back five feet and violently smacked into a giant oak. Dazed, he slowly slid down to the ground in a heap, but in an instant regained his feet. The three of us just stood there, amazed, saying nothing, while Tommy, snarling and foaming at the mouth, tried to rip the bark from the tree with his tombstone teeth and dog-like nails. He seemed restrained and/or unwilling to come back at me. Splendid I thought, drunk and "pigs-in-the-parlor." Now what? Perhaps his little demonic pals sensed the game was up. I don't know. Suddenly, he broke for his car, fired it up, rammed it into drive and buried the pedal, flew over the train tressel parking-lot border and into the backyard ... somehow swerved around several ancient oaks, jumped the curb and sped weaving down Dartmouth into the Inkster night.

"Let's go see if the band's set up."

· · · ·

Being a single pastor can be a bit awkward on a number of different levels as you might imagine. Couples who were experiencing marital difficulties were often hesitant to approach a young single guy for counsel. What could he know? Also, I didn't do much dating. Still, it was a bit safer than you might guess, with the combination of a largely fishbowl existence and a no shortage of married women who never seemed short on advice. The Beech Daly era "saints" did witness Pastor Joe get himself entangled in a couple of relationships that nearly ended, hmm ... that doesn't sound right, nearly culminated in a trip to the altar.

Monta, aka Gigi, was a wonderful gal, my age, grew up in the neighborhood, street wise, pretty, not easily intimidated, divorced mother with a young son; most important, she loved Jesus. In no time we felt comfortable enough with each other that I didn't hesitate to phone her late one night after I'd received an unusual call. One of the regular Shalom brothers had of late, been bringing by a gal who had a very troubled life, years working in strip clubs and various substance abuse issues, but she'd recently made a decision to follow Jesus. Sadly, we too often witnessed young men and women just like this gal, get sucked right back into the same destructive habits they'd been set free from. This is why it was absolutely crucial to offer practical aid such as employment, housing and the like, along with emotional and spiritual support. Thank God for places like *Teen Challenge*. Anyway, this gal calls me at 2 a.m... I assumed she was drunk by the way she was carrying on, and she pleaded with me to come get her. She was really tanked and it took some doin', but I finally got an address and directions. Hmm, this was a nasty neighborhood to be held up in (east side Detroit) ... might be a good idea to have some company ... a woman. Who am I gonna' get at this hour? Gigi. She was living with her mother in nearby Garden City and volunteered to accompany me. On the way out the door I grabbed a cassette tape I'd recently received from Florida; a fiery message by Evangelist Stalvey called "Power over the Devil." In the early morning hours of a starless night in the Motor City we got off the freeway and into a neighborhood where you'd better, as the Dan Amos Band would remind us, have an "...angel ridin' shotgun." On the way there, after picking up Gigi, I'd put the cassette tape in for a listen, prompted by the Holy Spirit I'd recall in retrospect, for another full throttle encounter with the dark side. When we arrived, for some reason, I slipped the cassette in my pocket. The dude who answered the door got my ol 'heart to pumpin'. He had a bit of a blank, annoyed look on his face, and had pimp written all over him, but not the usual John R. and Brush St., Detroit ghetto, *Baretta* TV show – Rooster character variety. This cat was tall, lean, Roy Rogers lookin' gone over to the Darth Vader dark side, steel-eyed cowboy, dressed in black from head to toe, including the hat on his head and snakeskin trimmed boots on his size tens. Well, figurin' this dude out would have to wait, because no sooner had we stepped into the dimly lit front room, there, slouched on an old, faded green sofa, unable to rise, intoxicated to the max; lay the object of our quest. Gigi sat on one side of her, I the other, and "Tex" pulled up a chair and went into Charles Manson stare me down mode. She was thrilled, and not a little surprised I'd actually come. Between tears, laughter, interspersed with language it had been some years I'd heard coming from the lips of a woman … rubbing my leg one moment, pleading for forgiveness the next. Well, you'd have to be spiritually brain-dead not to see what was goin' on here. Our delivered sister had fallen back into the clutches of her pimp, and had backslidden quickly into the lifestyle she'd so recently escaped from.[15] Ol' Darth Tex Vader's sly foxy little smirk let on exactly where he was coming from. Why had he gone along with these two strangers (Christians) comin' onto his turf to take his "property" away? He likely set it up. He was going to show his "girl" and us, who the real boss was, and we and no one else better ever interfere in his business again.

Out of the blue ol' Tex announced, "Hey Rev, got something for ya'll ta listen to. It'll explain where my power comes from."

Here we go … game on. Before I could say "Thanks, some other time," he slaps a tape into a nearby cassette player.

I really couldn't pay it much mind what with this gal hangin' all over

---

[15] See Parable of the Sower, Mt 13:3-9.

me, but it sounded like the same old occult crapolla propaganda; none of it was new to me. His sinister glare looked to burn a hole in me. I tried to focus on the young lady whose breathing grew increasingly labored. Minutes passed, and the might-intimidate little-ol-ladies and youngsters boogie man's occult power tape abruptly ended. Ol' Tex looked hard at me, a wry thin-lipped sneer painted on his mug. Then I remembered, "Hey, I gave your tape an ear, how 'bout you check out mine?"

"Go ahead," he hissed, lookin' like a reject from a *The Good, the Bad, and the Ugly* meets *Son of Dracula* movie.

Well, you may never have heard ol' Brother Herman preach ... best I can tell you is it's like Robert Duvall's character in the film *The Apostle* with both barrels blazin' ... at one point in his message Herman exclaimed, "You know how you put the devil to flight? You take authority over that rascal by pleading the blood of Jesus ... they can't stand it ... they gotta' go. Halleluiah!"

Snap! Ol' Tex couldn't take it no more and two things happened simultaneously. He'd been holding his tape while mine played. At the point where Evangelist Stalvey shouted the "blood of Jesus," he broke his tape in two and had that cornered rat look. The next moment the gal we'd come to aid, Terri, slumped up against me. "Passed out ... now what?" I wondered.

Only, she didn't just pass out, she'd stopped breathing. Ol' Tex grabbed her lifeless form off the couch and struggled to get her into a nearby bedroom. There, on a bed, he frantically went through CPR procedures while Gigi and I stood by in prayer. Does this guy know what the hell he's doin'? I asked Gigi to call an ambulance.

"No," barked Tex. "Don't even think about it."

Precious moments slipped by. Still no response, Tex was growing increasingly anxious and frustrated ... this girl was gonna' be dead shortly. Silently I prayed, "Lord don't let this girl die in this state; her eternal soul at stake." No doubt Gigi's silent prayers struck a similar note.

I gave Gigi that look like go make the call, I'll keep him busy. Suddenly, Tex reaches under the edge of the mattress and pulls out a bowie knife the size of Texas, waves it silently at me as if to say "don't interfere," and, unable to revive her, he decides he'll do a last ditch emergency appendectomy ... with a bowie knife! Gigi went for the phone. I tried to persuade Tex to wait for medical help and that God wouldn't let her die in this state. He almost spat at that notion and moved above her to make an incision. In my mind's eye the point of that blade piercing her slender ivory skinned neck made my hair stand on end. There was no stopping this guy. I didn't exactly want to tangle with psycho cowboy, demon possessed (can't say for certain but several of the signs were there), bowie knife wielding rodeo reject, so I rebuked him in Jesus' name.

The knife fell from his hand off the bed and onto the floor with a clang. He hit the floor next, clutching his chest, gasping for air, and slithered into the far corner. Heart attack! The young woman on the bed moaned, eyes flitting, short labored breaths ... breathing! Minutes later an ambulance and police arrived. I don't know what became of Tex ... if the police snatched him up ... was he dead, or did he crawl away into some hole? Our hearts and prayers were focused on Terri, and we had our work cut out keeping up with the ambulance en route to a nearby emergency room. Gigi and I walked alongside the gurney as they rushed Terri to an appropriate area for treatment. The attendants paused momentarily before two large chrome metal doors ... our young backslidden friend looked up at me ... then glanced beyond me while a grand smile spread across her face. I turned to look at what provoked such a response. There on the wall, unnoticed at first, was one of those paintings you occasionally see in hospitals, Jesus standing behind a doctor working on a patient. I'm getting goose bumps writing this ... power over the devil indeed.

There remains one final encounter with the dark side during the Beech Daly sojourn that I think bares telling. The details are a bit murky, but that it was a demonic encounter is not at issue here, at least in my mind and the two brothers whose memories I've had to call on to be sure I'd get it right, and so, with this one, I'm relying largely on their recollections.

Ken G. had ingested way too many psychedelics during his "turn on, tune in, drop out" career. Add dabbling with the occult and you've got trouble. I may as well say it right here. Both myself, Ken Hasper and Jim Heady who were also witness to this spiritual "no holds barred match," have all seen and experienced firsthand a laundry list of all things bizarre concerning the drug fueled, rock and roll, perverted sex, psychic mystic crapolla swirling under, in and around that lifestyle dubbed – 60s/70s counterculture. Kooks, wanna-bes, acid heads, speed freaks, junkies, whores aka street hostesses, gurus, cosmic troubadours, rip-offs, greaser hippies, knuckleheads and mental ward cases. In short, one of us is not easily duped ... to put one over on the three of us together would be a real coup. At Shalom, we had enough members who worked in various mental health and related fields, and on special occasions, a group from Shalom would take cookies and treats and go up and sing at the Ypsilanti Regional Psychiatric Hospital. Sometimes the line(s) between the demonic and mental illness are blurred and not easily discerned, and one must proceed with great caution until you're certain, lest you do more harm than good. Sometimes it's clear cut.

When Jim and Ken brought Ken G. over for prayer, none of us were quite prepared for what was about to transpire. You'd often hear us quoting Paul's encouragement to Timothy: "... be instant in season, out of season ...." (2 Tm 4:2). At Shalom, you better be ready 24/7! Alright, another guy whose done too much acid. Well, Jesus can fix that. It was an off night (no service or activities) at Shalom, perhaps a few people hanging out. The four of us went into the prayer room off the stage. After a few minutes of "warm-up" prayer, I went to lay hands [16] on Ken G. and two things happened simultaneously. First, in an utterly inhuman voice, he began to spew forth the most foul, blasphemous utterances imaginable. In an instant, he'd metamorphosed from a laid back dude to someone who'd give Jack the Ripper the creeps. Even more unnerving, a high- pitched banshee-like wail began to race around; outside the building it seemed, at an incredible high rate of speed ... far swifter than any human or animal. It was so real that an alarmed Ken Hasper went to investigate for himself, outdoors, searching for the origin of these inhuman cries. Seeing nothing he returned. Whatever it was it ceased. The effect on the young man we were praying over was apparent. He was highly agitated and altogether beside himself. Better to get him to the apartment upstairs for more privacy. All three of us were fully aware that we'd awoken something much more devious than the remnants of a few bad blotter acid trips.

Minutes later the conflict picked up where it had left off. Turns out downstairs had only been a "howdy do." Now all hell broke loose. The foul, hate-filled oaths and taunts resumed with fresh vigor and grew to an ear-splitting pitch. Roars, like some cave troll, accompanied with insults

---

[16]   Praying with people is often accompanied by the "laying on of hands." Acts 6:6

132

directed first at us, then at Christ. Was our imagination getting the better of us? Fangs, wolf like, dripping saliva, confronted us from a wide opened mouth. These verbal assaults would last about a minute or so and would be interrupted by bodily contortions; head back, feet digging into the bed, stomach/hips arching up like a cat's back but reversed ... then relaxed. Then what appeared to be a panic/fear induced effort to rip unseen hands from his throat ... again, the cursing and threats. In one particularly intense exchange, a strange voice identified itself by name (which none of us can recall) and threw down the verbal gauntlet that he/it, was more powerful than us and would never leave ... if we did not desist, he – Ken G and we three would die. At this point our tormented friend's body began to levitate off the bed. I placed a Bible on his chest which put an end to that nonsense; power indeed. The voice now pleaded, whimpering, "take it off, take it off," Gollum-like.

In what I guess you could liken to having your opponent on the ropes in the late rounds of a prize fight, I delivered a triple combination knock-out punch ... now, commanding the evil spirit by name to vacate the premises (Ken G's body) by the authority of Jesus Christ, our Lord. Suddenly he went limp. At first I thought he was dead. Thankfully, demons can't kill you. His chest slowly began to move up and down, and he looked at peace. The three of us, exhausted, left him and retired to the kitchen and some tea. Minutes later Ken G. strolled in. What a change. He reminded me of the demoniac in Mark's Gospel account (see Mk 5). Now seated and in his right mind, he described how this "thing" had been inside, tormenting him for months. He'd visited other local churches seeking deliverance, but the demon(s) inside would prevent him from speaking. Tonight had been different. Later, I couldn't help but wonder if the shrieking sounds racing around the building, and later the unseen hands at his throat, had been desperate attempts to shut him up and escape the inevitable which they sensed was coming when they (demons) walked into Shalom.

• • • •

Sunday evening services leaned on a mix of Catholic Charismatic, Assembly of God, and good ol' tent revival influences to stir the faithful and challenge the lost. Friday Coffee House was seed sowin' time. Sundays were, "Hey pal, you might never get another chance to accept

Jesus!" The format was fairly standard, dare I say traditional (since we prided ourselves in being non-traditional): opening worship with some lively folk rockish tunes, a traditional hymn or two ala "Amazing Grace" and "The Old Rugged Cross," testimonies, Bible readings with message, altar call, prayer and closing worship, and once a month – a special communion service. As far as a collection went, we sometimes passed small wicker baskets around, other times simply reminded folks there was a collection box in the rear; we encouraged tithing without being legalistic about it. We took pains to avoid any appearance of attempting to "fleece-the-flock."

The main Friday night concerns centered on bands/artists showing up as scheduled (winter weather concerns), and sound equipment working properly. Sunday evenings had more of the same with additional challenges. There was never a shortage of musicians around Shalom, but getting them to function as a cohesive unit … occasionally there were persons who felt "called" to the music ministry, and well, sometimes you had to wonder. You musicians out there know all too well what a "funny" breed you are … egos can clash … some detest rehearsal preferring to just "wing it" … others think the louder it is, the heavier the "anointing" will be … how long/short should the song service be? My take on volume was that if you couldn't hear the congregation singing (assuming they were), you probably needed to back it down. Also, it always helps to have a good sound person, preferably one that's not tone deaf, working the sound board. On the flip side, I had no problem with beefin' up the volume for special music if the occasion fit. I enjoyed experimenting with different music genres like singing Psalms to a reggae beat, but, overall, music at Shalom was our strong suit, and we were not ashamed to use it as a trump card on occasion.

The bulk of the preaching fell on my shoulders, although I was not shy about sharing the pulpit with anointed preachers from within and outside *Shalom*. It seemed worthwhile that "Shalomites" see/hear other preachers as it gave me a break and provided a venue for other up-and-coming preachers (see Appendix 2) to test the waters. Perhaps most importantly, I didn't want *Shalom* to become known and referred to as Shannon's Church, where everybody adopted the same narrow way of speaking, praying, same annoying Christian clichés, etc., that is so common to cult groups and also to legitimate expressions of local

Christian communities who too often get locked into a narrow, North American, homogenized brand of Christianity, often collected around one or more strong personalities. One month's special guest preacher might be someone who had a more scholarly, intellectual background, Dave Yetterock, an Assemblies of God minister, for instance. Next month it might be a foot stompin', holler call-back storefront preacher such as Julius Dodson from *Challenge House*. There would be no getting comfortably numb here.

Speaking of guests, my personal favorites were the brothers and sisters from *Challenge House* I just mentioned, a *Teen Challenge* type ministry located near Warren and Lovett in Detroit; a rough part of town to be sure. Their outreach facility, an old, stripped-of-everything-valuable convent, barely had enough electric and water service to make it livable. Julius Dodson, a black brother who served as director, and his associate Mike Kingsley, were a couple of characters. We loved having them.

Mike had been set free from the not so "gay" lifestyle while living in an apartment above a funeral home. When his turn came to take the pulpit and testify you'd better tighten your seat-belt. Like Neil Diamond's Brother Love, ol' Mike started off like a small earthquake, nice and easy, but once he hit his stride, well, you know that feelin' you get when the roller-coaster car you're in has just slowly reached the zenith of the first big hill … you know what's comin' next.

One Sunday evening some of our Adventist friends unexpectedly wandered in and grabbed several "safe" seats near the back. Till now, they'd only experienced Friday night coffee houses, which could get pretty rowdy, but, of all the Sunday nights they had to pick to drop in, wouldn't ya' know it, *Challenge House's* Mike Kingsley was our scheduled guest preacher. Before Mike did his thing we heard several moving testimonies of how God had snatched people from the jaws of death and hell itself. This was hard core, real deal, no pretensions stuff. Their matter-of-fact, humble, eternally thankful approach lent an authenticity to stories that elicited numerous "thank you Jesus," from swaying back and forth listeners gripped by the wonder of God's bountiful mercy and long-suffering love. Then, Brother Mike got behind the microphone, and having been perhaps the most enthusiastic listener during this time of testimony, he looked like a dam ready to burst. In a few minutes he got so excited (and very apologetic about it the whole time), he removed his shoes and began running around (best he could with people seated cross-legged, wall-to-wall, the few booths and chairs in the back full, and folks standing in the corridor leading to the rear entrance). He was shoutin' and carryin' on ... then finally, he'd slow down and resumed his place behind the pulpit, and somewhere between tears and "holy" laughter he'd apologize: "Brother Joe, Brother Joe, I'm sorry ... you'll have to excuse me ... but, Praise God! I just feel tonight like, like I'm on HOLY GROUND!" and off he'd go, running around again.

We loved it, well, most of us. I looked back and noticed an empty booth. Hmm, wasn't empty a minute ago. Guess our Adventist friends had had enough for one night. Oh well. Not everybody's cup-a-tea I guess. Weeks later, at my Adventist's friends request, I visited an Adventist service. The "straightest" service I have ever been to. There was little emotion. I mean come on, we're talking about eternal life ... smile at least! Well, I tried not to be judgmental or condescending, but I just couldn't see how you'd expect anybody to follow Jesus, especially young folks, in that kind of atmosphere. Nice folks though.

I thought I was an okay preacher and in time became fairly proficient. I was a bit of a Billy Graham fan ... keep it simple, to the point, and unless you feel a special anointing or some special occasion or other, keep it under 30 minutes. Indeed, twenty minutes is sufficient, and if you can't make your point by then, you've already lost most of them.

The unexpected and exercise (or lack) of spiritual gifts (see 1 Cor 12), occasionally got me rattled. In time it got to the point where Saturdays became a regular day of fasting and prayer on my part in order to be well equipped for spiritual discernment (a gift) and spiritual warfare. After a while you begin to be a bit more cautious as to who you're going to let do and say such-and-such. You gain a certain level of confidence born of familiarity with members of the congregation (and certain visitors), who have some experience with spiritual gifts including but not limited to prophecy, tongues, and tongues with interpretation. You also had a pretty good bead on who was "fishing," and/or manifesting 99% flesh 1% spirit. However, I was a novice myself and we tried to create an atmosphere of tolerance, but neither an "anything goes – let it fly" approach (although sometimes it did ... oh well, kept you on your spiritual toes). Most of our congregation were little more than babes in Christ, some transient and hardly staying long enough to get their feet wet, others wary of this

136

charismatic dimension of Christianity. We were fortunate to have several more mature, well grounded, and experienced in the Pentecostal way members.

. . . .

"Lord, why don't you use me the way you use ol' Herman down in Vero?" If I could call people out and reveal to them things only they and God knew to be true ... if only, if only. Who knows? God gives gifts to whom, where and when he chooses ... apparently these particular gifts (prophesy and word of knowledge) were not a right fit for me ... at least at the present ... perhaps I'd have grown big (bigger) headed. Sometimes these gifts come with their own unique challenges and pitfalls. I used to wonder how Herman dealt with the pressure of feeling that (and here I'm making an assumption) each new tent revival service had to outdo the last. Three healings last Saturday ... well by gosh there better be four tonight. I don't know. He seemed to handle it really well, and God had other ways of keeping him humble. I know at *Shalom*, we didn't have as much activity in the use of these gifts as I and others would like to have witnessed. It always made me a bit anxious when someone brought a message in tongues, and then that sometimes uncomfortable minute or two period of silence, waiting, hoping for someone to bring/give an interpretation. Back at the ol' Tent, Herman would "help out" in a pinch, and if an interpretation wasn't uttered by another member of the congregation following a message in tongues, he'd bring one. I don't recall having ever been so moved, and like a lot of folks I was a bit gun er gift-shy, but I'm the pastor for heaven's sake. By the way, does no interpretation necessarily invalidate the previous message in tongues? Or, I always raised an eyebrow when there would be a short utterance in tongues followed by a lengthy interpretation or vice versa. Hmm; fortunately, I recall few serious issues in this regard at Shalom, but healing and the Baptism of the Holy Spirit ....

As mentioned earlier, when I first took the reigns of leadership in early 1974, the Pentecostal issue was a bit of a "hot button" issue. Sadly, several left over the matter, but by 75/76 our identity was clearly bound up in charismatic experience. Yet, misgivings and issues related to the Baptism of the Holy Spirit always seemed to linger just below the surface. Chief among them, what, if any visible initial sign, should accompany a believer's "baptism" with the Holy Spirit? Most of us in various levels of leadership at Shalom at this juncture yielded to the traditional view of the Assemblies. Simply stated, there must be visible evidence accompanying a believer's baptism with the Holy Spirit, and that evidence will be speaking in/with tongues. I'd been influenced by a couple of books while taking courses at the Assemblies Bible College in Detroit including Donald Gee's *Concerning Spiritual Gifts* and Carl Brunback's *What Meaneth This?* Both authors argue, rather convincingly, for a visible, evidential manifestation that both the person being filled and any onlookers would find compelling and convincing that something supernatural had transpired. Their argument, which still makes me think they were/are on to something, became a regular part of our instruction. However, to our credit, or maybe lack thereof, it was not an issue worth battling over. Indeed, the type of thing congregations split up over. Still, sometimes sparks could fly if I'm saying one thing from the pulpit and I perceive my message is being undermined. Especially if the sheep whose care you've been entrusted with are confused and discouraged in part because those in authority over them can't agree. Also, "Hey, take responsibility for your own spiritual growth; you work out your salvation with fear and trembling (Phil 2:12). Don't expect me to figure it all out for you."

My personal problem with the issue (all things "Pentecostal") had a bit of a different spin to it. As I said, it made sound sense to me that speaking in tongues should accompany a genuine initial baptizing in/with the Holy Spirit as reported on several occasions in *The Acts of the Apostles*. An event that could be simultaneous with one's rebirth (born again) experience or subsequent; however, I rarely witnessed such in-fillings, and some that I did troubled me as to their validity. Some of you know what I'm talking about. These "tarry" services that sometimes go on for hours as people, and this is my subjective/objective observation here, speak in what appears to be tongues, but was it as the Spirit gave them utterance? ... Or were they mimicking and/or speaking out of frustration, fatigue, and/or the zealous promptings of misguided brethren? ... and in a similar vein, people who speak in tongues because some "loose cannon" saint is speaking a mile a minute in "tongues" themselves in the poor soul's ear insisting that they "Speak ... go ahead, just let it out ... the language is in your head ... go on, take that first step of faith and it'll come ... Lord, loose their tongue."

The person who is the subject of this misguided onslaught may speak in tongues, and it may very well be real, after all we're all God has to work with, but what if it's not? ... what if they were just mimicking ... speaking out of frustration and/or not wanting to embarrass (or let down) brother or sister big shot who'd laid hands on them ... or worse, have to return to their seat under the watchful gaze of the "blessed" ... dejected, wondering why the Holy Spirit had withheld something so special and expected that all believers would come into the fullness of ... what gives?

I wonder how many people have tossed and turned through the night following such a disheartening experience. I recall talking to more than I care to remember. At times like this I could have used a bit of Solomon the Wise's anointing. Sometimes I was just as perplexed as those persons feverently seeking an initial "infilling" experience and disheartened when outward manifestations were not forthcoming.

For my part, I refused to stoop to such questionable methods to "force" an experience on them that was not Spirit breathed. If they want it, lay hands on them and the "... Spirit will give them utterance" (Acts 2:4). I had no problem with giving instruction pertaining to spiritual gifts ... what to expect, not to expect, pitfalls, etc., but, if it's contrived, they, you and most others will know it. So what's the point? I didn't get into Christianity to "play" church. If we have to resort to gimmicks, I'd just as soon bail. I don't recall having ever laid hands on someone to be baptized with the Holy Spirit and have them then manifest speaking in tongues as visible evidence of said filling. I'm not sure why. It seems that my objective experience is at odds with my theology. I have been present when it has happened that people have been so filled, and heard plenty of testimonies of persons being so filled without anyone praying over them ... some have come up speaking in tongues after water immersion baptisms I've witnessed, but, at the end of the day, I've also witnessed too many questionable manifestations surrounding what should be a wonderful experience for all concerned. And may I add, in spite of the confusion and controversy surrounding the infilling and empowering of God's people with the Holy Spirit, this is an experience followers of Jesus need more than ever in today's world. Why is it that so many churches, mainline and independent, downplay the manifestation of spiritual gifts and seldom if ever experience them? While those who expect it, yearn for it, believe it ... usually do. One just hopes it's the real deal. I confess that in these matters I'm still very much "... looking through a glass darkly ...." (1 Cor 13:12).

• • • •

The gift of healing, or should I say lack of, nagged at me periodically like a dull toothache. I'd been healed (my ear-see Pt. 2), and I knew others who'd been healed ... true, these were not blind eyes being opened, twisted limbs straightened, leper cleansing variety, but we, along with our charismatic brethren near and far, affirmed that God does indeed continue to heal people both sovereignly and via those gifts (1 Cor 12) He has given to members of His body – the Church. Problem was, at Shalom anyway, we just didn't seem to be seeing, experiencing the level of healing manifestation we so adamantly proclaimed. When you adopt an almost boastful attitude (maybe that was the problem) that we, a twentieth century remnant of a "real" believing New Testament Church ... and scriptures like "These signs shall follow them that believe...." (Mk 16:17).And, "...call for the elders of the church . . . and the prayer of faith shall save the sick...." (Jas 5:14, 15) ... roll off your tongue with ease, but it's not happening, it becomes quite disconcerting. To say nothing of the mood that lingers like an unpleasant odor when some of the more obviously afflicted members/guests of the congregation are prayed over and grow worse or die! You pray, analyze, confess, study, and buy the latest "how to" books and tapes ... try again. Oh, the occasional troublesome headaches have subsided. The boil has burst and shows no evidence of infection or returning, but how about the "hard" cases ... the brother/sister who's totally deaf, the paralytic confined to a wheelchair who Sunday morning wonders if he should be wheeled down front after it's been announced following the service there will be prayer at the altar for those in need of healing. I eventually came to a place (few years down the pastorate road), where it became so uncomfortable preaching about divine healing, gifts, etc., I began to avoid it ... almost like I was embarrassed ... angry at God. For whatever reason it just didn't seem to be happening. Some days would be so spiritually dark you just grew weary of even thinking about it. No, we would not resort to the newest trend/fad – "Name It and Claim It," or as someone put it, "Blab It and Grab It" – wind of doctrine blowing through Pentecostal circles far and wide, aka the "prosperity" gospel[17]; an ill wind indeed. This whole healing business was one of several eating away at my spirit which would in time relegate me to the ranks of another burnt-out minister. Well, sort of.

However, if sensational healings were absent from our midst, there was no shortage of a steady stream of persons delivered from the bondage of drugs, sexual promiscuity, cult and occult bondage and materialistic pleasure slavery. The most dramatic healing, some would argue, was the healing of a broken relationship with God. At this moment I'm reminded of one of those wonderful Bible based epic films that so inspired viewers back in the fifties and sixties. I still have a copy – *The Robe*. In one powerful scene a Roman tribune, played by a young handsome Richard Burton, who'd played a part in Jesus' execution and was now fighting for his sanity, confronts a young paralytic woman in the town of Cana, following Jesus' "alleged" resurrection.

"Why," he sarcastically inquires, "did this Jesus, who'd allegedly healed others, not heal you?"

"Oh, but He did." is her response. Looking at her crippled condition with a slight sneer … she can easily read his mind. Apparently this young woman who'd been a cripple all her life was so full of malice and envy that the locals made a point of avoiding her. She alone of the townsfolk did not attend the Gospel recorded "Wedding at Cana" (Jn 2). As we know, Jesus arrived late. *The Robe* employs a bit of historical fiction here. Why was Jesus late? He'd stopped to talk to this young bitter woman.

"But He left you as you are."

---

[17]   In short, the idea that you possess what you confess (I have no problem with the benefits of maintaining a positive attitude, but we're dealing here with something that far exceeds this notion). As a Christian, if you are not prospering in your health, relationships, finances and so on, the reason can likely be traced to sin and/or a lack of faith. The notion that God sometimes wills and uses suffering (including sickness) as a means to work his purpose in those he has redeemed, they would argue, is a trick of the devil, planting their flag as it were on (3 Jn 2) "…and be in health, even as your soul prospers." God does not want you sick, poor, and in dysfunctional painful relationships. Of course this is not entirely new, America witnessed a "gospel of wealth" movement during the nineteenth century, which taught that wealth was a sign of divine favor rooted in personal virtue.

"No. He could have healed my body and then it would've been natural for me to laugh and sing. He's done something even better. He chose me for His work ... left me as I am so that others like me may know that their misfortune needn't deprive them of happiness."

Something of a similar nature comes across in one of my favorite scenes from Dickens's *A Christmas Carol*. Bob Cratchit is having a touching, serious conversation with his wife regarding how their young son, Tiny Tim, is dealing with the crippling condition he is afflicted with. Tim had recently confided in his father that he hoped when people saw him, especially at Christmas time, they'd remember who it was that made blind men see and the lame walk.

. . . .

Sunday evening services provided no shortage of drama. One evening my brother Jeff showed up with our beloved Uncle D.J. in tow. D.J. was one of my father's two elder brothers and this one especially was a bit of a legend. At this juncture he was living in Detroit's Cass Corridor, a seedy area south of Wayne State University, as its unofficial mayor, in one of those "skid row-ish" pay by the night, week, month hotels and boarding houses that had once been part of the city's proud heritage. For years now the Corridor had taken on the façade of a haven for pimps, hookers, bums and hustlers ... a goodly number of elderly folks ... too many, physically and/or financially unable to move to a safer neighborhood ... you wondered where their families were ... some, like D.J., actually liked it down there. Liquor stores, seedy taverns, burlesque houses and cheap eats establishments stubbornly sat like lingering shadows just west of Woodward. Uncle Don was our (Shalom's) go to guy for our ministry outreach down in the Corridor. He'd regularly collect names of residents who were particularly down and out and/or who had no family. We'd make formal visits at least twice a year (Thanksgiving and Christmas), armed with baskets of goodies, toys for kids, hygiene products, warm socks and gloves for adults. Before distributing gifts (dinners at Thanksgiving), we'd gather in the hotel lobby where old forgotten men and women sat staring out of lifeless eyes, to sing carols and hand out treats. What a joy to see the smiles, especially of children ... some folks rubbing their eyes, pinching themselves ... in wonder that anyone would come down to a place like this and spread a bit of holiday cheer and God's love. The hookers liked us too. They didn't often get fresh baked homemade cookies! However, this night D. J. was on our turf ... oh yeah, did I tell you he'd been drinking. He wasn't passed-out drunk, and I'm sure my brother made sure he left any unfinished bottle of cheap wine outside. Ol' D.J., like so many others, when he was sober, was an absolute delight to be around ... kinda' like an Irish version of Red Skeleton meets Fred Sanford, but when he'd hit the sauce harder than usual, he'd do a fine rendering of Dr. Jekyl and Mr. Hyde; in short, he could be dangerous following nine innings with the bottle.

I'd just launched into my sermon when three things happened almost simultaneously. Randy decided to hit the bar before he came into Sunday night service. He'd dropped his young wife and kids off earlier and walked down the street to minister to his own special need of getting into the "spirit" via spirits at a neighborhood tavern. It likely didn't take him long to drink up his perpetually almost empty pockets. He staggered in through the rear entrance and ambled into the middle of the in-progress service, and just stood in the middle of the sitting area like an old tree in a strong wind swaying first one way then the other; his one hand raised as though he wanted everyone's attention. No doubt he wanted to testify. You just wanted to smack the guy as your stomach churned while outa' the corner of your eye you noticed the knucklehead's wife, head bowed in shame and fighting back tears.

Suddenly the front door swung open and in stepped two Inkster police officers. After apologizing for interrupting, and which by the way, as soon as they'd walked in, my uncle D. J. dove behind the lone couch near the back. Guess he thought the cops were lookin' for him which wouldn't have been unusual as he occasionally had warrants out for his arrest. Meanwhile, Randy's giving annoyed glares at the police for having interrupted him as he was about to testify ... the police asked if such and such young lady were here ... she was. A young girl, seventeenish, who an hour earlier employed heavy persuasive tactics with her parents to not only let her attend this "cult" hangout, but drive the new family automobile (she'd just gotten her license). With some hesitation and another apologetic look towards me, I'd closed my Bible by this point and was just kinda takin' in this whole surreal scene. "Uh Miss, we've found your vehicle wrapped around a tree about a mile away ... totaled," an officer awkwardly tried to explain. Apparently it had been stolen from our lot just minutes ago. The girl freaked; she registered a ten on the Richter scale meltdown in no time. The police no sooner exited with the hysterical young gal in their wake, when....

Timber! At that point Randy, who'd been doing his best to act normal during the unexpected and no doubt daunting interruption by two of Inkster's finest, finally went down, face first like an old infested Dutch elm. Reckon he passed out.

Meanwhile my uncle is still hiding, peeking from behind the couch to see if the coast is clear, waiting to be certain that the police who'd taken the young lady outside to resolve the stolen wrecked vehicle nightmare she was going to have to explain to mom and dad, would not return. Not to be outdone, Randy stopped breathing. Penny, a young lady studying to be a doctor was fortunately on hand and rushed to work on him. I'm sorry, I admit ... I was thinking to myself, "Aw, leave him be." However, he was I assumed, not in the proper condition to meet his maker, and our mission was to help rescue people from the lake of fire, not give them a helping push. He pulled through.

So much for my sermon; use it next week. A lot of folks hung around for prayer and we had a good laugh about it later. These kinda' fireworks didn't accompany every Sunday service, but they did on enough of a regular basis to where as I said, Saturdays became a ritual fast day as I recovered from Friday night and prepared for round two on Sunday evenings. Oh yeah, my brother Jeff managed to calm D. J. down and get him home in one piece.

. . . .

Officiating weddings was usually a pleasant call to duty. I've performed thirty plus and don't recall any nightmares, but more than a few atypical ones. Wedding guests/families were often taken back a bit when the long-haired young guy with an earring took his place at the start of the ceremony. My first two weddings, each one different as night and day, are especially memorable. My buddy, Steve Matsos, who'd originally journeyed to Florida with me, was ready to make that lifelong commitment and wed his high school sweetheart Lou Ann; they honored me by asking me to officiate ... my first. Steve's mom, Mary, asked me to get a haircut and subtly hinted something about a suit. No problemendo ... got the split ends trimmed off so now it was only an inch past my shoulders. Next, I traveled cross town to fashionable Ferndale and a clothing store – Rags to Riches; paid $29.95 for a new soft corduroy tan suit. The ceremony and reception are a bit hazy, but I have the pictures to remove any doubt it was only a dream. Besides, I need only call them; Steve and Lou that is. Four grown kids and an overflowing quiver of grandkids, and they will indeed remind me, "Yes Joe, it happened!" And how's this for cool. My last wedding was Steve and Lou's first-born, Jana and her husband, Jason, (April '98); I briefly came out of minister retirement to bless them on their wedding day.

There were thirty something weddings in between my first and last. One at the Martha and Mary Chapel at Greenfield Village on a sultry August afternoon that was so hot we had to put out the candles even before the ceremony began ... they were slowly "coppin-a-lean" and wax was dripping everywhere. A steady stream of sweat ran down the middle of my back. I shortened my comments and sped through the ceremony without compromising the solemnity of the occasion before folks, especially the bride, passed out. Another one on a bridge at Elizabeth Park in Trenton ... one at Hines Park ... another outdoor one at Weller's in Saline, and a bit of a tricky one on a yacht on the Detroit River on a brisk early October afternoon; the Renaissance Center as a backdrop. Tricky I say because the water was quite choppy, and the bride, a bit nervous to begin with as you might imagine ... and well, I held my Bible in my left hand and used my right (at her waist) to steady her lest you'd hear, "bride overboard!" No indeed, chivalry isn't dead. The groom and maid-of-honor, whom you might think should have taken it upon themselves to steady the tense bride, both looked a bit queasy themselves ... now wouldn't that have been hilarious had the whole blooming lot of us got seasick ... they were grateful I was as steady as Captain Bligh going around the Horn.

I'm sorry, I said my two most memorable and here I am going on nearly forgetting the second, as in second ceremony performed and a standout for "better or for worse." In time I'd become much more selective about whose wedding I'd officiate. Seems word got out that there was this preacher who'd marry anyone, anywhere, anytime (not true I might add), "and, hey Rev, there'll be somethin' in the card for you."

I also had reservations about officiating a ceremony if one or both parties had been divorced. After a few years and input from other ministers, I developed a criterion that included counseling, workshops, questionnaires, etc. over a period of at least several months before I'd agree to officiate, unless mitigating circumstances existed. Okay, the second wedding. I don't recall if they were Christian or not. Funny how sometimes people have no room for Jesus in their life until it comes time to get married, get the babies dedicated/baptized, and die. Anyway, they were friends of a friend ... you know. I thought well, someone's gonna' marry 'em, might as well be me because everyone there will get an earful one way or another of the Gospel. The ceremony with reception following was held at an old National Guard Armory at the southeast corner of Huron and I-94 south of Ypsilanti. It was c. '74 and I had no idea so many hippies were still around. The last of the Ann Arbor/Ypsilanti breed, hang on till the last tie-dye shirt and hash pipe are gone, patchouli oil smellin', head-band, Birkenstock sandal wearin' crowd showed up like it was Goose Lake II. There was a dog in the bridal party! Fido took his place down front after trotting down in the procession (er, I don't recall for certain, but I don't think the mutt was best man, er dog). Clouds of smoke appeared as if on signal and the pungent smell of burning Acapulco Gold washed over us ... geez, I'm back at Haight-Ashbury. I've never met anyone nor heard from the couple joined in matrimony that day, so I don't know what if any effect my words had on the minds of the Woodstock generation of southeast Michigan. I never made it through the reception. I could only handle a couple songs from the live band, get this, *The Louisiana Cat House Blues Band.* Not exactly the Wedding Feast at Cana, but you get the picture. Far out man....

· · · ·

For a ten year run beginning c. '75, mid-July was a highly anticipated time of year at Shalom. Sandwiched between our Memorial Day and Labor Day campouts, usually up at Shoepac and Tomahawk Lakes near Atlanta, MI[18], was our Ann Arbor Art Fair outreach. This was our "takin' it to the streets" opportunity, born after a visit to an earlier Art Fair and fueled by a perplexity as to why the Gospel wasn't being proclaimed to this mass of

---

[18]   C. 1980 I met a Catholic priest at a funeral we jointly officiated. He invited me out to take a look at Camp DeSalles in the Irish Hills area and offered its use to Shalom at a very reasonable rate. While not quite the up-North vibe, we moved our camp-outs to this much more easily accessible location.

collected humanity ... especially in an area (corner of South and East University), set aside for non-profit, political, social activist, community sponsored groups and the like. Where were the Christians? Seemed many of the local churches just locked their doors and waited out the siege rather than embracing this golden opportunity. Well, instead of waiting for someone else to do it, a group of Shalomites decided this was a tailor-made-in-heaven opportunity, and after securing and going through the necessary channels, insured that Shalom Ministry would be represented at next year's fair.[19]

Our first effort was received rather coolly. The booth itself was well organized, neat, artistic, but the large sign "Mars' Hill" might have put a few folks off. Most students of the Bible would immediately recognize the reference from *The Acts of the Apostles* (Ch.17). What could be more appropriate? It may have been something of a self-fulfilling prophecy, but at least we could say in the face of a rough outing, so had Paul the Apostle fared in Athens (Ann Arbor). Heck, some folks saw the sign and figured we were some kinda' UFO group. Undaunted, and with a year under our belt, we adopted a new strategy for our second year, one we'd keep and tweak a bit, but we hit the nail on the head this time.

People travel to the Art Fair in search of that one, special, unique piece of art, but that's not all. Good food, people watching, entertainment and partying are also part of the Art Fair goers' agenda. If we were going to make contact, we had one shot at getting their attention, and being ambiguous (Mars' Hill) wasn't going to cut it. So, here's what we came up with. An aesthetically attractive booth, we were representing the second person of the Trinity after all, that took as its theme from C.S. Lewis' "Lord, Lunatic, Liar" approach. A large backdrop surrounded by the caption (the same question Jesus asked His disciples in the Gospel narratives: Mk 8; Lk 9), "Who Do You Say That I Am?" centered beneath one of the few pictures of Jesus I liked. Also, the not too subtle statements: on one side – Did Jesus Claim to be God? And on the other – Was Jesus Lord, Lunatic, or Liar? Make no mistake; our booth was a show ... I mean

---

[19]   Our run at the Art Fair ended after 10 years when due to limited space, the directors decided to limit groups in the non-profit section to those having a Washtenaw County mailing address. It was great while it lasted.

an Art Fair goer stopper. I'd get a kick out of the people who'd pause, do a double take, eyeballing us from a safe distance, discussing amongst their companions if these brash folk are for or against whatever. Some shaking their heads as they moved on. Others, a slow smile warming over a blank stare, step forward, "Nice to see you guys out here."

There'd also be a good deal of interaction between neighboring booths; not all of it amicable. One year the Communist Party of America had issues with us. Eight or so of them began to picket/demonstrate right in front of our booth, making it nearly impossible for us to conduct our business. One young gal in particular took it upon herself to initiate foul-mouthed, blasphemous chants, interspersed with derogatory digs at us personally and the Christian community at large. She had a wild-eyed, disheveled; "oppressed workers of the world" act going on, but she and her "comrades" didn't appear to be winning much sympathy from the throng of fair-goers. For much of the fair, I'd be close at hand to oversee setup and tear-downs and avail myself to give people breaks. The Commie assault was not during my shift, but I was nearby, waiting for them to grow weary and disband having made their point, and like that buzzing, biting horsefly you just can't seem to shake or land a good slap on; they were a persistent, obstinate bunch. A part of me was praying for them but, as the saying goes, "There but for the grace of God go I." Others had tried to engage them in dialogue, but this seemed to only further antagonize them … like throwing apples at a beehive, they just buzzed louder. Another part of me fantasized about walking up and slapping the "red wench" and decking a few comrades. Besides getting me arrested, it seemed a move that would likely be counter-productive to our evangelistic mission … just a delicious thought that briefly crossed my mind. While I wrestled with my emotions, a curious thing happened. Three of the biggest, crew cut, muscular, bulldog tattoo sportin' marines wandered up. These guys were intimidating … reminded me of my old *Sergeant Fury and His Howling Commandos* comics. Standing between our booth and the demonstrators, their gaze rested heavily on the Red Party. One by one our comrade "friends" slinked away like whining little puppies with twitching tails between their legs. The wild-eyed young gal with the Vavoom (cartoon character) foul mouth was the last to slither away. The marines turned, nodded to us, and without a word melted into the crowd. We sat there frozen, speechless, and before any of us could react and give chase to thank them … well like the lone (3 that is) ranger er' angels, they'd since blended into the landscape of art junkies. Hmm, "angels unawares"… (Heb 13:2). I wonder?

Each new year at the Art Fair had its own particular vibe to it. Friends made and fruitful conversations and opportunities to pray with folks gave a *Book of Acts* authenticity to it; one way to jump-start your faith. Real Christianity is not dull. Indeed, our Art Fair evangelism had numerous challenges, but the most irritating hurdle didn't come from the smorgasbord of cult groups, logistics getting in and out, pagans and hucksters, getting just the right blend of booth workers for each shift (male/female, talkative/listener type balance). The most annoying thing was other "Christians," usually of an ultra-conservative or ultra-liberal bent, whose passion for arguing over trivial issues as though they'd have no rest until at least one theological debate in the market square of ideas was in their win column. We had no qualms with honest inquiries, indeed, "…earnestly contend for the faith…." Jude's letter reminds us, but when you're engaged in an exchange with a couple of devotees of Sun Myung Moon aka Moonies, or Guru Maharaj what's his name, suddenly "pre, mid, post-tribulation" debates need to be put on hold, along with the "holiness" issues certain segments of Christendom were obsessed with taking "Jesus People" to task over (hairdos, hemlines, music); I think that about covers it (Col 2:21).

Finally, the Ann Arbor Art Fair was a splendid opportunity for members of our own congregation and a handful of others (even my mom sat behind the booth briefly), to get a taste of, as we said, first-century New Testament Christianity. A month of Wednesday Bible studies were set aside for Christian Apologetics 101 (good for all believers, especially those new to the faith), and an extended Saturday session to review literature, do's and don'ts of working the booth, what to bring, etc. Where else can you, in a three hour booth shift, run into a: Messianic Jew, Mormon, an Agnostic, the ever popular "I'm Catholic end of discussion," a Gurd Jieff devotee, Dead Heads (as in Grateful Dead fanatics), several TMers (transcendental meditation practitioners), a witch, followers of Scientology and Eckancar and a couple of Rastafarians, and way too many comfortably numb yuppies. By fair's end, Saturday evening, the above list may have been considered a slow shift; an exhausting four days to be sure, but spiritually invigorating.

. . . .

Meanwhile, the radio thing was about to take a new spin. First, you'll recall that I'd mentioned Evangelist Stalvey's prophecy (Joe and Ken Hasper will take the Gospel to the city of Detroit), and how this was at least in part realized on the air waves at WMUZ. Another opportunity fell into our laps; a onetime TV show (30 min.) on local programming called *It's Your Turn*. Ken and I hooked up with several other musicians and put together the first (there would be several incarnations) Shalom House Band; kind of a folk-rock vibe. We also played a one-nighter at the old Grande Ballroom (the Detroit House of Prayer Ministry got hold of the building and for a short time sponsored concerts there) ... on stage at a venue I'd been to so many times before (in the audience and typically stoned), now under a whole different set of circumstances. Indeed, a different "Master," and was at times, as you might expect, surreal. But, back to the radio thing, a couple of events put a bit of a damper on the *Shalom Coffee House* show on WMUZ. First, our generous benefactor had fallen on some tough financial times, and no Brinks trucks were pullin' up to *Shalom* on Monday mornings to load up the previous evening's collection to haul to a nearby bank. The burden of a $90 a week radio show was a bit tough, but what was more upsetting was we'd been bumped into a new and later time slot ... around eleven at night ... nothing wrong with that, but the programs following and preceding ours were, how shall I put it – embarrassing. They may not have felt too kindly towards us either. It got to the point where I didn't want to tell folks about our show because I feared they'd tune in early and or listen late and catch Reverend Right (Wrong) and his Miracle Largely Nonsense Crusade.

"Yes, you, you listening tonight ... you in the rocking chair. The Lord is speaking to you right now! Don't hesitate to make that faith offering check out for one hundred dollars ... sow that seed faith friend ... don't let the devil steal your blessing. If you act now, God says He's gonna' multiply that seed gift a hundredfold, but you got to act now, blah, blah, blah." Same kinda' moron stuff you see and hear way too much of today. I always liked the "We're gonna' send you a free tape, book, prayer cloth, oil, whatever with your donation." Free, donation ... hot, cold ... hmm. Upshot, as far as continuing to struggle putting a contemporary music program on the air, we're done. What's the point of struggling financially to put something on the air all the while worrying about it being counter-productive because of the yahoos on before and after you? So be it. Nice while it lasted.

Some of the folks from southwest Detroit involved in ministry and outreach to the heavily Latino population thereabouts sometimes liked to hang out at our Friday night Coffee House. They'd also put together a contemporary music program – *Love Song* – spearheaded by Randy Salazar, that aired on WMZK, F.M. 98, the *Station of the Nations*, serving Detroit's diverse ethnic population. I'd gone down to do an interview for their program and ended up chatting with the station manager. They were looking for someone (program) to fill the after midnight slot. How's about that ... they gave me/Shalom the midnight to 5 a.m. slot several nights a week. At its peak we were running Monday through Friday; we called the show *Nightlight* ... can you believe it. A year earlier we'd had 30 minutes a week on the "Christian" station at $90 a show, and now, a secular station offers us 30 hours at no charge!

Big deal, you say. Who listens to the radio that time a night? You'd be surprised: nursing moms, truckers passin' through town, men and women workin' the "graveyard shift." Best of all, our immediate neighbor to the left of the dial was the new, F.M. classic rock challenger kid on the block, WLLZ. Unbelievable; I couldn't handle five nights a week, so I did a couple of things. Several of us split the week up. Other DJs included Al Blade, Dan Navajar and Rufus Harris. We'd typically do 2 – 3 hours live, music focused, and we had a series of pre-recorded tapes that were updated and rotated from time to time to cover the last couple of hours. How sweet to sit and look out over the city ... the station broadcast from the 20 or 30 something floor of the CNB building aka Penobscot Bldg. on Griswold in downtown Detroit ... knowing that the tunes you're spinning were reaching out to who knows how many folks ... Windsor, Flint, Toledo. One night I let my mom do the weather; she did good being a first timer. If a three hour show was on the table and the munchies hit at 2 a.m., no problem. Put on a live album; say *How the West Was Won* with Phil Keagy and the 2nd Chapter of Acts for example ... grab the elevator, out and down the block to Lafayette Coney Island. A couple of those will keep you awake. When word got out we had all this air time everybody and their brother would send me their demo, 45, album, cassette, new release. Yep, I had lots of "new friends" suddenly. I especially enjoyed doing live shows with Kemper Crabb of *Arkangel*, another co-hosted by Al Kresta and special guest Dr. Walter Martin, author of *The Kingdom of the Cults*. Also, a regular at the *Shalom House* over the years and a natural on the airwaves, James Issac Elliot, whose spontaneity and wit, along with the utter ease with which he would settle into the on-the-air live chair, left me not a little envious. However, once again as ol' George Harrison put it, "all things must pass." For reasons I've long since forgot, WMZK went A.M., which meant for starters, a much smaller potential listening audience. This, along with a dose of burnout and wedding bells dead ahead, meant it was time to call it a day at WMZK; heaven of a run while it lasted.

· · · ·

One or two of you may have been wondering ... hmm, single guy, thirty years old, what's up with that? As I mentioned earlier, never was too keen for the dating game, bit awkward as you might expect, pastor and all that. Also, the sometimes well-meaninged, I suppose, but annoying attempts at "setting me up" with so and so ... she'd make the perfect pastor's wife (that would be thrilling since I'm far from perfect), and the proverbial – you know you really should get married if you want to be a more effective pastor – and similar comments from, ironically, persons who were married and often wished they were single. I stayed busy enough to keep the whole dating thing at arm's length, but on occasion I grew lonely for female companionship of something more than the sister-in-the-Lord, buddy type. On more than one occasion I had to reckon with the sin of covetousness while viewing with envy one of the men of the congregation who was married to that beautiful woman ... kids, home, 9 to 5 gig ... how nice it'd be. I suppose I adopted a bit of a fatalistic approach to the whole issue: dating should be between believers, and like all aspects of our lives it was to be Christ-centered, which meant, among other things, physical intimacy was reserved for the marriage bed. As for playing-the-field, well, as we used to say and perhaps it was just a cop-out, a cover for awkwardness, "Adam didn't have to go beatin' the bushes lookin' for Eve, God brought her to him. So, be about the Master's business, don't get caught up in worldly schemes of romance and love and, well, be patient and it will all work out somehow."

At one point a bit of a scandal ignited as some frustrated "sisters," chastised for dating non-Christian men, boldly retorted that there was an utter lack of eligible Christian men; eligible as in suitable husband material ... "so what do you expect us to do" the womenfolk protested? Some of our disgruntled "sisters" went so far as to comprise a list of eligible Shalom bachelors along with a rating based on a set of desirable qualities women looked for in that special man including financial security! I'm not sure if I even made the list, but if I did, living in the old pop/beer bottle storage room on a hundred bucks a week salary ... yeah, I probably didn't even make the list. Eventually, both sides were able to laugh about it while recognizing that this was a legitimate area of concern that needed addressing. I felt ill equipped in these matters, but again, had the good fortune of having built contacts along the journey with folks like Beth and Paul Patton, who presented workshops and spent time chatting with brothers and sisters concerning these and other like needs.

Once I'd directed a young high school aged fella to Paul for counsel whose story 'bout broke your heart mixed with a dose of anger. Bit of a nerd I guess ... bullied at school ... acne, you know what I mean. Loved Jesus and hangin' around Shalom where a few of the older brothers had taken him under their wing. One day he privately, nervousness written all over him, approached me with one of those delicate matters each man must square off against ... no, not the neighborhood bully, though that also seems to be part of the right-of-passage one must hurdle, not this time ... today it was girl issues ... actually as in lack of, and he wanted Pastor Joe (the guy who doesn't date), to clue him in. He had his eye on a young gal who'd been attending *Shalom*, but didn't know how to go about asking her out. That he was terribly shy would be an understatement. After a bit of a pep talk and prayer, we decided that at next Friday's Coffee House, which she usually attended, he'd ask her if she'd like to go out for a bite afterwards; many of us used to go up to the Ram's Horn at Telegraph and Van Born.

A couple weeks later, a downcast, lost- my-best-friend looking brother wandered back into my office.

"Hey, bro how'd it go? Did you talk to her?"

"Yeah."

"Well?"

With a faint smile that really didn't hide very well the teenage angst of opposite sex rejection, he whispered she'd turned him down. "I asked her if she'd like to grab something to eat after the concert like you'd

153

suggested. She said she had to be home by 11:30 and that wouldn't work."

"So, that was it?"

"Not exactly, I asked if maybe she'd like to check out a movie, concert or something ... she said no thanks ... also, as far as dating goes, that she was believing and waiting for God's best."

My jaw dropped. At that point I just put my arm around him. "Let's go down to Daly's and get a couple foot-longs. Hey, man, that's only strike one."

In time, I did hook up with a young lady, the gal who accompanied me to downtown Detroit that night to rescue our backslidden stripper friend. Our relationship was precarious from the start. She was divorced and had a young son. In time, as our relationship moved in the direction of engagement, my conviction that divorce and remarriage were not compatible with New Testament principles was now put to the test (Mt 5:32); could I, if we married, continue to pastor under those circumstances? Often, when faced with difficult decisions, moral dilemmas of one fashion or another, people will bounce like a pinball from one person to the next until they find someone who'll tell them what they want to hear, not what they need to hear. Same kinda' thing when you visit your local Christian bookstore, searching for that tape or book that will provide some direction. Pick a subject. You'll find some author, denomination, group, whatever, who'll provide you with an answer your flesh craves. This is sometimes difficult to discern because one may genuinely lack knowledge or hold an erroneous belief. I'd researched the divorce/remarriage issue before, for others, in my capacity as pastor ... now the shoe was on the other foot ... mine ... can I handle the medicine I'd been dishin' out? Hard as I looked, and there were plenty of authors who offered this and that loophole, nagging doubts always loomed in the divorce/remarriage shadows. On top of that were other concerns regarding my ability to financially care for a wife and son ... also, could I give proper love and affection to a child not biologically mine? In spite of these serious misgivings it looked more and more like we were bound for the altar. By then we'd fallen into that rut, that mistake so many couples get mired in. Our relationship took on a more physically intimate dimension I'd believed, heck, preached and taught, was reserved for married couples only. It's like quicksand, almost impossible to break free from. Nothing drains you spiritually more quickly than a relationship that crosses the line

154

of physical intimacy. She was my first love (as in a woman I seriously considered "tying the knot" with); no offense Michelle – my third grade sweetie.

This young woman taught me some wonderful lessons; one in humility that makes the red creep up from beneath my collar to this day. It was one of those days custom made for a day outdoors. We decided on a picnic at a local swimming hole, gravel pit turned beach it may have been, down Trenton way. First time to this place for me, and now, as I relive it in my mind's eye, could it have been that I was being set up all along for one of life's most embarrassing moments? No. I believe the whole affair to have been spontaneous; little consolation, however, at the time. There, situated at shore's edge where a bright sign heralded swimmers and divers alike of an immediate drop off, stood a wooden, ancient ziggurat-like structure, with three diving platforms; the top one was for jumping, and the tower itself was staffed with several life guard attendants to ensure the brave and foolhardy weren't jumping on top of each other, and met certain age requirements and so on. This happened to be the area where most folks spread their beach blankets and lounge chairs, and when not busy lathering themselves in Coppertone, or absorbed in some summertime romance novel reading, could enjoy and applaud first one then another dive, leap and so forth from the tower leaning out over the water like some ancient willow. The third (highest) level, from the ground at least, looked to be the height of a telephone pole, and only the occasional jumper risked so daring a feat. Several times couples had jumped together. This always got the crowd's attention, and when the daring duo surfaced following their "lovers' leap," as often as not they'd be greeted by cheers, whistles and applause once their heads safely bobbed above the surface.

"Let's do it," Monta said suddenly, a faint hint of challenge in her voice.

"Well, um ... ok." No big deal. I can swim well enough and have jumped out of my share of trees, off garage tops in Redford Township, and high dives on Union Lake (10 feet high); this should be elementary my dear, but why was there no sage Watson or Sherlock Holmes at the top of the platform to talk us out of it, and why is it, once you're up there, when there's no turning back, does it now seem like you're six stories up?

It was our turn. The attendants had given the all clear below. We walked to the edge, hand-in-hand. All eyes gazed upwards and an awkward silence seemed to bring everything to a standstill. I hoped my date didn't notice my shaking or the cool clammy grip I had on her hand. Then, totally unexpected, Monta let go of my hand, smiled and sprang off the third level of the platform and executed a twisting, turning, triple somersault, and just before impact, opened up and entered the water with nary a ripple. The crowd went wild. It was a 9.7 or better. I had no idea she could dive, nor had I long to reflect on what just transpired. It quickly grew silent again. Looking down, I could see she'd casually swam to a safe distance, and was now softly treading water, smiling devilishly up at me ... the crowd again grew silent ... I knew what they were thinking ... wow, if that's what she can do, this guy must really be somethin' ... Tarzan (Johnny Weismuller) off the Brooklyn Bridge in *Tarzan's New York Adventure* stuff. No doubt I was turning redder than the chubby dude on a towel who'd forgotten or just didn't care to use any skin protection, and who's white pale skin of three hours ago now shown crimson. I jumped. Hands raised over my head, doing my best to extend my toes and not land flatfooted. I cut through the water like an orca and remained submerged, stroking underwater with everything I had, searching for mental images of Lloyd Bridges in a thrilling *Sea Hunt* episode for encouragement, so that come what may, I would not surface within easy hearing distance of the jeers and laughter I knew awaited me when I broke the surface, like some kid's red and white bobber after several good yanks have freed it from a hidden underwater stump. Thankfully, a late afternoon shower sent us and everyone else packing, but not before half a dozen admirers stopped by our beach blanket to compliment Monta on what had to be, they exclaimed, "the best dive of the season thus far."

"No doubt," Pastor Joe grudgingly nodded.

Unfortunately I suppose, can't say as I haven't wondered "what if" some days, but the relationship came to be more than I could deal with. The issues loomed large and menacing and I initiated a break-up; a "clean break." She went her way and I picked up my own emotional pieces, sought forgiveness and spiritual renewal, and pressed on with my pastoral responsibilities. I think about her from time to time; hope she's well.

. . . .

Wouldn't you know it, six months later and history sure enough looks like it's repeating itself. I've said I didn't date ... well much, and that's true enough, but when I did take a fancy to a young lady, well, I guess it was time to make up for lost time. My first date with Bonnie was either Christmas or Christmas Eve. I remember because we had difficulty finding an open restaurant and ended up at a Chinese place near Ford Road and Telegraph; didn't seem right to take her out in my been-around-the-block too many times, red and white Ford pickup. So I borrowed our radio sponsor's sharp yellow sports car. It did dawn on me half-way through the evening that this slick move was destined to backfire. If the night was a success and a follow-up date agreed to, what was I supposed to do, borrow the sports car again? Well, it did go okay and she turned out to be the kind of gal who didn't especially care if I drove a fancy sports car or battered pickup.

Again, I was smitten ... infatuated. She had a little girl, but had never been married, so the obstacle that haunted my previous relationship (divorce/remarriage) would not be an iceberg dead ahead undermining wedding bells should they be in the cards. Physical displays of affection (okay, I mean necking), were largely kept in check as both of us were determined to get it right this time, and save for the wedding night that gift of God wherein man and woman become one flesh. After a couple of months it was "take her up to engagement speed Scotty" mode, and then, some of the same old doubts and fears that plagued my previous relationship came knocking. Financial concerns and could I be a proper dad for this little one? Panic took hold ... deja-vu ... and locked the brakes up on another "what if" romance; as in "breaking up is hard to do," as Neil Sedaka put it. I likely didn't communicate very well the misgivings I'd found myself mired in, and, I suspect she became vulnerable to a guy waiting in the wings for just this moment. Right about the time I'm thinking about giving her a call and seeing where we're at concerning "us," she took up with what's-his-name. You stoics would have been proud of me. No tears ... probably just as well ... didn't take her long to forget me. Yeah right. It hurt. She was my second love. I wonder how she's doing. Does she ever think of me?

Geez, maybe I'm called to be single. Some months later I heard that Mary, the woman whose husband did the falling tree act in the middle of a Sunday night service, had separated from him and was living in a one horse town northwest of Ann Arbor, Gregory; a pleasant hour drive from Dearborn Heights. Think I'll drop in on her, rather sidestepping the "now why would you wanna' do that Joe," question bouncing off the walls of my mind. She was such a lovely gal, beautiful spirit, my arms ached to hold and be held by someone like her. If ever there was a woman who had grounds for divorce I thought privately … and a couple of kids. Do you see a pattern here? I'd become so smitten with her that I'd made up my mind that if it came to it (marriage that is), I'd leave the pastorate, take an active lay person role at some church, pick up a "straight" gig as a bricklayer perhaps, and hope our souls would not be forfeited to Beelzebub. You may be thinking, "Good heavens, all this after one visit?" Of course not, it was after the second (just kidding). It would take several months for me to be ready to broach the subject. I recall our first real date at a movie theater in Milford for the premier of *Rocky 1,* and thinking, as I tried to casually ease my arm over her shoulder, that if Rocky and Adrian can get past the deck stacked against them (the loveable Pauli, Adrian's rough around the edges brother for starters), surely we could make a go of it. One problem … actually quite a few posers, but one loomed more menacing than the others. She didn't seem to feel the same way about me as I felt about her, and/or she was so conflicted about seeing someone while "technically" still married that it was too much for her to emotionally manage. Anyway, yours truly, the great communicator (not), strikes again. There seemed to exist too many real or imaginary, probably a bit of both, walls between us that I lacked the strength and she the will to tear down. I'm making assumptions here in her regard; my assumptions proving correct batting average then and now is pretty pathetic by the way. As pastor and you may be asking what on earth are you doing seeing a "technically" married woman? And that would be a good question … maybe sometime later … let me try again … as pastor and custodian of the unofficial Shalomite manifesto for all things relational, it seemed prudent to us at *Shalom,* that it made little sense to "seriously" date someone who would/could not be considered a suitable marriage candidate. I'm not referring to social dating, brother and sister in the Lord kinda' stuff, group of mixed couples hangin' at hayrides, concerts, bowling and so on; dating non-believers was discouraged. The relationship road I now tread, like Sam, Frodo and Gollum picking their way cautiously through the Dead Marshes was as the name suggests, dangerous. The pain of perceived or imagined rejection was more than I could reckon with. Strike three! And with bowed head trudged toward the dugout of single man blues despair pulled from the game still again. Mary continues to occupy a piece of my heart.

. . . .

The greatest threat to Shalom's existence during the "Beech Daly Years" was not external per se, but internal. Somewhere in the neighborhood of '76/'77 we'd embraced the popular Shepherding[20] movement sweeping primarily through charismatic communities/churches across the land. Down South, my old "Tent" church home had regrettably undergone a church split, with half the members staying put under Evangelist Stalvey's continued leadership at *World on Fire Revivals*, the other half, mostly younger folks, followed under-shepherd to Herman, Lance Fedick, and set out to establish their own church community. The latter group, like us, had also welcomed "shepherding." Some of the movement's prime American movers and shakers were based out of Fort Lauderdale (down the road from Vero Beach). How much, if any, the shepherding teaching contributed to their split I couldn't say, but I maintained relationships with both groups. However, I felt more of a spiritual kinship with the break-away group that had taken this "shepherding" direction and in turn that helped strengthened my resolve to pursue a similar route. Publications like *New Wine* and *New Covenant*, the latter a local publication published by the nearby *Word of God Community* in Ann Arbor, became a sort of catechism manual for all things "spiritual headship." The whole concept appeared like an answer to prayer. It hadn't taken me long as a pastor to grow frustrated at the "flock's" lack of spiritual progress (could be a reflection on me, I suppose). We seemed to be forever wallowing in the playpen of spiritual babes in Christ. This then, would be the cure for our stunted spiritual growth, especially that insidious rebellious nature we'd dragged along behind us from our counterculture tour of duty ... question everything ... trust no one over

---

[20] Shepherding (sometimes called the "Discipleship Movement") was an influential and controversial movement within some British and American charismatic churches, emerging in the 1970's. The teachings of the movement emphasized the "one another" passages of the New Testament, and the mentoring relationship prescribed by the Apostle Paul in 2 Tm 2:2. Buzz words: elder, headship, submission and covering.

thirty. And so, we set out to divide up the members of the congregation, assigning persons and households to various elders whose responsibility it would be to oversee their spiritual growth. This meant, among other things, we had to know with certainty who our members were. We had no formal membership up to this point. Something we'd have eventually gotten around to, but now, for sanity, organization and accountability sake, I/we, the Board, wanted to know who we could count on and who was counting on us. Initially I'd been more interested in discipling new converts, but in addition, and often contributing to the relationship crisis within the congregation ... people moving in and out wherever the winds blew ... shopping for a wife/husband ... disgruntled or no longer able to tolerate some crisis in full vigor where they'd previously cast their lot ... running from church discipline. Don't mean to lump everyone who moves on to a new church in the same basket. I've known and personally encouraged some of our own congregation to prayerfully consider God's plan for them may mean leaving *Shalom*. Okay, I admit it, there were a few I privately hinted around at, suggested, we and they would probably be a lot better off if they fellowshipped elsewhere. Indeed, at times we had so many musicians in our stable that if they were frustrated by a lack of playing/ministering time, I knew of places in the metro area wearying heaven with the plea, "Lord, send us some musicians." On occasion that's exactly what happened. Funny thing, there always seemed to be two or three more ready to take up the slack. I'd go so far as to argue that in some cases some of our new members came to us from other congregations in answer to our prayers. The Duncan family, as mentioned earlier, fit this description; after all there is a sense in which we were all one Body and if a congregation down the street had a need we could fill, and vice versa, good deal.

Still, too many folks just seemed to be drifting aimlessly, undisciplined, anticipating the so-called Rapture at any moment ... so, why make long range plans/commitments? I anticipated that shepherding would cure a good deal of what ails them.

Now, when brother or sister so-and-so are struggling spiritually, the first place to look for the culprit behind said condition was that most devious, pernicious of fleshly weaknesses (some referred to it as a spirit, not in the demonic sense, but, "you have a spirit of lust, anger, whatever"), rebelliousness- spiritual growth enemy number one. And, at some level gotten out from under their "covering" (care of the assigned spiritual mentor-elder, pastor, husband, etc.), which left them particularly vulnerable to that three- pronged assault: the world, the flesh and the devil.

Shepherding, at least in the manner in which we and a good many others utilized it, rather than that elusive spiritual miracle salve that would lead us into greener pastures, turned out to be nothing more than "spiritual" snake oil. In some cases, people's lives, their families were blown sky high and left to rot in a spiritual no-man's land. *Shalom* had come late to this "party" and slow to hit the dance floor, but we could see what was happening in and around us, in addition to ill tidings carried on the winds from afar. We may not have been in over our heads yet, but we were knee deep and heading that way. We were spared some of the trauma other communities experienced who had been "shepherding" months before us.

The alarm was sounded both within Shalom by some discerning brothers, and voices without were likewise warning the Body of Christ to put on the brakes and take heed. What at first appeared to be a solid, scriptural sound strategy for energizing local expressions of the Body of Christ, quickly took on the nature of a cult; power and control trips. Especially disturbing was the manner in which persons in various degrees of spiritual authority were usurping the sacred relationship between husbands and wives, children and parents. Could it be that we who were called to strengthen and build up God-fearing families were inadvertently tearing them asunder? Frightening thought, likewise, the manner in which spiritual heads/coverings would hear the voice of God for someone rather than with them. In reality, the movement as largely practiced couldn't help but lead to a "dumbing down" spirituality, the very thing it sought to remedy, and some men, many with sincere and honest intent howbeit misguided, put themselves into positions of authority no less dangerous for themselves than for those they'd lord it over (1 Pt 5:3).

For my part, I was slow to respond to the alarm, and some took this as a sign of an unwillingness to abandon this approach, others going so far as to describe the whole shepherding movement as demonic and left *Shalom* for greener pastures. I was not entirely persuaded that shepherding in general was heretical … unhealthy, but a tool like any other, which may be employed for good or evil. Historically, at least in monastic institutions, arguably the bedrock of western civilization, with their emphasis on obedience to the rule, a form of shepherding it seems to me, had been used largely to good affect. Perhaps we were using shepherding after the manner of inappropriate use of spiritual gifts which the Apostle Paul addresses in his letter to the Corinthian believers ... don't stop using spiritual gifts, but adopt such guidelines so that these gifts edify, not tear down. Perhaps, I reasoned, it's the same with shepherding. We simply need to tweak it here and there, not abandon it, and throw out the baby with the bathwater as it were.

The tide of resentment, confusion and fear of lingering in perceived "cult" waters tipped the scales of my mind. I didn't want to lose any more people, and so, we washed our hands of the whole shepherding business. Problem now was that we swung back to the everybody largely doing their own thing, and any exercise of spiritual authority, submitting one to another, church discipline, was too often written off as that shepherding snake trying to wiggle its way back in.

· · · ·

"God, you know my heart. I never got into this for the money, but can't you loosen up those heavenly purse strings some." It seemed like we were always struggling to keep our heads financially above water. Keeps you on your knees I suppose, but we'd long since outgrown this old storefront. Light, sound and recording equipment were a constant fixture on our needs list. I'd read a wonderful book on the life of George Mueller, a nineteenth century Brethren minister, who'd himself been profoundly influenced by the Pietism[21] movement, and his work with orphans in Bristol, England. He and his wife never asked for money nor would they accept any government and/or strings-attached donations. Instead of soliciting funds, they would in prayer present their needs and petitions before God, and trust in Him to provide their every need. Mind you, we're talking two thousand plus orphans here. Sometimes with not enough provision to see them into tomorrow! His story is full of countless examples of God doing just that, providing every need, and Pastor Mueller not so much as breathing a word of how the needs were often urgent and

---

[21]   A revival moment in Protestantism (18th cent.) that stressed prayer, reading of the Bible, religious experience, and committed Christian life in small communities.

162

seemingly insurmountable. How many radio/televangelists need to read his story and "sober" up? You don't need to hawk little green cloths, water from the Jordan and miracle anointing salve to keep your ministry afloat … that is if it should stay afloat. Anyway, back to Shalom and it's time to put up or shut up. As much as I admired Mueller, his work and his approach to secure financial support, we let our needs be known in what struck us as both scripturally appropriate and prudent, and usually to committed members only. No bingo nights, seed-faith, arm-twisting, solicited donations, or name-it-and-claim-it drivel to bolster our funds. I'd rather just call it a day. Still, we always seemed to get by, and with free air time on WMZK we didn't need to waste precious "on air" minutes soliciting dollars for our "faith" program because we didn't have enough faith that God would meet the need. Still, some days financial issues troubled me to no end. I wrestled with one of those seven deadlies – envy, when I'd visit a place like *Calvary Chapel* in Costa Mesa, California, or see a sharp looking mailing from the *Adam's Apple* in Ft. Wayne, Indiana, or the *Salt Company* in West Detroit … the big talent … big budgets. Of course size and almost unlimited resources doesn't necessarily translate into guaranteed success, and indeed, has its own hazards. Staying hungry did keep us in prayer 24/7 and I must say, it was an adventure.

· · · ·

God provided for my medical needs during the "lean" years (c.70/80s) in some unusual and at times, amusing ways. Following are two of the more memorable. I hope that my circumstances during these pastoral years didn't betray an irresponsibility on my part, as in adequate health care coverage, but in those especially early years we were nickel and dimein' it, and when you're young and in good health, barring some accident, one may feel a certain invincibleness. Upshot, I'm depending on the Lord should something out of the ordinary come up … and wouldn't you know it….

Could there be a worse time to be afflicted with a toothache than New Year's Eve evening. The throbbing starts slow and uneven and in no time morphs into a steady relentless pounding, and I'm thinkin' I'm gonna shoot myself. I wearied heaven with pleas for relief, but it seemed like for now, ol' Joe may have needed a little chastisement. I'd heard dousing said tooth with whiskey would ease the pain. "I'm not gonna make it two days

(January 2, my birthday incidentally), "I muttered over and over, assuming no dental office will be open until after the holiday. "Maybe I should just pull the damn thing myself." Wasn't there a *Three Stooges Episode* like this?

I never did like whiskey … abominable stuff, but desperation won out, and with a fifth of Jameson Irish Whiskey under my arm raced home to procure my only viable option at this point. Well, it didn't work. I gargled, swished, and doused the area and then some, all to no avail. Frustrated, I tried to knock myself out and slowly chugged the rest, and I'm basically a teetotaler at this time. Dumb, I know … lucky, er blessed it didn't kill me. You who have endured a terrible toothache can empathize with me. We can laugh now but at the time it's no joke.

I had been seeing a dentist in nearby Dearborn for periodic cleanings and up till now had been spared the need for fillings and such. Selden Skelly, my dentist, was quite a character. I'm guessin' he had seven or eight years on me, a "hip" Jew as in unorthodox, who, knowing I was a preacher just getting by, enjoyed cracking jokes pertaining to all things preachers/religion, while I, sitting in the chair could only nod, grunt and roll my eyes at his unsanctified attempts at humor. Why do dentists (dental hygienists) try to carry on conversations with you all the while fingers, instruments and tubes, drills whirling in one's mouth, hardly able to swallow let alone discuss the Tiger's bid for a championship or Crosby, Stills and Nash latest release? Upshot, with an utter matter of factness Dr. Skelly declared, "My lad, you need a root-canal." I immediately nodded a grim ascent as I'd do just about anything to rid myself of this tooth migraine. Now as he and his assistant who he jokingly referred to as the "Virgin Mary," no doubt to rile me, in vain I should like to add, went to work, I had a new problem to confront. How am I going to pay for this? No insurance, ten bucks in my wallet, no credit card … maybe they'll work out some kind of payment plan; so embarrassing.

An hour later Dr. Skelly pushed his chair back, removed his gloves and mask, and with a slight smile not entirely masking the seriousness of his tone quipped, "Hey Rev, no charge … say a few prayers for me." Before it all sank in, Dr. Skelly, like the Lone Ranger, quickly disappeared to tend his next patient.

• • • •

"What the...." A small lump just above the hairline on my forehead appeared suddenly out of nowhere. I first noticed it following a shower where/when it slightly protruded through my wet scalp. I paid it little notice. It didn't hurt and with my hair dried and combed, it was no longer discernible. "Just a knot on the head that will disappear shortly" I mused. Except it didn't, but was growing, and as the months peeled off what I now suspected to be a cist of some sort became increasingly noticeable. Also, the hair in that area, nickel size, fell out. My barber confirmed after several visits that indeed, whatever it is, it's growing.

While on sabbatical from Shalom down in Florida, I spent a good deal of time with Tim and Nancy Meyer. One day after an ocean swim, Tim noticed the "lump" on my head. "A cist of some sort ... I'm not sure what to do about it ... I've prayed but...." A wry smile crept across Tim's mug as he volunteered to flatten it with a two by four. He no doubt would have enjoyed it too. "Thanks, but no thanks."

Jennifer Brown, a young girl from Tim and Nancy's church, had a pediatrics practice in nearby Fort Pierce, Florida, and offered to take a look. No doubt I was her largest patient, laying there on the examination table with most of me dangling from both ends. "Yep, you've got a cist. I'll have it out in a jiff." While she carefully shaved the area and numbed it up, the anxiety of how am I going to cover this tab grabbed hold. A small incision and in no time there it sat, in a small petri dish, a yellow white, robin's egg sized cist. A few sutures later and she smiled warmly and said, "This one's for free. God be with you."

Yes, God provided for me during those lean pastoral years in many wonderful and diverse ways. Oh yeah, even the hair grew back in that area ... fortunately.

. . . .

It was time to move on from the old 3852 Beech Daly location. We got a bit of an unexpected nudge out the door. One evening several of us were "hangin'" in the chapel area when that sickening sound of screeching (brakes locked up), right outside on Beech Daly made you involuntarily grip something as you tensed up waiting for impact ... just waiting for someone to get rear-ended or broadsided.

"Bam!"

The building shook and the front end of a car made its own doorway

165

and sat halfway inside the front of the chapel. Fortunately no one in the vehicle or chapel was seriously injured; shook up a bit's all. Yep, time to hit the road.

Our official last night at the Beech Daly location was March 30, 1979, with perhaps our biggest crowd. Left the front door open (for air) and so folks who couldn't squeeze in, could hang out front and at least hear the music. Members of *God's Graffitti*[22], along with Jan Krist, Jan Mohl and Sue Love saw to it that we went out with a spiritual rockin' revival bang.

. . . .

The next two years saw us evolve into something of a gypsy church. A couple of miles east of our old location sat a Baptist Church that for reasons not entirely clear, had seen its membership wither away to a fraction of what it had been during its heyday. They agreed to rent us the seldom used adjoining fellowship hall that could nicely accommodate us at a reasonable rate. Large basement with classrooms and bathrooms meant we could continue and expand our nursery and Sunday school needs. Sunday evening worship, Friday concerts and midweek Bible study ensured business would continue as usual; well sort of.

During the warm months it was necessary to keep the windows open. In Inkster, noise concerns had never been an issue as residential dwellings were largely out of ear-shot or didn't care. Not the case here. Howdy neighbor! We're the first Church of Rock and Roll so hold onto your seat. Our Sunday services could get a bit noisy to say nothing of a full blown Friday night concert with featured groups like Servant (think REO Speedwagon for Jesus intensity and volume). The neighbors weren't too keen about all this. Also, the current pastor of the church we were renting from was, how shall I say it, odd! He ran a hypnosis clinic out of the basement of the fellowship hall during the day. We weren't too crazy about all that … too close to mind control occult techniques; taboo with most of us. Prior to our services at the new location, I'd make it a point to

---

[22] A group of Shalom musicians, some solo, some groups, sometimes all together, including: Debbie Ordus, Dawn Baird, Maureen Siler, Ken Hasper, Joe Shannon, Ken Pore, and Living Water – Roy Horton, Keith Savoie, and Al Blade.

be the first one to open up the facility for *Shalom's* use so I could stash all Dr. Rev. So and So's hypnotic clinic signs where no one might see them and get the idea it was something we promoted. For personal living quarters, I and my buddy Keith Savoie moved into a friend's mom's place, Glen Kough, on Culver near Oakwood in nearby Dearborn.

Little amusing side note – the house I mentioned above, a "brother's" mother owned and she was often out-of-town. Keith and I basically lived (slept) in the nicely finished basement, and made some use of the upstairs kitchen and family room with fireplace area. There was another boarder, a friend of the family, Sandra, often on the go, worked long hours, we rarely saw her … yes, her! She lived upstairs and it never was a big deal but provided a few amusing moments, as in when someone would stop over on church business and she might beat me to the door, and she just happened to be home at the time, in her dainty (small) sunbathing outfit and glass of Chablis in hand, lookin' like the model on the cover of a magazine. "Joe, you have callers … I'll be out back catching some sun … there's some leftovers in the fridge," she'd innocently holler. What could I say; sometimes you just have to laugh. I don't recall any ugly rumors being generated on account of our temporary awkward living situation, and it was kinda' nice having a woman 'round the house from time to time.

We'd just gotten settled into what we fondly referred to as Baptist Acres (several months), when suddenly we were told we'd have to leave. "You've got two weeks!" Two weeks! I went to their next board meeting looking for some answers for which I got the proverbial run-around. I ended up verbally chastising them for giving us such a short notice; we had no formal rental agreement.

"Not the way to treat anybody let alone brothers and sisters in Christ." I gave them my best you're disgusting look that implied, "No wonder your sanctuary is vacant Sunday mornings." I walked out, shook the dust off my feet and spat for good measure. Turns out neighbor complaints and a better rental arrangement with an Amway group were our undoing. Two weeks! That's on their conscience.

Now what? Two weeks to come up with something. I'd been using the weight training room at the YMCA near Ford Road and Evergreen. We approached the director who was altogether receptive to the idea of renting us the cafeteria area and a small adjacent room for child care on Sunday evenings. Great location but it meant that for now we'd have to suspend our Friday evening outreach/music programs. A brother in Christ, Jim Frazer, gave us use of his day care facility on Ford Road between Beech Daly and Inkster roads for midweek bible studies; same folks who owned Real Life Day Camp out on Geddes Road in Canton where we held our annual hayride/foot stompin' barn concerts.

Meeting at the Y meant a substantial amount of set up/tear down time. We were a portable (gypsy) church; many of you can empathize with that. When you're using someone else's facility, you often feel like you're walking on eggshells and take extra care to leave the place cleaner than you found it.

The motivation for finding a permanent church home moved from the back burner to the front. While I didn't think the Y, even if we eventually out-stayed our welcome, would give us a mere two weeks to make other arrangements as our former "Christian" landlords had, the whole setup was unsettling when cast alongside our vision for church growth and development. There were a few naysayers, but most Shalomites, I foremost among them, wanted a place we could call our own. Easy enough to understand if you and your family have rented an apartment/home and dreamed of owning your own place someday. How you'd fix/decorate it … landscape, kid's rooms. So the search was on, and with a committed group of 50 plus adults and legions of kids from newborns through teens; it didn't seem an unreasonable undertaking.

. . . .

Before you pronounce me daft, provided you haven't already, let me say one final, we can only hope, thing about the "dating game;" no, not the popular TV show … I think I watched it in full twice, years ago … got to where I couldn't watch the end and the cameraman's close-ups of those utterly rejected looking (which they were) contestants who hadn't made the grade. Why I avoid most reality shows today. "Okay you, pack it up and don't let the door hit you on the way out … I've seen better dances from chickens who's heads have been cleaved from their torsos … and you, how pathetic … forty-four years of age, insurance appraiser and not as smart as a fifth grader." Could it be I wonder, if we're slowly marching back to find our seat amongst those Romans who had nothing better to do than spend an afternoon at the Coliseum drinking wine and being amused by bloody gladiatorial battles, and "oh splendid, a crucifixion is on today's card." Hmm, dating and gladiators, how'd I get here, connection perhaps? Anyway, I'm about to launch into an account of my fourth and most significant, successful (I wonder), courtship. And yet, I've gone on and on (perhaps some denial issues from the past lurking below the surface) as to how I did not date. Well I didn't really, again, not in the casual manner with which most seem to undertake it. I hope, by the way, when I next check my emails, I shan't find one or more, "Hey Joe, remember me? … How 'bout the night we went out to the billiards hall on Schoolcraft and then to MaMa Mia's Pizza place at Grand River and Beech Daly? Well, how about it?" I shan't be holding my breath … on with it already.

During *Shalom's* "gypsy" sojourn, I'd taken a fancy for a young gal who'd hang at the *Shalom Coffee House* back in Inkster, and who'd graduated from Edsel Ford and currently attended Oakland University. Following high school graduation I didn't see her as much, although she still dropped in from time to time during home visits on weekends. She and a group of friends had joined us for one of our Tomahawk Lake camp-outs. One afternoon at the beach, I casually approached her about going for a swim … out to a little island 100 yards off shore. "No thanks," she quipped. Hmm, not sure what to make of that? Likely a good thing anyway as later I'd discover in the water she was a lot more like Jane than I Tarzan. Highly probable I'd been spared another one of life's most embarrassing moments (recall the diving platform).

Months later she surprised me by accepting an invitation to attend a 2nd Chapter of Acts concert at EMU's Pease Auditorium. Well, I was fairly smitten with her. However, I didn't expect much to come of it. Nothing so grand ever crosses my path. If you're not getting my drift here, I'm referring to the "Eve" God may one day bring into my life … is this the one.

The obstacles were nothing to sneeze at. First, a ten year age difference, which of course when you're "in love" you dismiss as no big thing, and any bumps in the road as a result are usually the stuff of good natured jokes and funny little awkward moments. For instance, whenever we talked about the Beatles. Once we went on a date to Beatlemania at Detroit's Music Hall, we had to confine our, you know trying to make a favorable impression, bit nervous perhaps conversation to Beatle's music from the *White Album era* on! "Good heavens," you say. Indeed I do. It would be just one, some small, insignificant example of just how far apart in years we were. She was too young to have firsthand experience of the "British Invasion," any Beatle's music prior to '68 … 5 years old! I suppose being with her made me feel younger; perhaps that's a good deal of what it was all about (at least in my only slightly sanctified mind). She was pretty, long gorgeous locks like Rapunzel, athletic, outdoorsy, seemed to be serious in her desire to follow Jesus … and not, I repeat, not "mousy"; a quality I could not tolerate. Oh, and I also enjoyed the paybacks I could give my (aged) buddies who'd been married awhile to women more their age. I choose not to elaborate. You figure it out.

My spiritual walk at this time was taking some pretty stiff "body shots"; six, seven years of pastoring under my belt, late twenties, and already some early burnout symptoms beginning to surface. My whole life since '74 revolved 24/7 around *Shalom* … ministry … what little personal social life I enjoyed was largely confined to the "fishbowl" environment of a pastor's life. Troubled also about not spending more time with my own immediate family, but then I was being about the Master's business, or so I reasoned. Even more alarming, actually two things … dark, intense, almost paralyzing struggles with unbelief, and regrettably, one day I found myself in the arms of a married woman, a member of the congregation. Spiritually, I'd done more than just shoot myself in the foot.

· · · ·

I'd had bouts with unbelief before. This was different and in part fueled by my disappointment, heart wrenching loss of several members (all young) of our congregation.

Kimmy Murdock was a cute little girl; reminded me of Shirley Temple. She was killed while retrieving a ball on Six Mile Road in Livonia. The young driver never slowed down; just swerved to avoid some kid … the kid jumped … the wrong way … she was briefly on life support. I recall singing at her funeral. We all knew she was with Jesus and in good time we'd laugh together again, but for the present, when you gazed into the grieving eyes of those parents … the hurt.

Pat Duggan was a young man who'd been attending Shalom for several years along with his wife Pam and little girl. One day, on a pastoral visit to their home in Lincoln Park, I couldn't help but notice a fair sized amount of martial arts awards on display. Never would I have suspected this guy was a skilled, respected martial artist. He was so laid back …

small in stature but stout. I'd been looking for something to do to stay in shape. Pat encouraged me to think about martial arts (his style was Chung Do Kwan, a Tae Kwon Do discipline). He took me to a club on Schaefer, north of Michigan Avenue in Dearborn, where some of his old associates had opened a school (Pat himself had not trained for several years). We also had some serious discussions regarding the philosophy behind martial arts (primarily Asian), and would practicing Tae Kwon Do compromise my allegiance to Christianity. Pat never embraced some of the questionable (for us at least) philosophical/religious components undergirding some aspects of Asian martial arts; both of us viewed it rather as an excellent cardio workout wherein you actually learned something – self-defense, which might come in handy some day. Anyway, I'd grown bored with racquetball and doing mindless aerobic moves to pulsating disco music with sweating Richard Simmons types squeezed into comical, unflattering outfits (legwarmers) that held no appeal for me.

In no time at all, here I go, thirty years old, putting on a gee (uniform) for the first time, trying to tie this white belt (beginner) around my waist, while keeping a wary eye on a slender young woman, brown belt strapped around her narrow waist, executing moves I know in my wildest imaginings I'll never approach. Oh well, I'm here to get a good workout and learn something, not square off against Bruce Lee.

The place Pat introduced me to, like many martial arts clubs springing up faster than arcades and video stores in the '80s, were in it to make a living as well as for the love of the art. To make a go of it, many club owners realized they'd have to tone it down a bit (Americanize it), in regards to both physical intensity and spiritual overtones. Of course, each club has its own unique personality, but the *Dearborn Academy of Martial Arts* seemed tailor made for a guy like me, and the proprietor, Rich Morrisey, and teaching assistants who were typically black belts seemed unconcerned with promoting "spiritual" exercises I would not be comfortable with. Actually, I thought a great deal more about just what did Jesus mean regarding this whole business about turning the other cheek (Lk 6:29). I've heard an astonishing number of clever ways to circumvent this one. I recall one big time evangelist declare, "Well now, the Lord didn't say what to do after he hit ya a second time." Inferring, in his mind that at that point, if you're still conscious, you can go on the offensive.

I like what ol' Evangelist Stalvey used to say (cut him a little slack;

remember he was an ol school military man; recall Clint Eastwood's role in *Heartbreak Ridge*). "I'll knock yer teeth out then pray God heal ya after ya get some sense. Halleluia!" Not exactly a sound theological approach perhaps (metaphors, analogies, New Jerusalem, Kingdom Age) way of sidestepping the issue, but, guess I'll cross that bridge when I come to it.

Sure enough, in no time I got in pretty good shape and nearly died (bit of an exaggeration here) in the process. Never much of a martial artist, although in time (5 years), I'd eventually be awarded a black belt having tested before Professor Sell[23] himself. Pat trained with me on occasion. He wouldn't admit it, but he held a little bit of a celebrity status in local Tae Kwon Do circles. After all, there amid the pages of perhaps the first Americanized TKD textbook, is a terrific picture of him facing off against an opponent twice his size. They called Pat the giant killer.

One day Pat told me he had bone cancer. What! In the area of one of his ankles and so he began treatment while the congregation got behind him and his wife and daughter with prayer and moral support. In a couple weeks he lost his hair, but still somehow trained with me on occasion, in a limited capacity of course. I tell you it was inspiring. I think most of us privately hoped this was some kind of test for Pat. God is going to heal this brother with or without medical science's intervention.

Word reached me that he'd taken a turn for the worse. I talked to his wife; it didn't look good. To myself I thought, "Yeah, well, it didn't look promising for those ten lepers either." Word spread through the congregation; time to turn it up a couple notches, pray and fast.

"Joe, it's me. Pat's lookin' pretty bad. He's asked for you," his wife whispered into the phone. I remember it like it was yesterday, thinking, and okay, just finish this laundry or something or other chore I was in the middle of and then head up to the hospital. An hour later I made my way towards his room when I met his pale, swollen eyed wife in the hallway surrounded by several family members. Pat had died fifteen minutes ago.

---

[23]   Professor Ed Sell, at the time was the highest ranked non-Asian Tae Kwon Do practitioner in the United States and overseer to a dozen or more schools throughout the country, including one in Garden City owned and operated by partners Chris Covert and Tom Allegian where I trained for two additional years before earning the coveted black belt.

"Joe, you can go in and see him if you like, it'll be a while before they move him," she trembled as she spoke.

I pulled up a seat next to his bed … just me and Pat … looked at him silently for some minutes. How absent, vacant a body looks at death. Fifteen minutes ago … fifteen, why did I fart around and not beat it down here. This guy, my friend, member of the congregation is wrestling with the "death angel" and I take my good ol' time getting' down here. True, I hadn't known just how urgent the situation was, but I still felt miserable having missed him. The thought did cross my mind that perhaps I should lay hands on him and bid, by the authority of Jesus, that life return to this lifeless shell. I didn't. I just silently prayed, thanked him for his friendship, "See ya soon." It was my honor, along with a Catholic priest at the family's request, to assist at both the funeral and graveside internment near Flat Rock, Michigan.

. . . .

Mark and Debbie had been members of our congregation for several years. Their two daughters, Amy and Megan, were the darlings of the church (before anyone bristles at the exclusiveness of that last comment, yes, we had an abundance of wonderful kids challenging our nursery and Sunday school staff). My affection for the Covert kids was in part an ordinary result of my friendship with their parents and the many hours I spent enjoying their hospitality at their residence in Wayne. The girls, like their folks, were warm, friendly and loveable. And ol' Pastor Joe, being childless, easily succumbed to a special soft spot for them which they used to their advantage procuring treats from my desk following Sunday services. No matter how down-in-the-dumps I might be, Amy (the older) and Megan could turn my gray skies blue.

One day Amy began to complain of headaches, so several of us prayed over her for healing. A week or so later, while Mark and I sat at the movies in downtown Wayne with Amy; she'd gotten all dressed up for a "date," there I go again, with Pastor Joe. Somewhat eccentric for one so young, she looked like a five year old Janis Joplin in her outfit. Our evening was shortened due to painful headaches nearly bringing her to tears. Were these migraines? Eye issues perhaps? The headaches persisted, and while we continued to pray for her, a visit to the doctor revealed something much more serious than any of us would have imagined. Extensive tests revealed Amy had a tumor the size of a baseball attached to the lower back of her brain. Surgery was scheduled for the following week.

The congregation immediately mobilized itself to pray and fast for Amy as the day scheduled for surgery approached. The operation took several hours. Finally, the lead surgeon entered the waiting room with news while we held our breath. The "operation was a success" was met with sighs of relief and quiet prayers of thanksgiving while he broke down the surgery in detail and what could now be expected. After hugs and reassurances, our emotionally drained group of immediate family and friends filed out of the waiting room and bid each other goodnight.

It seemed as though my head just hit the pillow when the phone startled me. It was Mark, Amy's father. With trembling voice he told me the hospital had just called and told them to hurry back down. Something had gone wrong. "Meet you there," I assured him.

I arrived shortly before Amy's parents. As I approached the ICU desk a team of doctors and nurses wheeled Amy's lifeless body hurriedly down the hall. In an instant they disappeared around a corner and I turned around to see Mark and Debbie hurrying towards me. A nurse took us to a private room where we waited, silently, for some word on Amy's condition.

Minutes dragged by when Amy's surgeon opened the door and stepped in. He appeared grave. After her initial operation, Amy had been moved to ICU for recovery and observation. All appeared as expected when suddenly her bedside emergency alarm sounded. She'd stopped breathing and couldn't be revived. Doctors were alerted while nurses gave her oxygen. Apparently her brain was swelling more than had been anticipated following the operation, and, if not relived quickly, she would die. The only way to relieve the swelling would be to open her up again. Precious time had already been lost; she was not expected to survive.

Amy survived the second operation but slipped into a coma. She was placed on a life support system with little chance of survival.

In the space of a week, a young, sweet, active little girl now lay lifeless in a hospital room. It was quiet there except for the sound of air being systematically forced in and out of her lungs. Her parents maintained a silent vigil nearby … prayerful, thoughtful, weary from an emotional roller coaster ride, not yet abandoning hope, secure in "Whatever comes of this, nothing can separate us from the love of God" (Rom 8:38).

The drive from my office to the hospital took 15 minutes. My mind searched for answers, comfort. "God," I pray, "what do I say to the parents of a dying child?"

Amy remained in a deep coma for several months. During this period I met with her parents regularly for prayer and encouragement. There were days when little was said. Comfort, I hoped, came from being in each others' company. Sometimes we would go for walks and dinner and there was time for conversation. Those who are suffering invariably come to the place of asking, "Why is this happening to me/us?"

Some folks discourage people from asking "Why?" They think such an attitude betrays a lack of faith and that the afflicted should simply and with a stoic's resolve put their trust in God and be content. I disagree. Solomon, Abraham, Paul, Job, David and other members of the Scripture's Faith Hall of Fame experienced moments of anguish when they looked to the heavens and cried, "Why?"

To the absolute astonishment of everyone, Amy came out of the coma, was able to come home, and begin the slow painful road back to what we all hoped would be a life of physical, emotional and spiritual health. She needed round-the-clock care. Family, friends, members of the congregation all pitched in. Progress was slow but she was still with us, able to communicate with some assistance, and able to receive a generous amount of affection.

Then, just as quickly, she experienced a sudden relapse and died.

Later that evening Debbie called and we discussed the necessary arrangements for Amy's burial. I was asked to conduct both the chapel and graveside services. I have conducted many funerals and none of them are easy. I slept little the night before Amy's.

Family, friends, neighbors and church members sat quietly as I made my way to the podium. It is for times like these that I am especially grateful for the Scriptures. Of all the earth's people, we have a sure hope in the resurrection of the dead. Hope … I knew that as I gently shared these beloved truths from the Bible, the Spirit of God would caress hearers' hearts with warm reassurance. "I am the resurrection and the life," declared Jesus; "whoever believes in me, even if he dies, will live… (Jn.11:25).

In the weeks and months following Amy's death, many in the congregation seemed to have more of a difficult time coming to grips with her death than her own parents. With Mark and Deb's approval, I encouraged several of the more deeply conflicted to call on them and talk about their shaken faith in the wake of Amy's death. My own interactions with the family and friends of Amy during her ordeal and following her death created many opportunities for thought provoking questions and conversation concerning life and death issues. It's been years, but hardly a week goes by that I don't think about the little girl who got all "dolled" up one night for a "date" with the pastor. I wonder if she remembers it. Guess I'll have to ask her.

. . . .

Rough waters ahead; the young lady I'd developed an interest in had returned to college. The *Shalom Ministry* seemed stagnant. Attendance on Sundays remained solid, but I was disappointed with our Friday night concert series' attendance. On occasion we'd pack 'em in, a *Found Free* concert (pop, rock and soul band from Philadelphia) who'd recently taken on *Shalom* guitarist Rob Bialowicz, turned out the faithful in droves (Rob's got a big family). On another occasion, we had one of the most dynamic nights ever, when a couple former Living Water band mates (now Soldier), teamed up with new convert to Christianity Ed Sell, fresh off a *700 Club* appearance and coincidentally, head of the Tae Kwon Do association I was affiliated with and had been interceding for, and who now fronted the dynamic *Sell Martial Arts Team*. Kids from all around Taylor and Dearborn Heights packed the joint, 'er sanctuary, to have their ears taxed by some sanctified rock and roll, and their eyes wide open beholding amazing displays of martial arts skills. The icing on the cake were the moving testimonies of the Sells, and how despite his earlier successes and world renown achievements in martial arts he declared, "It don't mean a thing if you don't know the King (Jesus, that is)."

However, these were the exception, and it troubled and sometimes angered me when groups (good groups) would travel some distance, *Foreign Legion* from Ontario and *Ground Crew* from Indiana for example, and play to a less than half full house. I was embarrassed.

The bouts with unbelief, rekindled following the recent deaths I've mentioned ... add a dose of loneliness, yes you can be lonely while surrounded by people, and none of my relationships with women over the past 7 or 8 years had come to anything (anything as in marriage). Nor did it look to me like my most recent lady interest, given for starters she's away at school, and I'm challenged by face-to-face relationships let alone

176

late night phone calls and weekly letters, would develop into a true, lasting romance. Upshot, I got an attitude ... a bad attitude ... with God, and spent way too much time feeling sorry for myself. "Hell with it." I danced around with a spiritual "death wish," a way to get out, and fell for the advances of a young married mother in the congregation, herself wrestling with marital issues and spiritual warfare.

I used to think about something I'd heard Billy Graham say. How he'd never, regardless of the circumstances and how innocent all parties might be, allow himself to be alone with a woman. Just to be safe and "avoid the appearance of evil," (1 Thes 5:22), to say nothing of what the tabloids and news reporters would do with such a high profile moral failing should one happen.

Well, my "I'm startin' to not give a damn anymore" attitude, coupled with a letting my guard down, and before I could/should have, like Joseph of old who fled carnal temptation while serving in pharaoh's household, I lingered too long, tempting fate. I/we found ourselves in each others arms; the single pastor in the arms of a married woman. A quicksand like relationship quickly threatened to overwhelm us; quicksand is often fatal.

I was horrified. But the weakened mental, spiritual state I'd let myself deteriorate into made it difficult, nigh impossible, it seemed to resist. I'd repeat, repent ... put my hands back to the plow and ... right back in her arms again. Sometimes going so far as to initiate circumstances where we might find ourselves alone with each other. Playing with fire indeed (Prv 6:27-29). How do you look the congregation, her husband, her, in the eye before you take the podium to deliver Sunday's message? I was already struggling with the exercise of spiritual gifts, especially healing. Now, given what I'd been about, what anointing, if any, could I expect? Now I was getting by on what little natural talent I had, and the fact that God will use even a "dirty" vessel to feed his people if that's all that's available. In the eyes and minds of the folks in the pew who at this juncture were clueless to my indiscretions, I was still the same ol Pastor Joe. I wish it was that easy.

My indiscretions (necking/petting) with this woman were not an every day/week occurrence. Sometimes we'd go a month or more thinking, "Well, that's done," only to fall once more back into that most pernicious of the seven deadlies – lust. It certainly, for my part at least, had little or nothing to do with "love," but as I said, a spiritual death wish and an "I'm angry with you God, sandwiched between flattery and loneliness. I've given it all up for you and what do I have ... so take this...." Childish, I know. What do I have? Duh, eternal life!

Well, I was getting nowhere fast. Perhaps a sabbatical would help cure what's ailin' me. I'll go visit my spiritual (born again) roots down in Vero Beach, Florida, and try to sort things out. Distance myself from this nightmarish spiritual suicide relationship I've failed to slam the door on, and as ol' Bob Seger might put it ... "see some old friends, good for the soul." Get my "spiritual head" back on straight. I left *Shalom* in the capable hands of the elders and my assistant pastor – Al Blade. I arranged for various guest speakers to help with the preaching load, anticipating an absence of two, maybe three months. At least my timing was right. I was rollin' like a river southbound on ol' I-75 on an early, gray January morn. I love the feeling of slowly removing one article of clothing after another with each stop headed south, until finally crossing the state line into Florida from Georgia, keeping a wary eye out for the next rest area so you can complete the transformation and don that Jimmy Buffet look.

Better yet, I was getting out from under, for a season at least, the immediate care and responsibility of my pastoral responsibilities to say nothing of that unwholesome relationship I'd become mired in. My staff knew how to reach me in case of an emergency, and I touched base with Assistant Pastor Al several times a week. Initially, I "crashed" on a boat (not exactly the Queen Mary, good thing was the privacy, nobody would park their boat next to it, afraid they might catch something, from the boat that is, not me), at a marina in Ft. Pierce, Florida, just south of Vero. Seems like I kept following in the wake (love those mariner metaphors) of my ol' church bouncer friend – Tim; the guy who to a large extent was initially responsible for me being at *Shalom*. Here it was, seven or so years later, and he, along with his wife Nancy and little girl Erin (I had the honor of officiating their marriage ... all I recall was it was on an April 1st and if he stopped the ceremony just before the pronouncement and yelled, "April fools!" ... I would have excommunicated them ...), had settled back in Florida and once again I was taken under his wing, 'er fin. The more troubling issues I was wrestling with I kept to myself. Tim had built me up (his sister-in-law Frannie was then boarding with him), as God's man-of-the-hour. Actually, I felt more like John Lennon's plaintive wail, "I'm a loser, and I'm not what I appear to be." Didn't want to let him down and so I said little about my pastoral woes.

We hung out and fished a bit. Fishing with Timmy is kinda' like being trapped in an ol sailor's yarn, as in a cross between *Old Man and the Sea* meets *Moby Dick* ... out in the Bermuda Triangle. As you can tell, I survived. Psychologically damaged, but lived to tell the tale. I appreciated the warm hospitality and friendship of Tim and his family.

My worship/fellowship time was split between *New Beginning's Church* (formerly *First Church of the Last Chance*, gotta' love that name) led by Evangelist Herman Stalvey, and a splinter group under Stalvey's former assistant pastor, Lance Fedick, *New Life Church*. It troubled me not a little to witness first-hand the aftermath of a church split. I had good friends in both groups. I hadn't come 1300 miles south to try and figure all that out. I had my own issues to contend with, and as time allowed I would fellowship with both groups and steer clear of any lingering discord between them.

An old associate in the construction business, Lee Calloway, provided a gig for me so that like Paul the Apostle I could pay my own way. I could just hear it now back up north at *Shalom*. We're going to take a special collection for Pastor Joe (resting down in Florida while all of us are in the throes of another Michigan winter), so, dig deep. Actually, they would have, and at one point I did need a bit of financial help with van repairs, but, work is also good for the soul, too much idleness can drive you mad and/or lead to despair. I even picked fruit again for a couple weeks, 'bout all I could handle. Swimming, running, eating right ... the physical man was making strides, spiritual fitness came at a higher price.

I kept a journal, developed a regular prayer and devotion regimen, immersed myself in the Scriptures; however, my resistance to confiding in someone, Tim and Evangelist Stalvey being the two obvious candidates, may have been the fly in the spiritual ointment. Still, a resolve was taking shape to finally douse these fires of lust and have done with it. Now, if I could just get a better handle on these spiritually draining battles with unbelief. I continued to keep in contact with Barb up at Oakland, her letters being the high point of my day. Indeed, looked like she might pay me a visit while on spring break visiting family on the Gulf Coast.

Astonishing! I had a few bucks in my pocket from the construction gig, maybe treat myself to some Fagen's barbecue over in Gifford. On Sundays, before the afternoon service at *New Beginnings Church*, I liked to catch some waves and sun at nearby Wabasso Beach. Afterward, I could never resist taking a ride down nearby Jungle Trail, stop and look around the ol' Orchid Island apartments we "Motown" boys invaded a decade earlier. What's this? One of the units was for rent ... the one we first stayed in! Would they let me rent it for a month? Yes, they would. Praise God.

Soon afterward, in something of a "this can't really be happening" to me mist, I moved in with what few possessions and necessaries would see me through a month's stay. "Hello ... what's this?" Who came bouncing out of the apartment directly across from mine? Dale ... Dale Campbell from Livonia, one of the '70s Wabassoites who'd came down from Michigan and spent some time with us after our initial arrival some ten years ago; and still here? Somewhere/somehow we'd lost track of each other and now I "bumped" into him at the very place we'd last seen each other ... ten years ago ... unbelievable! We enjoyed getting reacquainted and several other mutual friends from the "township-Redford" dropped in over the next few weeks; a pleasant reunion.

I was still working a construction gig (development called The Moorings, south of Vero on A1A), and met a lovely married couple from Boston (Joe and Cerene and their two boys) who'd moved to Florida to make a go of it. They resided in nearby Sebastian, and since we worked for the same construction company (how we met), we carpooled to work and hung out occasionally. Their Bostonian accents and sense of humor made laboring under the Florida sun more endurable.

In the meantime my dad had come down. By the way, Barb, the gal from Oakland University did drop in for a few days' visit ... great time as I recall ... still, my little ol' pessimistic nothing-good-ever-happens to/for you pathetic mentality incessantly nagged at me, "nothing will ever come of this." Hanging out with Pops was the highlight of my sabbatical. Some days I'd leave him the van for getting out and exploring an area new to him. Other days he'd just loll around the "crib" and wet a line off the dock stickin' out like a hangnail into the Indian River out front of our Jungle Trail "cottage." We buddied around in the evenings and his company just added balm to the spiritual healing I sorely needed. Well, 'bout time to head back to Michigan and face the music.

. . . .

Dad and I drove back to Michigan via West Virginia to take in some of his old stomping grounds and see who might still be around. The state of the ministry at Shalom appeared good … kinda' made me wonder … "Gee, guess they can get along without me." Best of all, it looked like *Shalom* would soon be renters no longer. A church facility on Ecorse Road between Pardee and Monroe streets in Taylor was available and within our budget. It wasn't much. Kind of a congregation built it bit by bit over time structure. But the sanctuary would accommodate 200+, and there were a couple of rooms, a kitchen, an office area and a fellowship hall … needed a ton of work … electrical upgrades, decorating, landscaping … it hadn't been kept up and looked tired, rode hard and put up wet as they say (cowboys, I guess).

We had a whole congregation just chompin' at the bit, unafraid of a little sweat and elbow grease. The deal done, we landed like the marines and in no time a beachhead had been established and – Open for Business. I would live there. From time to time others, families in need/transition, and single brothers also called it home. Once again the ol' Friday night concerts were back on the menu. Parking wasn't great, but a huge parking lot directly across Ecorse Road where there was a little used strip mall parking lot that ensured an overflow parking solution. A restaurant sat just to the west of us; a southern home cookin' style mom and pop place; really handy for socializing before and after church.

Then it happened. Just when I'd concluded the goings on between myself and the married woman were history, once again … kinda like re-breaking your leg after coming off months of successful rehab, and on the first day of practice prior to the new football season, right back where you started; like a roller coaster heading down fast. This time a wreck seemed inevitable.

Perhaps I should ask her to leave the fellowship. That didn't seem right. I then took a step I should have taken months earlier. I confessed my sin to a trusted mature brother in Christ. Bingo. I was freed. Any interest in this married gal other than as a fellow sister, laborer for the Kingdom, vanished like a hazy mist under the heat of a noonday sun. I suggested she do the same. Problem was … perhaps it wasn't a problem, but rather one of those "eventually you'll reap what you sow" harvests finally come home to roost. The person(s) she confided in was so blown away by these revelations, that they in turn needed someone to share the "heavy burden" with, a sympathetic soul, and/or possibly they just couldn't keep such a juicy tale to themselves. In time, well, you don't need to be Sherlock Holmes to see where this is going.

· · · ·

During the next few months my courtship with Barb blossomed, to the utter dismay of her not-pleased parents; a preacher ... ten years her senior no less, and a poor preacher by the looks of it. This will not do.

In the back of my mind it always seemed too good to be true ... this will never fly, and yet there the two of us were, Christmas '82 afternoon, opening gifts with her family in Dearborn. "Ah, what's this? One last gift, rather small, let's see ... Barb, hmm, looks like your name's on it." (Barb and I had planned this ahead of time. Neither her parents nor brother and sister-in-law had a clue till now that something was up). With a hard-to-hide knowing look on her face, Barb unwrapped and produced an engagement ring. For several moments time stood still ... no one breathed. Finally, Barb's brother broke the silence and approached me with a congratulatory extended hand. Barb's mother tried bravely to smile, one moment looking at Barb, the next to her husband. Quietly and I thought rather somberly, Barb's dad asked his son to fix him a drink, a double ... quite unlike him, however, circumstances being what they were.

Months passed and when it became increasingly apparent we would not be deterred, a non-verbal truce of sorts freshened the air and the talk could now turn to a summer wedding date, planning, invitations, you who have been there know all too well; planning a wedding is a task not for the faint of heart.

My dad half-joked to me privately that it wouldn't work. Perhaps he saw something I was blind or unwilling to see, but he'd stopped trying to tell me what to do years ago. Heck, I was thirty-one. Whataya gonna' say anyway. Whatever his misgivings were, he kept them largely to himself.

Privately her folks were not at all keen on this union, and while trying to make the best of it, I knew a bit of animosity for the man who'd "taken" their little, only girl, lay just below the surface. The whole concept of asking the parents for her hand in marriage didn't set well with me. I knew what the answer would have been. But, I/we convinced ourselves rightly or wrongly that this was God's plan for us and not even one's parents can derail what the heavenly court has ordained. Our matchmaker, as Tevye concluded when he learned his oldest daughter Tzeitel had promised herself to Motel the tailor, was the same one who'd hooked up Adam with Eve, or so we could argue. And here I take a solemn pause and pray God spare me the "what goes around comes around" with my own daughter and the wheel of fortune.

The wedding was set for upcoming July. Neither of us wanted the same old traditional wedding ceremony we'd witnessed on numerous occasions. I'd of late, thanks in part to friendship with a Texas musician and medievalist Kemper Crabb, become intrigued with all things Medieval/Renaissance. A year earlier, Barb and I, along with traveling buddies Mark and Debbie Covert, had visited a Renaissance Festival near Tuxedo, New York. We had a blast. It wasn't difficult to persuade her that just such a wedding would be just the way (fairytale like) to embark on our journey as one together. Her parents were flabbergasted. My parents shrugged it off as "Sounds like somethin' Joey'd do."

A medieval themed wedding turned out to be quite an undertaking. The patio of the Henry Ford Fairlane Mansion would be the site of the ceremony. *Dearborn First Baptist Church*, Barb's mother's church, was a nearby backup in case of rain. An outdoor reception lakeside at Camp Sokal (we reserved the entire camp) near South Lyon would be the site of revelry, feasting, and non-stop music and dancing for our medieval themed reception.

What a day. The morning of the wedding started out with a bang as a young woman rear-ended me on Ten Mile Road on the way back from taking some decorations and signs to Camp Sokal. Due to rain we had to go with Plan B, and moved the ceremony at the last minute to *Dearborn Baptist Church*; somehow we pulled it off. Kemper Crabb officiated with help from Evangelist Stalvey and Shalom Elder – Jim Duncan. Jan Krist, Rufus Harris and Kenny and Susie Meeks warmed our and all in attendance hearts with music during the ceremony. Many attendees and all of the wedding party, including Kemper, were in full medieval regalia. When's the last time you saw a groom in tights (not to worry, I had a custom-made leather, princely studded jerkin that reached mid-thigh). My soon to be father-in-law looked like he was waiting for someone to pinch him and send this bad dream running for the shadows. My best man, Mark Covert, looked like he'd just flown in on the wing of an arrow from Sherwood Forest. Of course, the bride, Barb Auxier (soon to be Shannon), stole the show, as it should be. Guinevere never looked so stunning. At the conclusion of the ceremony, halfway down the aisle, I stopped, picked up my new bride and carried her out the rear of the church.

It cleared up beautifully for the reception. We encouraged people to bring a change of clothes, or stop at home on the way to the reception and change into casual wear. Something for everyone: swimming, a grand feast complete with roast pig, strolling musicians, a gal Barb knew from Wayne State University came and led basic medieval ethnic round dances. Later we moved indoors to a hall on the grounds that we'd decorated for a little high energy music and dance. The only glitch was the caterer ran out of food (thankfully not beer and wine). Likely more our fault than his as we'd underestimated the number of folks attending the reception, and what with everyone working up quite an appetite dancing, swimming, volleyball (no jousting), and well, folks were famished. Not to worry. The caterer was very cool, professional while under the gun (crossbow), and in no time was lining up beautiful steaks on the large outdoor grill; he'd hustled up the steaks from a nearby market in South Lyon. I mustn't forget to mention the wedding cake. Several talented women from Shalom baked and assembled a one-of-a-kind, complete with a dragon, massive castle cake. In short, years later, no one who was there has forgotten that wedding.

· · · ·

You can't follow up a non-traditional wedding with a traditional honeymoon as in something Niagara Fallsish. Ours was anything but traditional, and for added spice, as if one's honeymoon should be lacking, ours had several terrifying moments: violent thunderstorm and bear encounter out on the Appalachian Trail; our one person raft (we tried to make it a two person, you know, newlyweds and all that) popped a seam while going down the Ichetucknee River in Florida – actually more embarrassing than terrifying; also snorkeling with a school of barracuda off Treasure Cay in the Bahamas; most harrowing of all, a near-death experience while white-water canoeing on the Nantahala River on the North Carolina/Georgia border. I know, sounds like an edition of National Geographic, not someone's honeymoon. I should begin by pointing out that while in high school, my future wife was a bit of a jock, an outdoorsy girl, including a veteran of Outward Bound. Camp Dearborn was my idea of roughing it. Anyway, it had been one of the things that attracted me to her and now I was going to begin to pay the price. Hence, our honeymoon took on the look of an eco vacation adventure as we went from one wilderness environment to the next.

What could be better, more bonding, more refreshing in the August heat than some white watering. I offered little resistance when she suggested that to get the "full" experience, to really feel the river, we should canoe it, not restrict ourselves to a raft in the company of seniors, screaming kids and out-of-shape city slickers … we could get that at an amusement park ride. I buried any misgivings; of course I hadn't seen the mighty Nantahala yet, and had I not on several occasions mastered more than one of Michigan's well-known rivers including the challenging Au Sable River itself? What could North Carolina throw my way that I was not more than equipped to tame? Duh … I don't know if the film *Deliverance* had made its way in and out of movie theaters by then, but, this is the neck-a-the-woods/rivers we'd be on … and in a few hours, struggling to survive in.

A few years later we were canoeing the Pine River in mid-Michigan, two canoes, each with a couple, were fifty yards ahead of us at one point. The Pine by the way, is the type of river that had it not so many meanderings one must navigate, you could read a book or take an extended nap as you gently let the current bear you to your destination.

"White water ahead, white water!" one of the women cried, urgency and concern marked her shriek.

We turned the bend and caught sight of them just as they gracefully jostled over some ancient willow whose resting place just beneath the surface made for a few bumps, bubbles and foam … white water indeed. I'd seen more white water in hot tubs; they high-fived each other and like Lewis and Clark, face to the wind, pressed on. We laughed so hard we nearly flipped … white water-pahleeze!

Meanwhile, back to the Nantahala, my new wife may have sensed some trace of apprehension and matter-of-factly assured me not to worry. She gave me a crash course in White Water Canoeing 101 in no time; "it'll be fun," she quipped. I'm twice her size so naturally I would be in the rear of the canoe. Her task would include reading the river and hollering directions to yours truly. My job – steer. Did I mention this was a class 3 river (5 is the highest). Our recreational honeymoon activity of the day, a seven mile run down a class 3 river with some twenty sets of rapids … in a canoe; whoopee!

I had 100 yards to develop and learn the techniques before the first set of rapids came into view. The current, compared to the Au Sable, was like being on the autobahn. Here we go … first set of rapids … the roar of the swift moving water smashing against half submerged boulders made it difficult to hear directions from "outdoors woman." Sure enough, over we went … not too bad … we were prepared and had anticipated this happening and so designated who would go for the canoe, paddles, stay composed till we'd float down to a calmer stretch of the river and regroup. Well, this was just a warm up. The big dance was just around the proverbial bend.

I can't recall how many times we went over, but I'd need both feet and hands to make a count. With each spill my irritation began to get the better of me. I don't know what upset me more … my own ineptness, or her misjudging our ability to canoe this river … right now bounding along on the "seniors" raft sounded pretty good. Some of you think I'm overreacting, exaggerating the peril we found ourselves in … in the middle of God knows where; Jethro Bodine country. We seldom saw anyone else on the river. No pay phones, hah, on the shore at periodic rest stops, "Say fellas, could you come airlift us outta' here? We're a bit hungry and have decided to call it a day." The only way out was to keep goin' forward; each new set of rapids more challenging than the previous. Figured out too late that rather than sit in the rear of the canoe, I should have knelt, which would have been more stabilizing and prevented most if not all our spills.

"Oh yeah, we can handle this," I recall her assuring Mr. River Outfitter hunk who dropped us off, gave us a few tips and what to watch out for before pushing us out into the current.

Think I'm exaggerating … painting the scene a bit direr than it likely was … watched Humphrey Bogart in *African Queen* too many times Joe? When you can hear the next set of rapids well before you can see them, and the sound reminds you of that time as a kid when your parents took you and your siblings out on the *Maid of the Mist* at the foot of Niagara Falls, well, one's throat (mine at least), goes bone dry. Not sure if we were wearing helmets, but over we went. We each grabbed a paddle, but the canoe shot forward and was lost to us. No sense trying to make it to shore … no back door here … remember what they said, "butt down, head up …

you'll come out of it." I know I'll come out of it, just not sure if I'll be alive. The rapids at this part of the Nantahala were no joke. My tennis shoes and wedding ring were stripped off; my wedding ring, not a week old, resting beneath the cool river waters waiting for some Smeagol like river adventurer to claim it. We found our canoe lodged against some rocks a quarter-mile down river. Both of us were bruised and battered, nothing serious, although I sustained a gash across the palm of my hand which caused me to wince a bit while paddling. I was steaming, but said little. Now it was survive ... can't be that much further, but ah, before the conclusion of this mad venture, one more "add insult to injury" icing on the cake would kick me where it hurts ... déjà vu ... back on that diving platform for another lesson in humility.

We made it. There at a bend in the river where the waters took a brief respite from their frantic impulse to find earth's lowest point was an area marked for all river traffic to exit and an area for pick up. Some twenty plus folks leisurely lounged about while outfitters secured rafts waiting for as-yet-not-arrived rafting parties. This turnout had not been chosen by chance. Fifty yards down the river, as several large warning signs left no doubt, was a fifteen foot drop, a waterfall, and only professionals and the foolhardy would risk it.

"Okay, you guys want to make the run?" Our outfitter who'd just arrived in a transport van asked. The kinda' young handsome lookin' guy who looked like he'd graced the cover of whitewater magazines and catalogs ... probably going down this river since he was three....

"Make the run. Whataya mean?" As a small crowd gathered round, he explained that he could take in our canoe, one or both of us... he shot me a glance, over the falls.

"It's really quite a rush," he grinned a bit too cockily I thought. Did I detect a hidden sneer, dare in his voice? He went on to explain that 99 out of 100 people who shoot the falls spill, but not to worry, his two partners thirty yards downstream would retrieve the canoe and paddles, and there, strung across the river was a low hanging rope attached to a winch, and you only need to grab hold while we reel you in. He didn't say but just as easily could have added, "What could be easier and more fun!"

The gathering crowd nervously looked at one another, fidgeting, no one saying a word, only the sound of rushing water in the background.

Then Mr. Whitewater rafting centerfold looked at us. "How 'bout you guys?"

"Like to mate, but my hand and all."

"Awesome, I'd love to," Barb chirped.

A dull red hue crept across my face as I struggled to smile. There was a viewing area adjacent to the falls where folks could assemble and watch thrill seekers, idiots (as in people who go over Niagara Falls in barrels), tempt fate ala extreme sports. Okay, bit of an exaggeration. I could hear people comment under their breath as my new wife and Mr. Whitewater, who'd gone upstream fifty yards to allow enough time to hit the falls just right ..."Wow, the chick's got guts."

Over they went. As predicted, guide and my wife were spewed from the canoe and momentarily disappeared below a whirlpool of white foam before bobbing to the surface, just in time to reach up and grab the rope before being hauled safely in. The crowd cheered. Ah, I would have applauded more enthusiastically were it not for my bruised palm.

What a ride back to the Outfitter Store. You recall how Ralph Kramden of the *Honeymooners* would throw dirty looks Alice's way when he was "steamed?" Still, had to admit, I was proud of her. I don't know anyone who's married to a gal who'd do that. Do you?

Enough about our honeymoon, it seems as though the Lord had seen fit to make me a contender for a number of Life's Most Embarrassing Moments episodes. Once, a few years later while out skeet-shooting (clay pigeons), she bested me quite soundly. Mind you, it wasn't a public exhibition or competition, but still, a man, at least this man, would like to think he could annihilate more clay pigeons streaking across the landscape than his wife.

She played on the Women's softball team at *Shalom*; I, the Men's. A good night for me would be going 2 for 4, only 1 or 2 errors in the field, and no significant injuries; groin pull, that sort of thing. A so-so night for Barb would be going 4 for 4 (1 home-run and three triples) ... her one weakness, not exactly a racehorse around the bases, flawless fielding, and like Elvis, who'd even if he got in a brawl in one of his films his hair never lost that cover of *Teen Magazine* look, Barb's hair just always seemed to retain that shine and light bounce. The first time up at the plate, especially if it was a first time meeting between teams and none of the opposition recognized who it was who nonchalantly strode up to the plate was always amusing. She'd launch these shots the air traffic controllers at Metro would pick up on their screens. Second time up, their coach waving everyone back ... boom, another missile launched deep into the night. If it was a diamond without fences, the opposing team would push their outfielders back so far when Barb came to bat, that you could hardly make them out as they nervously waited outside the lighted parameters of the outfield. If she wouldn't stand at the plate like Reggie Jackson watching her launches streak into the upper atmosphere, then jog around the bases, she'd have quadruple the amount of homers on her stats; liked the view from standing on third base I suppose.

Exceptionally sound on defense as well, her lack of speed her only liability; infield players balked at being on the receiving end of one of her throws. My favorite Barb defensive "replay" ... runner on second, sharp two hop single to Barb in right center ... lead runner rounds third and slows to a jog thinking it's a gimme ... Smack! An utter look of astonishment on her face ... there, waiting patiently at the plate, a grin plastered across her face, the catcher waits to apply the tag from a rifle shot throw from Barb.

Yep, she had a howitzer for an arm; could throw strikes (in the air) from the outfield. She couldn't best me at ping pong or at the pool table, but those are not typically spectator sports, so my athletic prowess went largely unnoticed; just as well.

We settled into a modest three bedroom brick bungalow in the south end of Dearborn Heights, coincidentally on the same street (2 blocks down) from where little Joey had likely been conceived. My parents lived with my dad's sister Angie in '51 while they waited for their home in Redford Township to be completed. I'd made it clear to our board of elders and the congregation that Barb was my wife and not the assistant pastor. She would complete her degree at Wayne State and embark on a career in physical therapy, eventually taking a position at nearby Heritage Hospital in Taylor. Our days/life was bright, but an ill wind was building ... storm clouds hovering over *Shalom* were taking on an increasingly ominous appearance; there were rumblings in the distance.

We, the congregation that is, were well settled into our new location. Things appeared to be moving along as well as could be expected. When we'd initially set foot into the Ecorse Road location, we for the first time moved our Sunday worship service to the morning (late morning). Small groups called Prayer and Shares met on a monthly basis, typically hosted by an elder, as a means of building relationships and getting new members acclimated. Jackson Prison outreach … did I mention the Men's softball team played the inmates (their home field – hah!) on several occasions. I'd get a kick out of the way the inmates would cheer us on and hoot at the prison team. On one occasion I launched a pretty good poke … longest of my "stellar" career, well past the left fielder's head and close to the foul line, but inside by at least a foot. "Foul ball," the ump, an inmate working behind the plate hollered. A moment earlier, just as I'd dropped my bat on the way to first I heard a voice like Jimmy Cagney holler out. "Call it foul you S.O.B. I got 5 packs on this game," a prison team player hollered a little too loud.

There were the typical squabbles and occasional grumblings … mostly relationship issues, but we were a slowly growing congregation still clinging to that contemporary, anti-traditional/ceremony vibe as best we could (actually in vain I might just as well throw in, from where I now sit anyway). Occasionally I'd find this or that tract, book, magazine article anonymously left on my desk, at my door, that were a way of saying "Pastor Joe, I/We really think you need to pay more attention to this or that issue:" to drink or not to drink (as in alcohol), proper beach attire for picnics and baptisms, believers yoked with unbelievers … that sort of thing, and once a book, *The Pastor's Wife*. All well and good I suppose, but I hope the manner with which these items mysteriously appeared was not an indication of an unapproachableness on my part. Regrettably, I was a bit of a moody sort. The dangers *Shalom* faced came not so much in the form of persecution, but the dreaded lukewarm state (Rv 3:16) that leaves you like a ship at sea in a dead calm; going nowhere.

It had been a good while, perhaps a year since I'd gotten that monkey off my back (relationship with a married woman), and now myself married; perhaps 6 months. During this time, slowly, like a storm far out at sea, building strength for a land assault, and unbeknownst to me, word of my failings with this woman had been creeping along the grapevine.

I was sitting at my desk 30 minutes before a Sunday morning service, reviewing my sermon notes, when one of the church elders walked in, closed the door and stood before me with an I have something to say look. The gist of which was, "Everyone knows about you and this woman. There were other serious issues of a similar nature infecting our members. People are upset and want answers … Oh, and I quit."

Feeling like I'd just been rocked by a sucker punch, I countered. "So the dam breaks and you, an elder, are gonna beat it outa here?"

He paused at the door, turned and gave me that "do tell" look. I continued, "These people elected you an elder and now because trouble's come you're gonna bail. I misjudged you. I expected more." To his credit he did stay on until things settled down somewhat and *Shalom's* direction was determined and people could decide to stay or not.

I've faced some tough preaching situations; this was the worst. The matter had burst like an abscess. The chapel was typically full, worship and praise over, collection taken ... all eyes on me now as I stood trying my best to suck it up and do what I'd been called, ordained to do – preach the Gospel. Was it real or my imagination; were these folks, my "charge," the flock I'd been entrusted with looking at me differently? Some eyes spoke pity, some shame, anger, understanding, but the only message I seemed to glean from those seated before me was, "How could you... our pastor, you who we put our trust in?"

Somehow, God's grace no doubt, I managed to finish the service without entertaining everybody with a nervous breakdown. An emergency elder's meeting was called. Our worst fears (mine at least) were confirmed. From here on out it rapidly escalated into a mess. Word on the street was that Joe had an "affair" with so and so. It riled me that folks, ones I'd trusted and laid my life down for, would refer to the "situation" as such, since we'd never actually consummated the relationship, and to use the "affair" word would lead people to make erroneous assumptions. Hey, confront me man-to-man, brother-to-brother. Well, what's to be done?

It was clear we needed outside help on this one. Someone or other from the Assemblies was suggested but that was quickly shot down (not by me). Pastor Dick Bieber of *Messiah Lutheran* was someone we respected, was not personally connected to the situation or any forthcoming outcome, and agreed to meet with us. The details of that meeting are a bit hazy, and to this day there is some disagreement as to what was said and what the advised course to pursue was. This was the last straw for me. My spiritual death wish had come to pass. I was done, washed up. Still, like an over-the-hill boxer, this was not the way I wanted to go out ... in defeat, disgrace.

After our board's initial meeting with Dick, I met with him privately. Not that I doubted he wasn't candid with us when first we dumped this mess out on the table in the hope he could help us salvage something. The upshot of my private meeting with him was that we both agreed that if I had enough board support, enough congregational support, and still believed in my heart I could still fulfill the sacred responsibilities that come with the call to pastor … then there should be no stopping me … we also talked at length about repentance, time considerations (he seemed to think it significant that at least a year had passed since the last transgression and subsequent repentance), how did the offended husband regard matters as they stood, and were there any scriptural warrants preventing my staying in the pulpit.

A special Shalom "family" meeting was called. All the cards were put on the table, including a question and answer session moderated by one of the elders. I sat in a pew towards the front, Barb next to me. Following the question and answer session, there was a vote. Joe stays … Joe resigns. I'd agreed to this vote in characteristic fatalistic fashion. I had no intention of pastoring a church where I wasn't wanted, and I would accept (I confided to only a few close associates) only a unanimous or near unanimous vote (roughly 95% or better), as an indicator that I might still be able to give it a go as pastor of *Shalom Ministry*.

My wife and I left the meeting just prior to the vote and returned home to await the call. I'd mentally prepared myself for the proverbial, well, this is it … best I could hope for was 60% ... ah, just as well. I was burnt out anyway, but damn, just not the way I thought I'd go out … the kitchen phone interrupted my dark broodings.

"Joe, Jim Duncan (Shalom elder) … only two dissenting votes."

To this day, after all that, I'm not absolutely certain staying on was the right call. I never quite recovered. The old bravado barely flickered. Every time I stepped behind the pulpit I knew people looked at me differently, and why not? Only a handful of members departed after it'd been announced that Joe would be staying. I bear them no grudge. I may have done the same had I been in their shoes. The gal who I'd had the relationship with, and I too often failed to take into account the agony she and her husband endured, stayed on, and thankfully, years later their marriage continued to remain intact. Shalom had been dealt a vicious blow, but rallied in the late rounds... at the last bell, we/I were still standing.

· · · ·

192

Now that the flames of controversy had died down it was all behind us, or was it? It was time to get down to business. Occasionally I'd get wind of this or that minister, church, individual … who'd "heard" about me. Toss up between hilarious and pathetic how these stories twist and turn in the telling … the fish always gets bigger. For my part, I tried to stay focused, but real or imagined I just wasn't the same. I lacked confidence, avoided certain topics in my sermons as you might imagine, and that spiritual grim reaper called unbelief continued its relentless pursuit.

Unbelief is not the type of subject you can bring up with just anyone over a cup of coffee at the Clock restaurant. Just what I'd now need circulating around the gossip mills, hot on the trail of my by now well-known indiscretions: "Pastor Joe's not even sure if he believes anymore … pity actually …." And don't talk to your wife about it, after all, she's looking to you for spiritual strength (by the way Barb never wavered from or fled my side during what had become "our" ordeal). I didn't like to bring "church" related issues home. As far as confiding my bouts with unbelief with my old mentor, Evangelist Stalvey, I don't guess I'd have discussed it with him anyway. He had enough on his own plate, and I certainly didn't want to let Coach down. So, I wrestled with it alone.

Shalom had grown stagnant, as most places would from time to time, and a good ol' fashioned revival, fueled by prayer and fasting, repentance, re-dedication, would turn things around (er forward one hoped). However, this torpid season, had in my mind's eye, no easy cure … no end in sight, and during my private prayer and meditations, I couldn't shake the idea that the pastor was the culprit … the one inhibiting spiritual growth. Images of Ezekiel's "dry bones" haunted me (see Ez 37).

Our numbers stayed steady. Some would leave, come back, leave again … new folks who'd become disenchanted with their own place of worship giving ours a look. Incidentally, when I'd interview people for membership, a fairly informal affair, but we did want to know something of their background, expectations and so on … sometimes I'd contact their former pastor for references and/or professional courtesy (safeguards too). I'd also get a kick out of (mostly fellas but occasionally the women folk fit this bill) who'd begin coming to *Shalom* (sometimes returning after a conspicuous absence), "satellites" we called them. What gives? Hunting … taking a look … any new prospects. Ah yes, "all the lonely people, where do they all come from …." Lookin' for Mr./Ms. Right. I bet some of them are still lookin'.

Trudging along, keeping your best front up, in the stinking mire of spiritual doldrums, feeling the squeeze of the ever-tightening noose of unbelief that leads to sulfurous pit like regions of despair. I need to get out from behind the pulpit. Step back for a while and sort this all out for mine and the congregation's sake. It had been two years since the Joe stay/split vote. Enough water had passed under the bridge and if I resigned now, I could go out with a bit of dignity. Some of you are thinking that Joe, you should have thrown it in two years ago … possibly. I would remind you however, that the "issue" presently harassing me (hence the flock I tended), was neither my failing of three years ago, nor some vote of approval, not my marriage … no, it was an unrelenting struggle with unbelief.

I was settled on it then, having discussed it with my wife. I'd give a couple months' notice and in the interim assist the elders with a pastor search … new waters for us. I'd pursue a teaching degree and Barb would be sole (primary) breadwinner; a physical therapist and fortunately for us, jobs a plenty in her chosen profession with respectable salaries and benefits.

Our list of pastoral candidates was short. Indeed I could think of only one person that could help *Shalom* regain its footing and move on (this does not mean of course that there weren't others who could manage the position, but neither was there a line around the building waiting to be interviewed). Al Kresta, a well-respected brother most of us knew, given the near proximity of Eden Books on Eureka near Telegraph in Taylor, which he managed and lived above with his wife, Sally, seemed a good candidate. He'd taught at *Shalom* on the cults, New Age groups and at special preparatory classes for the Ann Arbor Art Fair. He'd been a guest on the *Nightlight Show*, and a participant in two warmly received productions: *Gravity* and *Genesis Wars* (Al did make a splendid Francis Schaefer did he not?). I and the elders were satisfied he'd be a right fit. Al's wife Sally had some misgivings, but was willing to give it a go. Apparently, so did most of the congregation.

· · · ·

Just 33 years old, eleven pastoral years under my belt, calling it a day for now … half hoping someday I'll be back. The congregation gave me a warm retirement (sounds weird, retirement at 33 years old); let's call it a farewell party and dinner. *Sail*, with Henry Woodworth and Paul Patton, *Jubal*, Dave and Jean Mehi … speeches from the Heady brothers (Jim and Jerry) … were all quite moving, my dad sitting there smiling.

Inkster, MI., corner of Beech Daly & Dartmouth.

3852 BEECH DALY
INKSTER, MICHIGAN
JOSEPH SHANNON
MINISTER
562-4344

Promotional materials
for Shalom and
The Way Truth
and Life ministries.

GODS GRAFFITI

The Shalom Coffee House is an outreach of the Way, Truth, and Life Ministry. It began in 1974 with a handful of musicians, a minimal amount of sound equipment, and a desire to see Gods word go forth through contemporary Christian music in an informal setting.

As a result of this outreach many people have made the decision to accept Jesus Christ as Lord and Savior of their life. Many people have been set free from alcohol, drugs and occult involvement. Others have received both physical and mental healings. All this has been accomplished through the saving power of Jesus Christ.

Christian brothers and sisters of all ages and from all walks of life come together on coffee house night to fellowship together, and worship Our Lord, Jesus Christ. Coffee house night has proved to be a time of spiritual refreshment, of getting to know one another better and of establishing new friendships. These are just a few of the fringe benefits of this evangelistic out-reach.

WAY, TRUTH, AND LIFE MINISTRY

The Way, Truth and Life Ministry is a fundamental, non-denominational Christian Organization ministering primarily to the youthful subculture. Our purpose is to help free these people from drugs, spiritual deception, and the hate that has began to destroy them. To see them firmly established in a Bible believing church; ours or one convient to their location and needs.

In July of 1974 we incorporated with the State of Michigan, and in 1977 we received our tax exempt ststus from the Internal Revenue Service.

In the future we hope to be able to continue our work, and expand as God directs us. Our primary functions are: to be evangelistic (sharing the Gospel of Jesus Christ as found in Mark 16:15-18), and to build up and strengthen the saints in the faith. Your prayers and generous gifts are appreciated.

A special note of thanks to the Lord Jesus Christ, the giver of life, who truly is the Way, the Truth, and the Life. Also to evangelist Herman Stalvey, whose ministry and faithful dedication has been a source of real encouragement.

GODS GRAFFITI

Gods what!...Gods graffiti...and yes we're more than slang on the wall. Musicians is what we are. Each with a unique, personal and living relationship with Jesus Christ. We can perform individually or as a team. From left to right, up against the wall we are: Ken Hasper, Debbie Ordus, Joe Shannon, Dawn Baird, Roy Horton, Maureen Siler, Al Blade, Keith Savoie and Ken Pore.

Dawn Baird......................Dawn's music has a folkie flavor to it. It's as warm and personal as she is.

Maureen Siler.....................Maureen's music soars high and dives low, it's powerful and full of life.

Ken Pore.........................Mr. Versatile...jazz, rock, country, classical...it's all here. Kenny's first album will be available soon.

Ken Hasper.........................Ken's music communicates. It's folk with rock overtones.

Living Water.........................Rock & what!...Yea, that's right...rock and roll. These guys take literally Psalm 98:4...Make a joyful noise unto the Lord, all the earth: make a loud noise, and rejoice, and sing praise... Not only are Al, Keith and Roy fine musicians, but they minister, teach and counsel as well. They like to rock, but the rock, Jesus, comes first.

Debbie Ordus.........................Debbie is part of the Shalom House band and plays piano for Sunday Worship.

Joe Shannon ....Joe pastors the Way, Truth and Life Ministry. He also sings with the group and does a live radio show on WMUZ.

197

Chosen Few (Jubal) c. 1976

Shalom Band:
Dave & Jean Mehi,
Dino Vallone,
Joe Shannon,
Ken Hasper

Progressive Razz
c. 1975

Shalom "All the young dudes, carry the Good News."
Left to right: Mike Sherman, Jim Duncan, Tim Meyer, Glenn Kough,
Jim Heady, Joe Shannon, Ken Hasper

Bob Holt Band c. 1977

Sonquest c. 1977

Shalom House Band @
Old Detroit Grande Ballroom

Shalom Gang c. 1976

Shalom Hayride
c. 1979
Left to right:
Joe Shannon,
Kenny Meeks,
Steve Faunce,
Rob Bialowicz

Foundfree c. 1978 (from Philadelphia, PA)

Phil Paonessa
& Lifelight
c. 1978

Crystal River
c. 1979
(from Vero Beach,
FLA)

Nightlight Show
WMZK F.M. 98
Mark Covert,
Amy Wilder,
Joe

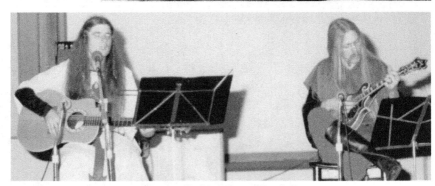

Kemper Crabb & Dave Marshall

Fletch Wiley c. 1980

James Issac Eliot & Jan Krist c. 1980

Joe: "Sometimes a way seems right,
but the end of it leads to death."
Prv 14:12

Paul McKenzie & Bruce Labadie c. 1981

Shalom Women's Softball c. 1980

Joe & Keith Savoie c. 1980

SHALOM
MINISTRY

22400 ECORSE RD.
TAYLOR, MICHIGAN
48180

291-7040

Ann Arbor Art Fair c. 1982: Kenny Meeks,
Mark & Debbie Covert, Joe

Living Water: Keith Savoie, Roy Horton & Al Blade c. 1984

205

Shalom Men's Softball c. 1982

Shalom Women's Softball c. 1982

Sail: Henry Woodworth, Paul Patton, Bob Couch, Dan Rimer c. 1984

Foreign Legion from Ontario, Canada c. 1982

Kenny Meeks Band

Foundfree c. 1982

Mylon c. 1984

Joe chillin with
Water, Blood &
Wine Band
from Miami,
FLA
c. 1982

Shalom Campout - Camp DeSalles in Irish Hills, MI c. 1982 (Above & below)

Jubal c. 1982

Joe and
Mark Covert
at Fairlane
Mansion,
Dearborn, MI
July, 1983

210

PART FOUR

GET BACK JOE JOE

I never had much of a backup plan. Figured since that day back in '73 when I'd been "called" to the ministry, once I started, I'd see it through till the end. One of my favorite contemporary Christian album covers was Paul Clark's *Hand to the Plow*. Those old gnarled hands, glued to the plow, fidelity to the task the clear message. The past few years I'd been troubled with the thought of what a drag it would be to find oneself down the road, pastoring largely because there was nothing else I could do, and/or because that's what others expected of you. That would not be sufficient to keep the fires burning, especially during prolonged crisis situations, periodic bouts of burnout, and crippling ordeals with unbelief. There I stood, unemployed, just moving out of the newlywed stage of marriage, looking at four years of school followed hopefully with a teaching career. What about pastoring? Some way, somehow, I'd be back. In the interim, it's back to the classroom in pursuit of a teaching degree with certifications in both English and History. A combination most of my advisers discouraged. Since history is your passion they reasoned, you need to pair it with something more marketable; math or science ... History/English teachers are a dime a dozen. "Thanks but no thanks," I thought to myself and stubbornly dug my heels in. Me and math have never clicked (I still struggle with long division), and science, well ditto that. Besides, if advisers are steering everyone away from that History/English combo, good, I'll be the more marketable. Furthermore, History and English better suit the needs and responsibilities of being a minister ... sermon preparation, newsletters, teaching, extensive reading and so on and as I said, I fully expect to be back in the preacher saddle someday.

First stop, Henry Ford Community College in Dearborn, Michigan, and by all accounts one of the better community colleges in the Midwest.

It was Fall '85 and things started off with a bang, or perhaps more of a dull thud. I'd taken an "Introduction to Logic" course, and the instructor, a brilliant logician, was a militant, in-your-face atheist. This was entirely unexpected and I was quite unprepared for such an encounter. I'm thirty-three ... most of the other students are fresh out of high school; what about them I wondered? My personal faith, which had taken some hits and been roughed up a bit, was in no condition to lock horns with this new adversary, especially in the classroom and on his turf. He could rattle off syllogisms faster than Jack Van Impe could dish out Bible verses. His fallacy analysis seemed airtight. I was one perturbed dude on the way home following this class. I lacked both the confidence and skill to respond in some articulate Thomistic dialectic regarding the utter reasonableness that we may indeed conclude God not only exists, but loves and desires a relationship with each of us. Oh how I longed to shut his arrogant trap from rambling endlessly on as to how stupid and illogical it was to entertain these childish notions that God, especially the Christian concept of a personal relationship with the divine, was the domain of suspicious, ignorant morons. The young students around me cringed before this blasphemous Protagoras.[24] A few could care less one way or the other. The grade on their transcript was utmost on their agenda, and they would nod their head in blind assent to most anything that might favorably impact their GPA.

Once I tried the "loose and bind" approach (Mt 16:19). I hoped he'd choke on his own words, or better yet, be struck blind like the sorcerer Elymas who'd so tried the Apostle Paul's patience. Well, he just continued to ramble on. Further reflecting on this incident, I carefully read over Paul's run-in with the sorcerer (see Acts 13). I noticed Paul was "filled with the Holy Ghost" when he cursed Elymas. I'm not certain what I was filled with. My instructor in logic was filled with "crappola," of that I was certain. Ah well, live to fight, er, debate another day.

I dropped the "Introduction to Logic" class. After a couple of weeks listening to God heckling, coupled with the frustration of not being able to go toe-to-toe with this guy in his "ring" I wondered, "why am I paying for

---

[1]   An ancient Greek philosopher credited with coining the phrase: "Man is the measure of all things...."

this? I don't need this BS." It was starting to wear on me spiritually, and while I would have liked to script a much cooler ending, kind of a spiritual *Rocky I* movie … the no name student comes out of nowhere and flattens Apollo (the arrogant atheist) Creed; no, I slipped out the back door. Don't recall if I ever prayed for the man; guess I should have.

Speech class was a better fit. Five years of hosting a radio show under my belt and eleven years of presenting the Gospel before friendly and hostile audiences. Public speaking did not intimidate me. Ah, here's something I could hold my ground in and perhaps even excel. Lord knows I needed a heavy dose of confidence builder. Our final speech assignment was a demonstration speech. Most of my classmates' presentations went pretty well; one poor soul's "How to Make a Smoothie" demonstration went awry … poor gal nervously hit the high speed when she should have hit low … it erupted like Mt. St. Helens; blew the top right off. There was guitar tuning (a former band mate and Shalom member – Rob Bialowicz), dress hemming, and yawn, how to set a formal dinner table. My demonstration was last at my request since I knew I'd be making a bit of a mess. With ten minutes left I slipped out like Clark Kent and returned decked out in my crisp Tae Kwon Do uniform pulling a wagon loaded with cement slabs and other paraphernalia necessary for this stunt. This certainly got everyone's attention. After a several minute lecture on the how and why of risking breaking your hand at what first might look like a silly endeavor only adolescent boys, Chuck Norris wannabees, and adults who still feel the need to prove themselves (uh, the latter might be me), I deftly went cleanly through the stacked slabs accompanied by a deafening yell (breathing technique), and when the dust cleared I was certain, "that one's in the bag." Indeed, I earned an A in the course, just the lil shot of confidence booster I sorely needed.

· · · ·

I think I invented the vice-grip Lamaze method technique. You guys who've been in the delivery room assisting (yeah, right, where's the smelling salts) your wife during delivery, know that hopeless feeling you have as she glares at you with that, "Oh my God this hurts, do something" look.

"Okay, breathe honey." Hmm, was that who/hah or hah/who? At one point, towards the end when we, or at least I and the attending physician, could see the baby's head, I dutifully manned the soft music and ice chips. You ladies may be thinking big deal and I can't fault you for that. Still, I was there … I tried … could there be a moment when husband and wife feel closer than immediately after the birth of a child?

Our firstborn (7/10/86), a son, had so much black hair, even sideburns …"maybe we should name him Elvis." We settled on Cory James. Turned out to be good timing though can't say we timed it thus. Actually, all three of our kids were a surprise, well, not entirely. You know what I mean. As one of my married lady friends pointed out, "If you're not using protection, get ready … God loves children." Since Cory was a midsummer baby, we could arrange my upcoming fall classes around my wife's schedule. She would continue to be the primary "breadwinner" until I earned my degree and hopefully secured a teaching position. This would put me in a bit of a "Mr. Mom" role.

You arouse a great deal of interest when you stroll into a restaurant, library, supermarket, with an infant. Plop, still asleep in his car seat, diaper bag with a bottle or two slung over my shoulder. At first folks pay you only casual interest … well mom must be slow making her way in … along any moment I expect. In time it dawns on them, "my goodness, just this big guy with a newborn." Here they come. Like timid autograph seekers. "Oh, can we see the baby? How old is he? Look at his hair!"

Fortunately, my wife worked nearby at Heritage Hospital in Taylor, and we often coordinated her lunch with the opportunity to bring Cory up for his "lunch" (nursings).

As much as I would have liked to zip through school and secure a decent paid teaching position, the time I spent with Cory … bathing, feeding, changing diapers (I got pretty good at it), allowed me an opportunity to interact with my son on a level most dads are unable to, what with work, military. Okay, so changing diapers isn't all that fun. I use to tell myself, "Hey, someone (mom) used to do it for you, so…." I had a buddy down South who occasionally found himself in that, for him, unaccustomed role of having to change a dirty (#2) diaper. He'd take his boy outside and hose him off. Count your blessings Cory.

When Cory moved into the toddler stage and I needed time to study, I'd like to thank whoever invented the Jolly Jumper. I'd put Cory in that

215

contraption suspended between the kitchen and living room, put on some classic rock ... and bing, bang, zoom ... he'd bounce around like a pinball, laughin, spinnin ... after 15 minutes it'd begin to taper off ... 5 minutes later, he'd be slumped forward, out on his feet. Getting him out without waking him was a bit tricky. Ah, an hour or two of quiet.

. . . .

The close of the eighties witnessed several big changes. During the spring of '89 I earned a teaching degree from EMU. Our second child, a son – Jesse, was born; a St. Patrick's Day baby announced on WJR by the late great J.P. McCarthy. We moved from our modest home in the south end of Dearborn Heights to a beautiful brick bungalow with family room and natural fireplace on Hipp St. in Dearborn; perfect for the kids. St. Sebastian playground to our south, Elmhurst-Schemansky neighborhood park along Outer Drive to our north, and the Whitmore-Bolles Elementary School with outdoor pool an easy bike ride away.

Now, with a teaching degree in hand, the cold reality that teaching jobs weren't exactly plentiful hit home. Subbing (Dearborn School District) gets old real quick. The Gulf War was in high gear, and several of the classes I covered at Dearborn's Edsel Ford H.S. included students with extended family members on both sides of the conflict. Tense? You bet! On top of that, subs weren't exactly "bringing home the bacon"... maybe adding a little broth to the soup. While it didn't pay very well, one could gain a wealth of experience ... kind of an initiation, welcome to public education, and some days, a baptism of fire.

A teaching position at Wyandotte Hospital caught my eye – Adolescent Psychiatry. "You're hired!" Boy, hope I haven't bitten off more than I can chew. Sure is a great view though; seventh floor overlooking the Detroit River. At any moment, football field length freighters making their way up and down the river. Gulls, suspended like kites, peering through the large, thick paned windows, with that annoyed look wondering how these mere mortals got up into their air-space. The small student body at Wyandotte Adolescent Psych was a mixed (male/female) population. I was expected to teach all subjects (hope I don't get any Algebra and above students), and well, it was a Psych ward. If a kid "flipped" out, he/she would be "bum rushed" by the staff, restrained until a nurse arrived with a hypo, and lights out.

I recall the staff being a caring group. One of the clinical psychiatrists, Wendy, was a musician; acoustic guitar, folkie genre. I thought the kids would get a kick out of hearing themselves on tape. Lugging up an old, Sony reel-to-reel tape recorder left over from Shalom radio days to the seventh floor is no easy task. After a few days of rehearsal it was "ready or not, here we come." Students, staff, visitors, accompanied by the "Joan Baez" of the seventh floor, and we produced a not too shabby version of "Lean on Me." Think Michael Jackson's and Quincy Jones' "We Are the World." But, instead of a who's who from the music industry, a crowd of "troubled" kids, staff, and me smack dab in the middle. That recording (long since misplaced), was the highlight of my short-lived employment there, followed closely by winning (for the entire hospital), a January through April weight loss competition … 30 lbs.! Of course, much more fun putting it back on.

The hospital changed hands, endured some restructuring including employee cutbacks, and being one of the new kids on the block, I was let go. Months later a line from a Phil Keaggy tune put this episode in perspective, something about, "disappointment is His (God's) appointment;" seems God had arranged that brief stint at Wyandotte Hospital (minor leagues), as a warm-up for the majors. Stay tuned.

I took a summer school teaching position; such a move often betrays a healthy dose of desperation. My new employer, Vista Maria, Michigan's largest home for girls, set on a 38 acre campus along the Rouge River in the northeast corner of Dearborn Heights bordering Detroit. Young ladies (12-18 years) placed there by the courts for a myriad of reasons, whose lives by the age of 15 were often the stuff of your worst nightmares … abuse, neglect, abandonment. Many were runaways, and in many instances when you looked into their family history, you'd run too.

You're all aware of that first day on the job jitters. Teeth brushed, hair trimmed, casual but professional apparel … here I go, and as I headed east down Warren from Outer Drive towards the secured entrance of the lock-down facility the butterflies began their dance. "How tough can this be," I murmured trying to calm myself. "Hell, if I could handle a mixed population at Adolescent Psych. Wyandotte Hospital, this should be…."

"Good morning, do you have your I.D.? Great, teachers use the parking lot on the west side, right over there."

Well, two hours into my first day and so far so good. Often teachers experience an initial "honeymoon" period with their students, and so the young ladies took me for an unexpected component, something new on the menu for a change, a welcome respite to their drab, monotonous routine … it's summer and I hate being here while all my friends are having fun … locked up in this wannabe rehab center. Also in my favor, for the moment at least, I was a male and someone new to converse with.

"Uh, excuse me, Mr. Shannon; we're going into a CTA – Clear the Area (lock-down) … ladies, to your rooms … no talking. Mr. Shannon, the staff over at BEATA Hall needs your assistance right away. It's the building to the right as you leave. Your key will get you in."

"Hmm, what's this all about?" I wondered to myself as I bound up the steps. Before I could insert the key the door flew open nearly knocking me off the porch. "Quick, up the stairs," an anxious woman, breathing heavy, managed to mumble. Screaming, cursing … sounded like a wrestling match coming from the second story. "Get away from me you … I'll kill you mutha … go ahead grab me bitch, I'll bite yo mutha – ass." There, huddled in a corner of a dark, foreboding hallway, at once sobbing, and then cursing, crouched a young girl of about 16. Like a cornered mountain lion, hissing, hands extended claw like, waiting for the pack of hounds to move in; she would not be taken (restrained) without a fight.

Staff didn't have time to brief me on the situation; they huddled nearby after unsuccessfully trying to extract her. Four Vista Maria staff planned their next move. As one they regarded me. "Who are you?" One of them asked.

"Why do they need me," I wondered to myself. "Is this some kinda first day initiation?" I'd only been on the job two hours. "There are four of them. What's the big deal?"

They reminded me of the County Road Commission crews you sometimes see along the highway. One guy in a hole digging away while several others stand idly around drinking coffee and having a smoke. Now, these Vista staffers have decided I need to grab her and get her out of that defensive cornered position so we as a group could restrain her.

"Uh, be careful, she's a biter," one of the staff anxiously warned me.

"If this girl tries to bite me, she'll be eatin soup with a straw for awhile," I mused to myself. "I don't need this gig that bad."

"Okay, honey, c'mon, get up … this is my first day, give me a break, huh." Lord, help me to take charge of this situation I silently prayed.

Shouldn't there be a nurse here with a hypo ready to put this kid "out." Well I'll be. Dracula's daughter stood up, smiled at me and walked to the behavior-mod room like she was going to the mall. The Vista staff was dumbfounded. I didn't stick around to chat. I was assigned to teach in one of the four resident living quarter buildings – Beata Hall, the psych unit where the "crazy" girls live, as they like to half-jokingly describe themselves. Incidentally, psych unit ... sound familiar? The second floor classroom was small, and twelve students was a tight fit. Hot? Lord have mercy ... no air, cheap, noisy fans strategically positioned bringing little relief. Some days you could feel the sweat trickle down your back. And smell? Like a chicken coop in August thanks to pigeons nesting in the windows, who, in spite of daily evictions, managed somehow to reclaim their turf by sunup the following day. The adjacent room (behavior mod room), think padded cell, and if occupied by one of the young ladies "goin off" conveniently while you're trying to conduct class, good luck. First screams and shrieks that Linda Blair in the film *The Exorcist* would envy, followed by sobbing, swearing ... and after having exhausted venting thus, then faintly, but steadily growing in volume and intensity, the pounding, rhythmic beating against the walls that can go on for hours. The staff here, more often than not, just let the girls go on like this expecting in time they'll have had enough, take a nap, and the whole episode will likely be forgotten. Okay for staff, they're way down the hall. I'm in a classroom with an increasingly angry mob about ready to storm the adjacent room and ring little miss goin off's neck. Why don't they send for the hypo nurse like at Wyandotte? My "Vista Maria" attitude may have been born that day.[25]

On another occasion, "Okay, ladies, let's continue with our lesson on *The Red Badge of Courage* ... hey, sit down, you just got here ... I haven't eaten either ... Okay, so I wear an earring ... your dead mother appeared to you last night ... what war? The Civil War...."

A bit of a commotion down the hall grabbed our attention. I had a direct line of vision from behind my desk and what appeared to be several "suits" were making their way straight for us!

---

[2]   See Appendix 3 for an unusual memo teachers received one day while employed at Vista Maria/Clara B. Ford School. You teachers will go, "Wow!"

"Hi, we're from Dearborn Public Schools ... on a tour of your campus." Following a few nods and awkward introductions including giving me the once over ... I'm in shorts, tank top and flip flops ... I'd quickly ditched a few weeks earlier my first day casual yet professional look ... in this heat and at any moment you could be called upon to restrain one of these gals ... anyway, the Vista folks didn't mind and that's who I worked for.

"Dearborn Public Schools eh ... hmm, something's up."

Up indeed, Dearborn Public Schools was slated to take control of the education at Vista Maria beginning the next school year (Sept. '91), just a few weeks away! The Vista campus was buzzing with excitement. They (Dearborn Public Schools and incoming principal Terry Campbell), would interview current Vista Maria teachers (ten or so of us), if we were interested in hiring on with Dearborn and teaching at Vista Maria. Interested! Are they kiddin'? This is too good to be true. Talk about right place at the right time ... slow down Joe, you're not hired yet. My interview with Terry Campbell was scheduled last.

This guy isn't gonna wanna talk to me after interviewing a dozen other potential hires. It'll probably be a 5 minute "how ya doin?" Make it look like we're giving all former Vista teachers a shot. We talked for an hour. I decided not to be shy about my past, including eleven years as a minister. Why should I ... teaching at Vista Maria would be no stroll down Piccadilly Lane, and I wanted Mr. Campbell to know I could handle it.

Following two days of little rest and less sleep ... ring, ring. "Hello ... hi, yes this is Joe ... oh; hey hello Mr. Campbell ... the position is mine if I want it. (Okay, Joe, don't act so shocked, yet) ... yes, of course ... thank you." There was great joy in the Shannon-on-Hipp-St. household that night. Only downer was I had to cut out early from our family vacation on Glen Lake up on the beautiful Leelanau Peninsula to get back for a three day orientation before school starts. Wonder why we need three days ... and come dressed in loose, gym clothes ... what's up with that? Volleyball tryouts or what? This would be a new experiment. Union member Dearborn Public Schools would partner with non-union Vista Maria in providing education for the residents. Bit of a no brainer to see this venture's going to be a bumpy ride at best. Dearborn teachers' role as educators didn't always fit in comfortably with Vista's primary role – treatment, and so began for the most part, a friendly, professional relationship. There were "pot holes" a plenty however, and a few eighteen-wheeler swallowing sink holes, but what work environment this side of heaven is always smooth sailing? Oh, the loose clothes for orientation, that was for two days of NCI (Nonviolent Crisis Intervention) training. I suspected as much. Two days of restraint training … take downs, holds, how to come out of restraints without teeth marks. During breaks and lunch you would have overheard anxious new teachers whispering amongst each other, "Hey, aren't we in the union? We need to look into this … what's up with this restraint stuff? What if I get hurt or accidentally injure one of these girls?" Recall this is something of a new experiment … uncharted waters … none of us are tenured … breath deep and move easy … there's a dozen of us (new hires). We're all in this together. We'll make it.

And, make it we did. Several of us went the distance (1991-2007), when the grand experiment came to an abrupt end. Vista Maria had decided to go charter school, and so we parted ways, somewhat amicably, but it had always been somewhat of a strained relationship, like a mixed marriage between a believer and nonbeliever, sometimes pulling in different directions and obsessed with your own agenda, and unwilling to spend time traveling in the other fella's shoes. The Vista tales are legion; here are a couple of the more memorable ones.

"Oh … oh … this could be the big one, I'm comin ta meet cha honey … oh, it won't be long now," cried Fred Sanford on yet another episode of *Sanford and Son*, while gripping his chest, staggering around in the living room like the town drunk, pained expression, eyes heavenward, and often as not, little more than an act usually fueled by an altercation with "you big dummy …" his son, Lamont, or the feisty Aunt Esther. It was the last day of school that first year ('91) at Vista Maria. It had been an especially sweltering day in the second floor classroom of Lourdes Hall; me and seven or eight students. Last days are traditionally laid back, even celebratory … all seemed well, just countin' down the minutes … Alice Cooper's "School's Out" playing for the umpteenth time in my mind. What's this? Dull, foreign chest pains unlike anything I'd ever experienced, nor could they easily be cast aside as just some uncomfortable "afterglow" following a spicy lunch from the rundown storefront Chinese restaurant across the street. "Oh, they'll pass in a moment," I reassured myself.

"Excuse me, ladies, let's just chill a bit. I'm gonna put my head down … the heat and all. I don't feel so hot."

"Dang, Mr. Shannon, you ain't lookin too good … you paler than a snake's belly."

"Could one a you guys ask the staff to call the campus nurse … my chest hurts." Zoom, zam, gone … you'd a thought someone just hollered, "Clear the Area," in which case residents must immediately proceed to their rooms, remain silent (lockdown mode), or risk disciplinary consequences. As one of them beat it down the hallway I heard her cry out, "dat man havin a heart attack … I'm gone. I don't wanna watch him die."

I don't recall a nurse rushing over (may not have been one on campus), and while the chest pains didn't intensify, they stubbornly hung around, and it seemed prudent and at the urging of the in-house principal, Susan King, I drove myself over to nearby Fairlane Hospital (I declined an ambulance). Here's one for the dedication record books. While being evaluated from the emergency room a nurse brought me a phone so I could call my grades in which were due at the end of the day. Turns out I had some sort of stress attack. Summer vacation couldn't have come at a better time.

On another occasion, back at BEATA Hall, it became nigh impossible to conduct a class one afternoon due to the constant, can't hear myself think pounding, coming from a nearby BMR (Behavior Mod Room), where an older, good-sized gal, seemed determined to beat the door down. The steady blows against the heavy door reminded me of the rhythmic, and at times crucial, beating of a solitary drum with heavy drumsticks, more like clubs, to ensure that the rowers, usually slaves and/or criminals temporarily forestalling a death sentence, kept the vessel moving at the commander's ordered speed. Think, *Ben Hur* …"what is your name, 41?"

This young gal had steadily progressed to a "ramming speed" rate and I'd had it. I was just about to call my principal when one of the Vista staff poked her head inside the classroom and in a controlled firm tone said, "Ladies, we are going into a CTA. Go quietly to your rooms. Mr. Shannon, we've got a problem."

Boom, boom, like some orc drum deep in the mines of Moria, and you know it's about to get interesting. What's this? The door is starting to come off the hinges … in a few minutes she'll be … this is no hollow wood, cheap, closet door … this is the door to the BMR room in a lock down facility … you know, where they could securely lock up Norman Bates should he join the party.

The three female staffers, that desperate pleading look in their eyes, asked me to stay. They couldn't leave, not with a dozen other residents locked in nearby rooms. We huddled in the nearby office while one staffer put out a couple of calls; one a campus wide alert and call for backup, and a second one to the cavalry – Dearborn Heights Police. In the meantime, I helped the other two barricade our office door … desk, couch, and file cabinets. In order to break out of the unit, she'd have to go through us (we had the keys). The film wasn't out at the time, but you'll remember that great scene from Peter Jackson's first installment of the Tolkien trilogy, *The Fellowship of the Ring,* when the nine members of the fellowship were barricaded behind a thick, heavy wooden door, awaiting attack by a host of orcs accompanied by a cave troll while deep in the mines of Moria. Our plight might not have been so desperate, but once our "cave troll" broke out of the BMR room and went to work on the less heavy office door, I seriously began to wonder what I would do should she succeed. You'd think four of us would be enough to restrain her. Maybe, but some of these gals possess almost superhuman demonic strength, and she'd just come through one door. Three nervous staff women, one praying, one swearing, one rolling her eyes, made sure I was between them and the pile of office furniture against the door. And, just like the first door, the hinges on this one began to break free. In another minute she'd be through. Suddenly she stopped … shouts from without … keys rattling to unbolt a door giving access to the second floor. Had help arrived in the nick-of-time? A new husky voice broke the odd silence. "Okay now miss … you stay calm … don't resist, we're gonna cuff you."

The cavalry had indeed arrived. Two Dearborn Heights police officers and several Vista administrators, and at the sight of such a show of force, especially from two cops who were in no mood for a confrontation, and like a scene out of *Dr. Jekyll and Mr. Hyde*, our unhappy camper marched docilely to another BMR room in a nearby building to await an updated psychiatric evaluation.

Back home that evening. "So, hon, how was school (work) today?"
"Oh fine."

• • • •

Vista Maria, after several years of debate, finally agreed to conduct most of the education classes in the main building on campus. Getting out of the units (the girls' on-campus living quarters) would be a plus for students and teachers we reasoned. Vista was concerned about the issue of transporting the girls to and from school, a distance of a hundred yards or less, and the risk of girls using transport time as an opportunity to make a "break" for the fences. Transport, especially during inclement weather, was something of an inconvenience, laziness perhaps, but in our minds (Dearborn faculty), the pros far outweighed the cons. Running during transport never became a big deal; however, on a couple of occasions, it could be quite entertaining as you watched Vista staff do a pretty good rendition of the Keystone Cops[26] while trying to chase down a resident before she could make it over a fence; if she did, the Heights police would be called for assistance. Vista and the police knew once outside campus, the girl's "M.O." was to beat it down Warren east towards Evergreen (Detroit), where they could access a phone at a gas station/donuts shop. A convenient place for the cops to intercept them … don't cha think? Running north or west was a bad move. If you did get over the Rouge River (west), the poison ivy, mosquitoes, and the creeps lurking in the bushes (what I use to tell them) will get ya … kinda paint a *Pappion* (Devil's Island) picture for them. Still, from time to time, one of them would scale the fence in spite of the barbed wire, and risk a west/north escape, perhaps since they knew most girls who headed south/east were returned in cuffs and usually within an hour. I use to wonder what would/could we do if 20, 30, hell all of them bolted at once. Dearborn faculty didn't normally participate in the "chase." I wish I had video of the dozen or more times a gal dashed by my window like some track star, followed momentarily by half a dozen "staffers," some of them pretty big … huffin' and a puffin', slippin' and a-slidin', hollerin' like they were bein' chased by the devil, knowing the girl stood a good chance of scaling the fence before they could take her down.

"They ain't gonna catch her," I'd say to myself. "Lord, if she makes it, please don't let her get hurt." It's a jungle out there, but many of our girls were willing to take that risk.

---

[26] A bunch of bungling cops featured in early 20th century cinema comedies.

In time, I had the good fortune of securing one of the better classrooms. Best of all it was furthest from the principal's office (you teachers understand what I mean … kind of an out-of-sight out-of-mind thing). The room had one wall of windows with a northwest view and sometimes an entertaining show: student shenanigans, staff and custodial personnel that at times reminded one of *The Three Stooges* meet *The Jeffersons*. All visitors come up the sidewalk leading to the entrance and up the stairs outside my classroom door leading upstairs to Vista administrative offices. Lots of traffic, and with the girls (and me) so easily distracted, our classroom door usually remained closed (though never locked, in case a classroom brawl broke out and I needed staff assistance … happened maybe once a year, and I think I called a CTA maybe three times in 16 years), and the blinds drawn, in the event that whenever a stranger walked by, especially a young male, UPS delivery man or whatever, and the girls rushed the windows to gawk … most embarrassing.

I've never quite figured out how/why the girls from the Psych. Unit (BEATA), that the other residents and they themselves sometimes referred to as the "crazy" girls, seemed to be able to pick up on the Shakespeare lessons, character analysis, plot complications and so on, at a much deeper level than the other, mainstream residents. They seemed to understand right where Lady Macbeth, Ophelia, Cordelia and other, usually tragic female characters were coming from. Indeed, many of their "stories" mirrored the tragic figures the Bard introduced us to. One girl in particular, a tiny thing who couldn't have weighed more than 75 lbs. soaking wet, whose name escapes me and face just a hazy memory, stood head and shoulders above her peers in this regard. Indeed, she'd tell me what was going on in the minds of some of these characters. I'd think to myself, "Vista staff better hope this girl doesn't organize a revolt, mass escape … she's way smarter than the lot of them." She hated the place, and nothing unusual about that. "Wonder why she hasn't made a break for it?" I'd mentioned to a few colleagues.

The school had one ground floor restroom in an area called the quad where staff typically placed themselves to be centralized in the event of a classroom CTA, and to monitor the bathroom; a favorite excuse/time, if a resident was going to make a break for it. I'd just sent a girl down to the bathroom (with a pass), and noticed that my petite, Shakespeare scholar from BEATA wasn't in class. "Absent," I thought to myself.

"Clear the area," came echoing down the hall like a foghorn at sea ... louder and with a more serious than usual edge to it. Pandemonium, screams, and then "call 911," somebody yelled. More screams.

If that girl I just sent down there caused all this fuss, I'll ... hmm, maybe she ran ... can't be that hard to catch ... doubt she could do the 100 yard dash in under a minute. "What? No way. Is she alright?"

Seems the girl I sent to the bathroom opened a stall door to find my Shakespeare scholar student – hanging! Fortunately they got her down in time. Of course this caused a great deal of concern including a thorough review of procedures. It was decided the young gal needed more intense psychiatric care than Vista Maria could provide. She was quickly and quietly transferred to a more secure psychiatric care facility. I wish I'd gotten a chance to speak to her, but I couldn't help wondering if she'd engineered the entire episode, after all, she wanted out, as in out of Vista, in the worst way.

I don't know why I took on a summer school assignment one year; must have needed the extra bucks. There had been some higher level racial (white-black) tension between the residents of late ... name calling mostly, posturing, a few fights. Be on the lookout for gang "stuff:" rolled up pant legs, tattoos, and hand signs. Ah, but today would be different. Wouldn't you know it? We'd be working with a "skeleton" crew of Vista staff, and it being Friday and summer, most of the administrators would be "down the road" long before the school day ended.

"Clear the area. Clear the area ... we need help out here!"

A dozen long strides found me in the hall. "Oh, boy, this is gonna be good."   A group of African American girls had a white girl down and were giving her what for. The white girl I recognized and it surprised me as I knew her for keeping to herself, quiet ... why would they go after her? No time to launch an investigation. Students in other classes could hear the commotion and knew the "game" was on. It may have been planned ... hall against hall maybe, white/black, straight/lesbian ... all of the above? The CTA directives fell on deaf ears. Staff was quickly overwhelmed as a half- dozen fights went into overdrive the length of the hallway. The staff (woman) assigned outside my door, whose main job was to be sure no residents exited the west building door near my room lay slumped against a wall. "Sucker punched," I guessed.

"Take your pick," I quickly mused. The white girl on the floor somewhere beneath a group of girls bent on hurting her big time was where I waded in and decided not to be too gentle about it. These are, after all, high school girls, and a few looked like they could wrestle in the popular-at-the-time World Wrestling Federation. After giving the heave-ho to several, I managed to pull the now hysterical girl and target of the assault up and behind me. As we eased back, her attackers prepared to make another rush for her, and sought to embolden themselves with loud yells, cursing that would make a sailor blush, and "git out da way, Mr. Shannon, or we'll…."

"Where the hell are the teachers?" I wondered. I hope someone dropped a dime on the Heights police. Administrators, if they were on campus (the floor above us), should be piling down here. A quick look down the long hallway revealed staff outnumbered and overwhelmed by a half dozen separate fracases; they may not have been able to use the lone phone in the quad could they get to it. We were fast approaching riot level. We were alone and with each turn of the minute hand more girls joined the brawl.

Fortunately, the stairs leading up to the second floor were but a few yards behind me. The dazed girl and I bumped up against the first step just as the "pack" decided to bum rush the both of us.

The young lady, paralyzed with fear, would be slow to respond. Tarzan-like, I slung her over my shoulder and bounded up halfway to the first landing, turned, executed a make my old Tae Kwon Do instructor proud sidekick into the gut of the first girl leading the pack, down she/they went with a howl of curses and momentary confusion; thankfully, none were seriously hurt but for a few scrapes and bruises; the kick, incidentally, was a thrust (push) technique, and given the situation seemed appropriate ... I'd do the same thing again under the circumstances.

This brought us enough time to find an office with a startled lone administrator, jaw gaping at me as I plopped a girl down in front of him. "We got trouble downstairs. A group of girls wanna kill her. Lock yourselves in. Call the police. I gotta go."

Wide-eyed, all he could muster was a, "ah, yeah, sure." How he could not have heard the wild commotion by now in high gear one floor beneath him; maybe he's just hard of hearing.

Well, which brawl shall I join? Might as well take the one nearest my class and work my way down the hall. I noticed out of the corner of my

227

eye that the school counselor Bill Fundaro had finally joined the festivities. He'd come late but at least he'd come. Guess we disturbed his nap, hah. These girls can be feisty but are generally low on stamina. In the end we got the upper hand. The police never showed. Maybe no one called; we were after all quickly and overwhelmingly engaged (pre-cell phone era). Maybe the Heights police were on a donuts run; just kidding. I was kind of hoping to see the "pepper spray" swat team join the "dance."

For balance sake, at least one good time, and there were many, should be mentioned. I am easily amused. On this occasion I nearly got myself in hot water, but once again dodged the bullet.

The CBF principal and Vista "high command" had given me leave to take 8 plus students and two staffers to a presentation of *Macbeth* down at the Hillberry Theater near the Wayne State University campus. The students were hand-picked from my Shakespeare classes, and the most important criteria was zero to very low expectation that they'd use the outing to "run." Particular details, location and specific times were kept confidential in case anyone had the idea of getting "picked up" if the opportunity presented itself. The principal, Larry Simon, graciously worked into the outing money for a late lunch (the weekday matinee ended at about 2 p.m.), and we all thought it would be cool to eat somewhere downtown. I knew just the place. I'd surprise them.

"Uh, Mr. Shannon," one of the staff exclaimed, "we can't take these girls in there."

"Why not?"

"They serve alcohol … Vista regulations forbid takin kids into any place that serves alcohol."

"Don't worry about it. I'll take responsibility for it," I reassured her. The smell of barbecue that hung heavy on the sidewalk outside was likely the real persuader. Both staff deferred to my logic. "Look, we're hungry … it's getting late … I'm not drivin around lookin for a White Castle. Besides, the girls are psyched!"

"Wow, Mr. Shannon, the Hard Rock Café!" I wanted this to be a day my girls wouldn't soon forget, and no doubt seeing a stellar production of *Macbeth* already hit a home-run with them (only glitch was one of the staff fell asleep during the performance … kids were more embarrassed than I was); the Hard Rock Café would be the icing on the cake. My own two older kids were in their teens, and I'd have no qualms about bringing my own in here ... not like we're going to belly up to the bar for a round of Bloody Mary's. We ended up sitting in an area outside the bar section – perfect. Soft drinks, iced teas and several platters of appetizers capped off an awesome day.

. . . .

My sixteen Vista years include a dimension most teachers don't care to think about let alone discuss. Well, here it is. We've heard plenty of stories concerning the school day crush most of us carried for a favorite teacher or two. I even had one for a nun during eighth grade. I thought she was kind of cute and she encouraged me to sing, especially leading worship at Mass for the elementary grades, but that lil crush was short-lived. And, you've likely heard the Police (Sting) tune – "Don't Stand So Close?" How about when a teacher gets a crush on a student? This would happen to me not once, twice, but three times during my 16 years at Vista Maria. The last one almost did me in. It's likely no accident that all three, especially the last two, transpired during the "dark" years of my marriage ... a topic I'm still debating whether to address. I probably will, after all, it's the proverbial elephant in the living room, so I suppose I'll deal with it before I put the final period down.

The first "crush" incident was not a reciprocal type of thing, and so it was the least dangerous. Oh, she liked me well enough as a teacher. She was warm, friendly, but that was it. I kept my feelings, which terrified me, under wraps. She may have had a bit of a "father" figure vibe for me. Many of these young ladies at Vista Maria have no father figure, and a poor image of men (given many have experienced abuse) as well; many suffering trauma at the hands of mom's boyfriend. Add to that the general loneliness of being separated from family and friends in a lock-down facility, at such tender ages, starved for attention ... you get the picture.

I hated to see her go. It's nice to have a friendly, warm, and in this case very attractive young woman greet you with a smile and a cheerful hello each day. The sigh heard round the world escaped from deep within me the day she left Vista Maria; we reconnected years later and keep in touch.

The second episode was of a more serious nature. At this juncture my marriage was entirely void of romance, and my expectations of that dimension returning null. Nor was I actively looking for romance in all the wrong places, but I knew I was an accident waiting to happen. This was the kind of girl I use to dream about in high school … total package: smart, great sense of humor with a magical laugh, a stunning gorgeous redhead, mature beyond her years. It began innocently enough. She'd stop by my classroom to chat. Her story, like so many others on campus, was the stuff of nightmares. Her warming up to me I assumed to be nothing more than a need to talk with someone other than the Vista staff, and the peers with whom she didn't relate well … mentally and emotionally she was years ahead of most of the residents. Since she'd never known a father, perhaps it's a simple case of the old "looking for a father figure."

As the weeks turned into months it dawned on me that I'd begun to develop "feelings" for this young gal. Now what? I didn't want to shut her down. She didn't appear to have many friends. Would I just be another in a long list of adults who'd let her down? And, to be sure, I rather liked the way she'd flirt with me, as though she expected nothing in return … no grade inflation or breaks. Unless I was gullible, blinded by infatuation, ego tripping … all of the above, that she'd come to view me as more than a "father figure" became increasingly apparent. Well, what's the harm? Nothing will come of it anyway. She was confined to a lock-down facility, me, a loveless marriage. At the conclusion of the school year that would be, as before, the end of it. If you think me way too casual about the whole "affair" I can assure you I was sorely vexed. Give these fantasies, romantic urges (still don't like to think of it as old fashioned lust), an inch, and I knew they'd take a mile; possibly pass the point of no return … a dead end. "How can you so much as think," I'd chastise myself. "You're married. She's young enough to be your daughter. Wake Up! You're playing with fire…." The attention became addictive.

"Mr. Shannon, I want to be with you," she softly whispered one day after sliding up a desk next to mine … "when I get outta this hole … you could even adopt me." The lost puppy in the pet store window look spoke as clear as her words.

Inside I'm thinking, "Done! Yes, let's do it."

Fortunately, I heard myself responding, "No girl, it would never work. One day you'll meet a young guy more your age and you'll be glad you waited."

Terrific, now here come the tears and the "but Mr. Shannon."

A month later the last day of school finally dawned. I know I had it bad because I should be ecstatic … school's out! That vibe was tempered with the realization I'd likely never see or hear from this young lady again. She'd be going to a girl's home in Belleville, MI while finishing her senior year of high school. I wouldn't give her my phone number or email at her repeated requests; I didn't want to hear from her.

The school had emptied out the last day, and I sat behind my desk tidying up and batting down the hatches before heading off for summer break. A melancholy mood weighed down my mind. Occasionally, I'd stand, stretch, gaze out the window at a nearby low-risk residents' unit, thinking I might get one last look at her. Later, deep in thought, head down, glued to my chair when I should have been long gone. Most everyone else had split. Staff and teachers had all bidden each other, "Have a great summer."

Head still down, I could faintly hear someone slowly, quietly approaching my desk. Another last to leave teacher perhaps come to shake hands on the way out. No, it was her, my student. I could tell she'd been crying. She said nothing as she slid a desk up next to mine like she'd done dozens of times before, sat down heavily and gave me that I'm hurting will you please hold me look. The classic guilt, how could you do this to me written on her Lady of Shallot countenance? "You know we could make it work. I could care less what people would think" she whispered.

The halls were strangely quiet. Looking her square in those beautiful green eyes I fought the urge to take her in my arms, and in a low voice declared, "because I do love and care about you … I know it wouldn't work … it would eventually turn on us, consume us … you'd come to rue the day we first met." It seemed odd, almost a betrayal to so easily express my love for her in word, something I hadn't been able in years do with the woman I'd sworn to "love as Christ loved the Church"(Eph 5:25). She sat there quietly, staring at me hard … probing. Did she realize deep down I was right? I stood to leave, "Come on," I said, "walk with me to the parking lot."

As she rose she stepped directly in front of me. Here comes a hug I guessed to myself, and why not? We could both use one. It was a warm, affectionate embrace. She glanced up with a sorrowful smile and moved, I thought, as if to give me a little peck on the cheek. She had something else in mind. And for the next few moments I no longer gave a damn. A shudder ran threw the length of my body as I came to my senses. How would I explain this "kiss" to someone should they poke their head in at that moment?

"C'mon … we need to go." Something in my voice must have convinced her that was it. She stoically walked alongside me. Neither of us said anything. Both of us occupied with our own deep thoughts.

As I pulled out of the parking lot and slowly made for the Vista Maria entrance/exit off Warren, I paused for a moment and glanced in my rear view mirror. There she stood, sobbing in the driveway, looking after my slow moving truck.

Keep going Joe … keep going. For weeks it was nigh impossible to shake that image. A sense of shame crept over me now and again. How had I ever let things come to a near unmanageable level? Surprisingly, I also felt a little bit of pride, as though I'd past some Herculean, trial by fire test, and would perhaps be rewarded with a reborn marriage … maybe even rediscover those infatuation, puppy love, high school romance vibes once more … where they belonged … in my marriage. Guess again.

· · · ·

Oh, those precious years watching your kids grow and pursue their own ventures. Jesse, my second, a boy, is really something special (as are the other two of course). There's something unique about Jess however, maybe even a little magical. He was after all a St. Patrick's Day baby '89. We originally named him Ethan, but a week later we thought better of it and changed his first name to Jesse; Ethan now his middle name. What a pain in the ass changing all those documents. I won't make that mistake again. Jess has also given me, and it certainly wasn't his intention, maybe my most difficult "dad" experiences; several perhaps. Jess had serious wart issues as a youngster; hands and feet. It came to be my responsibility to take him over to Fairlane Hospital on Evergreen in Dearborn for his periodic wart "burnings" (liquid hydrogen). Someone, probably Jess, should smack me for being so "out-of-it" when it came to his treatment. What did I know? Not much it turns out. I just assumed the physician would make the right call(s). It's an unnerving experience to have to forcibly hold down your kid while he's pleading with you to make them stop in between sobs and violent shaking. "Just a little more, Jess. We gotta get em or they'll be back with a vengeance." More screams until I said, "Okay, Doc, that's it."

The crowded waiting room had nearly emptied out as I carried Jess quickly out. The few remaining parents eyed me disapprovingly as their toddlers clung to them wide-eyed. I could well guess their thoughts, "How could you?" being one of the more charitable.

Later, when we moved to the Saline area, Labor Day '96, we secured the services of a wonderful Indian woman physician – Flommy Abraham. Soon it came to be that time again. This would be the first warts treatment with the new doctor, and as in the past, the lot fell on me to take him in.

"Shall I hold him down?" I inquired as she prepared to treat him.

"Why?" She gave me a puzzled look.

"Well, uh, you know … the pain, burning."

"He'll hardly feel a thing. I'm going to numb the area around them first."

"Shots?"

"No, a bit of salve I apply with a Q-tip. In two minutes the area will be numb enough to hit them (warts) good and hard."

Anger, jubilation, regret … I could kick myself, and that psycho doctor back in Dearborn. Why didn't I ask? Why didn't she offer? Man, do I feel stupid. "Lord, think you might … uh, could erase perhaps the memory of all those previous visits from Jess's memory?" I don't think he holds it against me. Wonder what he'll think when he reads this?

• • • •

Our Saline home was all and then some we'd dreamed of. You had to pinch yourself now and again just to be sure you were awake. A mile from town, with a country, up-north vibe courtesy of dozens of towering pines scattered all around the lot. Inside the contemporary ranch were two fireplaces, a deck that wrapped itself around half the house, finished walk-out and nearby lake access. Nothing like an old gravel pit, deep and clean, excellent for swimming. A nearby dairy farm which some nights made it seem like the neighbors were watching *Rawhide* or *Bonanza* reruns with their windows down, volume up … we could sometimes hear the cows moving in and out of the distant pasture. Deer, fox, great horned owls, we loved it.

One frigid January afternoon I thought I better look in on the boys who'd gone down to the lake earlier for some pick-up hockey. I could walk, but better take the truck in case they're ready to pack it in. As you pull in the small parking lot of the "Commons" picnic/beach area, you can park with a panoramic view of the 15 acre or so lake and surrounding waterfront homes.

"Hmm, there's Cory," in the middle of a high school aged group of guys in a shoveled out area of the lake ... goin at it like it was the NHL. Where's Jess? Hope they didn't stick him in goal ... doesn't seem to be here. Wait .... ah, that's him ... wow, look at him go." Indeed, way out in the center of the lake on a windswept clear patch of ice, a young kid twirled and spun like a dervish. It fairly took my breath away. "Where'd he learn to do that?" He'd been dancing since he was 7 or so, had great balance and was fearless (which accounts for more than a few gray hairs gracing my crown), but I'd never witnessed him skate like this.

We hooked Jess up with some lessons at the nearby Ann Arbor Cube and in no time he was competing at the local level. Between dance and skating he stayed in excellent shape. What a thrill to watch him glide smoothly around the ice arena ... twisting, turning, spinning through the air ... moving to the loud, pulsating, techno beat sounds accompanying his routine. Up in the air for a turn ... arms crisscrossed, spinning like a top before coming to an abrupt halt accompanied by a wide grin; nailed it. Oh, occasionally a spill. Your gut churns at those moments, but when they (he) bounces back up and press on ... what character building athletic competition potentially offers on a variety of levels.

. . . .

My most vivid, early on memories of Hayley, our third and last child born in February '91, is the sound of a rattling cage (crib) at dawn's first light. There she'd be, bounding up and down, broad grin, giggling like a running brook ... desperate to escape the confines of her "cell." Her smile still grabs me.

Many know Hayley for her dancing. My little angel seems like she's been fluttering around like a butterfly since the toddler years. In Middle School however, she also took up softball, a pitcher, taking after her mom perhaps who had been an exceptional player for Edsel Ford Dearborn during the late seventies. I also pitched in high school. I reckon Hayley made good use of both gene pools in this regard. Oh, did I mention I led line dances at school dances, and actually had guys come over to the house (when no one else was home) for a crash course in 1960's dances: Bristol

Stomp, Boogalloo, Cool Jerk and so on … go ahead laugh, but both Jess and Hale got their "dancing shoes" from "funky" Motown Joe!

Hayley was a tall skinny thing with long slender arms. Like many of us did in days gone by, she also began and honed her windmill style softball pitching technique out in the backyard, and boy, er girl, she could whip that thing. On game days, I'd get a kick out of watching the other team's coach checking her out as she warmed up, a look of growing concern clouding his/her and the opposing teams' players' faces. On her first outing she retired the first nine batters (pitchers are only allowed to throw three innings). Some girls didn't want to bat against her. Others would be a foot or two out of the batter's box and the ump would have to repeatedly, patiently, nudge the apprehensive girls forward. I'd be lying if I didn't tell you I'd be sitting in the stands grinning like a prize hog in slop. At the end of the "day" however, dance won out, and the demands of daily rehearsals ended a promising softball career.

It's a different kind of thrill when you're sitting in a dark auditorium … the lights ease up and the music kicks in, and your million dollar smile daughter goes fearlessly into a dance routine that takes your breath away. And, truth be told, some of her numbers/routines, typically with several to a dozen sometimes additional members, made me a bit anxious, especially as she got older and the outfits sometimes more revealing.

"She's too young for this," I'd worry, "Shouldn't there be a few more years of braces, playing hide & seek, catching frogs, watching old school spooky movies like *The Blob* with dad…?"

The companies she actually danced for were fairly good with regard to tasteful dance routines and outfits. At several competitions I sat perplexed watching young girls between the ages of 10-14 (from other dance schools), gyrating around like seasoned strippers in go-go outfits. "Hey, coach, what are you trying to do?" I'd bite my tongue from saying (maybe I should have), "Prepare those girls for a career at the local strip joint!"

Some of Haley's "hotter" numbers towards the end of high school, as I said, often led to a strange emotional cocktail. A mixture of pride and sometimes reflection, "Hmm, wonder what the Lord thinks of this." And, "I hope the other men sitting in here aren't looking at my daughter like…?" Like the way you're looking at theirs perhaps? On more than one occasion I had to "check" myself. "Look at Hayley. Stay glued to her," I'd admonish myself. When the music faded I'm sure I beamed like Chaucer's Chanticleer; the occasional brother-sister dance team (Jess and Hayley) usually made for misty eyes.

. . . .

I haven't forgotten about the third (and hopefully final), teacher/student crush episode that transpired over a sixteen year period at Vista Maria. Again, one might ask why even bring this up? For my sake, if not for yours/theirs. Was it Bilbo who said, "Third time pays for all?"

I'd noticed a young lady limping along the hallway in a temporary cast. "Hmm, pretty ... must be new," I thought to myself. I didn't think more of it until she hobbled in the following day and made her way up to my desk.

"Hi, I'm ….Where would you like me to sit," she smiled and handed me an admit slip from the counselor's office. A stunning Chaldean girl with long, jet black hair, large, dark brown eyes and a warm smile. Most of the residents are in a melancholy if not a bad mood 24/7. Can't say I blame them, locked up and all. I've had girls staring teary-eyed out the window looking after state workers carrying their baby away after a brief family visit, and now I'm supposed to teach them the difference between adverbs and adjectives. After a couple weeks I knew my newest student didn't fit this mold. Of course she didn't want to be here, but her upbeat, pleasant-to-be-around attitude revealed a girl who wanted to do her time, make the best of it and move on. As with the previous two, I began to look forward to seeing her. Most of my students don't come bouncing in the room with a big toothy grin and a, "Hey, Mr. Shannon, what's up?"

Here I go again. I might have the lyrics for a great country, maybe blues tune, if I put these episodes to music. The infatuation, the starved for a little "innocent" flirtation/romance ... I still hate to call it lust, the word has such a disgusting hollow ring to it. I like to think that I simply appreciated the warmth and friendliness she directed my way. Once more the emotional old-school roller coaster began to jerk and slowly make its way up that first big hill.

When I'd catch one of the more sensational so called "sexual predator" stories on the news, some involving teacher-student relationships, I'd look at these "cuffed" teachers standing limp, emotionless before a judge and I'd think, "Yeah, throw the book at em.

236

They'll have a great time in prison." And if some old, Alfred Hitchcock looking teacher "hit" on my still in high school daughter, I'd be hitting on him; baseball bat to the knees. Yet here I am, flirting dangerously with the same business. Oh, I'd tell myself it was no big deal. I had no intention of running off with anyone. Yet I liked, maybe even craved the attention; that old high school like, crush buzz wasn't unpleasant either. The class of eleven young ladies ranging from 14-18 years of age was occupied with an in-class writing assignment. A little muffled chatter, but it seemed far off. It was one of those days when the memory of my father, who'd died ten years past, lay heavy on my mind. It was time to stand, stretch, gaze out the window in the direction of Rouge Park and distant Redford Township. Pleasant memories of "pops" played like a newsreel in my mind's eye ... sit back down, head in my hands and turned away from my students as if to give them the impression, if they were even taking notice, that I was deep in thought or struggling with a headache. Both code for "don't bug me." Instead it became increasingly difficult to fight back the tears as I "beat" myself up wishing I'd done this or that for my dad ... been with him when he died.

"Mr. Shannon, are you okay? What's wrong?" A soft arm caressed my shoulder and warm, sweet breath spoke tenderly in my ear.

Startled, "Oh, hey ... I'm okay, just got a lot on my mind ...bit of a headache. I'll be alright. Thanks for your concern."

The rest of the class eyed me quizzically. They'd never seen me like this before. I was a bit embarrassed myself at my lack of professionalism. A couple of class clowns sought to lighten the somber mood. "Dang, Mr. Shannon, want me to hook you up with some meds? Dis place be stressin you more than us."

"Mr. Shannon, you fah real? You ain't playin us is you? I know you a wannabe Shakespeare actor but...." Another young gal quizzed me.

I glanced over at the girl who'd come up to check on me and who had returned to her seat. She alone wasn't giggling. A concerned look remained etched on her face the rest of the hour. Thank God this mini meltdown happened when it did. Had we been alone it may have ended in a repeat of the "kiss" incident of a couple years earlier. I kept my growing feelings for her well hidden. I'm certain she suspected nothing.

What to do? These mental "Lolita" episodes will be the spiritual death of me. I dare not confide this struggle with anyone. If this leaked out, even though no real harm has been done yet … could be my teaching "curtain call." For the next few months, up until the end of the school year loomed on the horizon, I gave her the cold shoulder. Wallowing in a mire of self-loathing, fear, and unable or willing to seek out spiritual guidance. Gone were her warm smiles and magical laughter. Anger hadn't dislodged them, but a hurt, pained, why look. I deserved her loathing, but for the present she wouldn't play that card.

We had a picture taken together at the school year-end picnic. Our icy relationship had thawed somewhat as neither of us I suppose wanted to part ways on such a cold emotional note. And so we did, very proper, professional, wish you well on life's journey kind of sentimental stuff the last day(s) of school often resound with. I've thought about looking her up over the years; curiosity I think, hope … but so far I've resisted the urge. She's probably got two or three kids of her own by now. "Joe who?"

· · · ·

"So Joe, what about the pink elephant in the living room?"
"The what?"
"The elephant … you're marriage. Married 20 years and you're just gonna dance around it? And what's up with the Catholic trip?"
"The latter issue is the easier of the two … well, maybe not … it's a bit complex in its own way and not without its share of pain … my marriage however…."

I'm very much aware of both how sensitive and careful I need be plying these waters. It would be easy enough to say it just didn't work and leave it at that. Equally tempting would be to load up the big guns for a defensive and if necessary grand assault against my former spouse. However, since it is a significant part of the puzzle behind this journey, and largely the motive behind this book (my journey away from and back to Catholicism) … for my kid's sake, mine and hers, I shall proceed with caution and as much charity as I can muster. Critics should keep in mind, if such a thing be possible, that I view these events, and mine and my children's lives, against the backdrop of eternity, serious business to be sure. That is the lens one should strive to look through.

You might say I came late to marriage, thirty-one (she was ten years my junior); I was quite taken with her. Attractive, beautiful Rapunzel-like hair, pale blue eyes, outdoorsy, athletic but feminine (half the guys on the

Shalom softball team were afraid to play catch with her), focused – endeavored to be a physical therapist, attended Oakland University while we dated, and most importantly – a Christian. She'd make a great pastor's wife. My parents liked her, although my dad half-kiddingly remarked privately to me that it wouldn't work. But I was 31. I knew what was best, and no doubt saw myself as operating on a higher "sensitive to the Holy Spirit's leading" than my dad. He's just being Fred Sanfordish and I'm that big dummy – Lamont.

Her folks, on the other hand, were horrified at the prospect that our relationship might be heading towards the altar. Now that my own daughter has reached "marrying" age, I can in hindsight at least, somewhat empathize with them. I was a far cry from what they would consider a good catch. Ten years their daughter's (only daughter) senior, whose economic earning prospects were moderate at best … and he's a preacher! The latter being quite preposterous and the worst scenario possible, at least by her father's reasoning, but their daughter was a stubborn minded thing, and once they realized she/we were not to be deterred, to their credit they made the best of it. I thought I'd die one evening when her mother pulled me aside for what I could tell was going to be one of those sensitive little conversations. Still, I could hardly believe my ears.

"You know Joe; she really doesn't have that great of a body…."

One of those rare moments when a witty comeback momentarily escaped me; she'd really delivered a knuckle-ball. In a moment I regrouped. "Great," I said. "Neither do I." That did it. End of conversation.

I won't bore you with (you may be already) too many "if onlys," but I do regret not having made more of an effort to "bond" with my future in-laws. I usually don't tread down paths where I feel I'm not welcome. And, understandably, her family eyed me with at least one suspicious eye and not a little discomfort at their daughter's unwillingness to listen to "reason." Formally asking Barb's father for his daughter's hand was off my radar screen. I know well enough what the answer would have been. Besides, we were adults and needed no consent. The upshot – we were married in a wedding ceremony and a reception that years later, folks still talk about. Why? Not often the groom wears tights! Ours was a Medieval/Renaissance wedding right out of a storybook (7-30-83). *Renaissance Magazine* (Vol.6, Issue # 21, p.52), features a picture of us in medieval wedding garb.

I don't guess either of us saw one of life's "curve-balls" heading our way as in my leaving the pastorate after eleven years and the ensuing pressure cooker we found ourselves in. Still, we stayed the course and in '91, I entered the teaching world full-time as an employee with Dearborn Public Schools. That dark cloud of guilt of "abandoning" the pulpit never entirely disappeared from the horizon of my tormented mind. I don't know that my wife and I discussed it much, and neither of us was prone to deep, dark, chronic bouts of depression. Still, as the years peeled off, my spirit remained troubled, and in time, the busyness of life, two careers, three kids, and we found ourselves drifting apart and unable to find our way back to each other. Perhaps it would have helped had I been more open, communicable, in spite of my lingering doubts and fears; especially of a spiritual nature. To become so transparent seemed counterproductive to the role of "head" of the family, but likely it was just foolish pride.

Following the birth of our third child, Hayley, it dawned on me that a vasectomy might be a smart move. Three kids ... perfect, and we now have our little girl. Our desire for intimacy will no longer be hampered by unplanned pregnancy issues; this might be just the thing to help turn our marriage around. Well, it wasn't. Ironically, it may have been just another "nail in the coffin." The real intimacy inhibitors went largely unaddressed. Any moral conflict regarding the vasectomy itself I wouldn't allow myself to entertain. Many of my friends had had the procedure. They were Christians ... they seemed okay, marriages intact, so why not me. Sometimes there are those days, usually when I'm alone and looking at pictures of the kids, and on occasion I might imagine one or two more ... what would they have been like? What if my own parents had stopped at three? Getting a vasectomy didn't ruin my marriage, nor did it help. Still, I count it as one of my big "life's regrets."

· · · ·

I've heard (read) Barb say that I was a great dad, but a lousy husband. Probably sums it up quite well. I was more of a stay at home, help with the chores/kids kinda guy ... so far so good, however this didn't necessarily insure that her emotional needs were being met. She wanted her husband to be a friend and in this I failed. One can become so preoccupied with their own issues that they wind up neglecting the one they've been called to love (in the case of husbands), as Christ loved the Church. Maybe it's a form of narcissism, and/or misguided thinking that my family's well being is so tied up in my welfare, that I'd best tend to my needs first then we'll see about you. Being ten years her senior, and the one who should take the lead in guarding and guiding the spiritual growth of our marriage/family … in this I dropped the ball. As the years slip by you wake up in the morning wondering who it is you slept with. That great destroyer of marriages – despair, edging ever closer … this isn't getting any better … no end in sight.

"I love you." This simple phrase rarely passed my lips. Those couples who utter this mantra several times a day to each other make me wonder. How meaningful can it be? Perhaps it doesn't matter … just to hear it. No doubt to seldom, if ever hear it from one's spouse must be tough; especially for a woman I'm guessing (I've vowed not to let this happen with my kids). My wife seldom heard words of affection from her husband.   Part of my own inadequacy may have stemmed from a misguided understanding that one can still verbalize, express tender thoughts, even if the "feelings" aren't there. I no longer "felt" love and it's all about being real isn't it? That came with a "heavy" price tag. Feelings come and go … can be deceptive, and love is so much more than a feeling. Upshot, if certain needs aren't being met at home, one may be tempted to look elsewhere.   For her part, intimacy was largely contingent on the energy derived from her emotional needs being met. Now, we're in a stalemate, a perilous place to be, not unlike an ancient mariner at sea who fears the "dead calm" and now you're stuck … going nowhere, and if the wind (energy) eludes you long enough, you waste away and perish.

· · · ·

"What do you get for a room?" I inquired of a middle-aged gentleman who rented several rooms out of his home in Detroit just east of the Dearborn border. So this is what it's come to; another in a growing list of mistakes. It only lasted a month, getting a room that is, but I knew well enough the scriptural admonition not to let the sun go down on your anger (Eph 4:26), and that my place was at home with my wife and kids, not at "Gomez Adam's" home in a seedy neighborhood off a once vibrant section of Michigan Avenue currently littered with worn out looking party stores, bars and the occasional business (cleaners, barber) hanging on for dear life. Perhaps a temporary separation will serve as a wake-up call to the both of us.

Depressed, angry, lonely, the strip club on the corner, like some siren beckoning men to their doom, sucked me in after a brief spiritual battle in which I gave a pathetic performance. Why do these places have dimly lit rear entrances? You know why. I pulled around back and hastily hustled passed one of several bouncers who looked like members of a once formidable motorcycle gang.

What a dive. As Three Dog Night put it, "Don't turn on the lights, I don't wanna see ... mama told me not to come." While some barely legal young gal slithered around a pole in nothing more than a thong on a dimly lit stage, cheap looking disco ball glittering overhead, pulsating, way too loud music, a dozen or more shady characters slowly came to life as my eyes adjusted to the smoke filled shadows of this neo-hedonistic cave. Several men sat around the main stage nursing beers while offering unflattering comments at the expense of one or more of the dancers.

"Hi, my name's ... like a dance?" (as in lap dance), offered a young, just out of high school looking gal whose smile chilled me as her eyes revealed an empty, zombie like appearance.

"Uh, thanks, but no thanks."

I wished to be left alone ... a foul mood had me in a vice like grip, and I was in no hurry to chase it off. She didn't get the hint, or just ignored it. This was her turf and she knew how to play the game. Perhaps pickings were slim tonight and this non-regular might need a bit more persuasion. I didn't find her particularly attractive, and didn't feel like sharing my woes with someone who would nod politely enough, for a fee. Instead of just politely saying I'd like to be left alone, which no doubt would have sounded particularly stupid from a guy who just wandered into a joint like this ... no, I had to say, "How's it goin?"

Thinking I'd get the "Oh, okay," and then seeing I was indeed not interested, or after other prospects wandered in, and she'd hit on them while I'd finish my beer in "peace," then get the hell out of here before, Lord help me, someone I know wanders in.

· · · ·

The temporary separation experiment was short lived. In January of '96 my wife surprised me with a special birthday gift – the trip of a lifetime; one of those eco/adventure vacations to Belize and Guatemala, arranged with an outfitter out of Ann Arbor. On a frigid February morning we bid Detroit adieu and later that day stepped out to ninety degree weather at the Belize airport.

The trip was designed to be a mixture of vigorous outdoor challenges including long hikes thru jungle wilderness, cave exploration and cave swimming … the latter is not for the faint of heart … doing an easy breast stroke for a half-hour, miner's like light affixed to your head, cool, but not numbing water, dark and very quiet but for the occasional low voices of your group to ensure we're all together … and any moment, you're waiting for some massive, slimy tentacle straight out of a Jules Verne tale to wrap you in a death grip and take you under never to be heard from again. I loved it.

The outfitters, all veterans, carefully planned overnight accommodations at comfortable lodgings as we crisscrossed Belize and Guatemala. Cha Creek, deep in the jungle, near the Belize Guatemala border was awesome. You could have shot the film *Jurassic Park* here. No electricity, no screens on the windows of our thatched huts (few insects in mountainous rain forest terrain), lots of macaws and howler monkeys to stir you from the comfort of your bed, and the slow moving Macal River a stone's throw from our lodgings.

"Back in a few, goin for a swim before breakfast," I whispered to Barb.

Alone, careful not to make any unusual noise, stroking easily upstream, eyes trained on the opposite river bank in hopes of catching a glimpse of what many who've dwelt here for years have never seen – jaguars. Could I be so lucky? They're here alright, but more elusive than a will-o'-the-wisp. Might one of these great cats even now risk an early morning appearance while quenching its thirst, unaware that floating midstream…"Gee, I hope that guy at the lodge was right about this river being too clear and cool for crocs around here." The morning mist still lay heavy on the river, the Central American sun not yet able to pierce the towering trees guarding both banks and burn it off; the whole vibe reminiscent of a scene out of the film *Apocalypse Now*. "Shucks, no jags today."

On another occasion our adventure took us to Mayan ruins at Tikal, Guatemala. After an exhausting day of exploring and with twilight fast approaching, our merry band of a dozen (the dirty, sweaty, tired dozen), were ready to call it a day, head for our lodgings, a shower, drinks and some local cuisine.

"I've gotta go up this temple. I'll catch up with yas at dinner. Sam Tillett (local guide), wanna come with me?" He nodded his ascent accompanied by his signature toothsome grin. We were alone.

He was a bit fatigued and half way up the steep, headed for the clouds ancient stairway, some Central American take on an ancient Sumerian ziggurat perhaps, and he paused shooting me that, "Far enough for ya?" look.

Moments later, I stood alone at the top of the Jaguar Temple. The growing darkness tempered by a tropical full moon. I fought back the urge to beat my chest as I gazed out over the forest canopy, half expecting King Kong to burst thru the trees and challenge this violator of the sacred temple. "Hmm, maybe I should look around up here. Fay Wray might be shackled up to one of these pillars"… no such luck … best not to linger. Don't want to navigate these obscenely steep steps downward if clouds obscure the moon. Wow, what a tumble that would be.

Several days later our adventure wound down at a tropical storybook paradise (very laid-back, few tourists), at Placencia, off the southern coast of Belize. While relaxing alone on the beach one lazy afternoon, a few young local guys thought they'd get a laugh at my expense.

"Hey, mister, wanna see our pet."

"Sure." I set aside a cool Pina Colada to give them my full attention.

One of them carefully uncovered his hands and delicately placed a large black/blue scorpion on my forearm. They were grinning like Styme on the Little Rascals, proud of themselves and the momentary heart failure of this Yankee tourist.

I suspected something from the get go and immediately noticed the absence of a stinger (how else could he have held it) … obviously they'd removed it.

Not one to wish to ruin a good joke. With an ear piercing shriek I jumped up and bolted for the safety of my cottage. They howled with delight. I could get used to this "Margaritaville" way of life.

To my wife's credit, I suspect she engineered this special get-a-way in part to perhaps rekindle the faint embers of our troubled marriage. The trip was a blast, but romance remained elusive … a will-o'-the-wisp. If you can't make it happen here….

. . . .

I don't recall having ever had a boil. A month following our Belize/Guatemala adventure, a small, nickel size lump developed on the top middle area of my right forearm. I paid it little notice and expected in time it would disappear as quickly and quietly as it had appeared. Well, it didn't. Not only had it grown to quarter size in diameter and a noticeable lump shape, it began to bleed from the top; just enough to be noticed and in need of daily bandaging. Naively, I stubbornly assumed it would, like a lingering headache, eventually fade into the sunset and that would be the end of it. Not so fast. Now it started to pain me on occasion and now and then I'd awaken with a sharp, throbbing pain where this "boil" had taken up residence; time to see a physician.

I'd made a doctor's appointment after school (C.B.F./Vista Maria) at nearby Fairlane Hospital in Dearborn. It was the last period of the day of my appointment and I anxiously watched the clock sluggishly make its way towards the dismissal bell. Fifteen minutes to go, the class of some ten young ladies were wrapping up an assignment and my arm is throbbing something awful, and now blood is seepin' through the bandage. "Keesha, go get Ms. Claramunt (principal) … tell her I need her down here, NOW!"

I'd some gauze handy and while the other students looked on curiously, I carefully unwrapped the now soaked old bandage when the thing erupted like Mt. Vesuvius, blood spurting out. Patrica Claramunt rushed in at that moment and in a short time we had it rewrapped and the bleeding under control. "I don't need a ride … I'll hustle over to Fairlane and get it looked at … I'll be in tomorrow, no big deal … No, I can drive. I'm alright."

Nearby Fairlane Hospital in Dearborn was the next stage of this odd adventure that I now suspected had its origins somewhere in Central America a month earlier. Dr. Mungulu, who hailed from the Caribbean, greeted me with a warm toothy grin enhanced with a glittering gold front tooth (I'm not making this up), and after a few questions about my recent eco-vacation, began to carefully probe my exposed "boil" with a delicate instrument. Then, calmly leaning forward, face inches from mine, his eyes twinkled: "Mahn, I gots tah tell yah … yah got sometin' growin' in yah ahm."

"Say what!"

"I'm gonna schedule you wit a specialist tomorrah. He'll git it out. Not to worry mahn."

"Get it out. Get what out?"

"Dat we won't know till it's out. It's some kinda larva, I can tell yah dat. Yah know doubt brought it back wit yah mahn. It's been growin in yah evah since."

Don't bail on me yet folks. It gets weirder. The following late afternoon at Fairlane Hospital the receptionist checked me in as – Joseph "larva man" Shannon – I'm serious. A small crowd of fifteen plus doctors and staff gathered in a room normally used for plastic surgery to see for themselves the guy with "Somethin' growin in his arm;" a first for Fairlane Hospital. A physician sat to my right with several surgical like instruments at the ready, and a nurse to my left with smelling salts should I pass out. Yikes! They would not be numbing up the area or putting me under, and I would need to remain perfectly still as it was vital to extract all of the "creature" out at once so no parts break off, enter the bloodstream and cause further complications.

My arm resting securely, I glanced around the room at the faces of the curious onlookers, some who offered looks of encouragement, others looking stoically on, come what may … now, my eyes closed like some little kid who doesn't want to watch him/herself receive a shot … trying to remain motionless while the doctor began to probe. It smarted some, but tolerable. It was dead quiet … no one breathed … I noticed the nurse's hand holding mine seem to go limp as gasps erupted from several onlookers. Then, as if planned, a chorus of "Oh my … Oh my … Oh my God."

Now, before I can muster the courage and see for myself what prompted these outbursts, the doctor cries out inches away from my ear, "It's alive, it's alive, it's alive…."

"Wow, your name wouldn't happen to be Baron Von Frankenstein would it?" You'll recall him making a similar outburst when the creature (monster) first wiggled its fingers revealing life had awakened in the lifeless flesh. Nothing quite so dramatic here, but I couldn't keep my eyes closed any longer. There, slowly wiggling on a petri dish was a yellow/white larva the size of my thumbnail, not unlike what you might uncover under your sod or while turning soil in the garden. I'm not making this up. Had I waited a few more days, a bott fly (think horse-fly) would have crawled out from my arm, kissed me and flown off. Apparently they're a real nuisance in Central and South America, especially with cattle; reckon I looked like a Holstein cow sleepin' in that hammock, and unbeknownst to me, one of those rascals laid an egg in a fresh scratch following a day of hiking in the jungle.

Months later I relayed this tale to our guide-Sam, then visiting Michigan. He laughed saying, "We git dem all da time, but we find and evict dem witin a week ... we don't leave dem in for a month mahn."

Incidentally, Belize and Guatamala are beautiful. Don't let a few bugs scare you off. Oh, and a bott fly, dig the technical name-Larvae Dermatobia Hominis. I wanted to get it back from the lab. Maybe display it in a showcase, paper-weight, or in a neck medallion. That never panned out; however, I did manage to get a photo from the hospital that I'll gladly share with you skeptics.

. . . .

What do folks say, "A change of scenery will do you good?" Here's hoping. Saline, here we come. We purchased, thanks in large part to my wife's trust fund left from her mother, who'd died a couple years earlier following a lengthy and courageous battle with breast cancer. Now, on Labor Day weekend '96, we settled in a home years earlier we could only dream about.

Kids are enrolled in school, we're settled in, and now all we need is a church. Spending a dozen Sundays visiting local congregations was not very appealing, nor had we any contacts out this way to turn to for suggestions. Seemed odd to be thumbing through Yellow Pages to seek out potential local church leads ... unspiritual somehow ... what's this? A Vineyard Church[27] located in nearby Milan ... worth looking into. Set on a side street a block off one of the main streets that make up the small town of Milan, south of Saline, this Vineyard congregation settled into what looked like a traditional mainline small town Protestant church, but one

---

[4]   An association of some 1,500 churches worldwide who see themselves as "empowered evangelicals"; a reflection of their charismatic and evangelical roots shaped during the post Jesus Movement of the mid/late seventies in California.

glance up at the altar with an array of electric guitars, drums, piano and all the trimmings, I couldn't help but compare it to the church I'd pastored fifteen years earlier ... now I was the stranger ... visitor.

From the very first "twang" of an electric guitar and on into a vibrant, scripture fueled message, warm enthusiastic folks, some in suits, most in faded jeans. Ahh, this is too good to be true. With the wife and kids in tow the following week, we immediately became regulars at the Milan Vineyard Church. In time I helped out with Sunday School, but maintained a pretty low profile which suited me just fine. The next few years witnessed all three kids (Cory, Jesse, Hayley) being baptized into the Body of Christ. In the meantime, however, our marriage continued to deteriorate and my wife increasingly spent more time out evenings; some of the folks she took up with didn't sit well with me, but we were largely well past the point of any civil discussions regarding such issues. I wasn't grinning, but tried to bear it. Perhaps with her being ten years my junior, and my disposition largely content to be a stay at home with the kids type, it was just as well. Seemed harmless enough ... maybe it'll even help in some way. The nights out grew in frequency and when your wife wanders in at two, three a.m., you start to wonder. So did friends (of mine) and family. "Joe, wake up man. Can't you see what's goin on?"

I'd begun to take note of on the surface, innocent things that taken together painted an increasingly bleak picture. Now golf outings took precedence over church, and at dinner time, an annoyed rolling of the eyes from her if I suggested we say grace. I grew weary, frustrated and angry, lying in bed night after night wondering where and with whom my wife is. Our home had a beautiful walk-out basement where the boys slept. I joined them, and thus our storybook medieval marriage dissolved into a business partnership concerned only with paying the bills and keeping the kids on track; what a discomforting message we must have been sending them.

· · · ·

"I think I'm gonna puke." My first inclination was to throw the picture away, when did I get so heavy? ... But my three kids were in it and it was a nice shot of the "famous" Jungle Trail apartments on Orchid Island (see Pt. 2). We were vacationing at a Disney Resort near Wabasso Beach, FLA '98, just a stone throw from where I'd "crashed" on the beach (for free), 27 years earlier. Now it cost us $300.00 a night! Disney wrecked (civilized) it … ah, nothing ever stays the same, but the beach was still awesome, great waves, Cory and I had a nerve rattling shark encounter while body surfing (and I use to skinny dip on this beach). Of course I had to show the kids where their ol' man and his buddies use to live. I should have taken the picture I mentioned above, not been in it. I looked like one of those guys in the before/after pictures you see accompanying the latest diet craze and or new piece of high tech home gym equipment guaranteed to produce eye catching abs in just 30 days. I suspect a good many of the "after" pictures are enhanced or outright fakes. There I stood (in the picture), looking like some bloated biker at Bike Week at Daytona Beach. Only problem, there's no after picture. I've kept the picture, tucked away in a basement office, a periodic reminder of why Nestle's chocolate milk and a cherry, cheese Danish twice a day, coupled with a fried food diet, might inhibit the success of any "after" shot to rest alongside the "before" one that was difficult to gaze at. Still it was a great vacation and a real nostalgic buzz for me.

. . . .

I'd had some success with diets and workouts at local gyms, but my battle of the bulge had been a roller-coaster affair, and now, weary with the struggle, I fell prey to what at the time seemed like a reasonable solution. "Joe, meet Lipo Man." I'd reasoned since I found my appearance disgusting, my wife must feel the same way; I don't recall her ever having verbalized that sentiment. I further reasoned that while my physical condition might not be the sole inhibitor to intimacy, it likely contributed to a lack thereof.

Working in Dearborn provided convenient access to a clinic specializing in the procedure, and with little consultation between me and the wife I went ahead and set up an appointment. It might not help my marriage, but it might resuscitate my self esteem. The cost, as you might expect, was "high rent." Medical insurance wouldn't kick in a dime for this largely "cosmetic" viewed procedure. I cashed in some bonds at a significant penalty that were designated for retirement. Excluding my wife from any medical and financial input only drove the wedge between us deeper. I'd made up my mind. "Damn the torpedoes … full steam ahead."

Well, where on the list of Joe's 10 top colossal life's mistakes should

I put this one? I had the maximum procedure ... four cuts, four tubes and slurp, out comes the sludge, er fat. I recall thinking I could drive home after the procedure (when the anesthesia wore off) back to Saline from Dearborn. They wouldn't release me if I didn't have a ride. Good call. I couldn't have driven around the block. By the time we rolled up the driveway of our Saline home I was popping pain pills like M&M's.

"Okay, God, just kill me ... I give." In spite of the pain pills it felt like I'd just endured something out of an Edgar Allen Poe tale that hadn't quite been resolved. Adding insult to injury, the subsequent swelling (that lasted several weeks), appeared to make me look bigger than ever.

"Be patient," the doctor admonished.

I'm running out of patience. And, if this guy's conned me, I've got plans for him. Several months later when I'd check myself out in the mirror, I'd swear I was lopsided. That knuckle-head of a doctor; incidentally, he did warn me that if I didn't change my diet, get sufficient exercise, blah, blah, blah ... I'd be right back where I started from.

Well, this is one episode I can look back on with a good deal of regret, including not seeking my wife's input on the matter. Guess I knew she'd try and talk me out of it, but I'd made up my mind, ironically no doubt, further alienating her by my unwillingness and/or inability to communicate. She'd managed to stay in good shape and wouldn't understand I reasoned, the self loathing eating away at me; Lipo, miracle diets, amphetamines ... all easy way outs that are not ways out at all ... just a maze with nothing but dead ends.

Best thing is what I did a couple of years down the road. In addition to eating less and more nutritional foods, I jumped in the judo ring with my two sons (Thurs. nights we laced up the gloves for boxing), instead of playing the spectator, I wrestled around and joined in conditioning exercises with them. Cory was the better boxer, best at the club (Cory had some boxing experience a few years earlier including 5 matches, as well as training, at age 14, with the U of M boxing club in Ann Arbor), but Jess had the judo moves. He's the only student I'd seen enter the ring by jumping over the top – head first, then go into a tumble and bounce back up on his feet in ready position. All that dancing and skating comes in handy in unexpected ways.

· · · ·

No question, our marriage was on the ropes, and if we were going to make it we needed help fast and mainlined. Retrouvaille, a program to help couples heal and renew their marriages sounded promising, so we traveled to the east side of Detroit where a program was offered. I was apprehensive and didn't expect much, but we were running out of options. One look at the other men suggested that indeed, pessimism hung heavy in the air. The women, though weary, seemed inclined to cling to what little shred of hope the facilitators held out. Turns out the program exceeded both our expectations and offered at least a little light at the end of the tunnel. But, like the diet and exercise program you neglect after some initial success, you quickly find yourself back where you started, maybe worse, if you don't "stick to it."

· · · ·

Shakespeare's *Hamlet,* followed closely by *Macbeth,* are my favorites along with *King Lear.* The first two formed the bedrock of my "Introduction to Shakespeare" class at Clara B. Ford (Vista Maria). During a particularly low point in our marriage, and while at my wit's end, red flags popping up like so many dandelions, I found myself wrestling with a Prince Hamlet like dilemma. During oral readings with my students I'd typically take on the role of the young prince, whose world had been turned upside down by the untimely death of his father, followed shortly by his mother's hasty remarriage to her late husband's brother (Hamlet's uncle and current king of Denmark), and the appearance of a ghost resembling Hamlet's late father who reveals the true nature of his death (murder) at the hands of his treacherous brother – Hamlet's uncle/stepfather. These plot complications are all revealed in Act I and the next four acts are largely concerned with Prince Hamlet's quest to determine with absolute certainty the authenticity and truthfulness of the ghost's revelations. Throw in some romance (Ophelia), comedy (Rosencrantz and Guildenstern), best friend relationship (Hamlet and Horatio), and, of course, mayhem, more tragedy, and revenge. It's no surprise that this play is largely regarded as the Bard's masterpiece.

Twisted or no, I sat back after having read the ghost scene for the third time one afternoon and it dawned on me that like young Hamlet, I too shall go mad if I don't determine with certainty if there's any fire behind these smoking red flags in my marriage, or, is this all just paranoia and vain assumptions leading me into dark places wherein the mind confuses night with day.

"The play's the thing, wherein I'll catch the conscience of the king," quipped Hamlet following an encounter with a troupe of traveling actors and the sudden realization that here just might lay the means of determining the truth or not of the apparition's confessions concerning his father's untimely end at the hands of his own brother. Hamlet, with the unwitting aid of these actors, will have them perform a piece that bears a striking resemblance to the circumstances surrounding his father's death. Hamlet and his sole trusted friend, Horatio, will carefully scrutinize his uncle during the performance. If his guilt does not manifest itself during a particular scene, then the ghost has lied and indeed may be no ghost at all. However, as Hamlet suspected he would, his uncle, during one particular scene, becomes so distressed that his uncle now king must leave the performance. Convinced the apparition has revealed the truth, Hamlet plots revenge. To further complicate the matter, Hamlet's uncle now knows Hamlet knows.

So what am I to do? Take my wife to a movie, play? Indeed, we did go to Stratford, Ontario about this time to share one last weekend … to see if there were yet any coals buried deep in the ashes of our marriage that might yet, with a little coaxing, spring back to life. This was my initiative … a couple of plays and relaxing, intimate dinners, away from the kids and numerous distractions. I'm not quite sure why she went along with it as it was fairly obvious she'd "checked out," and was only waiting for the right moment to make her move, as in divorce. The weekend turned into one long uncomfortable date.

The desire to know just what the hell is going on, as in my wife's frequent and increasingly lengthy intervals away from home was maddening. Better, I reasoned, to know for certain than let one's mind run wild with vain imaginings no doubt greatly exaggerated.

There's a way. A store in Southfield provided all I needed; phone tap and computer spy ware. While the underhandedness of the venture gave me pause, under the circumstances it seemed warranted, and to my knowledge, not illegal. Spying is after all, a violation of someone's privacy. My need to know trumped any other concerns including someone's right to privacy. Could I have afforded the services of a private detective (spy), I may have gone that route.

The trap was set. Will it spring? Come up empty? Like Hamlet, I sensed I was in for a hell of a ride, and after a week passed by the opportunity I'd both dreaded and anticipated materialized. I'd have the house to myself for several hours. No interruptions and plenty of time to check the "trap." Then, I would see if, indeed, the computer spyware's the thing, wherein I'll catch the conscience of my wife.

Swallow, take a deep breath, and order your hands to stop shaking, ignore the silence of the grave foreign to this household and pull up the spy ware site. Minutes drifted toward the hour mark. How long have I been staring out this window into nothingness. Familiar landmarks slowly rearranged themselves and my other senses confirmed this was no dark dream. What I did/didn't discover, I'll leave between me, her and God.

Okay, now I know for certain ... now what? Nothing for now and the advantage mine; I'll accumulate as much evidence as possible. At this juncture some might be rolling their eyes thinking, "what a jerk, spying on his own wife ... invading her privacy ... pathetic." To you I'd say, "you're clueless ... walk a mile (hell, a block) in my shoes." I found it telling when this all "hit the fan," that some were more appalled by the means I used to gain information than what I'd uncovered. I suspect they found the "what" I'd likely discovered no big thing; little more than fodder for a *Desperate Housewives* episode or two. Their opinions meant/mean nothing to me.

The game was on and battle lines drawn. It didn't take long for me to hear from her attorney that I had violated federal laws, and she all but threatened me with a gallows' date. My wife's slick little Jane Hathaway looking wench of an attorney never did get it. I could care less about any real or imagined legal threats. At the end of the day the only thing that mattered(s) to me was what does God think and how will my actions impact my kids.

Home alone several weeks following the confrontation, late one evening, and a loud knock at the front door startled me out of a sullen, dark mood; a fella with a large envelope gave me a questioning look. "Joe Shannon ... I have a summons for you." So be it.

At my wife's suggestion we hired an arbitrator to assist hammering out the details of our looming divorce and avoid excessive attorney fees; it seemed, in her mind at least, reconciliation was no longer on the table. These sessions, while saving thousands of dollars in attorney's fees, were beyond annoying. I felt like some over-the-hill boxer in the ring with an up-and-coming contender; me at seventy-five percent with a few injuries, my opponent in his (her) prime. Outside of my attorney, I only confided in a select handful. Strange as it may seem, I still thought a miracle lay just beneath the surface, unseen, unlooked for, but lying submerged waiting to surface none the less. Like Lazarus (see Jn 11), our marriage would be raised from the dead, and while it would be tough we'd make it work somehow. You might think that such unrealistic musings might put me at a disadvantage while negotiating the terms of the divorce. Would taking a "bulldog" approach in negotiations suggest a resolve that no miracle was at hand … best fight pharaoh's host and not look for the sea to part, for now at least. Perhaps I went through the motions of negotiations halfheartedly, content for the most part to trust in the Father's hand to deal out what is right and just on our kids' behalf, and at the end of the day in the restless quiet of my own troubled thoughts, I knew a good deal of the anguish I currently wallowed in was of my own making; a "reaping of what I'd sown." My foggy state of mind left me in a vulnerable position to negotiate. She'd likely been planning her move for months, a battle strategy in place, no shortage of advisers (most if not all the living embodiment of the blind leading the blind), and here I stood, "Yeah whatever," all I could muster when confronted with her demands. Except that is, when it came to the issue of joint custody.

· · · ·

The big day finally came. I sat nervously in the coffee shop of the Washtenaw County Courthouse, waiting for a last minute "huddle" with my attorney; he was late! Outside the courtroom, my soon to be "X," even now I don't like referring to her that way, chatted with her attorney who made a beeline for me and without so much as a "Good morning," started going off on me over some money issues. "Money doesn't grow on trees you know," she began.

She doesn't know how close she came to being launched thru the upper story window. I turned to my attorney. "Did you know that?"

"Know what?"

"Money doesn't grow on trees … gee; I'll have to remember that." Then to Ms. Smug Attorney, "Go to hell!"

Before the matter could escalate further our case was called up. It couldn't have lasted more than ten minutes. I periodically shot a sideways glance over at my wife searching for any sign of doubt. She never looked my way. My parting of the Red Sea level miracle didn't happen, or maybe it did.

The judge called me before the bench. "Your honor," I chose my words carefully, "I can't sign this document. I took a vow before God 'till death do us part.' I'm still breathin and so's she … I won't sign."

"The court understands Mr. Shannon. However, we don't need your signature." And with a rap of his gavel bellowed, "Next case!"

A block from the Washtenaw County Courthouse in downtown Ann Arbor and "Damn, now what … what did I do?" As one of Ann Arbor's finest flashed his lights and motioned for me to pull over.

"Excuse me, sir. Can I see your driver's license … say, what's wrong with you? You okay?"

"Yeah, I'll be alright … just got out a court … divorce court. Sorry 'bout rollin thru the stop back there."

This cop actually laid a hand on my shoulder and in a low voice almost whispered, "Look, you be careful."

I must have looked like hell. It wasn't about losing her at that point. That happened a long time ago. Somehow, I felt once again, I'd let God down … and that in a pinch, He'd let me down, and my kids … Damn!

The next two weeks were incredibly awkward. She'd agreed to let me finish out the month prior to my moving into a house in nearby downtown Saline. I wanted to be close to my kids. I'd procrastinated about looking for new "digs"…"why bother, this thing's gonna work out." Heading into town a week after the divorce I took a side street through a neighborhood I don't normally traverse. "Hmm, For Sale … not bad … kinda close to downtown. Wonder what they're askin?"

Bingo! A need made and met in heaven. I needed a place and fast. They wanted out before Christmas (it was November). It turned out to be a smooth, quick, good for everyone done deal.

Backing out of my former wife's driveway that gray afternoon with the last load of my stuff, kids standing on the porch, "Don't worry," I yelled, "I'm only a few minutes away." That was tough.

The divorce contract was part joke, part nightmare. Prior to the divorce hearing, my attorney initially wanted to go after (at my urging) full custody of the kids based on my fears of the lifestyle my now former wife embraced they'd be openly subjected to now that I was out of the house. In time, I came to understand that the Court (especially in Washtenaw County), is not concerned with certain moral issues, unless it's something like child pornography, heroin addiction … and can be shown to be putting the kids in harm's way. From where I stood that's exactly what I saw happening. Still, even if I could have it my way, could I force the kids to live at my place 24/7 and leave the beautiful surroundings of York Woods, their neighborhood friends and lake access? At the end of the day there simply was not a lot I could do about it. "God, please don't let my kids be deceived because I'd fallen asleep on watch. Please protect them…." Sometimes my prayers gave way to dark thoughts. I can get my kids out of that house. Ah, Joe, remember Hamlet and where the dark road of revenge led him. "They that live by the sword shall by the sword perish" (Mt 26:52).

One evening I sat quietly rocking in the dark, listening to some classic rock, enjoying the nostalgic "buzz" and temporary relief from the mental anguish in large part fueled by the stark reality that I no longer possessed parental controls; we presume to be parents until children metamorphose into adults and strike out on their own. The tune "Hey Joe" (Hendrix version) suddenly startled me from my slumber. The room seemed darker, as though some unseen hand turned down the lights until only a faint glow remained to illuminate familiar objects. The familiar lyrics and guitar licks took a surprising, sinister hold over me, and in my despair I argued back and forth with myself. I should just do it … was Jimmy talking/singing to me …"Hey Joe, where ya goin' with that gun in your hand?"

Evangelist Herman Stalvey's authoritative voice echoed in my ears as if I was sitting in front of one of the speakers at a tent revival on one of those "hot August nights" Neil Diamond turned into a hit. "The devil," Herman began in a low, steady voice, "the devil … if he can get ya thinkin' 'bout it long enough will before you know it sure 'nough have ya doin' it!"

As much as I like Jimi, that's one tune I avoided for awhile. Besides, the kids need their mother.

· · · ·

You know what's strange, it's been going on 14 years (the divorce), and not once, not once have any of my kids brought it up. I try not to "snoop" about their mother. If the kids have something to say, a question perhaps, I'll let them bring it up. To their credit, especially Hayley and Jess, who were most affected by the joint-custody arrangement, neither ever whined about having to cart their stuff back and forth between my place and their mother's. It was a hassle as you might expect, but they didn't complain. I'd been careful not to interrogate them when I had them. I didn't want them to feel like they're going to get the third degree every time they walk in with a suitcase and school backpacks bulging with a week's necessaries. They attended church uncomplainingly. Still, my time with them always passed too quickly, and the anger boils deep within when I consider the time I've been "ripped off," especially with my daughter. While I pray for change, it seems I'm ever forced to face the hard reality that while I may have been forgiven for shortcomings that led to this sorry state, the consequences are not so easily escaped. The "things could be worse," approach never seemed satisfying. Many fathers are separated from their kids for months, years … work, war, illness. Mine were just a stone's throw away. I never imagined it would be this tough, compounded with the irritation at finding out relevant "kid data" second and third hand, and being left out of important decision making on occasion.

I was not entirely alone during these struggles. People were praying for me, her, the kids; that was a source of comfort. The few months leading up to the divorce, my principal at Clara B. Ford, Larry Simon, offered to help me out if I wanted some time off. "Thanks, but I need to keep busy … work, I'll go crazy(er) sittin' around sulkin', thinkin' about it 24/7." He gave me a lot of breathing room and it helped to know he and others were prayerfully interceding on my behalf, perhaps even more so in the months following the divorce and you start to beat yourself up over what the Father has already forgiven.

Cory, Jess and I, as I alluded to earlier, belonged to the *Academy of Martial Arts* directed by Sensai Dan Powers up near the Ann Arbor Airport. We tried to get up there at least twice a week; one for judo, and one for Thursday nights which were especially set aside for boxing. To spend some quality time with my sons coupled with a serious workout was a tonic for mind, body and spirit. I could still go toe-to-toe with Cory in the ring (he might dispute that), but my endurance rarely exceeded two rounds … then, I'm like a ship without a rudder or sails. "Hey, Cory, go easy on me, will yah?" I'd have liked to seen Hayley join us, and she likely would have had not dancing taken up so much of her time.

· · · ·

"Hey, ya heard about Shannon? Back doin' the Catholic thing!"

"No way."

"Yep. Talked to him the other day."

No one was more surprised than me, howbeit during the final preceding months before that day (re-commitment to the Catholic Church), the reasons in favor eventually gained on and then surpassed any significant misgivings clouding my mind. I expected a few raised eyebrows and indeed, some from my own family as it were. Glad I didn't spend the last thirty-five years Catholic bashing. Under the present circumstances that would have been some "crow pie" to choke down. Still, I proceeded quietly and with caution, mindful of Paul's admonition that "For now we see through a glass darkly...." (1 Cor 12:12).

Al Kresta and I had continued to maintain our friendship long after I'd left Shalom; he briefly took the helm (pastor) before himself returning to the Catholic fold. We'd occasionally get together for dinner, "catch up" and what not. I knew something of the spiritual path he currently trod and at times it would be up for discussion (the whole Catholic "thing"), in a laid back manner. He took care to allow me space to raise the matter, or not at all; I liked that. During one discussion he'd mentioned how much a Thomas Howard[28] book, *Evangelical is Not Enough*, impacted his thinking on his then role as a pastor of Shalom Ministry. Hmm, have to check it out. In the meantime, Al patiently listened to what I suspect were some of the usual objections and issues he and his wife Sally experienced from family and friends when they "crossed the Tiber" and embraced Catholicism: purgatory, indulgences, the priesthood and sacraments for

---

[28]   Howard, himself a convert to Roman Catholicism and emeritus professor of English at St. John's seminary in Boston, in a gentle, straightforward "layperson" terminology, helped me put a finger on what I sensed for years I'd been missing, including eleven years as an evangelical-charismatic pastor; while at the same time helped ease fears/dread that if indeed I returned to my old Catholic roots I would have to endure stagnant, largely lifeless, uninspiring and even unbiblical liturgical and sacramental practices. Well, it's been 14 years, and my appreciation of the Mass, Catholic liturgy and sacraments continues to grow.

starters.

. . . .

The completion of my master's work at WSU during the mid '90's culminated in an essay on "Eucharistic Controversies during the Middle Ages." While I wouldn't at this juncture put myself in the Catholic "real presence"[29] camp, the institution and celebration of the Lord's Supper took on fresh meaning and importance during the months I spent researching the topic. One Sunday at the Vineyard Fellowship we attended in Milan, MI, and a Sunday typically set aside for a monthly "breaking of the bread" to be incorporated into the worship service, it was announced we'd have to put it off because we'd run out of time.

"Out of time ... how can you run out of time for the Lord's Supper," I wondered to myself. This really gnawed at me. I don't recall having discussed it with the pastor (a mistake). While I continue to respect and appreciate my local Vineyard brothers and sisters, I thought they dropped the ball on this one. Lord knows I fumbled more than a "few" times myself.

This also happened to be around the time my marriage had been torpedoed (the uncovered email revelations), and I'd asked the Church to address my wife's now not so "secret" lifestyle according to Matthew 18:15-17. The response I received to this inquiry left me dumbfounded. The gist of which went something like, "Well, we don't do that ... we've rarely if ever seen it work, so we don't do it."

I was speechless. Since when do we do or not do what the Scriptures admonish us to do based solely on tangible results. The "Parable of the Sower" (Lk 8:5) immediately comes to mind, or how about Paul at Mars' Hill (Acts 17:22)? "So be it," I muttered to myself. "So be it."

One Sunday I decided to take in a Mass over at Christ the King Catholic Church in Ann Arbor. It had been awhile since I'd attended Mass. Most of my Catholic Church appearances over the past thirty-five years had been an occasional wedding or funeral (for a short period c. late '70s I occasionally "sat in" and helped with the worship at St. Elizabeth's in

---

[29] Catholics hold that following the consecration at Mass, Jesus is present with his body, blood, soul and divinity under the appearances of bread and wine; sometimes referred to as transubstantiation.

Wyandotte). "I'll sit in the back and pick it up quick enough," I thought to myself. "All those years at St. Agatha ... heck, I still remember a smattering of Latin. Hmm, don't think they do much in Latin anymore."

I did know a few folks who attended Christ the King, but it's a big place and I'd just as soon kind of slip in unseen and unnoticed. I picked up a church bulletin on the way in (not out), so I'd have something to look over before Mass began. I did have enough spiritual sense about me to "nip in the bud" those initial misgivings that reared themselves as soon as my butt hit the pew. "Ah, wouldn't ya know it ... there's a statue of the Blessed Mother ... hmm, where's Joseph? Ah, there he is ... what's this lady next to me doin? Rosary ... figures."

No, this kind of attitude will not do, and the Apostle Paul's admonition to "esteem others better than ourselves" (Phil 2:3), echoed in my mind's ear. I didn't have much to feel self-righteous about anyways. I'd skim the bulletin, and then focus on the crucifix and the choir who were warming up and who didn't sound half bad.

Interesting ... no bingo announcements, no upcoming annual church fair with pleas for help staffing the blackjack table at the Vegas tent. On the other hand announcements concerning pro-life groups, charismatic prayer meetings and Bible studies ... Bible study? Since when did Catholics start reading let alone study the Bible? A quick flip back to the front of the bulletin assured me that indeed this was a Catholic Church.

I may be slow, but it was crystal clear I'd stepped into an unusual Catholic Church. This was immediately confirmed as the processional hymn announced the start of the liturgy. "Good heavens ... everyone's singing ... they're drowning out the choir. Gee, they even look happy!"

Now I'm starting to get a little nervous. However, I managed to settle in and tried my best to focus on the liturgy. What is it proclaiming? These words, many of them a distant memory, had the ring of truth to them. I'd forgotten the typical Mass had so much scripture, including readings from both the Old and New Testaments. The presiding priest delivered a sermon as challenging and inspiring as any I could recall from my "tent revival" days. I had to throttle myself several times from blurting out a few hearty "Amen, Brothers!" Minutes later an odd thing happened. During the singing of the Angus Dei (Latin for Lamb of God), tears came to my eyes. I bowed my head and put my hands over my eyes lest anyone should take note. I later shrugged it off as a "nostalgic vibe" that took me by surprise.

Likely a flashback to when we Shannon kids attended Mass as a family, and my dad would be next to me immersed in the Eucharistic celebration. "That's all it is" I reasoned. However, that would not be the end of it. To this day I often find myself getting all misty-eyed at that part of the liturgy.

．．．．

The next few months witnessed me bringing my "Catholic baggage" before the Lord. Presently, though a regular at mass, it continued to be a bit awkward, especially at communion time when I remained one of the few if only person(s) sitting in the pew while the congregation made their way down front to receive the bread and wine (body and blood of Jesus). I respected that I'm in their "house," and need to "play" by their rules. Until I could come to a place wherein I wished to be back in full communion with the Church, make a good confession in the Sacrament of Reconciliation, and say, "Yes/Amen, this is His body/blood," not just some mere symbolism, some reenactment … I'd have to be content with being an observer. Questions, issues, I knew most of them: purgatory, priesthood, papacy, Mary/Saint "worship," the Mass itself … on and on. Okay, I'll take them one at a time. Indeed, one at a time, my primary concerns came to be largely (not entirely in some cases) satisfied. The Christ the King Bible Studies and RCIA – Right of Christian Initiation for Adults classes (the latter with my two younger kids in a year long program), shed light on questions that had troubled me for decades; a few still do. I became a student of the Catholic Catechism, astonished at the depth, clarity and profound beauty of the Church's teaching and insights on matters so important to disciples past and present wishing to follow Jesus: sanctity of human life, sin, redemption, and the sacraments. Why had I not looked into these years ago? What was it I missed as a kid back at St. Agatha … pride, arrogance, ignorance … all of the above? Other books like Steve Ray's *Crossing the Tiber*, and especially Thomas Howard's *On Being Catholic*, helped dispel a great deal of misunderstanding I'd carried around for years and never bothered until now to seriously look into.

At the same time, two fundamental pillars of Protestantism I'd long held dear began to waver and ultimately collapse: Sola Scriptura (**Only** Scripture), and Sola Fide (Faith **Alone)**. While I've largely left the reasons for my new attitude concerning these two fundamental issues to persons far more capable of addressing them (see suggested reading), their importance argues for some explanation here and now. If these matters interest you please see Appendix 8 – *Catholic Issues.*

. . . .

On the east side of Dearborn, tucked away in what was once a school on a side street off of Warren on Pinehurst St., sat Alba Books; a Catholic bookstore staffed by priests and brothers of the Society of St. Paul. Whenever I found myself in that part of town I liked to drop in and browse and on occasion chat with the brothers. During one visit a new publication called *The Rapture Trap* sounded like an interesting read. Hence began a several month inquiry, including reading several other related books and discussions with both Protestant and Catholic believers concerning particulars, time and nature of Jesus' return. To cut to the chase, I have since abandoned the position I'd held since my Jesus Movement days of the seventies, of a "secret" church rapture in any of its popular manifestations. And, while I do not consider it as serious a topic as Sola Scriptura and/or Sola Fide, it certainly was an important ingredient for me and thousands like me who embraced it without question. On this matter, and a good many others, I just assumed the people I was listening to and reading had got it right. Concerning a more careful look at the secret "rapture" (from the Latin verb meaning "caught up"), that so called secret snatching away of believers just prior to (midway or after according to some interpretations) an unprecedented period (seven years or so) of unparalleled evil, persecution and mayhem. A view largely based on a few misread portions of scripture and books like *The Late Great Planet Earth* and the *Left Behind* series, as well as contemporary Christian tunes like Larry Norman's "Wish We'd All Been Ready" and, of course, let's not forget bumper stickers like "In case of Rapture, driver will disappear." That the Church for 1800 years never held such a position (2nd coming of Jesus – yes; secret Rapture – no), came as a bit of a shock to me. Furthermore, most Protestants reject the Rapture theory and the dispensationalism from which it derived. What else, I wondered, had I innocently or perhaps blindly jumped on board with, ignoring and sometimes mocking two-thousand years of Church teaching embodied in the sacred Scriptures, Tradition and Magesterium of the Catholic Church.

. . . .

Lenten season 2004 and the path leading back to the faith of my "fathers" seemed straight, narrow, and beckoning with open arms. This would be an Easter (Resurrection Day) to remember. The time had come to talk face to face with Fr. Ed Friede, pastor of Christ the King Catholic Church in Ann Arbor.

A bit awkward pouring out your heart at a booth in a Big Boy's Restaurant during the lunch rush; however Father Ed listened patiently, nodding here and there. He must have been hungry and I had a lot to say; good combination on this occasion actually. Anyone who knows me, however, knows I don't have a problem talking with my mouth full … Sorry, mom. After thirty minutes it was time for my closing argument.

"Well, Father, that's about it. In spite of all that's happened, I can't help but wonder if this whole "trip" (contemplating a return to the Catholic Church), is nothing more than a way of dealing with the stress and depression fallout following the demise of my marriage, and a bit of attending church with my dad as a kid nostalgia … nothing more?" Looking back on it I might have told myself to just hold on a minute. How about the years of study, the questions and issues I'd wrestled with and largely resolved. Surely that counts for something. But, I'd just emptied myself and no doubt my thinking had become a little muddled. Now I hoped Fr. Ed might be able to shed a little light on the matter; unravel the knot.

"So, what's wrong with that," he quipped between gulps of ice tea. "If that's what God chose to use to lead you back, so be it."

That took me a bit by surprise. "Is that it," I thought to myself? Father Ed glanced at his watch. Code for lunch is over and time to go.

At first I was a bit disappointed. I'd hoped for some sign, word, more on the "walls of Jericho collapsing" level. What did he say? "So what's wrong with that?" Maybe it's that simple. Didn't the Apostle Paul say something about, "all things work together for good to them that love God …?" (Rom 8:28).

. . . .

263

Passion week 2004 and I sat in a rear pew of the beautiful sanctuary of Sacred Heart Seminary in Detroit. Quiet, alone, just enough light to make out the surroundings including the breathtaking stained glass windows along either side. My mind raced ... heart pounded like a singer poised to step out into the spotlight.

Ah, but there's one thing lacking. I need to go to confession. What am I to do about that? I have quite a laundry (dirty) list. Think I'll go for a stroll to the library and read a bit. In one of the corridors a young priest with a quick step approached. Hmm, what the heck I thought, "Hello, Father ... I wonder if you might have time to hear my confession."[30]

"Sure. Let's go down to my office."

After a few pleasantries and introductions the matter at hand took center stage. "Bless me Father, for I have sinned," I spoke carefully, just above a whisper, seems to me that's how it went ... wonder if they've changed things ... "uh, my last confession was about 35 years ago." We both looked at each other and laughed. "Uh, not to worry Father, I've condensed it into the big 5." Father eased back into his chair unable to hide a small sigh of relief. You patient readers of this tale don't get too excited. I don't intend to reveal the particulars; not entirely anyway. My vasectomy was high on the list. The other four had something to do with the "7 Deadlies"(wrath/anger, greed, sloth/laziness, pride, lust, envy, gluttony). Had time allowed I likely could have hit all seven of them.

What a pleasant ride back to Saline. Resurrection Day 2004, including receiving the Eucharist, was glorious indeed. Yes, Dorothy, "there's no place like home." In the weeks and months to come some well intentioned friends expressed concern regarding my "old" found faith. I suspect it was a wake-up call of sorts for a few of them to carefully consider why and where they were at spiritually. Most folks just seemed

---

[30] The sacrament of Penance (Reconciliation) wherein penitents acknowledge their sins to a priest, who may then offer absolution and some form of penance. Catholics distinguish between venial (lesser) sins, and mortal (grave) sins. Confession typically takes place individually, but general absolution may be given under certain circumstances. Following Jesus' resurrection, he breathed on his disciples and told them, "Whose sins you forgive are forgiven them, and whose sins you retain are retained" (Jn 20:23).

pleased to hear I was still following the Master; as far as being Catholic, "Well good for ol Joe."

. . . .

A bit of a lump sometimes rises in my throat sitting alone in a pew minutes before Mass watching families come in together. My mind drifts back to those endless Sundays during the 50's/60's at St. Agatha's in Redford when we attended church as a family, and now, I couldn't help but wish my own kids were seated alongside me.

At this juncture, Cory had pretty much left the nest, and according to the joint-custody arrangement, I'd have my two youngest a couple of long weekends per month. On those occasions they agreed to attend RCIA classes in order to prepare for admittance into the Catholic Church. They both made their First Communion and Confirmation in '06 Spring. Jesse took St. Patrick and Hayley St. Brigid of Ireland as their patron saints. I pray one day Cory will come into the Church, and if I'm still around, strong-arm him into taking St. Columba as his patron saint, then we'll have the Irish patron saint trifecta.

. . . .

Life moves along like a river, sometimes slow and sluggish, other times rapid and uncertain. In Spring 2007, I got blindsided at work. Vista Maria, where Dearborn Public Schools had furnished education for more than 150 adolescent female residents for sixteen years, had decided to pursue plans to implement a charter school. The current Dearborn Public Schools personnel, approximately fifteen of us, ultimately would be assigned somewhere in the district. Our assignments would be based on seniority and on the subject areas in which we are certified by the State of Michigan. In my case, these subject areas are History and Language Arts. My first choice for an assignment was Dearborn High School. I'd done my student-teaching there back in '89 and thought that it might be kind of interesting to be back. It turned out, though, that I was assigned to Edsel Ford High School. "That's cool," I said to myself.

Christ the King Catholic Church, Ann Arbor, MI

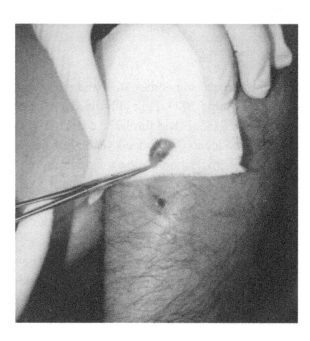

Bott Fly larva
(larvae dermatobia
hominis) removed
from Joe's arm (Henry
Ford Medical Center -
Dearborn, MI)
a month after a trip to
Belieze, Central
America, April 1996.

Joe performing a brick break with the Garden City
Tae Kwon Do Team at Vista Maria/Clara B. Ford.

Troubled girls get chance at new life at Vista Maria

By Angelo B. Henderson
The Detroit News

They are never alone.

Eyes watch them during the day and a ceiling microphone listens over their beds at night.

From wake up nudges at 7 a.m. to lights out at 9:30 p.m., time is not theirs to manage.

Although Vista Maria, Michigan's largest home for girls, is perched on a sprawling, grassy 38-acre campus, tucked alongside the Rouge River in Dearborn Heights, no one wanders alone in its buildings or grounds.

Vista Maria is as close as Michigan comes these days to an old-fashioned orphanage. Institutions such as Vista Maria share some of the same characteristics as their predecessors, but there is one major difference: Children and teens are in these institutions because they are in trouble.

Runaways. Drug users. Prostitutes. Petty criminals.

"This is the last stop," said Phillip J. Synder, associate executive director of business at Vista Maria. "After residential treatment centers, boys may end up at Maxey Training School, but this is it for girls. This is where they have to succeed."

Synder refused to allow residents to speak with a reporter because of the state's child protection laws, but he did agree to a tour.

Vista Maria is one of the largest teen treatment centers in the Midwest.

It takes keys to get in or out of every door, and all are double-locked.

Girls are escorted by a counselor when they go from one building to another. They walk silently in lines, grouped in twos and threes — locked arm in arm.

To 143 girls, ages 11-18, this is home. Some will call it that longer than others.

Most of the girls — 115 — are under tight security, living at Vista Maria for eight to 20 months, depending on their willingness to abide by the rules.

Twenty others are in a temporary shelter. They had just been picked up by police and their future depends on a review by the home. The remaining eight are in short term rehabilitation — 120 days at the most.

"We are committed to treatment, which is different than an orphanage, which just provides care," said Snyder.

Clarence Tabb Jr. / The Detroit News
Instructor Joe Shannon speaks to a classroom of teen-age girls at Vista Maria which offers "a very structured environment."

Christmas 2006 - Cory, Hayley, Jesse

268

Fordson High School
Dearborn, Michigan

PART FIVE

FORDSON

"Hey, Joe," said the voice on the other end of the phone. The voice belonged to Cheryl Flynn, a colleague of mine from the Clara B. Ford days. She then continued casually, "See you're goin' to Fordson."

"Fordson! Where'd you hear that?"

"Oops, sorry … thought you'd have checked your district e-mails. Talk to ya later. Good luck."

"Let's see, let's see what the hell's my password?" The e-mail from the Dearborn School's Human Resources Department was brief and to the point: "You've been assigned to Fordson High School. Please report Tuesday…." I thought, "Here it is Labor Day weekend and you're just now letting me know this."

Incidentally, these things do often happen and not always as a result of someone's procrastination and/or incompetence. There were contract issues in the Dearborn school system as well as late retirements and the bumping and moving according to seniority and building needs, all of which contributed to the "it's-just-the-way-it-is" climate of the final hectic days preceding the start of a new school year. I'd expected to be at Edsel Ford; indeed, I'd spent the previous week cleaning what I expected to be my classroom from top to bottom. I even redid the bulletin boards. "I'd be ready that first day of school," I congratulated myself. "Ol' Joe's ready for the move from the 'Outback' (Clara B. Ford/Vista Maria) to the big time – Edsel." By the way, Edsel Ford was the alma mater of my used-to-be wife and a bunch of folks I've known for years who stalked the corridors back in the late sixties. This would add an interesting twist and vibe to my new placement. Not for now, though, it seemed. "Fordson … man, what's up with that? Lord, you got something to do with this?" I hope whoever got that made-over classroom will appreciate it.

School begins the Tuesday after Labor Day. Here it was, Saturday, and no one would be there during the holiday weekend. I couldn't get my stuff (the materials that I'd likely need at Fordson). Also, I wanted to get my stuff out of the way of whoever was taking the room at Edsel. However, I had no idea what I would be scheduled to teach. On Tuesday morning, hopefully I could get in early to Edsel to collect my things. Then I could beat it over to Fordson, which was just ten minutes away, and get somewhat oriented and settled in before the students arrived. Like most of you, I like to feel in control. This was not the way that I expected to start the next phase of my teaching career. It was daunting enough to be leaving an environment of an all-girl school with the class sizes of a dozen or so and move to a mixed male/female population with class sizes of 25 plus. I felt like I was heading for a Shadrach, Meshach, and Abednego[31] experience. In this story from the Old Testament, three young Hebrew men were cast into a fiery furnace at the whim of a pagan king – Nebuchadnezzar II who wanted them to renounce the God of Israel (Daniel Ch. 1-3). When I started at Clara B. Ford/Vista Maria, I started much the same way. However, I adapted, survived, and thrived there. "I can do this," I said to myself. "I hope...."

I managed to get in and out of Edsel that Tuesday before the cock crowed. Still, by the time that I walked into Fordson, the halls were already approaching the levels of mall madness on Christmas Eve. Students, staff, security, and administrators scurried about, some nervous, others excited. Some bewildered freshmen were trying to find their way in unfamiliar surroundings, like me.

"Ah, the main office," I said to myself. Sporting my best confident smile, I walked in and introduced myself. The secretary seemed cordial enough, in spite of the first-day-of-school craziness. She greeted me with a sympathetic smile. It just so happened that the principal (Imad Fadlallah), whom I'd never laid eyes on before, came striding in at that moment. Nodding to me, the secretary announced to him, "This is Mr. Shannon, one of our new teachers." Without breaking stride or turning to make eye contact with me, he simply muttered, "I saw him."

Well, now, that's a fine howdy-do. I tried to make light of it. There

---

[31] These three young men even have their Hebrew names taken from them: Hanamiah (Shadrack), Mishael (Meshach), Azariah (Abednego). Sentenced to death for putting the One God of Israel before earthly rulers and are thrust into a fiery furnace, but they are saved by divine intervention.

was no sense in letting a little thing like that rattle me. I thought to myself, "This guy must have a thousand things on his mind, hectic first morning and all." Still, it would have been nice if he'd just paused a moment, extended his hand, and voiced a simple, "Welcome to Fordson ... nice to have you." Later, it occurred to me that principals must find it annoying on those occasions when they're "forced" to take on teachers that they know little or nothing about and have little control over placing in "his/her" building. There is no doubt that principals get burned in this regard on occasion. However, going to Fordson wasn't my choice, either. If indeed this was the case, I should like the benefit of the doubt along with at least a token of professional courtesy.

During the following three years, this principal and I did develop more of a professional relationship, yet it remained somewhat cool. I felt like a bit of an outsider and that I was viewed with a certain level of suspicion. I confess that I may have encouraged this – you know, keep `em guessing, which was a bit of a control technique, I imagine. Perhaps he and some of the other administrators and teachers, many of whom were Middle Eastern, were having a bit of a challenge dealing with my "Irishness." Hah! I worked with this principal and his staff for three years. I hope that I left him, a Muslim, with a good impression (witness).

As a history teacher, I spend a good deal of class time on matters of religion; it's part of the package. I took it upon myself to pick up several books about Islam as well as a copy of the Qur'an so I could lecture more authoritatively on related matters that were bound to come up. I've had numerous, wonderful conversations, sometimes debates, with my Muslim students, my colleagues, and a security guard (who, incidentally, happens to be African American). These took place before and after school, at lunchtime, and during my prep periods.

One day after school, the guard popped in to chat. During the course of our conversation, I said, "Oh, so you're a Black Muslim." I got an earful on that one. "No," he exclaimed pointedly like he'd been through this before, "I'm a black man who happens to be Muslim." The guard promptly launched into a well rehearsed lecture. No doubt I'm not the first poor unenlightened soul to cross paths with him in regards to this matter. He carefully explained the differences between traditional Islam and Black Islam. The Nation of Islam, a dominant sect within Black Islam, is considered a heresy by orthodox Islam, since it claims that there is a prophet after Muhammad, namely, the Honorable Elijah Muhammad. Since our first discussion, this guard and I had many conversations; our dialogue could get spirited but always remained amicable. I have learned a good deal from him with regard to Islam. I pray that he is well.

By the way, wouldn't you like to be a "fly on the wall" (okay, maybe not a fly) when I'm teaching a class on the Crusades, the Reformation, the Jesuits, the Holocaust, the Six-Day War, or 9/11! I don't pull any punches and I try not to come off as a know-it-all. Indeed, most of my students don't realize it, but I'm learning as much, perhaps more, than they are in regard to a host of historical issues. When I have addressed historical matters of a sensitive nature, I sometimes have had to reexamine them in order to discern any of my own bias. For example, let us take the lingering unrest and conflict between Palestinians and Jews following the establishment of the statehood of Israel. Many of my students are more sympathetic to the Palestinian cause, and I have found that I need to take my students' historical/cultural backgrounds into account when these issues surface during class. Many of my students are AP (Advanced Placement) kids and seniors, and I see little value in watering things down. I like to heat things up, knowing that these kids soon will be encountering these topics in settings that might be out of their comfort zones, such as college. My "M.O." comes from what I learned during my radio days. You want listeners? You gotta make them either happy or mad enough to listen. Nobody likes bland.

· · · ·

"I've got a feeling we're not in Kansas anymore," Dorothy breathed anxiously to Toto in *The Wizard of Oz*. Fordson is not your everyday American high school, by any stretch of the imagination. Take out your notepads; time for a history lesson. The school, which was named for Henry Ford and his son Edsel, has a rich tradition that dates back to its completion in 1928 near the northwest intersection of Ford and Schaefer Roads in East Dearborn, where it still sits regally. You'd be hard pressed to find a high-school building in this state with a more beautiful facade. Fordson is the first American high school to cost more than one million dollars (roughly 2.5m). Its neo-Tudor style was inspired in part by Rushton Hall in Northhamptonshire, England. The inside of the school has seen better days, as you might expect given its 90 plus years. However, it still

273

possesses a good deal of the architectural charm that characterizes the exterior. The 2nd floor library and the main foyer are both exceptional, and help Fordson to retain an institution-of-higher-learning vibe. In both of these locations, a goodly number of statues of ancient scholars and philosophers stand as silent witnesses to what education has been and should be. I sometimes jokingly tell my students that my statue and/or bust will take its place one day alongside Mercury, Euripides, and Homer. The best counter for that, which none have thrown back as yet, is that wonderful line from *The Wizard of Oz*, when Auntie Em, after hearing farmhand Hickory (the future Tin Man) declare that their town will erect a statue in his honor one day, fires back, "Well, don't start posing for it now!"

A large number of well known alumni have left their stamp at Fordson, for good or ill: Russ Gibb (the proprietor of the Grande Ballroom during the 60s), Chad Everett (film and TV actor), and Walter Reuther (union activist and one of *Time* Magazine's 100 Most Influential People of the Twentieth Century) to name a few. They tell me that my room – A107 – was once occupied by teacher James Osterberg, the father of Ann Arbor rocker Iggy Pop. This fact didn't impress me much. I'm not really a fan of Iggy and the Stooges ... more of an Amboy Dukes, SRC, Mitch Ryder fan myself. However, it's not just the building and alumni that puts Fordson into a league all of its own. This is not your father or mother's high school. Today the school's population is comprised of students, 90% of which would identify themselves as Arabic. Most of these students would identify themselves as Muslim. Of course, this runs the gamut from culturally casual (sometimes clueless) to sincerely passionate and reflective adherents, and a dozen blends and varieties sandwiched in between.

· · · ·

My first several months at Fordson turned out to be more interesting than intimidating. Every day, someone or something sparked my curiosity as I drifted on a rollercoaster of emotions: one moment, intrigue, the next, amusement, and, occasionally bewilderment. Some things about high school never change: bullies, pranksters, punks, jocks, loudmouths, and drama queens, shy types, guys who send the message "grab me before I melt." Fordson is largely like *Grease* taken into the new millennium with a mostly Middle Eastern cast. When I first went over my class list, I thought, "Huh?" It seemed like every class had several Alis and Muhammads (nicknamed Mo); sometimes Ali was a first name, sometimes a last name. "Hmmm, not too many Sues, Nancys, or Freds on here," I remember thinking.

It may be true that some things never change, but much has. Cell phones in the classroom are a royal pain. Cell phones are almost impossible to control, like trying to fend off a locust swarm with a few branches and a can of Raid. My teachers never had to worry about kids taking a snapshot of the test and passing it on to their buds. By the way, while we're on the subject, an issue that has perhaps vexed me more than any other is the widespread practice of cheating among students. I've tried to make sense of it but, since I've taught at only one other school, I don't have a lot of varied teaching experience. I don't know where Fordson High School sits on the national student "cheating scale." Cheating wasn't a huge problem back at Clara B. Ford. This may be due in part to the mentality of "I don't give a damn about my grades anyway" that some of the girls carried. They also might have thought, "Why take the risk when getting busted might lead to a suspension of privileges like home visits, late stay-ups, and what not?" I've discussed the cheating at Fordson with my own kids, all of whom are recent high-school grads, and they're not sure what to make of it, either, though by their reckoning, cheating at Saline High School never reached the epidemic proportions with which Fordson is plagued.

"Maybe dad's just exaggerating," my kids probably have said to themselves. I don't think that I am. I hope that this doesn't reflect too negatively on the entire student body. I'd like to think that a good many, even most, of my students maintain academic integrity. My mind drifts back to my old high-school days to recall a certain amount of contempt with which students that regularly cheated were regarded. Oh, but get ready to grab hold of something: There may have been a time or two or three that I stooped to cheating; more along the lines of copying a friend's homework and turning it in as my own. In any event, I still regard this kind of behavior as cheating. On occasion, I have discussed the subject of cheating with my students, both privately and during class. I have received a full gamut of responses. On one end, there is an indifference marked by an attitude of "So what? Who cares?" On the other end, they have bewilderment that is akin to my own about why cheating at Fordson is so widespread. If I want to heat up the conversation with my students, I can sometimes ask, "Does the Qur'an address this subject?"

One day after school, a young female student approached me with tears in her eyes and anger threatening to boil over. She was beside herself with discouragement because she'd taken the "high road" and didn't score as well on an exam as some of her classmates. She knew with certainty that several of them had stooped to cheating. In her mind, they had not only gotten away with it but benefited by doing so.

"For now," was my response.

"Whaddaya mean, Mr. Shannon, for now? It's just not fair."

"For now ... you can take it to the bank that it'll come back to haunt them one day."

"How so?" she said, not unlike a judge searching for answers "I'm so pissed ... I need an A in your AP class or I'm out a potential scholarship. I could just scream!"

"You're Muslim?"

"You know I am."

"Does the Qur'an have any passage similar to this Bible verse? 'You reap what you sow.' (Gal 6:7)? Try to take solace in your taking the high road (not cheating) as pleasing to God and He will reward you for that. It may be tomorrow, years down the road, or both, but He will."

At this point, the discussion about cheating can go in a lot of directions. I admire those students who don't cheat, and there are many, who endeavor to walk the true path and do the right thing. Like the Psalmist, we are sometimes dismayed when we see the unrighteous prosper and nice guys and gals seemingly finish last. I like what Evangelist Herman Stalvey used to say, "God's markin' it all down and payday's comin'." This ought to give you pause for thought. I suspect that this cheating business may be a nationwide phenomenon with fluctuations here and there. We adults haven't always been the best role models.

· · · ·

It took awhile, but I finally got used to about half of my female students wearing hijab (head scarves, which typically cover both the head and neck). Actually, many look quite attractive thus attired. This is not the point, of course. Still, I've come to appreciate not only the look but the motivation behind it; inner beauty is more important than outward. Some of my students refer to themselves and each other as "scarfies." I don't, but nobody, including the staff, seems to get too uptight about it. Many of the young ladies are quite proud to don the hijab. Still, from where I sit, it's sometimes difficult not to look at them and wonder how these girls might look without their scarves. I think it was my former wife's beautiful head of hair that first caught my attention. I've had a good many conversations with both scarved and unscarved young Fordson ladies as to the significance of this attire. We discussed questions like "Why I do or don't wear a hijab. What does the Qur'an instruct in this matter?" and "Was I forced to wear a scarf?" Then there's the whole thing with students who wear a scarf in part as a sign of modesty but then, from the neck down, they wear tight shirts and jeans. Not all, mind you.

Many of my female students are attired in more traditional, conservative hijab. This is abaya, the "head-to-toe" gear that many of the female students of Yemeni and Iraqi backgrounds adopt. However, the latter may not feel as pressured as the former to wear the abaya. I have noticed women dressed with niqab (face covering) on only a few occasions, howbeit, in 2017 I've noticed an increase. Typically I'd see these women in the halls and at parent/teacher conferences, not in my classroom until Fall of 2015, a delightful young lady originally from Yemen. Seeing women dressed in niqab still rattles me a bit, but no doubt some folks see yours truly and don't know what to make of him. Many of the young ladies at Fordson, Arab and non-Arab, look and dress pretty much like you'd see at most American public high schools; as do the guys. It's fascinating to sit back and observe the dynamic of how the whole "dress" thing is played out in the classroom. It seemed so much simpler back in the day when you just had to decide if you were frat, greaser, or continental – later, straight or freak (hippie). Actually, now that I think about it, that could be rather stressful, too.

There is a perceived "pecking order" within the Arab student community at Fordson. This is based on nationalistic ties. Currently, the top of the heap is occupied by the Lebanese, due to their numbers and the fact that they are more Americanized than other Arab nationalities. The Yemenis cling precariously to the bottom rung of the pecking order. They are fewer in number, dress more conservatively, and generally have darker skin and slighter builds. The Syrian, Iraqi, Palestinian, and other Middle

Eastern groups fall somewhere in between. It is hard to say how the non-Arabs are placed on the pecking order. However, you know how most minority groups have to clamor to be noticed or opt for the fly-under-the-radar approach and stay cool until the storm passes. I'm still sorting out the pecking order and try not to make too much of it, but one should be aware of these and other dynamics that shape the work environment.

Some kids will fight over the most trivial matters. In their minds, you gotta carry a rep, especially if you're the underdog. Here at Fordson, doing so is not quite as simple as the Jets and Sharks of *West Side Story* fame. Did I mention "boaters" (those students who have just gotten "off the boat")? They are looked upon as being extremely uncool; not yet Americanized enough yet I assume. Also, divisions exist beyond national lines. There are religious differences, too, stemming from a seventh-century division within Islam concerning the rightful successor to Mohammad. This split caused Islam to be divided into two main groups, the Sunni and the Shi'ites. The Sunni, who comprise about 80 percent of all Muslims, hold that the true line of succession from Muhammad is found in the four Caliphs: Abu Bakr, Omar, Uthman, and Ali. To many of the Shi'ite, Muhammad's son-in-law, Ali, was the true successor to Muhammad in the leadership of the Islamic community. I have both Sunni and Shi'ite students in my classroom. On the world stage, Sunnis are the more dominant group within Islam. Here at Fordson, the Shi'ite is the more dominant group on campus, due to the large number of Lebanese students here. Consequently, my students and I have some very interesting discussions. It's a delicate dance at times; sometimes I'm like the guy in the center cage at the circus who keeps the lions and tigers from going after each other or, worse, turning on me! I can take the heat as long as it enhances the educational objective and no one gets hurt. When I've had time to reflect, I often marvel at some of the conflicts within Islam, as alluded to above. Sunni/Shi'ite issues over leadership mirror ongoing conflicts between Catholic, Protestant, and Eastern Orthodox traditions. Occasionally, I'll have a kid say to me on the sly, "I'm not Sunni or Shi'ite, I'm Muslim." "That sure sounds familiar," I think to myself. How many times has someone thrown the line at me, "Joe, I'm not Catholic or Protestant, I'm Christian"? Indeed, I could high-step with that one.

This leads into something that I wanted to mention, an aspect of my current job that I enjoy thoroughly. On numerous occasions, kids –

Muslim, non-Muslim, male, and female – stop by before/after school to discuss matters that we either ran out of time to bring closure to in class or to clear up misunderstandings. These students sometimes come alone or at other times with a "support group." Perhaps they felt uncomfortable taking a position in front of their peers while in class, so they come to see me privately. It's gotten so I usually eat lunch in my classroom to accommodate these kids. Many of them (for example, seniors who are getting a jump on their liberal-arts credits for college) take classes over at nearby Henry Ford College in the afternoon. They have a difficult time stopping by after classes end at Fordson. Some drop in during my prep period, some even before school (7 a.m.ish). Sometimes they want to discuss religion and or Middle Eastern politics. With regard to Christianity, most of their inquiries concern historical issues, such as the reliability of the Scriptures. For example, how does Evolution square with the account of Creation in the Book of Genesis? Faith/Science issues are big on the menu. Sometimes, we discuss the Crusades, including primary accounts from both the Muslim and Christian camps. In these discussions, my students and I confront the question, "How could Christians have done this?" Or theologically oriented matters like, "Mr. Shannon, what's up with this Trinity thing you guys are into?"

Typically, I confine these sensitive subjects to my AP classes. I try to keep these matters within an historical framework, and I hope that my motives are appropriate. Outside of the regular classroom, I have shared a bit of my own personal spiritual journey with my students, in response to their youthful curiosity. They find my responses intriguing and often are compelled to consider their own spiritual journeys, or lack thereof. Many of my students have been surprised at how much Christianity and Islam have in common (I have been surprised at this as well). For instance, how both traditions hold Mary, Jesus' mother, in high esteem … significant differences concerning Mary? Yes, but it's a starting point with which to build on. On those occasions when the Christmas break/vacation (sorry, I don't refer to it as the Winter Holiday since everybody really knows what it is and why we're taking a break at this time) coincides with a unit in World History called "The Birth of Christianity," I've shown the 2006 film *The Nativity Story.* The students seem to really enjoy it; a rare thing by the way, a film both they and I like. I've had them write papers in which they compare/contrast the way Mary is portrayed in the film and New

Testament with the Qur'an's account of Jesus' birth and depiction of Mary. I've had young ladies, typically of a more conservative Muslim personality, tell me privately how much they admire Mary and the way the film depicted her as someone unwilling to compromise her beliefs. If students are not comfortable with this question other options are offered, typically dealing with the film's accuracy, or lack of, portrayal of life in first century Palestine. To be sure, I take exception to many Islamic beliefs and practices, but I do not disrespect or make light of the ones to which I disagree. Indeed, I also teach a unit on Islam and I must endeavor, without favoritism or bias, lay out the historical facts as best that we may ascertain them, allowing for scholarly disagreement and debate, and reach our own conclusions and let truth lead us where it may. If I am called out on something during class – for example, "How could God have a son?" – I'll dive into it if it fits into the historical context of the class. If not, and the student(s) still want to pursue the subject, they know when and where to find me.

· · · ·

One day, a couple of kids hit me up: "Mr. Shannon, we're starting a History Club, and we'd like you to be the teacher-sponsor. Don't worry, you won't have to do anything, just kind of monitor it."

"What's the matter, couldn't you find anyone else?" I shot back.

Once a month after school, I hosted meetings of the History Club in my classroom. Open to students and staff, these meetings last an hour or more. They include presentations, discussions on the historical theme(s) that the students had decided on the previous month, with my approval. These meetings are concluded with mingling and snacks. Somehow, I ended up the main presenter for three of these gatherings during the first year of the club. One meeting was oriented around Christmas, where we looked at the origin of many traditions and how they have evolved over the years, such as carols, decorating trees, Santa Claus, and the Three Wise Men. I did a similar presentation with Easter – Good Friday, chocolate bunnies, and colored eggs. The kids responded to this subject with a resounding "Huh?" I enjoy trying to sort out the subjects for them, fielding their questions and marveling that so many know so little. I'll never forget one meeting of the History Club, a special Irish edition, which took place in March 2009. We had fliers posted in the halls and announcements flashing across the TV monitors in the school that warned Fordson, "Grab a hold of something. The Irish are coming!" The History Club presented to a classroom that was standing-room only. Our audience included several counselors; heck, even the principal dropped in. Rumor had it that we'd be serving Guinness and that I'd be in a kilt (both of which turned out to be untrue). I told the story of St. Patrick to our attentive audience and followed this with a question-and-answer period that covered anything 'Irish' – the famine, the Troubles, the IRA, pubs, leprechauns, the Orangemen, and America's first world-famous athlete, heavyweight boxing champ John L. Sullivan, Boston's Irish Strongman – until time ran out and we dove into a mountain of snacks and drinks, including potato skins. "Erin Go Braugh!"

For me, part of the attractiveness concerning the History Club was to present history in a setting where most of the kids who attended our meetings had a genuine interest in history in general and the month's theme or topic in particular. Treats and some occasional extra-credit points may also have been part of the attraction. However, after presenting at a few of the sessions I have mentioned above, I would just sit back in quiet amazement at how God worked in this setting. I had the opportunity to share the mysteries of the Incarnation and the Resurrection and their resultant joys. While holding Jesus in high regard as a prophet, most Muslims do not believe that he died on a cross and rose on the third day. It will come as a surprise to many Christians that Muslims do believe in Jesus' birth by a virgin, Mary, whom they also hold in high esteem. For my students, I can help to separate fact from fiction with regard to the historical narrative and traditions associated with these events, point out where the controversies lie, and give them a setting in which to raise questions. I also can help to satisfy their curiosity regarding matters that many teachers would just as well dance around because of either a warped understanding of the place of religion in the public-school classroom or a lack of training and expertise in such matters, perhaps both. In addition, it's no secret that many history textbooks are biased, more commonly by what they leave out than by what they do include. While I may not be able to address all of these biases, there is a time and place when they must be addressed, without exchanging one bias for another. I "get off" on this. When it comes off well, it's a nice counterweight. Sometimes, though, it didn't. We had a few meetings that were duds. There were occasions when

I felt like I had failed to make the point that I wanted to make. The historical climate on which I wanted to share light had remained clouded in obscurity. Ultimately, though, the History Club bore great fruit. In 2010, it morphed into the Debate Club, an explanation of which will follow.

It was nice to have a few successes on which to fall back. On numerous occasions, I find myself whining and complaining like Old Jonah during my drive home from work (50 minutes plus). I can get depressed at what a pathetic, miserable witness for Christ I am as a teacher. The Scriptures are replete with examples of men and women who have stumbled along a similar narrow path. In spite of their shortcomings, though, they persevered. The reality is that their sanctification was not complete until they were in the arms of Our Heavenly Father. Following in their wake might not be such a bad thing. Disappointments, though they were legion, did not hinder them from their pursuit of "the prize" (in Paul's words) that waits for us in glory. These role models from Scripture and the lives of the saints provide a light at the end of the Tunnel of Doubt. Thus far, my teaching experience at Fordson has not left me free of a few cuts and bruises. However, I'm not yet ready to throw in the towel (c.'17).

Despite the overall success of the History Club, it failed to generate interest with students in 2010. However, when a group of students, primarily from my AP History classes, asked me to sponsor the Debate Club, I accepted, with reservations. (Since I already had a full plate at Fordson, I didn't want it to be added to unnecessarily. Both the History Club and the Debate Club were time-consuming, after-school activities. I wanted to be sure that the students were genuinely committed and that they would hold up their end, organizing, participating in, and promoting the club.) The principal gave the Debate Club a thumbs-up. I thought to myself, "This could be even more interesting than the History Club." We did have a couple of historical debate presentations during History Club that were okay. I saw potential in them and wondered why Debate wasn't pushed more at Fordson. By having formal debates, students can learn and develop skills that are useful in every walk of life. My thinking is that, if you expect an interested, enthusiastic audience to show up, then you need a stimulating debate topic. Here, we must take care where we tread. I don't dodge the controversial, per se, and just about anything can fit somewhere into a historical context. However, I've had to say "No" on a few occasions and expect I will again. What do you think high-school kids want to debate? (Remember, ol' Joe's not in Kansas anymore.) They didn't want to debate subjects such as abortion, freedom of speech, the legalization of pot, immigration laws, gun control, and stem-cell research. Usually, many of my students do want to debate "Middle-Eastern" issues. I'm okay with this as long as we have a specific agenda. Typically, narrow topics work better. For example, a couple of participants wanted to debate what they saw as the Occupation State of Israel and the suffering and subjugation of Palestinians and other Arab nationalities that are subject to their rule. In addition, these students felt that the United States had become too cozy with Israel. Consequently, these students used this setting as a platform to "Jew-bash" and to blame them in general and the U. S. in particular for many of their ills, both at home and abroad. I told my students that there had to be representatives from both camps to have a legitimate debate. If no one wished to present, to argue the position of Israel and/or the United States, then I would step in and would try to present an argument. After considering this, my students decided to explore other topics that were focused less on Middle-Eastern issues. One day, several students approached me concerning a debate topic: "Did the Holocaust Really Happen?"

"No," I told them, "We're not going to debate if the Holocaust happened. If you want to get into the who, what, when, where, why, or the numbers, we may be able to come up with something." I wondered where they get this stuff. It comes up from time to time, but I usually shut it down immediately. As you might have gleaned from the two topics that were proposed by my students for debate, a significant number of them sprinkled throughout my classes are not shy about expressing their dislike, indeed hatred, of Jews. I take into account the painful experiences that many of them have endured first-hand due to violence and centuries-old disputes in their (or their parents' and grandparents') homeland. During their adolescence, many kids just spout as a means of getting attention. When push comes to shove and they are pressed into giving some intelligent articulation to justify their taunts, they quickly wither away, a stream of vulgarities the best that they can muster. Make no mistake, though: Some of these kids have been traumatized. We all know that there's plenty of blame to go around. Think that I'm exaggerating? I met with a counselor who was concerned about a young fellow who was failing my class. "This kid's father is gonna beat him good," the counselor said.

"Maybe that's what he needs," I thought to myself. She went on, "I talked to dad. He told me, 'Look, I didn't carry my two young sons through several miles of land mines (Iraq, I think) so they could make it to the U.S.A. and fail.'" Yep, these kids/parents have had some experiences I've never known. In teaching, I am often confronted with a question that I hope to turn into an object lesson (and to see if anyone is actually listening). The dialogue goes like this:

"Mr. Shannon, what are you?"

"I'm an Irish Jew."

"Huh! Say Wallah, Mr. Shannon!"

"For real … I am."

"No way!"

This gets 'em every time. If eight kids have their heads on their desks, I can guarantee that six will raise them with an expression of, "Did he say what I just think he said?" Before you roll your eyes one more time, tis truer than you think. I'm Irish (Shannon), and no one in my family has come forward yet with the announcement, "Well, Joe, it's time you were told. You were adopted from a rural German orphanage." Yikes! No question I'm Irish, and likely a sizable dose of continental strains given that Grandma Shannon's maiden name was Bastien. Maybe even a bit of a German, French and Scandinavian blood swirls along the corridors of my bloodstream; but Jewish? In a unit on Judaism that I teach, I usually do a lesson on "Father" Abraham; this precedes the ones that I tackle further down the road on Christianity and Islam. Abraham is a key figure for all three monotheistic religious traditions. We discuss Abraham's sons, Ishmael and Isaac. Unlike Jews and Christians, Muslims believe that Ishmael, Abraham's firstborn by his handmaid Hagar, was the son that God promised to Abraham and rightful heir. Through the seed of Ishmael, the destiny of humanity would be realized. Typically, this account sets the stage for some interesting discussions. "How is it," I put to them, "that these three groups of people, who all esteem Abraham as Father of the Faith (Jew and Muslim by blood and faith, Christians by faith), have grown so far apart? Why does way too much animosity exist among us?" These questions give the students and me something to ponder and to revisit during the weeks and months that follow. I also like to point out to all of my students that many Christians consider themselves "Jewish" (hence my comment that I'm an Irish Jew) in light of the Apostle Paul's comments in his letter to the Romans (Ch. 11). Here, Paul uses the allegory of Israel as the olive tree of God. Paul likens Gentile believers in Jesus to wild olive branches that have been grafted onto this tree. As you might suspect, I need to take a slow, steady-as-she-goes approach in these waters with my students. Many of them are seniors. At this time next year, some will be occupying seats in local universities and community colleges. The classroom debates there can take a "no-holds-barred" approach, and too bad if your little ol' feelings get hurt. So I have no problem with heating things up a bit to give my students a taste of what they can expect. You want them to have some experience under their belts before you send them into the big game. I also know when to cut the heat if things threaten to boil over. It usually leaves a mess, and I don't like messes.

Students learn to read you faster than their textbooks. They know your strengths and weaknesses. I like to imagine that I remain largely shrouded in mystery, but I may be kidding myself. Still, here goes: My two biggest personal liabilities in the classroom are my mouth and my moodiness. Both of these qualities play off each other in their own devious manner. It troubles me to know the shadow that they cast over my witness. Plus, it's embarrassing to approach my confessor with the same old story month after month when I go to Confession. My tongue … I can't seem to control that little "rudder" that steers the body (Jas 3:4-10). James points out that the person who can control his or her tongue has mastered their whole body. The kids at Fordson tell me that I'm sarcastic. I usually jump to my own defense (no one else does) and point out that what they perceive as my sarcasm is nothing more than good old Shakespearean wit that they should learn to appreciate. This is hard to do, I suppose, if the verbal barbs are flung in your direction. I reckon that wit has its place in the classroom. It can be a useful teaching tool, and a bit of humor on occasion can lighten the mood of the class. Part of my strategy in the battle of wits that I have with my students is awareness and careful examination of conscience; these have become new weapons in my arsenal in my attempt to make some spiritual gains in my own walk. Furthermore, my memory bank still holds images of being on the receiving end of several verbal attacks from an exasperated nun or a frustrated lay teacher back at St. Agatha. These attacks hurt back then and are locked in my memory. "Gee, Joe," I think to myself, "Maybe they are reminders that you should take pains not to go that route with your students." No doubt I deserved some measure of what

I got back in the day. Still, no one likes to be humiliated publicly, especially before their peers. I think to myself, "You're supposed to be an ambassador for Jesus?" I've beat myself up pretty well over the "tongue" issue. Like my body weight, this is a lifelong struggle that will take more than willpower to overcome; it takes grace. Our cooperation with the Father's gift of grace, won for us by Jesus and delivered by the Holy Spirit, is just what the doctor (Jesus) ordered. When you as a child of God square off against the world, the flesh, and the Devil, the battle plan is your will working in sync with His grace. "I can do all things through Christ who strengthens me" (Phil 4:13). So, press on.

. . . .

When you've been teaching for twenty plus years, you sometimes pause, and in your mind's eye, the faces of countless former students race by, kids who left some kind of imprint on you for good or ill. "Where are they today?" you wonder. There are a dozen former students that I can see just as clearly as if they were sitting here with me. Then there's that one, or maybe two or three, whom you quickly hone in on, like with the collection of faces covering the Beatles' album *Sergeant Pepper's Lonely Hearts Club Band*. Currently, one or more of these kids may be in their thirties. Several of them have stayed in touch over the years. Following the graduating class of 2011, I have had to squeeze in a few more on that album cover. One young lady in particular is one of those once-in-a-career kids with whom you cross paths.

This girl, who wears the hijab, struck me as a moderate conservative Muslim in the way that she carries herself, both in appearance and in conversation. Since she is a bright kid, I would chide her for not taking my AP Euro History class. She'd often stop by to chat, sometimes alone, other times with one of her like-minded sidekicks. This girl has been one of my several "go-to" kids concerning all things Islam. I think that she liked me in an "uncle-ish" manner, or maybe as a big, older (much older, in my case) brother. All of her siblings are female. Many of the Muslim girls do not date, and boyfriends are usually taboo. So perhaps this student would have liked to have had a big brother. Back in high school, I recall thinking that having an older brother would have come in quite handy. My younger brothers may have wished that they didn't have an older brother at times. Anyway, back to my student, she could get on my nerves, in a playful kind of way. She could be attention-seeking, but in general was a delight to be around. On one occasion, we had this exchange: "Mr. Shannon, I brought my IPod for you to check out. Let me pull some music up on your computer. You'll love it. Come on, please?"

"Not a good time. I've gotta put these grades in … some other time."

"Oh, come on," she pleaded. "You can do grades later. I have tons of cool stuff on here you're gonna love. Some surprises, too. Pahleeeeze?"

"Yeah, right," I thought to myself, "Just what I want to listen to at 7 a.m. in the morning." Oh, boy, here it comes. The sad, droopy-eyed pout, not unlike the one that my daughter used to cast my way when she had something special to show me and I'd say, "Not now, hon."

In my experience, most students at Fordson have limited musical tastes. It may be much the same elsewhere. I can't really use my own kids here as a litmus test. Their musical interests run the gamut from classic rock to alternative country, Celtic, and funked-up hip-hop and R&B, for which, by the way, they can largely thank ol' Dad. On numerous occasions, they have frequented the Ark (an intimate music venue in Ann Arbor that is near at hand) as well as wonderful summer celebrations in downtown Ann Arbor called "Top of the Park." These offer a musical smorgasbord sure to please just about everyone's palate. It seems that most kids at Fordson listen largely to garden-variety pop and rap, sometimes with a little Arabic seasoning. My opinion of their tastes is based primarily on my having chaperoned talent shows, proms, and homecomings; the song lists there are tilted heavily in the direction of the latest hip-hop drivel. Wow, I just thought that I heard Pops (Harold) there for a moment. Dad couldn't deal with Dylan's nasal-powered vocals or with the Chambers Brothers' screams spittin' out my eight-track player. Harold was more of a Perry Como kind of guy. Pops just couldn't get the message behind meaningful lyrics like "I've got a girl named Rama Lama Ding Dong." Go figure. Anyway, the hip-hop, teeny-bop trite music fare clogging the air waves sounds like they all use the same bass and drum "canned" soundtracks. On occasion, when I'm at my local gym, I'm compelled to endure such cultural dung when an aerobics class is going through its routine. Anyway, back to my student from 2011. "Maybe tomorrow with the music." … she'll probably forget all about it and that will be the end of it.

Next day: "Good morning, Mr. Shannon. Ready?"

"Uh, ready as in …?"

"You know, tomorrow. You said tomorrow you'd give it an ear."

"Hmm, so I did. Well, let's hear whatcha got." What else could I say? As I surrendered my favorite chair and computer to her, she was so excited. She acted as if I'd just turned over the wheel of the *Starship Enterprise* to her. She was in DJ mode in no time.

I gotta tell ya, I was impressed. During the next fifteen minutes, I heard snippets of songs by the Beach Boys, U2, Luciano Pavarotti, the Big Bands, Patsy Cline, cuts from the soundtrack of *West Side Story,* some current stuff that I recognized vaguely from my daughter's listening playlist, and a healthy helping of Beatles (I still can't get over the fact that sometimes I'll mention John, Paul, George, and Ringo and maybe Led Zepplin or the Doors and the entire class lets out a collective "Huh?"). In addition, my student highlighted her favorite group – the Bee Gees – on her IPod. She must have had a hundred songs on this thing. By the time that I had finished listening, I was hooked like a largemouth bass on a sleek rapala lure.

Hearing just snippets was a bit annoying, especially if it happened to be a tune that I actually liked. It reminded me of some jock on CKLW-AM radio playing the hits back in the sixties. These jocks always seemed to run their mouths at the beginning of a song (which sometimes is the best part) or faded it out too soon at the end. I wanted to reach into my transistor radio and give these jocks a good smack. Now, I smiled patiently at my student, amused to see how excited she was. I thought about how little effort that it sometimes takes to bring a little joy and laughter into someone's life. I suppose that my student kept jumping from one tune to another knowing that she only had a fifteen-minute window.

"I don't believe this!" I exclaimed.

"What?" She gave me a quizzical look.

"This tune, this tune …" I shook my head in mild disbelief, "You've got a Jerry Lee Lewis song on here I haven't heard in decades. Pull it up, and then don't touch it."

She clicked on the song, "The Lewis Boogie," and turned up the volume. I sat back, closed my eyes, and rode the winds of time back for a few precious moments. I went back to 1969: I was over at the house of my buddies, the Engel brothers, Tom and John ... on Brady Street in Redford Township. Another poker game was underway in the basement and Jerry

Lee's "The Lewis Boogie" was a welcome musical diversion from the latest psychedelic tunes on FM radio of which we were currently fans. Now, here was this cute little "scarfie" (I say that affectionately) sitting at my computer with a C-note grin on her face, silently giving me that smile that said, "Mr. Shannon, don't put me in your little stereotype Arab-Muslim girl box. So there."

On a later occasion, my musical Muslim protégé casually mentioned how her little sister, who was in elementary school, had surprised Mom and Dad with a question. No, it was not a birds-and-bees inquiry. Instead, it was "Why do we hate Jews?"

"What? Wherever did you hear such a thing?" Her parents questioned.

"That's what the kids say in school."

"Well, we don't hate Jews."

My student went on to explain how her parents carefully explained to the youngster that this belief is not their way. They have issues with Zionists but not with Jews, per say. I might have guessed as much. This is a special kid – my music-lovin' young lady – from a special family. In 2009, I had her older sister in my AP Euro History class; unlike her sister, she was very quiet but shared with her a love for the arts. As I said, this family had all girls. This got me thinking about Tevye and Goldie's brood of girls in the wonderful musical *Fiddler on the Roof*. My student and her older sister displayed a penchant for learning along with seriousness about their Muslim faith. I suggested that my current student rent the DVD of *Fiddler on the Roof*, given the similarities between her family and Tevye's (notwithstanding that one family is Jewish and living in Russia at the turn of the twentieth century, where life for the Sons of Isaac was becoming precarious – you know, "Like a fiddler on the roof"). My student rented *Fiddler* and loved it. It turned out that the whole family watched it. She laughed as she explained that her father sang along with several of the songs. "Did he?" I wondered, amazed. I have much to learn. I should have liked to discuss the personal relationship that I have with Jesus with my IPod-totin' student. Currently, she is a graduate of Wayne State University, married, mother and teacher, and we remain in touch. Someday, perhaps, I'll have an opportunity to share my testimony with her. However, in the mind of St. Francis of Assisi, perhaps I already have.

A few paragraphs ago, I referred to Zionism. Now, let me tell you about my first open house at Fordson. It was a low-key affair, but I took it seriously. I had my room looking good, with textbooks on display. I rolled on a couple of extra strokes of deodorant. Then the open house began: A trickle of parents wandered in and out and we exchanged pleasantries. Since it was early in the year, no real student issues were on the table yet. Formal parent-teacher conferences were still a couple of months down the road. Then, a husky, forty-something Middle-Eastern fella wandered in. He walked around carefully. He eyeballed me, then my name on the board, and then back at me again, waiting. A few other folks in the room bid me a good evening. I was left alone with this guy. Now that it was just the two of us, he swaggered up to me briskly and said, "Mr. Shannon, eh? How do you do … I'm … Shannon, what's that?"

"Excuse me?"

"Shannon, are you Zionist?"

I fought back the urge to say "Yeah" just for the amusement, but thought better of it. "No, I'm Irish," I answered.

"Okay, but are you Zionist?" he persisted.

"Well, explain to me just what a Zionist is," I offered, turning it back to him. He rambled on for a couple of minutes but had little to no understanding of Zionism in its ancient or current context. The man just seemed to have an ax to grind. Satisfied with his brief dissertation, he abruptly pointed to the textbook on the history of the United States that was on my desk.

"Those, those," he barked, "All Zionist."

"The textbook?"

"Yes, Zionist."

"Indeed." I handed the book to him with this challenge, "Show me the pages." He whirled about and left in a huff. "Good day," I said. "Uh, thanks for stopping.…"

Incidentally, both texts I use (U.S. History and World History) are decent enough. The challenge comes for instance, when a topic like World War 1 is largely confined to one chapter; and you could easily spend a quarter of a semester on the "Great War". Both publishers and teachers have to pick and choose what they consider most relevant. I/we incorporate a lot of supplemental materials; pull up *World War 1 Weapons* on U-Tube for instance, to "fill in any perceived gaps in the narrative or something that might arouse student interest. For instance, while many texts (high school and AP-Advanced Placement) mention Margaret Sanger as a pioneer in Women's Rights and founder of Planned Parenthood, it's pretty much left at that. "Would anyone venture to guess," I throw out somewhat rhetorically to the class, "why Sanger (famed twentieth century eugenicist) was invited to and indeed spoke at the women's branch of a Ku Klux Klan rally?" Silence, quizzical looks, a few yawns and a couple "Huhs." "Or perhaps you've heard," I continue, "that she once expressed her vision for the "Negro Project" (collaboration between the American Birth Control and Sanger's Birth Control Clinical Research Bureau) saying, 'We don't want the word to go out that we want to exterminate the Negro population."

These discussions can go in a lot of different directions, nowhere at all, or so it may seem. Speaking of the Klan, students are bewildered that they (the Klan), had it in big for the University of Notre Dame during the 1920s; most students are at least familiar with Notre Dame Football-the Fighting Irish, but know little of its Catholic roots and ongoing heritage. In case you were unaware, the Klan was also not fond of Catholics and Jews. One way or another, these conversations/lessons all fall under the umbrella of the history courses I'm expected to teach. I'd like to think I also have an obligation not to use my position to project my own historical "bias," but to remind my students that there's often more to the text account (often due simply to limited space) than meets the eye/ear. So, if it arouses some interest, look into it, give us a presentation, perhaps you'll solve the lone shooter theory in the Kennedy assassination, and/or was Constantine's Donation indeed a forgery, and how about Columbus-hero or villain, the Illuminati, the "Summer of Love"… don't get me started.

My first parent-teacher conference was super, overall. However, the first 30 minutes of it puzzled me a bit. Some women (moms or perhaps older sisters, I assumed) would carefully ease up to my table. However, when I stood up to greet them with an extended hand, they pulled back abruptly, almost startled. Then they gave me a sheepish, apologetic look and mumbled something that I couldn't quite make out before putting a hand across their chest, nodding, and sitting down. "What's up with this?" I wondered. The odd thing was that this didn't happen with all of the women at the conference. Most simply smiled, shook my hand, and exchanged pleasantries. Then we'd get down to the business of "how's my kid doin'?" Looking around at how other teachers at nearby tables were interacting with moms, I sort of figured it out. Some Muslim women make absolutely no physical contact with the opposite sex, other than immediate and extended family. It annoyed me a bit that no one at Fordson told "the rookie" about this custom; a "heads-up" from an administrator would've been nice. "Perhaps this is part of my initiation," I thought to myself. Later, I laughed about it. I have a lifelong reputation for learning things the hard way.

Many of my female students make no physical contact with males unless it's their father or close family relative (cousin, uncle). I've tripped over my feet in this regard a few times. I'll be walking up and down the aisles during class, checking and monitoring student work. Forgetfully, I might pat a young lady on the shoulder, saying, "Nice work ... can I get five?" This kind of thing can be embarrassing for both of us. I'll get the "you-know- better" look, but nobody has a panic attack. Still, I forget now and again. I come from a culture that likes to shake, hug, poke, tickle, smack, and elbow. After all, we Irish even hug people we don't like (and then we'll beat the hell outta ya ... then hug ya again). Hah!

· · · ·

Do you remember the slang that you and your crowd used back in the day when you had to serve that four-year sentence called high school? In my day, we said things like, "Far out, dig it, groovy, reefer, bad short (tough car), jive (don't give me none), trip (LSD)." You old timers might be thinkin' more along the "Daddy-o" and "Squaresville" type of jargon. At first, two expressions that I hear regularly around Fordson amused me. Now, though, they really get under my skin and make me cringe like much of America did when Roseanne sang the National Anthem a few years back. These expressions are "Say Wallah!" and "On my mom's life." Hey, spend a day with me and keep your therapist on call. Any former Fordson student of mine reading this is chuckling right now.

"Say Wallah!"

"What?"

"Say Wallah, bro!"

Okay, this is for you who, like me, haven't run in these circles before: "Wallah" is short for "I swear to God." Some of my students who fit the more conservative mold disapprove of the expression being tossed constantly around so nonchalantly. They see this phrase as a sign of disrespect for Allah as well as just another example of immature behavior for which some Fordson kids are legendary. The more mature students resent the undeserved stigma of being bunched in with many of their knuckle-headed peers. Some of my students desperately want to shake free of these stereotypes. They make statements like, "I can't wait to get the hell outta Fordson and away from these idiots." I've heard this sentiment expressed on many occasions. A few kids even resent their Arabness. Didn't most of us go through something similar, an identity crisis with who we are and where we're from? Although we can resent these things, ultimately we usually come to accept and maybe even embrace them.

"On my mom's life!"

"What?"

"Mr. Shannon, Wallah, on my mom's two eyes, I handed it in yesterday. You know I did."

Perhaps I should take a kid who says this more seriously; otherwise there would be an acute shortage of mothers in East Dearborn. Every generation of school kids develop their "language." One way for kids to stay a step ahead of the "law" (teachers, parents) in the "us-versus-them" struggle to educate. My folks and teachers laughed at us and insisted, "Speak English." I was the same with my kids. They'll be the same with theirs. Also, I tend to overlook "light" vulgarity (for instance, 'hell" and "damn") when students use it in class. However, I don't tolerate sexually charged comments, jokes, and so on, or bully language. The latter is the more difficult to pick up on as it's often so subtle. Also, I don't allow Arabic to be spoken in class unless it's used in an instructive manner. Why? I don't know Arabic. If I'm going to be in control of my classroom, I need to know what's being said. I don't know if the guy sitting in back just hollered at the kid three rows over, "You're mama's a whore," if he's speaking Arabic. This kind of thing has happened before in my classroom, and you know where that can quickly lead. I'm laughing to myself, thinking that I have my hands full with derogatory comments slung in the King's English, let alone one that's foreign to me (and I'm too old to learn Arabic). On a similar note, I recall the first time that I was correcting a writing assignment. This is one of those exercises that I give early in the school year in which I ask my students to tell me about themselves in a couple of paragraphs. From reading their papers, I can pick up some clues as to where their writing abilities lay and learn some of their likes and dislikes. In several papers, students were putting (pbuh) after the name Muhammad and sometimes if they happened to mention Jesus or an Old Testament patriarch. "Hmm, curious," I thought. It didn't take a literary Sherlock Holmes to decode this acronym: P-B-U-H stands for Peace Be Upon Him, a sign of respect.

. . . .

Another one of my hijab-sportin' gals, a delightful young lady I had for first hour who often arrived early, before 7 a.m.... This is very unusual, as most of my students come staggering in just at the 7:20 bell and promptly go back to sleep (with their eyes open). This is my best behaved class. Hah! Anyway, my early arriver would be all "perked up" like she'd just filled up on high-octane stuff at Starbucks. If I was busy, which I usually was, she'd sit quietly and catch up on her text messages. We usually chatted for a few minutes about this and that before the other students filtered in. Towards the end of the school year, she walked in one morning and, rather than settle in her assigned seat, plopped in a front-row desk an arm's length from mine. She had a tired, "Can-we-talk?" look about her that was quite uncharacteristic.

"What's up?" I asked.

"Mr. Shannon, you won't believe the weekend I just had. Oh, my, gosh!"

"Work?"

"No, no. I told you...." She rolled her eyes in dismay that I'd so soon forgotten the issues that had been plaguing her of late.

"You mean...." I started before she cut me off.

"You know what I mean," she countered. "Oh, My Gosh, I'm not even gonna lie. I told you it was gonna happen. I got divorced this weekend!"

When one of my students announces that she just got divorced, well, that's a new blip on my radar screen as a teacher. Okay, time to shift into Pastor Joe gear, in a subtle sort of way that is. "So talk to me," I said gently, as if she really needed any encouragement. "Was your marriage an arranged deal?"

In her milieu, the Muslim world that many of my students are in, things aren't always what they seem, to me, at least. It pays to just shut up at times and listen. For the next ten minutes, my student proceeded to pour out her heart. I nodded occasionally and only interrupted for clarification. In her culture, the marriage process isn't complicated (her marriage was not arranged), but the divorce process can be. Muslims think of engagement as a "getting-to-know-one-another" period that is as binding as marriage. Officially, you and your partner are a couple but are not yet living together, nor have you gone through the civil process. Here's where it can get sticky: In order for the engagement (marriage) to be dissolved, both parties must go before a sheikh (religious leader). If both parties want the divorce, it will usually be granted swiftly. However, if one of the parties wants the relationship to continue, it can get complicated and can lead to lengthy negotiations. When a sheikh hears a divorce case, things such as children, abuse, length of marriage/engagement, and other significant issues also must be carefully weighed. My student was still at the engagement level. The other party, who initially resisted her wish to terminate the relationship, eventually gave in. She had to return her dowry (ring and jewelry) and a sum of four thousand dollars. At this point, the sheikh agreed to the divorce and granted it. This was a lot for an eighteen-year-old who was still in high school with which to deal. This young woman has a certain strength about her; she'll be okay. I miss our morning chats: "I'm not even gonna lie."

. . . .

A few more things before I put the last fat period on this thing, grab my walking stick, and head out on my next adventure: While I was at Vista Maria/Clara B. Ford, I wrestled with three teacher/student "crushes" during the course of my sixteen-year teaching experience at that location. There were years between each episode. Nothing ever came of them. Only one of the three girls involved guessed that I may have had romantic feelings for her. When the student/resident left the facility, I'd breathe a sigh of relief and vowed that a crush would never happen again on my end and moved on stoically. Now, at Fordson, I had put a good many miles between the last incident and myself. Being both older and wiser, I little entertained the notion that this sunken Atlantis of teacher/student Crush Land would ever again resurface to threaten my sanity and my witness. Don't look now, but here we go again, and with a vengeance. "What the hell is this?" I groaned to myself, "Déjà vu?"

She was a wonderful, attractive, Lebanese/American, a bright young lady with a million-dollar smile and a personality to match. She is one of those girls about whom you might think to yourself wistfully, "Why didn't I meet someone like you way back when?" Perhaps that's all it was, a bit of wishful thinking for what might have been. Fordson is loaded with physically attractive girls, but I've been around long enough to know, like the Temptations sang, "Beauty's only skin deep...." Inner beauty, virtue, is the real deal. Should you discover someone who possesses both; this is indeed a rare treasure. In this regard, I like a couple of comments from the Book of Proverbs in the Old Testament. "As a jewel of gold in a swine's snout, so is a fair woman which is without discretion" (Prv 11:22). Many of you also are familiar with the description of a virtuous woman from Proverbs 31, which gives a synopsis of admirable qualities that the writer believes that a woman of noble character should possess. For example, she fears the Lord, is savvy in business, sees to the needs of her family, is talented and creative, and willingly extends herself to the poor.

My student struck me as the complete package, at least potentially. First of all, she was friendly in an appropriate way (not the old "suck-up-to-this-dude-for-the-sake-of-my-GPA" kind of friendliness, which I can spot a mile away). On a crummy day, a smile from her could roll back the gloomy gray clouds. I liked the sound of her voice, which had the light spirit of an elf maiden from Rivendell in *The Lord of the Rings.* She was pretty in a "country-girl" kind of way. I sensed that this girl was truly genuine. At first, I brushed off the subtle feelings that began to stir toward my student. As the weeks went by and she began to become the only motivator to keep me looking forward to going to work, it slowly dawned on me that as in the past, stormy emotional seas lie dead ahead. At this point, I'm sure that I wearied Heaven. "God, don't let me say or do something I'll regret," I prayed. "I can't take this. Please grant me strength and wisdom." I kept my pleasant but unwelcome feelings to myself. I was too embarrassed to mention this infatuation, even to my confessor. Besides, I reasoned, it's only a mental struggle at this juncture. Therefore, I could weather it until the year ended, when she would be just a memory and calmer emotional seas would prevail once again. I considered having the girl moved into another class. However, this was always a hassle, and what reason would I give to the counselor? "Well, if you must know, I have a terrible crush on her and...." Half of Fordson would know before the day was over. No, in typical Joe fashion, I decided to suffer and to bear my anguish in silence and solitude. I felt like some wounded beast lying in the shade of a mighty oak, waiting for the cover of night before venturing out. Despite my best efforts, my feelings for this young lady continued to escalate. I tried to resist the effort to flirt with her, but not always successfully. I would go home disgusted with myself. "I'll gut it out," I thought to myself. No Dr. Phil types for Joe. Didn't Jake Blues (John Belushi in the movie *The Blues Brothers*) say something like, "Me and the Lord got an understanding"? I really had no one (mortal that is) with whom I felt comfortable to reveal my little secret. I chalked up my crush to little more than old-fashioned loneliness. I thought, "Since nothin's gonna come of your pathetic little fantasy anyway, get over it." Even an avalanche comes to an end. I love those stories where they dig out some skier who just happened to be in the wrong place at the wrong time. In this case, it was gonna take a big St. Bernard to dig me out, alive, I hoped. Then there was the age thing. I knew that it was absurd, insane, and obscene perhaps. Even so, I found ways to rationalize my infatuation. For instance, this young lady possessed a maturity well beyond her years. During my dance with insanity, my class and I watched the film version of Victor Hugo's classic *The Hunchback of Notre Dame* starring Charles Laughton, a film that I like to use after we've wrapped up a unit on the Middle Ages. A favorite scene of mine is just minutes into the picture. The King of France and his entourage are taking in some of the sights and sounds of a big festival in Paris, from their box seats, of course. At this point, the gypsy girl Esmeralda (Maureen O'Hara – what a beauty) dances before them in a moderate but sensual fashion, lightly beating her tambourine and gently swaying to musical accompaniment. The old king is pleased and tosses her a coin. Then, turning to his doctor, a man seated behind him who looks older than Methuselah, the king comments, "Well, Doctor, doesn't she make your heart beat faster?" The ancient man of medicine nods, then sighs deeply and intones, "I'm a widower five times, but I could start all over." Everyone chuckles. Esmeralda so stirs a man's heart. During the movie, I stole a glance at my student. I wondered momentarily if my "innocent" crush on her was like that of the old doctor for Esmeralda in the movie. (I'm not quite as old as Methuselah, thankfully.) Quickly, I turned my attention back to the film, not wanting my own Esmeralda to start putting two and two together.

In my other situations, I was weak-kneed and felt like I was on the ropes much of the time. In this one, I felt more in control in spite of the spiritual battle in which I found myself entangled once again. This was due to the profound respect that I had for this young lady and my belief that real love serves not its own interest but the interest of others. I sincerely wanted the best for this young lady, and I knew that I wasn't part of that equation. Importantly, I was aided by personal prayer, fasting, and my openness to allow God's grace to empower me in this situation. I had an assurance that this thing wouldn't take me down. Ultimately, it did not, but I breathed a sigh of relief when the school year came to an end.

I've been celibate for years now, and there are days when I crave a woman's gentle kiss and caress. "With somebody more your age," I hear some of you add. Are my Ancient Doctor/Esmeralda infatuations just my cross to bear, not to mention opportunities for spiritual growth? Or are they plots from the pit, some attempt to destroy my soul by the Evil One? The good news is that I have come through these occasions, which have occurred over twenty years, largely unscathed. His grace has won the day, coupled with my feeble efforts. However, I shall not soon forget my last "Esmeralda," nor have I forgotten the other three.

· · · ·

It should have been a great day. Great days at work are not commonplace, and I suppose that's what makes them so. It was a Thursday, and I'd arranged to take off the following day, something that I don't do very often. At that time, which was about a year after my last "Esmerlalda" experience, I had planned a night out with my brother Jeff and my oldest son Cory, a concert at the Michigan Theatre in Ann Arbor that starred English guitarist Jeff Beck, formerly of the Yardbirds. We had looked forward to this show for months. Before the concert, Jeff, Cory, and I had planned to hit the Blue Tractor Pub in downtown Ann Arbor for some southern soul food and a couple of cold ones. I knew that I would enjoy the night more without that nagging little black cloud (work tomorrow) shadowing me, to say nothing of the fact that my students think me grumpy enough in general. However, when I don't get a good night's sleep, well, you can imagine. I'm sort of like a hungry grizzly in a bad mood. Also, a former student, a delightful young lady who is currently at Wayne State University planned on paying me a visit at the end of the school day. This was something else to which I could look forward.

Teachers at Fordson are expected to help monitor the halls during class changes; a necessary, somebody's-gotta-do-it deal. That Thursday was my day to get tripped up. Outside my classroom, I had a run-in with four or five smart-ass male students, for which I was in no mood. These underclassmen liked to congregate by their lockers, which were right outside my classroom. I grew weary of constantly having to shoo them away. The issue (loitering in the hall) was not as important as their unwillingness to comply with my directive, which was to get to class. As they moved down the hall away from my "turf" (A 107), the obscenities and insults that they hurled back my way were too much. I came close to going into a blind rage, almost blacking out, and in the words of Billy Jack in the movie of the same name, "Sometimes I just go berserk." I wanted to hurt these kids. I imagined my fist breaking their jaws and teeth littering the hallway. I went after them, hoping that one or more of them would be stupid enough to take a swing at me or, better yet, to jump me. They didn't. Security guards and other teachers intervened. Two of the more belligerent ones were escorted to the office and later were suspended.

This whole episode lasted less than two minutes but left me angry and shaken. I had a class with which to tend. Fortunately, we were viewing a video about Genghis Khan (whom I briefly admired, at the moment). I sat in the back of class, my eyes partly closed, trying to make sense of what had just transpired as well as my murderous emotional reaction. "Am I that burned out?" I thought. "Has that Deadly Sin – anger – gotten the better of me?" To make matters more interesting, several of my students – the huge, scary, knuckle-dragging variety of senior boys got wind of what had happened. They insisted that I point out these kids to them. "Mr. Shannon, we'll take care of it," they joked wryly, but were deadly serious. "Don't worry. We'll tend to it off campus. They'll never mess with you again." For a moment, I almost nodded a silent "Thanks, appreciate it," but I checked myself. Not only would this have been grossly unethical, but likely it would have escalated into something out of control. "Thanks but no thanks. I'm on top of it, guys. Don't worry, I'll deal with it Shannonator style," I joked half-heartedly. Fortunately, my young female visitor stopped by, true to her word. She was just what the doctor ordered. This girl has that rare gift of brightening up a room just by walking into it. Without her realizing it, she calmed me down considerably. I decided not to mention the recent fiery episode to her. We chatted about this and that before taking a nostalgic stroll down the halls and out to the athletic field where she'd offered to help with the girls' soccer team. We bid each other farewell, the memory of her warm smile etched on my heart.

I had a fantastic night out with Cory and Jeff. The next day, I awoke with a bad taste in my mouth from my run-in with the wannabe thugs at Fordson. "This will not do," I thought. "My weekend will be a waste if I let this eat away at me." It being Friday and the Lenten[32] season, I decided to go to the devotions called the Stations of the Cross at Christ the King Church in Ann Arbor. As I walked into the church, I noticed the pastor, Father Ed, enter the confessional. No one appeared to be waiting there. I thought to myself, "Why not get this off my chest and confess this sin of anger before it really takes root? And nothing like the Sacrament of Reconciliation to help one come to grips with sin." As well as the grace offered by the Sacrament itself, Father Ed offered some practical advice on controlling anger and not letting it taking control of me. My taking care of business prior to doing the Stations of the Cross made these devotions all the more sweet. Praying the Stations helped me to understand that everything I do, including my work, is part of the same package, the commitment that I have made to shoulder my cross and to follow Christ to Calvary. "Well, since I'm already in church, why not stay for the Friday night charismatic prayer meeting?" I mused. All in all, this was a Buffet Table of Grace, to be sure – Confession, prayer, reflection on Christ's passion, scripture, praise, and more prayer. Just thinking about it, I feel like getting up and dancing, Alleluia! Now I have a new awareness that anger has been more of a hindrance to my spiritual growth, such as it is, than I'd hitherto realized. (I'm not talking here about righteous anger and indignation.) Perhaps that's half the battle. Maybe I should watch Robert De Niro's portrayal of a troubled gangster in the movies *Analyze This* and *Analyze That* for more insights on anger management. Capice?

. . . .

---

[32] Lent is a 40 day period proceeding Easter which through prayer, fasting, almsgiving and conversion, prepare Christians for the greatest feast day of the year.

Student-reflection papers, which are part of my teaching strategy at Fordson, can pitch you the proverbial knuckleball. The responses of the students can catch me totally off guard. No doubt this can happen anywhere. Still, as I have noted, this isn't your mama's high school. My AP class on World History had just concluded a series on World Wars I and II, including the Great Depression. Before we dove into the Cold War, I had assigned a reading, the article "Seven Lessons in Manliness from the Greatest Generation" by Brett and Kate McKay. In this article, the authors list their own observations coupled with quotes and anecdotes from *The Greatest Generation,* a nonfiction book by Tom Brokaw. The title refers to those men and women who were born between 1914 and 1929. They endured the Great Depression and, later, trudged off to Europe, Africa, and the Pacific to support the Allies in World War II. The article puts flesh on the bones of those wonderful traits that most of us admire and seek to emulate, including "Love and Loyalty; Don't Make Life So Damn Complicated; Be Frugal; Embrace Challenge; Work Hard; Be Humble; and Take Personal Responsibility for Your Life." I asked my students to pick two of the seven lessons that they thought might be crucial to their own realization of the hopes and dreams to which they aspired. In addition, I asked them to write about someone who embodied any or all of the seven, such as a parent, grandparent, relative, or friend.

Every day at Fordson, I'm reminded that there's something unique about this place. Two student responses were especially telling in regard to those person(s) in their lives who embodied the spirit of "Lessons from the Greatest Generation." One student pointed out the hardships that family members endure while living currently in the Gaza Strip. Their trials, she pointed out, are not unlike those who struggled to endure amidst the want and uncertainty of millions of Americans who had to cope the best that they could until the Great Depression, like a terrible lingering storm, finally wore itself out. How long, she wonders, will her kinfolk have to endure hardships that most of us have never experienced, in a land that has known too little peace in one generation after another? Another student recalled how a relative, currently residing in the U.S., had survived torture at the hands of Saddam Hussein and his thugs. These hardships have not embittered him. Instead, they have built strength of character forged in the fires of hostility and tribulation. Many of my students and their families face struggles not unlike my Irish forbears, who often were treated with suspicion and hostility in Nineteenth-Century America; no doubt many of you have seen the Martin Scorcese film *Gangs of New York*. Kids who are Muslim and/or Arabic face daily reminders of the wariness with which much of the world views them. I imagine that this is not an easy burden to bear.

. . . .

During the 2010/11 school year, I had Malak Sabri Alkanani as a student in her senior year. I assumed that this memorable young woman was Muslim. Gotta be careful about assumptions; mine seem to always come back and bite me you-know-where. Anyway, Malak was very knowledgeable and outspoken concerning all things Islam/Muslim. Whenever a question came up in class, most of the students glanced over at her collectively, as though she were the preordained spokesperson. Malak knew her stuff: she would clear up the matter at hand capably and would share information in a matter-of-fact manner that was not condescending. In addition, she also displayed a willingness to hear other opinions. I liked Malak's attitude, her beyond-the-surface-level opinions, and her willingness to research topics of interest, not just to fly by the seat of her pants. Religious matters had particular interest for her. Malak would often pepper me with questions about Christianity which I initially attributed to youthful curiosity. She seemed especially bent on the reasons why I had returned back to Catholicism after 35 years of Protestant Evangelical Christianity. The subject of Calvinism[33] was also on one of her front burners. I have to admit that sometimes I had to do a bit of research in order to give Malak a reasonable response, especially in regard to the theology behind my Catholic beliefs.

Eventually, I found out that Malak had abandoned Islam in favor of Christianity, after a great deal of soul-searching and anguish over the obvious ramifications. In her junior year, she accepted Jesus as her Lord

---

[33]   A branch of Protestantism which traces its origin to the Swiss reformer John Calvin (1509-64). An emphasis on God's sovereignty, the predestination of the elect to heaven and the reprobate to hell, and the church as a well-ordered community living in solidarity are some of their more notable characteristics. Calvin's theological system is formulated primarily in his *Institutes,* and accepted with some modifications by most reformed Churches.

and Savior. After graduating in 2011, she was baptized at a local Reformed/Calvinist congregation who had been shepherding her. Consequently, her senior year at Fordson was a tough one. She still entered my classroom all bubbly and smiling, more often than not. Still, in her personal life, the stuff really hit the fan. As you might imagine, it has been difficult for many of Malak's family and friends to come to grips with her new "life." I'll let her explain:

> *I've lost many friends, and people who don't even know me seem to really dislike me. My family has no intentions of supporting a Christian, and life at home has been pretty unbearable. But, I have made new friends and been welcomed into a huge and loving family. Best of all, I've come to know, love, cherish, and treasure my great God and Savior-Jesus Christ. There is so much that He's done in my life, and if I were to list off every single thing, I suppose that the world itself could not contain the books that would be written.*

There is more to Malak's story that bears telling. Allegations were lodged against one of her teachers, who allegedly had invited her and other students to his church. He was accused of using his position at Fordson to proselytize. There was no denying that this teacher did bring up religion during class, on occasion, in the context of biology (in discussions on the Theory of Evolution, for example). He was not shy about discussing religion in both talking with and listening to students who would drop by to chat after class. But proselytize?

One Sunday, Malak and another female student showed up at this teacher's church, with parental permission. Malak returned a second time, alone. Not long after this, someone put a bug in the ear of the current (Sp.'10) principal that one of his teachers was encouraging Muslim kids to come to his church. The principal demanded an accounting. On an undisclosed school day in May, both students, as well as Malak's mother, were whisked into the principal's office. There, they were interrogated behind closed doors by both him and an attorney for the school district. During the "interrogation," which largely appeared to be an effort to secure data with which to go after the teacher, the principal was astonished to learn both Malak's mom and the mother of the other girl had given their daughters permission to attend the teacher's church. Though shaken, Malak defended her teacher. Unmoved and angry, the principal told her that she should take a look at the document "A Teacher's Guide to Religion in the Public Schools." She did and, what's more, returned with it. Malak had highlighted various sections of the teacher's guide to substantiate her defense of her teacher, who now was facing the principal's wrath. At this point, the matter remained unresolved. Exasperated, the principal told Malak that, even if the teacher did not abuse his position by ignoring the guidelines for discussing matters of religion, he (the principal), was the law at Fordson. (I should point out here that I have discussed this at length with Malak and the teacher separately, whose accounts dovetail perfectly. However, I have not discussed the matter with the principal or the attorney). After the principal met with Malak a second time, I suspect that he thought that he had seen the last of her.

Perhaps the principal and the attorney thought that they had enough ammo, so next they went after the teacher. Later, he, the teacher on the hot seat, told me that he sensed that something was up. At the time, though, he was not quite prepared for the manner in which he would be interrogated. This teacher is a bright, articulate young man who is not easily intimidated. The principal and the attorney didn't have much of a case against him. Before the end of the school year, the teacher was exonerated. The Superintendent of Dearborn Public Schools was also in the loop. Apparently, he was satisfied that no serious breech of teaching ethics had transpired in this case. I couldn't help but wonder if much of the fuss was because a Muslim had converted to Christianity. Had it been the other way around, I wonder what would have happened, if anything? The experience left such a bad taste in the teacher's mouth that he requested and was granted a position at one of the other high schools in the district. This was too bad; he was/is an outstanding teacher, and we need more like him at Fordson. What he didn't know when he put in for a transfer was that the principal who'd marked him would not be returning; he "retired." This whole episode calls to mind "Touch not my anointed, and do my prophets no harm" (1 Chr16:22). About a year after the ordeal,

I had an opportunity to sit down and talk at length with the teacher. Given that he is still with Dearborn Public Schools; I can only conclude that both his and my student's accounts are reliable.

On one occasion, Malak said to me, "Mr. Shannon, I'm surprised you've never been called out."

"Whaddaya mean?"

She pointed out that I'm always talking about Christianity. True, I admit, and a lot of other things, such as sports, music, politics, and food. Indeed, when I do discuss Christianity (or Judaism, Buddhism, Islam, Atheism, Deism, and so on) in the classroom, I do so under the umbrella of history. Christianity has and continues to play a significant role in much of what I'm responsible for teaching (U.S., World, and European History). So, deal with it! As I have noted, many of my students shortly will find themselves in a university, college, or community college classroom, where virtually no topic is taboo in a no-holds-barred arena of learning. They will be called out to take a stand for what they believe and why they believe it. Shouldn't you let the pitcher warm up before you send him/her into the game? As for my part, "I tell you, everyone who acknowledges me before others the Son of Man will acknowledge before the angels of God. But whoever denies me before others will be denied before the angels of God" (Lk 12: 8, 9).

. . . .

If you, like me, work a traditional Monday thru Friday workweek, you likely would nod in the affirmative, that indeed there exists a stark contrast in one's mental state between Monday and Friday mornings. Mondays typically begin with a resounding, "Good Lawd it's mornin' " rather than Friday's more optimistic, "Good morning Lord." This particular Friday morning in the Fall of 2012 was fairly typical. It would be a laid-back day as my four U.S. History classes viewed clips from the film *Iron Jawed Angels*, a historical-fiction film documenting the ups and downs of the women's suffrage movement, prior to the students following week's test on women's suffrage in the United States during the early decades of the twentieth century. Being well acquainted with the film, I settled into a vacant seat in the rear of the classroom (easier to monitor the class), and popped open a window, as for some inexplicable reason, I was sweatin' like the proverbial pig on its way to market; an open window at this cool early autumn hour will remedy that I thought to myself.

Towards the end of the second period, something just wasn't right; physically that is. Perspiration continued unabated while cramping in places I'm unaccustomed too (my cheeks/jaw), and now my heart racing as though I'd just been kissed by Angelina Jolie coupled with a dull, aching sensation across my chest and shoulders, and I'm thinkin' "Uh oh." The latter, chest pains, I attributed to a recent workout at a local gym in Saline, but something was clearly amiss.

"Ring, ring goes the bell ..." Chuck Berry crooned in the popular 50s rocker "School Days," and as third period students drifted into World History class, a nearby security guard agreed to look after my class. "Back in a minute, "I quickly explained, "need to see the nurse." That minute turned out to be my dismissal bell for the day. Fordson school nurse, Mary Baker, knew well enough that I had some blood pressure issues, and that I'd been taking Triamterene to help keep it in check. Also, atrial fibrillation (irregular heartbeat) was part of my medical history ... "You have a "strange" (irregular) heartbeat" medical personnel over the years would puzzle over while struggling to take my pulse.

"Not to worry," I'd joke, "it's from growin' up in Detroit's shadow during the 60s ... all that Motown stuff ... I have a 'funky' pulse beat!"

After shooing several lingering students out of her office, the school nurse turned her full attention to the Shannonator (current name students have dubbed me with), and she sensed this was something more serious than one of Joe's bimonthly drop-ins to have a blood pressure reading. As I described my symptoms and she carefully went about reading my blood pressure and checking my pulse she calmly but firmly put it," We need to call 911."

"What? No ... just let me chill here for a few ... I'll be alright..."

"Joe, we need to call 911, now!"

Doggone, I'm thinking to myself. I was so lookin' forward to some chili-cheese fries, a few cold ones and some laughs with my colleagues after work ... I don't wanna go to no hospital.

"Okay Mary, you're the boss."

In a few minutes the familiar sound of sirens could be heard in the distance. Now, however, they were coming for me. Maybe they'll determine I'm okay, false-alarm, bad case of heartburn, something.... Fordson principal Youssef (Joe) Mosallam and fellow Social Studies teacher, Ben Harmon, joined me in the nurse's office. "Ben," I joked, "maybe you better step out … they'll probably grab you."

Soon the small nurse's office was cluttered with emergency equipment and three Dearborn Fire and Rescue members; I was rather surprised at how young and in what good physical shape they appeared. "Look like Navy seals," I thought to myself. They were all business and in no time they had me hooked up to some contraption while one of them peppered me with questions: symptoms, family history, recent behaviors that might have triggered this. A nearby monitor flashed the number 250.

"What's that mean?"

"It means sir that your heart is racing 5 times faster than it should. You're supposed to be between 60-90."

Guess it wasn't my imagination after all. "Ouch."

"Sorry sir, we're putting a couple IVs in to bring your heart rate down."

Minutes whisk by while the number 250 on the heart monitor screen barely budged. Time to get this dude to Oakwood emergency, and with the school in temporary lock-down mode in order to keep the halls clear, ol' Joe, who always said he wanted to leave Fordson with a bang, now strapped to a gurney, IVs dangling along both sides, with three Dearborn Fire and Rescue personnel alongside, sped me down the hall and put me in the back of the rescue vehicle where things were about to get more interesting … lights on, siren wailing and we're off.

Up to this point I'd probably been way too casual about the whole affair; coping measure perhaps? This is all likely "Much Ado About Nothing" the bard (Shakespeare) might have chimed in. Still, "better safe than sorry," as we often plead. My request to swing by McDonald's was not found amusing. Guess they know what I don't know. In a few moments I'd be shot up with something (adenosine) that kicked me like a mule to the chest; another attempt to slow my ticker down below autobahn speed. Now, feeling like an over-the-hill boxer who'd just been flattened, dazed and confused, crawling around the ring, faintly hearing the ref shout out: ...Three … Four … Five....Then I heard, unmistakably, off in the distance yet strangely near, faint but firm,"I can't get a pulse, get the pads ready."

"Our Father who art in heaven," I began to myself … my head in a whirl of in and out consciousness. The EMS technicians must have gotten a weak pulse as moments later we pulled into Oakwood emergency. Hittin' me with the juice was shelved for the moment as a team of ER folks quickly took charge, ran some new IVs with drugs apparently not on the rescue vehicle, and minutes later my heart rate finally began a slow descent to a more manageable level.

"You'll be in the ER for awhile sir while a room is being readied for you," a doctor who looked too young to be out of med-school assured me.

"Oh man, can't they just write me a prescription and let me out-a-here," I pleaded with my principal who joined me in ER, but looked none too sympathetic concerning my making a hasty, stage-right exit.

Upshot, I spent the night and better part of the next day while tests were conducted, including a heart scan, and a meeting with a cardiologist. While it appeared there were no serious heart blockages or lingering irregularities, I all but had to sign an agreement that I'd get further tests (ultrasound), seriously consider some lifestyle adjustments, and take it easy for awhile. I was hoping to hear that it would be prudent to take a few months off work, but no such luck. [34]

The outpouring of concern, prayers, and kind thoughts from family, friends, co-workers and students was heart-warming. The nurses at Oakwood were patient and caring. The food was well ... ah, let's just leave it at that. Hard to complain about food when so many fellow inhabitants of planet earth are hungry and go without. In retrospect, I'd say God was sending me a message, a reminder, something like, "Hey Joe, tomorrow is promised to no one. So live your life in a manner that is pleasing to me ... today, tomorrow might be your time. Are you ready?" Jesus' words in Mark's Gospel echo in my mind's ear, "What does it profit a person if they gain the whole world, but lose their soul"(Mk 8:36)?

. . . .

I've learned firsthand as a card carrying member of the school-of-hard-knocks that male teachers who themselves initiate, or are somehow coerced by their male students, that bein' "boys" with them is fraught with

---

[34]   On April 15, 2013 (day of the Boston Marathon bombings), I had a catheter ablation procedure to correct a heart rhythm issue performed at Henry Ford Hospital in Detroit.

its own particular set of pitfalls. If they perceive you to be one of their "buds," it almost certainly means that they will expect some break when it comes to their grades, attendance/audit concerns, and discipline issues in general. I've learned not to paint myself into that corner; it's a delicate dance all teachers must eventually come to grips with … keeping student-teacher relationships in the proper equilibrium. For my part, don't be a prick-bastard, or the flip side, Mr. Easy Goin Nice Guy will likewise get you burned. No, one must move somewhere near the center in this regard. I sometimes have my AP students, typically at the beginning of the school year following a summer's reading assignment of Machiavelli's *The Prince*, write an essay with a bit of a Machiavellian twist to it. "Is it better for a prince to be loved or feared," he challenges. You see where I'm goin' with this … substitute the word teacher in place of prince. Indeed, it makes for some interesting and amusing reading; students must choose one or the other, a little of both is not an option. Okay, I won't leave you hangin', they're usually split 50/50 on it, and as far as my approach in the classroom? Tuff but fair … I like to fancy myself as a bit like Beorn, the sometimes ferocious bear other times gentle woodsman in Tolkien's *The Hobbit* tale, but you'll likely have to track down some of my former students for their take on The Shannonator.

I've enjoyed numerous healthy relationships with guys (students) here at Fordson, and many have maintained contact years after graduation; thank you Facebook. I've especially enjoyed those fellas who, usually AP World/European History kids, who also participated in the Debate and History Clubs I'd sponsored; after school hours, many liked to stop by and engage me in no-holds barred discussions with virtually no topic off limits: politics, religion, the Middle East, and one of my favorites which I confess to stealin' er borrowin', *How the Irish Saved Civilization,* a bit of a controversial book by Thomas Cahill that documents: The Untold Story of Ireland's Heroic Role from the Fall of Rome to the Rise of Medieval Europe. "Yes, hah!"

Ali Hachem didn't exactly fit the mold of the students mentioned above; howbeit I did sign a recommendation for him to take AP Government in'14. He was my U.S. History student, Semester 1, '12/13. Ali was a big kid (center for the JV football team), big smile, big voice … who felt his day was somehow incomplete if he hadn't bear hugged, fist pounded, chest pounded me … "Mr. Shannon," he'd declare, "you and me are gonna be boys … Wallah we are!"

"Ali, sit down, and if you think you have to perform Aaron Rodgers touchdown dance at the beginning and end of every class … you're Kaboomed! Code for you lost points towards your weekly participation grade.

At the end of class, Ali typically assumed that my desk was his hangout, and we were boys and the remaining few minutes were to be devoted to guy interests; usually sports, hunting, that sort of thing. Annoying at times? Yes, but he was hard not to like. As much as I'd try not too, it was difficult not to laugh at his vain attempts to sing, dance and play the comedian. He was actually a pretty good student (academically), which is likely why I didn't shut him down more firmly; kinda like bronco bustin' I reckon.

I'll say it one more time, "You can't be "boys" with your guy students; not at this stage of the life game. Among other things, it will be perceived as favoritism. I imagine Ali liked me in a big brother, uncle kind of way, and truth be told, when I learned he wouldn't be on my roster the following semester I was part relieved yet disappointed. I knew I'd end up missing him … he could certainly liven up a class single handedly.

During winter break Feb.'13 I received a text message from a coworker that Ali had died (heart failure); a quick look at my school emails confirmed the sad news. I attended his funeral at the Dearborn Community Center and talked briefly to his dear mother. She wore a large button with a picture of her beloved son with his signature smile. "That is how I'll remember your son," I whispered, nodding at his picture. As I sat with family, friends, students and faculty, several of whom took the podium to reminisce and express the heartfelt love many carried for this young man, my eyes seemed continually drawn to the front side where his mother sat. I couldn't help but wonder, "What if?" What if it was my child lying cold and still in that coffin. An image of Theoden-King of Rohan in Tolkien's tale-*The Two Towers*, flashed across my mind's eye as he declared to Gandalf after having just recently buried his only son, Theodred who'd recently fallen in battle defending Rohan's borders that, "No parent should have to bury their child." While a local Imam read from the Qur'an and reflected on the shortness of life and impending judgment, my mind wandered from one passage of sacred Scripture to another, seeking understanding and comfort that the God both of Ishmael and Issac wills

310

that all people be saved (1 Tm 2:4). I hope that Ali, a young Muslim and given the light he received, found grace and mercy and that one day we might meet again, and if he still wants to be "boys," I'm okay with that (Ali H. Hachem March 3, 1997 – February 17, 2013; RIP).

. . . .

I'd expected that 2016 would have witnessed at least several years' publication of this book, and that I'd have since moved on to other endeavors including employment, or better yet, retirement … alas. Concerning publication (as of summer '17), I have scant notion if/when that day will ever dawn as some of the content troubles me and I go back and forth wondering if I should drop or retain it. Well, if you've read this book in its entirety, now you know and can likely guess why some portions gave me pause. Of less, but still a concern, is updating the back cover photo; the one I originally submitted to my artist (Tom Roy), was c. '13 … a bit dated. Don't want to be one of those folks still using an enhanced high school senior photo when they now bear more resemblance to Rip Van Winkle, Gandalph or Methuselah … not quite there yet thankfully. The past few years at Fordson ('15, '16, '17) have just kind of drifted by with little to note other than I seem to be getting grumpier and rather disenchanted with the whole business of public education (standardized tests, common core etc.); add a dose of burnout coupled with a 50 minute commute both ways and well…. Upshot, the 2017 school year turned into one long bout of depression (very unlike me), and the thought of another year(s) in the classroom does not make for soothing sleep or lighthearted jests. "The thrill (teaching) is *largely* gone," as B.B. King crooned. "Hey Joe, retire!" I'd do it in a heartbeat were it not for financial constraints. In 1968 Frank Zappa and the Mothers of Invention released an album "We're Only in it for the Money"; a musical, satirical jab at both the far right and left wing climate of the sixties. I laughed at the notion of only being in something for the money then; not now. On the other hand, when those occasional rays of optimistic light pierce the despair of dead-end blues, there's likely a good reason I'd been originally placed at Fordson and perhaps my labors there might not yet be completed. My work ethic, which I often fall short of, comes both from the example of my two hard-working parents, coupled with the Apostle Paul's admonition to the Colossians: "Whatever you do, work at it with all your heart, as working for the Lord, not for men, since you know that you will receive an inheritance from the Lord as a reward. It is the Lord Christ you are serving" (Col 3:23, 24).

. . . .

"You want us (teachers) to do what?" They can't be serious. Let me back up a bit. At the close of the '15 school year, the principal conducted my year-end evaluation. The entire year he/they (administrators) had been encouraging teachers to abandon the traditional "Stand and Deliver" classroom approach to instruction in favor of one more *student led*; whatever that means. At my post-observation meeting, the principal remarked that he didn't mind me lecturing. "It works for you … you know how to do it." We also agreed that it wouldn't hurt to implement some other/newer teaching strategies especially given the wide diversity, culturally and otherwise, of our student population.

"Sure, I'm okay with that."

I kept the meeting and principal's remarks largely to myself, and the following school year ('15), went about business as usual. Faculty were advised that the current principal would be moving to a new position outside the building, and that it might be some months until a replacement was installed; in the meantime the assistant principal(s) and soon after an interim principal would see that things continued to run smoothly … well, hopefully. During this period it was made known to faculty that teachers were to cease both lecturing and using power-points in the classroom, or from another angle, ditch the "stand- and- deliver" approach for more statistically verifiable, improved teaching techniques. "Here we go again," I mused.

I shan't trouble you with all their reasoning and what they now expected in place of the old, outmoded and ineffective methods … dreadfully boring stuff. Now mind you I'd fully concur that some teachers shouldn't, or at most seldom, lecture, especially if it's not their strong suit and not yielding positive results. But, this new dictate, as in none whatsoever, left me annoyed and angry. I simply chose to ignore it and let come what may. As teaching goes I guess I'm a bit of a dinosaur (Sasquatch), and I'm not tossing out my "meat and potatoes" just like that, especially in light of what the previous principal shared with me in my post-observation meeting.

There was significant discontent over this and other "new" directions.

Many folks struggle with change (yours truly), but there are instances when there's good cause to resist. Colleagues I respected confided to me in private how dissatisfied they were the way the Fordson winds were currently blowing. "Give it time" you quip. Perhaps ... when they first installed promethean boards in the classrooms (think large screen TVs) I was not thrilled. Now I don't know how I got along without one.

Sadly, teachers who don't tow the new status quo line are often "marked." Fear of bad reviews, loss of employment, or other means of making a teacher's work environment so stressful, even dangerous, silence many. "Don't you have Union protection," you say? As I said, there are creative ways within the law/guidelines to circumvent any Union voice. You/They can make a teacher so miserable they'll quit, transfer if that option is on the table, retire, or have a nervous breakdown. Well, not the dude in A 107 ... not yet anyways ('17). Incidentally, a new principal came in during the middle of the school year ('15-'16), and while sitting in on a meeting of teachers being in serviced in these matters mentioned above (I was present), when whatta you know, the whole business of lecturing in the classroom surfaced; not by me. The new principal was quite taken aback and not a little surprised about the "lecturing" controversy, and modified with a new directive right there on the spot, basically saying it has its place and time. Indeed, I quietly chuckled to myself while trying to restrain my Cheshire cat grin. However, other matters, as in health issues both physical and mental, were knocking at my door of a serious enough nature that I requested and was granted an FMLA (Family Medical Leave Act); the second semester of '16 was over for the Shannonator.

Christmas '15 was a joyous affair, especially with 2 young grandsons (Ryder and Reece) to frolic with, but for one "fly in the ointment"; chronic lower back pain. These typically plagued me for no more than a few days perhaps two, three times a year. Well this flare up didn't see the exit sign, and after several weeks of limping around like Grand Pappy Amos on the "Real McCoys," and I was not exactly flourishing in the fruits of the Spirit: love, joy, peace, patience. A decent night's sleep remained elusive unless I popped a couple Ibuprofens and chased it with a "Sea Breeze"; vodka, cranberry and grapefruit juice on the rocks. You know how you are when you come off a bad night's sleep ... and when these nights turn into weeks, look out. And here I am in a classroom of high-schoolers, me grumpier than an old dog that can't scrath an itch, and by noon the back spasms so intense that I have to remain seated for fear of going down like some ancient oak struck by a bolt from above. After 2 months of waiting for it to run its course, I visited my old chiropractor. It had been 12 years, and after several adjustments (it briefly got worse before it got better), suddenly the pain subsided. However, a more serious storm than back pain was on the horizon, bearing down … heart issues … déjà-vu.

During and lingering after the back issues trial, I'd experienced what I described to my physicians as "episodes." Typically at night I'd be awakened (I'm a light sleeper to begin with), by an irregular heartbeat. Not so much the "racing heart" and subsequent procedure I had to correct it in April '13; this was different. The old ticker just wasn't hittin' on all cylinders. "Man, what's this?" … and as you lay there praying, trying to regulate your breathing and remain calm, the head-games (anxiety attacks) slink their way in. These "episodes" generally last about 30 minutes; a few for better than an hour; fortunately they, for whatever reason, happen at home where I can sit/rest undisturbed, waiting for it to subside. But, what if they strike while I'm on the highway, in the classroom, out to dinner….

It took the better part of Spring '16 to determine what the heck was goin' on, and a procedure to correct the heart problem at Henry Ford Hospital in Detroit was scheduled for July of '16. What to do in the meantime. I'm in no condition to be in the classroom; fortunately over the years I'd not squandered my sick days and had a 160 plus in my "sick bank." Now it seemed prudent to make use of them; hence FMLA. Stuck in one's own house (prisoner), and in my case the constant concern of a "heart episode" and anxiety attacks could lead, I worried, to an extended bout of depression. And so, two trips that Spring, I hoped, would serve as a sort of mental/spiritual healing balm while I awaited the heart procedure. First, a short week at Gethsemane Abbey south of Lexington, Kentucky, to hang with Cistercian monks who have devoted their lives to prayer, contemplation and work.

The setting was beautiful (rural Kentucky foothills), peaceful, numerous daily opportunities for prayer and worship as well as quiet, private walks on abbey grounds covering some 2,000 plus acres. "Well God, where do I/We go from here? What am I to do with the remaining years of my life? The way is obscure, lost in shadow … some light please." And come what may, I'm resolved, "As for me and my house, we will follow the Lord."

The Cistercians at Gethsemane maintain themselves in part by selling a wide array of products produced on abbey grounds; holiday fruitcakes and fudge being two of the more popular items. Should you chance to wander through the cafeteria between meal times, you will notice a table laden with small samples of fudge and fruitcakes beckoning you to break your fast. On my first day I grabbed a couple of pieces (the size of a small tootsie-roll) of a light, carmelly looking fudge that looked different than what I'd been accustomed too; not a big fudge person unless it's in ice cream. Hmmm, a slight warm glow seemed to wash over me after the second piece when I met the gaze of a young gal sitting nearby. "How'd you like it?" She grinned.

"Different ... not sure what to make of this warming sensation ... cinnamon perhaps."

"Umm, that would be the bourbon," she grinned again.

"Bourbon?"

Indeed, I should have paid closer attention to the small cards identifying/describing the dozen or more types of fudge. The one I chose happened to be spiked with Kentucky bourbon, which by the way, is everywhere down here. Every town/city I drove thru seemed to have a bourbon warehouse/factory(distillery) ... when I enquired about this at a nearby grocery market that looked straight out of the *Andy Griffith Show*, the clerk laughed and said, "Yep, and every other house/farm hereabouts has a "still ouch yonder." Now you may be thinking that ol Joe brought back a couple "bricks" of Abbey Bourbon Fudge. Well, I thought about it, but I decided I have enough issues on my plate without adding bourbon-fudge addiction to the pile.

All in all it was time well spent; however, the discernment I'd been hoping for remained elusive. Also, I'm not entirely naïve, but even secluded in a cloistered abbey, wrapped in an atmosphere of prayer and worship, the battle with the world, flesh and the devil continues, howbeit sometimes in different forms: spiritual pride, envy, despair, lust. Fortunately, His grace is sufficient.

Later, that same Spring, a visit to my old Florida haunts seemed like "just what the doctor ordered." I'm not talkin' bout some old dude, spring-break fantasy, but a time to visit my church family from days gone by, and take advantage of the ocean's healing aspects (physical/emotional/ spiritual).

The city of St. Augustine just south of Jacksonville always intrigued, and, as an A P Euro teacher I figured I owed to myself and students to become acquainted with the United States earliest permanent settlement (Spanish) ... but of course.

Three days just wasn't enough. Three weeks, three months ... I could see myself living here someday; might be as close as I'll get to Europe. In the historic part of town, attending Mass at Cathedral Basilica, and also a stop at arguably the oldest school-house in the States-The Father Miguel O'Reilly House Museum @ 32 Avilles St., a quarter mile from the cathedral, are a couple of must-sees. I was the only one at the museum one morning and struck up a conversation with a little, elderly nun sitting in a rocking chair in the vestibule, praying the rosary and paused to welcome me.[35] We chatted for a bit but the one thing I recall is her carefully explaining that I, at present, was standing in the very spot where freed slaves were first given a formal education in the United States. I took a picture of a small book/pamphlet on display we desperately need back in the classroom entitled-*Politeness: A Little Book Prepared for the Children taught by the Sisters of St. Joseph* ... hmm, mighta done me some good back when. Hiking/Shopping around Old St. Augustine builds quite a thirst/hunger and I (surprise, surprise), found a couple of commendable pubs; Meehan's Irish Pub on Bayfront (and a short distance from Castillo de San Marcos-Spanish fort) is first-rate, and a spectacular view of the channel the first Europeans sailed into.

As expected, my visit to the Sunshine State ended far too soon. I'd spent as much time as I could splashing in the waves, tearing into southern barbecue and key-lime pie, visiting old friends as once again Bob Seger crooned, "...good for the soul." Incidentally, you may have wondered how I managed the flight there and back. Indeed, I was a tad apprehensive ... what if I should have an episode at 20,000 feet. Won't I be Mistah Popular when the pilot announces, "Hey folks, change of plans ... gonna do a lil

---

[35] The rosary is a popular form of prayer, especially amongst Catholics. It consists of 15 decades, each commemorating a mystery concerning Christ or Mary and including the Lord's Prayer, the Hail Mary and "Glory be to the Father."

stopover in Memphis ... not to worry, only be an hour delay." But I rolled the dice (prayed actually), and made it both ways without incident. When we first left Metro, a sudden mild wash of anxiety rolled over me. "Please God, not now." When we leveled off minutes later the pilot came over the intercom and after the usual flight business announcements, said, "I'd like to give a shout-out to a Mr. Joe Shannon flying with us, from your son-Cory." Cory's an air traffic controller at Metro and was working that flight. Yikes! I laughed and immediately calmed down; well sort of ... my son is a professional.

. . . .

Having a heart ablation is not considered "heart surgery" per se, but it's no joke either. This would be round two, I'd had one earlier (Sp. '13) you may recall, which went quite well and resolved the issue. This procedure, similar to the first, would be in a different area of the heart, and likewise to correct an irregular heartbeat (a tune-up). They go through the groin, "ouch," and it is expected you'll be released, barring any post-procedure issues, in 24-48 hours.

On the earlier occasion, I came out of anesthesia (recovery room) greeted by replay after replay on the TV monitor of that morning's horrific Boston Marathon bombing; this time, the Nice, France terrorist attacks. Plus, I always seem to have "interesting" roommates. Some of you might want to skip over these 2 hospital roomie tales ... you queasy, too much-info.-types. So, I'm still in somewhat of a groggy state, sipping juice (I should have smuggled a flask in), and watching the news. The only thing separating me and my neighbor was a flimsy curtain. He had some heart procedure scheduled for later in the day, and meanwhile a steady stream of family, nurses and doctors, and it was like trying to nap in Grand Central Station. If you've ever spent the night in the hospital, you're likely nodding to yourself, "Been there, done that." Anyway, to cut to the chase, this guy was all bent outta shape about having a catheter used during the procedure. Four times ... four times, I had to listen in detail (only inches from his bed) the nightmare he went through months earlier when a nurse, who apparently had little training in this case, botched removing his catheter resulting in excruciating pain and bleeding. "Put a diaper on me, whatever," he exclaimed, "you ain't puttin' no damn catheter on me ... I'd rather die." I don't recall how it was resolved, but guess what, this whole time (couple of hours hearing over and over again as he explained in detail first to one than another doctor) yours truly is laying there with a catheter on wondering when a nurse is going to get around to removing it. I'm not kidding. When that moment came, and fortunately my roomie and his medical team were gone, I gripped the side rails of my bed like Rocky Sullivan strapped to the "chair" in *Angels with Dirty Faces*. As the nurse slipped my gown up, I thought she gave me a rather peculiar part smile, part smirk glance as she quipped, "Ready?" On no, I've got nurse Ratchet from *One Flew Over the Cuckoo's Nest*. I must have looked like Don Knots about ready to blast off in *The Reluctant Astronaut*. I felt it, but gratefully nothing in comparison to my roomie's nightmare. By the way, nurses have a tough job; I was fortunate to have very professional, good-natured, helpful ones. No doubt my two "roomie tales" are just the stuff of another day; especially working ER.

So, two days after busting out of Henry Ford Hospital I'm at home, supposed to be taking it easy, whatever that means. It was a steamy, sweltering July afternoon and I was restless, so I putzed around the yard/garden for a bit, pulling some weeds and what not. Later in the evening I had a couple of beers, chillin'. Feeling lousy I decided to turn in early and soon began to shake uncontrollably. I could barely grasp my phone but managed to call my son Cory who lives nearby. "Hey, you better come over here and sit with me for a bit, I'm feelin'…." I thought I may be having some kind of seizure, plus I could barely talk, having recently had a tube down my throat for a couple hours.

Cory apparently didn't like what he saw and immediately called 911. The "I'll be OK" approach didn't resonate with my son or the EMS techs. Upshot, two days at St. Joe's in Ann Arbor while they ran a battery of tests to try and determine what triggered a 103 temp (why I was shaking uncontrollably).

Warning, second roomie story; rated disgusting. So why bother mentioning it you say? For my sake, if not yours; a kind of an emotional healing type thing. So, once again I'm up on the 5th floor … IVs and monitors making it difficult to move, let alone use the toilet. Also, if you roll over or try to change your position, you wind up untangling first one then another tube of some kind. And as before, there are few secrets in these rooms, but something the nurse said to my roomie put me on high alert. "OK sir, your procedure is scheduled in one hour, and since you haven't had a bowel movement in several days, we're going to administer a double enema. I'll bring in a portable toilet." Double enema, toilet, you're kidding me; three feet from my bed, separated by a cheap Wal-Mart curtain.

"Hey Joe, where's your compassion for the poor dude?"

"It's out the window."

After 10 minutes, rumbling, gurgling sounds began slowly, steadily growing and in no time, Mt. Vesuvius erupted. I did a barrel-roll off my bed, grabbed my IV cart and bolted. Once in the hall, and like Chuck Berry crooned in "No Particular Place to Go," I gave myself a tour of the 5th floor until the coast (er air) was clear. On a lighter note, they actually have quite a nice menu at St. Joe's.

. . . .

Meanwhile, back to the subject of Fordson; you know you're getting up there when several times a week you hear something like, " Hey Shannon, when are you … ain't it bout time you retired ol' man?" How much longer? Wish I knew. As of this writing (2018), I'm still officially employed with Dearborn Public Schools at Fordson High School. Of course, that could change in a heartbeat. Yikes!

Here's another one I often hear. "So, what's it like … what are **they** like?" … referring to Fordson and my students.

Well, purchase my book for the long answer; the short one, "Well, it's kinda like the movie *Grease* with a largely Middle Eastern cast."

. . . .

"How can I wrap up this part of my adventure?" I hear myself asking. I have had the proverbial love-hate relationship with Fordson. I have wrestled with teacher burnout, long commutes, too many spoiled brats who want an easy out and an undeserved A for a grade, and too many teachers and administrators who are willing to accommodate them. There are lots of great kids at Fordson, too, some I shall not soon forget. These kids have challenged me both intellectually and in the rethinking of some of my own cultural biases. These are the students who understand that academic integrity, in addition to playing honestly, demands a lot of good old-fashioned blood, sweat, and tears. Now, if we could just bring back Latin and Speech/Debate classes and work some good Old-School sentence-diagramming exercises – remember those? – into our Language-Arts program, we'd really be on to something.

. . . .

During my ten-plus years of teaching at Fordson, I've learned much about Middle-Eastern culture. There is much to admire about it, and no doubt I've only skimmed the surface. I pray that a good many relationships I've developed at Fordson with students and staff of Middle-Eastern descent (and, certainly, non-Arabs as well) will continue and prosper. May we continue to learn from and respect one another, not trivializing about what makes us unique and/or different but embracing them as a means to become more fully sons and daughters of Abraham, acknowledging our spiritual kinship; howbeit the Apostle Paul and the New Testament in general do distinguish between *physical* descendants of Abraham and *spiritual* (Gal 4:22-26, 28-31; Rom 9:6-9).[36] For my part, the same spirit that guided St. Francis of Assisi and the first Franciscan Brothers in their special approach to and relationship with Muslims during the High Middle

---

[36] I presently have, and hope to continue, both professional and friendly relationships with Muslims (colleagues/students) largely as a result of my educator tenure at Fordson High School in East Dearborn, MI. I recognize many of the positive contributions adherents to Islam, both historically and in the contemporary world, continue to make on the sciences, literature and so on. However, I do not regard Islam as compatible with the Judeo-Christian tradition nor Muhammad as a legitimate prophet of God. Furthermore, while Islam (Qur'an) and Christianity (Bible) share many commonalities concerning Jesus' life-His virgin birth and the ability to work miracles for example, however, and more importantly, Islam rejects the very heart and core of the Gospel: that Jesus claimed to be God and that He was crucified and rose from the dead. Hence, Christianity and Islam are simply incompatible. This does not mean, of course, that they cannot peacefully coexist if they both so choose, and if all parties labor to make this world a better place. Still, I must be clear that I accept neither the authentic prophet status of Muhammad, nor the divine inspiration of the Qur'an. Indeed, I embrace the Catholic Church's position concerning other religions: "The Catholic Church rejects nothing that is true and holy in [other] religions. She regards with sincere reverence those ways of conduct and of life, those precepts and teachings which, though differing in many aspects from the ones she holds and sets forth, nonetheless often reflect a ray of that Truth which enlightens all [humanity]" (Vatican II, *Nostra Aetate* 2).

Ages, and may it likewise be a present witness in my walk. It was paramount, taught Francis, that one's deeds be aligned with one's words. As we use to say back in the Jesus Movement days of the '70s, "Don't talk the talk, if you don't walk the walk. " Salaam, Shalom, Pax vo Biscum, Peace out.

Hippy Day

Fordson Library

Steve Faunce & Joe, 2013

EDUCATOR'S AWARD OF MERIT

Presented to

Joseph Shannon

at
Superintendent's Honors Night
Dearborn Public Schools

You were selected by Nadeen Zaiat for the contribution you
have made to this student's education.

May 8, 2014

Brian J. Whiston
Superintendent

Abbey Gethsemane, 2014

Joey the Chin: Prohibition Days,
U.S. History

U.S. History: Celebrating the 60s-Greasers, Frats, and Beatniks; 2017

Tower Tribune **November 2017**

Teacher Spotlight
By: Noor Sami

For the past several years at Fordson, Mr.Shannon, nicknamed by his students as "The Shannonator", has educated students primarily in regards to the historic content of which our great country was built upon. Although his title as a US history teacher restricts him to being just that, the majority of students who currently, or for-merly have had him as a teacher, beg to differ. Personally, going into sophomore year and having to take US history, wasn't some-thing I was to be ecstatic about. This was mostly due to the fact that throughout most of my educa-tional career, we've been taught repeatedly about the same things in regards to the same people, through the same way; textbook analysis and worksheet prepara-tion. Although he uses his fair share of worksheet and textbook preparations, what is really ad-mired, and appreciated about Mr.Shannon's way of teaching, is his consistent use of the elabora-tion of personal "real life" experi-ences, in connection to the les-son(s) he is required to teach. The stories he tells, although they are seemingly hard to believe, sparks students' interest to want to look into what is being taught. It has been, and I am sure, will contin-ue to be, a joyous pleasure to have the opportunity to be enlightened with listening (and choosing to believe) Shannon's' crazy stories, about which he is in the process of publishing a book. Although I surely can continue the list as to why this man should undoubtedly be recog-nized, I would like to wrap up my statement with a simple thank you from the Fordson family.

EPILOGUE

"Don't give 'em all you got. Leave 'em beggin' for more," veterans of the entertainment world offer sagely. "Beggin'" might be a bit much to hope for, but inquires are most welcome. Indeed, there's much yet to tell. The spiritual treasures from my Catholic upbringing that I had neglected for so long now have revived. They continue to nourish and to sustain me. Shortly after my return to Catholicism in 2004, I started taking classes at Sacred Heart Major Seminary in Detroit. These classes, which address my interests in theological, ministerial, and philosophical matters, have been a wonderful means to mine the riches of Catholicism. When I began my classes, I hoped that they would help to shed light on the long list of questions with which I still wrestled. In addition, these classes would prepare me for future service in the Church. Currently, I still am discerning whether to go in that direction. Still, we are to be ambassadors for Christ in whatever vocation God calls us to pursue.

I continue to be blessed by, as well as thrilled and challenged by, the spiritual direction that my adventure has taken. After more than thirty-five years away from Rome, it's good to be Home. To all my brothers and sisters in the Christian faith, in whatever tradition that you feel best suits you and your family, God bless and keep you all the days of your lives until we, as one, sit down at that Great Feast, with our host, none other than the King of Kings – Jesus.

. . . .

You may recall the first sentence of this book: "History," I began, "has the potential to reveal where I've come from, where I've been, and where I may be headed." At this juncture, it seems fitting to revisit this subject. As a young child, I had the good fortune of being set on the right path. My parents, Harold and Gloria, chose to have me baptized. Baptism is the first of three Christian sacraments of initiation. My mom and dad also took care to see that the other two, the Eucharist and Confirmation, were realized during my youth. Now, half a century later, I find myself on that same road on which they took the pains to put me. My parents did their best to offer encouragement and guidance in this walk of faith.

I had hoped that my reflective writing effort might help me come to grips with why my path took so many strange twists and turns and had so many dead ends and narrow escapes. I was Joe the Redford kid, Joe the Catholic-school student, Joe the hippie, Joe the Born-Again Christian, Joe the pastor, Joe the married man, Joe the father, Joe the History/Language Arts teacher, Joe the Returned Catholic, and so many other things. In reflecting on what I've written, I wonder, "Am I a wiser man? Do people catch a glimpse of Christ in me? Are the fruits and gifts of the Spirit a living reality in my life?" The truth is that I still struggle with anger, lust, and gluttony. I'm still tripping on my tongue (on my spoken words) far more often than I should. Struggles with doubt and unbelief still raise their sinister heads and glare at me with those red, intimidating eyes, no doubt, to paralyze with fear, or worse, to create indifference in my faith in Jesus. Yet as sorry a saint as I may be, I'm still pressin' on. If my journey has taught me anything, it's that nothing can separate me/us from the love of God (barring an act of free will, wherein one rejects the saving message of the Gospel). That, brothers and sisters, old and new friends, keeps me going. Until Jesus calls me home, I am determined that like the apostle Paul, I "have fought a good fight ... finished my course ... kept the faith ... (2 Tm 4:7). I am grateful to have had such wonderful parents; a fantastic sister and brothers (Sue, Dan, Jeff, Ken); and three awesome kids (Cory, Jesse, Hayley); a wonderful daughter-in-law Samantha; and the joy of lil boys-Ryder and Reece-grandsons; all gifts from God to be sure.

A final thought, I promise. You may have thought that a more appropriate title for this book of mine might be something like *The Good, the Bad, and the Ugly*. Actually, this was my second choice; I love the theme song by Enrico Morricone to this classic "Spaghetti Western" of the same name. One day, I thought, "Gee, Joe, you're putting some dark stuff in here. You might end up creepin' folks out." This is a risk I've decided to take. The Old and New Testaments, as well as certain lives of the saints, don't whitewash events be it Job's trials, David's infidelities, Peter's denial of Jesus, or Augustine's struggles with sexuality as a young man. [37]

---

37   Sending the *Confessions* to a friend, Augustine wrote," In these behold me, that you may not praise me beyond what I am. Believe what is said of me,

In the five snapshots of my life in this book, I wanted to tell it like it was and like it is. At the same time, I wanted to fulfill my intentions for putting myself through this – the oftentimes emotionally painful aspects of reliving some painful events in my life – by using what little discernment I possess. I want to offer a ray of hope to others who have lost their way; like Steve Winwood sang in "Can't Find My Way Home," his song with the English band Blind Faith, "I'm wasted and I can't find my way home." Home as in Jesus and, perhaps, the family that now I affectionately call my own, the Catholic Church. As I've said, I spent ten plus years writing this book (off and on). I'm not the same man I was at the beginning and middle of this tale. Some parts likely are more tinged with anger, disappointment, confusion, and fear, especially following the months and first few years of my divorce and annulment.[38] It is what it is. I hope that you, the reader, find yourself ever moving in a more blessed relationship with God. As for me, this chunk of clay is still a work in progress.

All of our lives read like an adventure. I should like to hear about yours. I congratulate and thank you for sticking with me through thick and thin, like good ol' Gandalf did with the members of the Fellowship of the Ring until the destruction of the One Ring of Sauron was accomplished in Tolkien's *The Return of the King*. Well, we can set our walking staves in the corner for now. What say we go up to the Irish Pub (the Green Dragon in *The Lord of the Rings*), where we can celebrate over a pint and have a laugh or two. However, not before we take the time to kneel and give thanks to the Blessed Trinity, the source and summit of our existence. By

---

not by others, but by myself." This sentiment largely mirrors my own.

38   An annulment or, more properly, a decree of nullity, is a declaration by the Catholic Church through a diocesan agency known as a tribunal. The tribunal determines that what appeared to be a valid marriage was defective in some way at the time that the couple exchanged their vows. The annulment is not the dissolution of a valid marriage; rather, it is a decree that a valid marriage never existed. However, this does not mean that the children of that union are illegitimate. See Appendix 4 for a legal copy of Joe's annulment.

the way, are you doing anything on Sunday morning? If not, you're welcome to join me for Mass.

. . . .

Traveling eternity road

What will you find there?

Carrying your heavy load

Searching to find, a peace of mind.

–Ray Thomas, "Eternity Road," The Moody Blues, *To Our Children's Children (Threshold Records, 1969)*

. . . .

My wanderings you have noted; are my tears not stored in your vial, recorded in your book? My foes turn back when I call on you. This I know: God is on my side.

Psalm 56:8

. . . .

The Road goes ever on and on

Out from the door where it began.

Now far ahead the Road has gone,

And I must follow, if I can,

Pursuing it with eager feet,

Until it joins some larger way

Where many paths and errands meet.

And whither then? I cannot say.

-Song by Bilbo Baggins in *The Fellowship of the Ring*

by J. R. R. Tolkien

APPENDICES

Being a collection of lists and documentation that

shed light on events in the life of Joe Shannon.

The Musicians that appeared at Shalom, 1974 – 1985

Bands

- Al Blade Band
- Albrecht, Roley, and Moore
- Believer
- Caleb
- The Rob Cassels Band
- Choice
- The Chosen Few (Jubal)
- Crystal River
- Disciple
- Foreign Legion
- Foundfree
- Beverley Glen and the Living Epistles
- God's Graffitti
- Ground Crew
- The Heaven Reachers
- Heavenly Day (Sail)
- John Vass Band
- Little Flock
- Living Water
- Mac and the Bees
- The Kene Meeks Band
- Morning Star (The Bob Holt Band)
- Mylon LeFevre and Brokenheart
- New Dawning
- New Day
- New Wine
- Paul Ruehl Band
- Pilgrims
- Phil Ponnesa and Lifelight
- Progressive Razz
- R.B. Band (Rob Bialowicz)
- Ransom
- Refuge
- Renaissance
- Saving Grace
- Servant
- Shalom House Band
- Shekinah
- Shelter
- Soldier

- Sonquest
- Virgin Birth
- Water. Blood, and Wine
- Zoe

Solo Artists

- Dawn Baird
- Rocky Berra
- Al Blade
- Dennis Byrum
- Scot Crozier
- James Issac Elliot
- Erlandson
- Steve Faunce
- Ken Hasper
- Dale Hirt
- Gary Houston
- Mike Johnson
- Mike Kelly
- Jan Krist
- Tom Messink
- Ron Moore
- Kathy Moyer
- Orion

- Paul Patton
- Phil Ponessa
- Kenny Pore
- Paul Ruehl
- Vince Samulian
- Keith Savoie
- Maureen Siler
- John Waycaster
- Fletch Wiley
- Barry Woods
- Henry Woodworth

Duos

- Al Blade and Keith Savoie

(Duos Cont.)

- Al Blade and April Harma
- Kemper Crabb and Dave Marshall
- Dave and Jean Mehi
- Sonship (Howard Mandel and Nancy Helms)
- Just Love (Steve Waters and Carol Lehikoinen)

- Jan Mohl and Mayreen Siler

- Karen Labowitch and Larry Bell

- Pat Quinn and Ted Boswell

- Kene Meeks and Scott Roley

- Christian Stephens

- Gerald Olsen and Paula Cook

Guest Speakers at Shalom

(Sunday Services, Bible Studies, and Special Occasions)

- Seth Balmer, Fred Smallchuck, Dave Ytterock (Ministers, Assembly of God, MI)

- Julius Dodson, Mike Kingsley (Directors, Challenge House Ministry, Detroit, MI)

- Al Blade, John Mozug, Jim Duncan, Jim and Jerry Heady (Ministers and Elders)

- Sam Dabronka (Director, Teen Challenge, Detroit, MI)

- Herman Stalvey (Founder/Evangelist, World on Fire Revivals, Vero Beach, FL)

- Boyd Chavis

- Kemper Crabb

- Al Kresta

- Paul and Steve Patton

- Scot Roley

To: Clara B. Ford Faculty
   Teachers of Rosaland

From : J.   T.C.

Re: Rosaland's Voice Plan

To help Rosaland cope with the voices she hears, a plan has been developed with Dr. Green. Rosaland has a special prayer that she finds helpful in eliminating the voices, and she has been given a copy of this prayer to keep with her at all times. (But just in case, there is a copy at the bottom of this page.)

When Rosaland reports to staff (or faculty) that she is hearing voices:

1. She should be removed from any area in which her peers are able to aggravate her (i.e., direct her to Lourdes Hall staff if she is in a classroom).

2. Rosaland should NOT be left alone, under any circumstances. Staff should keep her within eyesight in order to ensure that Rosaland does not harm herself or others.

3. When Rosaland hears the voices, she reports that the aforementioned prayer, or self-statement, helps to eliminate the voices. The bottom of this page may be given to staff if, for some reason, Rosaland does not have her copy available.

One of Rosaland's medications has the side effect of blurring her vision, to the point that she will probably be unable to read in class. She has access to books on tape, and can benefit from group discussions, textbooks or other materials read aloud in class, etc.

Finally, Rosaland is NOT on the Special Education caseload at this time. We do not have any knowledge of any previous Special Education services, nor do we have any of her cumulative record on file as of this date.

Rosaland

John 3:16

"For God so loved the world that he gave his one and only Son, that whoever believes in him shall not perish but have eternal life."

Self-statement:

"I rebuke you in the name of Jesus"

336

CATHOLIC DIOCESE OF LANSING

300 WEST OTTAWA STREET
LANSING, MI 48933-1577
PH (517) 484-8870
FAX (517) 484-9060

Case Name: Shannon-Auxier

NO. L05/000102

LACK OF FORM

The following facts are manifest from the evidence presented regarding the attempted marriage outside the Church of Joseph R. Shannon with Barbara A. Auxier:

1   Joseph R. Shannon was obliged to observe the Catholic form of marriage in accordance with Canons 1108 and 1117 of the Code of Canon Law;

2   This attempted marriage was contracted contrary to the prescriptions of the above-mentioned Canons;

3   This marriage was never canonically convalidated in the Catholic Church.

In accordance, therefore, with Article 231 of the Instructions issued on the 15th day of August, 1936, by the Sacred Congregation of the Sacraments, We hereby declare this marriage invalid because of the total lack of the Canonical Form.

Given at the Tribunal of the Diocese of Lansing, on this the 11th day of March, 2005, by virtue of a special mandate of the Ordinary of the Diocese of Lansing.

Ecclesiastical Notary

Rev. Msgr. Raymond Goehring
Judicial Vicar

Submitted by: Mr. William Spencer
Christ the King Church
Ann Arbor, MI 48105

"Hey Joe, am I in the book?"

Matsos, Jana: 145
Matsos, Lou Ann: 144, 145
Matsos, Steve: 46, 52, 53, 55, 56, 62, 70, 71, 103, 144, 145
McCarthy, J.P.: 216
Meeks, Ken: 183
Meeks, Sue: 183
Mehi, Dave: 112, 195
Mehi, Jean: 112, 195
Meyer, Nancy: 165
Meyer, Tim: 70, 71, 78, 79, 90, 91,100, 102, 103, 124, 165, 178, 179
Mohl, Jan: 166
Moody, Troy: 80, 86
Morrisey, Rich: 171
Mosallam, Youssef (Joe-principal): 307
Murdock, Kim: 170

N
Navajar, Dan: 151
Nicholson, Mark: 80, 86

O
Orosz, Antoinette (Toni): 105, 125

P
Patton, Beth: 153
Patton, Paul: 111, 153, 195
Patton, Steve: 119
Penman, Tom: 86, 87, 88
Pore, Kenny: 106, 109
Posada, Al: 78, 79
Powers, Dan: 257

R
Ray, Steve: 261
Reid, Fr. John T.: 10, 11, 23
Roa, Tom: 26, 32, 35, 36, 37, 46, 52, 53, 55, 56, 62, 65, 70
Roy, Tom: 106, 311
Rundel, Bill: 24, 83, 84
Rundel, Gidget: 83, 84

Wyatt, Jack: 102, 126, 127

Y
Yetterock, Dave: 135

Catholic Issues

The following are some of the more important theological/doctrinal issues I wrestled with as I made my way back, after a 35 year hiatus, to the Catholic Church. It would be misleading to say all of my "issues" were/have been resolved, but the fact that I've been back fourteen years (since 2004) argues that indeed some significant resolution has/continues to be made. I am not a theologian, but if these matters interest you there are many wonderful resources available; the Catechism of the Catholic Church has been especially helpful. God be with you as you seek a deeper relationship with the Savior and the truth(s) that will set you free indeed.

Protestants hold the Bible to be the rule of faith – *sola scriptura* (Latin: by Scripture alone), arguing that it contains all of the material one needs for theology and that this material is sufficiently clear with the aid of the Holy Spirit that one does not need, as Catholics contend, apostolic tradition or the Catholic Church's magisterium (teaching authority) to help one understand it. Furthermore, many Protestants would point out that only the Bible is infallible. They acknowledge the place and authority of the Church and even tradition to an extent, after a fashion of sorts, but they remain fundamentally lesser than Scripture because they are not considered infallible, or protected against error in the way that Scripture is.

A brief Catholic rejoinder necessitates saying something not just about the Scriptures themselves, but Tradition and the Magisterium. First, *sola scriptura* is both an illusion and itself unbiblical. The Bible makes no such claim (sole authority) for itself. "Useful," yes. "Profitable," yes (2 Tm 3:16). "Sole," no! Furthermore, you cannot understand one word of the Bible without putting some meaning into that word. The meaning you give it inevitably reflects your background (your tradition). Scripture and your tradition(s) are an integrated fabric; they are inseparable. James Drummey states well the Catholic position on the matter:

> Catholics believe that we get divine
> truth not only from the Bible but also
> from sacred Tradition. This kind of
> Tradition, says the Catechism of the

Catholic Church, comes from the
Apostles and hands on what they
received from Jesus' teaching and
example and what they learned from the
Holy Spirit. It says that the first
generation of Christians did not have a
written New Testament, and that the
New Testament itself demonstrates the
process of living Tradition.[39]

The Traditions Drummey refers to, it should be noted, do not refer to myths and legends, nor transitory customs or practices that may change as circumstances warrant, including but not limited to devotion to saints, styles of priestly dress, liturgical rubrics and so on. What it does refer to are those traditions, e.g. meeting on the first day of the week to celebrate the Eucharist. When Catholics use Tradition with a capital "T," they are using it in reference to the Apostle Paul's admonition to "hold fast to the *traditions* you received from us, either by our word or by letter"
(2 Th 2:15).

Mary Healy's comments in her discussion on Mk 7:1-8 on "tradition" further help crystallize the Catholic position:

This passage regarding "human
tradition" is sometimes cited against the
Catholic understanding of the authority
of Tradition together with Scripture as
the rule of faith. But it is crucial to note
that Jesus is not rejecting tradition per
se, which becomes an important term in
the early Church for the handing on of
the authoritative apostolic teaching (1
Cor 11:2, 23; 2 Thess 3:6). Rather, he is

---

[39]   James J. Drummey, <u>Catholic Replies.</u> Norwood, MA: C.R. Publications, 1995, p. 35.

rejecting *merely human* traditions that are not based in God's word, that in fact negate the intent of God's word. Paul himself exhorted Christians to "stand firm and hold fast to the traditions which you were taught, either by an oral statement or by a letter of ours" (2 Thess 2:15). The apostles handed down what they received from Jesus and the Holy Spirit first in oral form through their teaching and example, and later in the written form of the New Testament (see Catechism, 96-100). Indeed, the formation of the canon of Scripture was itself an exercise of apostolic tradition.

This passage is also sometimes cited in disparaging Catholic liturgical and devotional practices as mere "human traditions." This misunderstanding is due in part to a real problem: religious practice is often superficial and routine among those who have not been adequately evangelized and whose faith fails to impact their choices and behavior in any significant way. Jesus is speaking about an attitude toward God that he saw in the scribes and Pharisees and that can be found among Christians in every church: the tendency to substitute religiosity for genuine obedience to God and his word. What is needed is a personal encounter with Jesus leading to a deep transformation of heart. When that occurs, religious practices come to life and serve their true purpose.[40]

Third, the Magisterium (Latin for "office of teacher"), is the power given by Christ to the Church to instruct authoritatively the revealed truths of Scripture and Tradition. It is through the magisterium of the Church that the concrete action of the Holy Spirit's guidance maintains the historical continuity with Christ, the Head of the Mystical Body. To be sure, all baptized believers, Catholics posit, are anointed and to the extent they willingly yield are guided by the Holy Spirit (1 Jn 2:27). The CCC points out this wonderful gift (magisterium) is the living, teaching office of the Church, whose task it is to give an authentic interpretation of the word of God, whether in its written form (Sacred Scripture), or in the form of Tradition. The Magisterium ensures the Church's fidelity to the teaching of the Apostles in matters of faith and morals (CCC 85, 890, 2033). There are a great host of issues, both moral and faith related, historical and contemporary, that are complex and not for the faint of heart, however well intentioned, to unravel: slavery, stem-cell research, abortion, homosexuality, scriptural inerrancy, revelation, divorce and remarriage, hell and social justice, just for warm-ups. What a rich storehouse the Catholic has been given (Scripture, Tradition, Magisterium), with which to come to grips with these and whatever else confronts the people of God. Spiritual pride, ignorance and laziness too long kept me negligent of these gifts ... no longer.

The second Protestant pillar I mentioned earlier is called Sola Fide (Latin – "faith alone"); this, along with Scripture alone, has for my part given way to the traditional Catholic view. I am mindful that in trying to be brief and not being a theologian, I risk understating both positions, and that the non-Christian observer (some of my Muslim friends for instance), may see this "faith alone versus works issue" as a semantics issue, hair splitting ..."much ado about nothing." I ask your patience. Both the Catechism of the Catholic Church and The Oxford Dictionary of the Christian Church (2nd ed.) have helped me sort through the extensive

---

[40] Mary Healy, *The Gospel of Mark* (Grand Rapids: Baker Academic, 2008), 137, 138

terminology associated with this debate, including terms like justification, sanctification, regeneration, grace, imputation and so on. Thomas Howard's chapter "Are Catholics Saved" in his book *On Being Catholic,* has been most valuable in helping me to come to terms with my "born again" experience of the early seventies as I wrestled for years to make sense of, "hmm, just what did happen to me?" Howard speaks eloquently to this.

If I may digress here for a moment, Catholics would agree that indeed, one must be "born again" (Jn 3:3), and that they are *saved* to the extent that they have and continue to cooperate with the grace of God offered to them as a free gift in Jesus. For the Catholic, this work of redemption (salvation) begins at baptism. In retrospect, I view my "Tent-Born Again" (see Pt. 2) experience as a "reawakening" of sorts (commitment to be a disciple, not just a casual believer in Jesus) of a work begun in me at my Baptism and continued at my reception of the other two sacraments of initiation, Holy Communion (the Lord's Supper) and Confirmation. Why my "reawakening" should have transpired in a Protestant-Pentecostal setting (Tent Revival) and not in a traditional Catholic setting? I can only surmise that God uses who/what is available to Him, and when a heart truly seeks and yearns to meet the risen Lord, He will make a way: sometimes I think God gets a kick out of throwin' us a knuckleball or two, keeps us on our toes, or better, on our knees. I will be forever grateful to/for my brothers and sisters in Christ at Truth and Life Ministry for helping this "backslidden" Catholic get back on track.

Here we go. Sola Fide is historically known as the doctrine of justification by faith alone, which distinguishes most Protestant groups from Catholic and Eastern Christianity, howbeit with slight variations not addressed in detail here. The "faith alone versus works" issue is part of a larger, fundamental query. "What must I do to be saved?" That is, saved from eternal damnation (separation from God). Had you asked me that 20 years ago I would have dutifully replied, "…if you confess with your mouth that Jesus is Lord and believe in your heart that God raised him from the dead, you will be saved" (Rom 10:9); that's it. Indeed, today I might also quote this verse as a starting point and present to the best of my ability a Catholic response to said inquiry. Most of my Protestant friends (Evangelical, Fundamentalists, Calvinists, and Pentecostals) with some variations … sorry, can't speak for the liberals here … would respond to that confession of belief on the Lord Jesus Christ (forgiveness of sins realized by accepting his sacrifice on a cross at Calvary), by faith *alone,* nothing else (some would say baptism is necessary as an act of obedience and public confession, but as a "work" plays no significant role) ... it is, faith alone ... nothing else, there is nothing you can do to earn this gift of grace (unmerited favor). While all Christians would agree good works are important, most Protestants would argue they play no role in your salvation ... it is a free gift secured by your confession of faith (a one time event if you are from the "once saved always saved" eternal security camp); Protestants are divided as to whether a "believer" may lose their salvation.

Catholics, on the other hand, might posit that while its true works in and of themselves don't save us, they are part of the equation; faith is perfected by good works. James' letter in the New Testament addresses this concern, indeed, "...faith was completed by works" (Jas 2:22). While the Catholic Church does not teach justification by faith *alone,* it does teach justification by faith, but as noted above in James (and other biblical texts) faith *alone* is insufficient. Regrettably, many Catholics swing too far in the other direction, believing they can work (earn) their way to heaven. For them, the Final Judgment will be a scale of sorts weighing one's good deeds against one's evil doings ... and well, most people think I'm a swell guy/gal ... and yea, I believe in Jesus (well sort of) ... so as I see it, I'm good to go ... right? Wrong. This is not a sound Catholic approach. The Catholic Church has never taught a doctrine of salvation by works. The Council of Trent (1545-63), in response to challenges from the "Reformation Camp," clarified its position on key issues including justification.[41] In short, justification includes the remission of sins, sanctification, and the renewal of the inner man. But getting back to "sola fide," an informed Catholic might ask their evangelical friend just where do the Scriptures say that we're saved by faith alone? Can you direct me to the passage? They cannot. The only scripture passage where the phrase "faith alone" appears is in Jas 2:24: "See how a person is justified by works and *not by faith alone.*" Is it any wonder Luther was not fond of James'

---

[41]   See Article 2: Grace and Justification in the Catechism of the Catholic Church, 2nd Ed.

epistle. Both Luther and Calvin held that faith was not considered to be genuine at all if it lacked evidence – good "fruit." Catholics would say that these works, while always caused and initiated by God's grace, are part of the overall faith-works equation; two sides of a coin as it were.

An informed Catholic might also point out the many New Testament passages that make it clear our works will be a factor in our judgment and not solely on "faith alone" (Rv 20, 22; Mt 15, 16) for starters. Furthermore, if one is saved by "faith alone," why does 1 Cor 13:13 say that love is greater than faith? It seems like it would be the other way around.

At this stage of my spiritual journey ('18), I'm convinced we are saved by God's grace alone and that we can do nothing apart from God's grace to receive the free gift of salvation. I/We must respond to God's grace. This response is something most Protestants would nod their assent to, but maintain the only response necessary to ensure salvation is an act (confession) of faith. Catholics hold that a response of faith and works is necessary, resting their case in part on: "For in Christ Jesus, neither circumcision nor uncircumcision counts for anything, but only faith working through love" (Gal 5:6). It may be that Catholics and Protestants are closer than many of them/us think on this issue; it is encouraging to witness civil dialogue and debate on these and other matters of faith and morals between Protestants and Catholics. Well then, do we Catholics believe we're saved? Absolutely, as baptized Catholics we are born again (Water and Spirit) and we believe we are saved as Paul declares in Rom 8:24, and that I'm also *being* saved (2 Cor 2:15; Phil 2:12), and I *hope* that I will be saved (Rom 5:9-10). Like Paul the Apostle, I am working out my salvation with fear and trembling (Phil 2:12), with hope filled confidence in the promise of Christ (2 Tm 2:11-13).

Just to heat things up a tad, "So Joe, do you think non-Catholic Christians will be saved? How about non-Christians?" I shall try to speak on behalf of the Catholic tradition – teaching regarding these matters I now embrace. The CC, unlike some denominations, movements and other religions that often take a narrow and limited view of anyone outside their group, recognizes the possibility of salvation for non-Catholics and even non-Christians. The CC recognizes that God works in many and sometimes surprising ways to effect his desire that "… everyone be saved and to come to knowledge of the truth" (1 Tm 2:4).

The Catholic Church holds to two very important tensions in reality:

God's loving mercy and God's revealed Truth. God is merciful, the Church proclaims, and gracious to those who sincerely seek Him, but this grace and mercy is balanced with his revealed truth. While we pray for the salvation of all people and embrace the mandate to" Go forth and proclaim the Gospel (Good News)," and acknowledge the reality that Hell exists for those who willfully reject God, and that those who chose to be separated from God in this life will get what they want in the next ... for eternity. Hence, while the plan of salvation aims for all humanity, it does not guarantee that all will be saved. Still, not all have been the recipient of the Gospel effectively proclaimed. The Catholic Church leaves the final determination to the Lord of how culpable one is concerning their rejection/acceptance of Jesus Christ.

Concerning the Catholic Church's relationship with non-Catholic professing Christians: "The Church knows that she is joined in many ways to the baptized who are honored by the name of Christian, but do not profess the Catholic faith in its entirety or have not preserved unity or communion under the successor of Peter. Those 'who believe in Christ and have been properly baptized are put in a certain, although imperfect, communion with the Catholic Church.' With the Orthodox Churches, this communion is so profound 'that it lacks little to attain the fullness that would permit a common celebration of the Lord's Eucharist." (CCC 838).

Joe, "How does the Catholic Church relate to Jews and Muslims?" With regard to the Jewish people:

> When she delves into her own mystery,
> the Church, the People of God, in the
> New Covenant, discovers her link with
> the Jewish People, "the first to hear the
> Word of God." The Jewish faith, unlike
> other non-Christian religions, is already
> a response to God's revelation in the
> Old Covenant. To the Jews "belong the
> sonship, the glory, the covenants, the
> giving of the law, the worship, and the
> promises; to them belong the patriarchs,
> and of their race, according to the flesh,
> is the Christ"; for the gifts and the call
> of God are irrevocable (CCC 839).

Concerning the Catholic Church's relationship with Muslims:

> The plan of salvation also includes those
> who acknowledge the Creator, in the
> first place amongst whom are the
> Muslims; these profess to hold to the
> faith of Abraham, and together with us
> they adore the one, merciful God,
> mankind's judge on the last day

(CCC 841).

With regard to the Catholic Church's attitude towards Jews and Muslims, it should be noted that this in no wise is meant to minimalize or distort the orthodox Christian view of one God, in three divine persons: Father, Son and Holy Spirit, aka the Blessed Trinity. The Church recognizes a kinship of sorts with Muslims in that we both profess to be monotheists. However, the monotheism of both Judaism and Islam differs significantly from the monotheism of Christianity. Christianity's Trinitarian understanding of the one true God which includes Jesus' divinity is at odds with Judaism and Islam. Indeed, Islam would describe Christianity as a tri-theist religion, rather than a monotheistic religion.

Concerning other religions:

> The Catholic Church recognizes in other
> religions that search, among the
> shadows and images, for the God who is
> unknown yet near since he gives life and
> breath and all things and want all
> women and men to be saved. Thus, the
> Church considers all goodness and truth
> found in these religions as a 'preparation
> for the Gospel and given by him who
> enlightens all men that they may at
> length have life' (CCC 843).

In short, the CC casts a very wide net, trusting in God's mercy, while not denying the sobering reality of divine justice: "How narrow the gate

351

and constricted the road that leads to life. And those who find it are few" (Mt 7:14). It might be well at this point to take a break and ask yourself, "What road am I on?"

Please see *Recommended Reading* for a short-list of books I found helpful while initially wading through these matters.

Nicene Creed

A creed is a summary of the principal truths of the Church/Christianity written as a profession of faith. The two earliest are the Apostles' and Nicene Creeds. The Apostles' Creed is a development of the Apostles' practice (Acts 8:37) of having persons who desired baptism profess their faith. The Nicene Creed ratified at Nicaea c. 325 A.D. by the Church Fathers, is sometimes known as the "Creed of the Trinity." Against the Arians, it proclaimed the eternal divinity of the Son, who is "of the same substance" (consubstantial—*homoousios*) with the Father. Likewise, the Holy Spirit is to be worshipped and glorified with the Father and the Son. The Nicene Creed is the most commonly accepted creed amongst Christians; the creed of the Catholic Mass is the Nicene Creed.

* * * *

I believe in one God,

the Father almighty,

maker of heaven and earth,

and of all things visible and invisible.

I believe in one Lord Jesus Christ,

the Only Begotten Son of God,

born of the Father before all ages.

God from God, Light from Light,

true God from true God,

begotten, not made,

consubstantial with the Father;

through him all things were made.

For us men and for our salvation

he came down from heaven,

and by the Holy Spirit was incarnate

of the Virgin Mary,

and became man.

For our sake he was crucified

under Pontius Pilate,

he suffered death and was buried,

and rose again on the third day

in accordance with the Scriptures.

He ascended into heaven

And is seated at the right hand

of the Father.

He will come again in glory

to judge the living and the dead

and his kingdom will have no end.

I believe in the Holy Spirit,

the Lord, the giver of life,

who proceeds from the Father

and the Son,

who with the Father and the Son

is adored and glorified,

who has spoken through the prophets.

I believe in one, holy, catholic and

apostolic Church.

I confess one Baptism for the

forgiveness of sins

and I look forward to the

resurrection of the dead

and the life of the world to come.

Amen.

Pop Culture References

Leave it to Beaver
(Pages 7, 25, 63, 93)
Ward and June Cleaver were the archetypal suburban c. 50s
parents of Wally and Theodore (the Beav) on the popular baby
boomer TV sitcom *Leave it to Beaver.* Eddie (wise guy) Haskel
and Clarence (Lumpy) Rutherford were also popular characters.

Maynard G. Krebs
(Pages 7, 26)
The goateed beatnik sidekick of the title character, and ultimate slacker,
in the TV sitcom *The Many Loves of Dobie Gillis.* Noted for his "beat"
slang bohemian appearance and aversion to employment, "Work!"

Ozzie and Harriet Nelson
(Pages 7, 93)
An American sitcom – *The Adventures of Ozzie and
Harriet,* aired 1952-'66, and starred the real life Nelson family including
brothers David and teen idol singer – Ricky.

Bonanza
(Pages 19, 233)
The 2nd longest running American Western (behind *Gunsmoke),* 1959-
'73, and is included in TV Guide's 50 Greatest TV Shows of All Time.

Ma and Pa Kettle
(Page 24)
Loveable "hillbilly" couple with 15 kids who move back and forth
(city-country) and their comic "cornball" adventures.
Universal Studios produced a number of Ma and Pa films in the
late '40s and 50s.

Charles Manson
(Pages 30,76,129)
A convicted serial killer whose late 60s "hippie cult" – Manson
Family, were responsible for the August 69 Tate-La Bianca
murders. Manson ordered the killing but was not a participant. His
name became synonymous with pure evil. Manson died in

November of 2017, an inmate at Corcoran State Prison in California.

The Beverly Hillbillies
(Pages 8, 31, 35, 38, 186)
An American situation comedy (1962-'71), about a poor backwoods family from the "hills," who after striking oil, head for "Californee." My favorite character was the brawny, half-witted but likable son of Jed Clampett's cousin Pearl on the popular "boomer" TV show *The Beverly Hillbillies.* Jethro was known for his ability to eat, ciphering ("go-zin-ta's"), and endless unfruitful pursuit of love and a career; the latter including a brain surgeon and double-naught spy, howbeit he only had a sixth grade education. Other popular characters include Granny, Elly-Mae and their beloved hound – Duke.

Bomba
(Page 53)
Based on a series of American boy's adventures books, and brought to the big screen and TV during the 50s/60s. The films starred Johnny Sheffield who was no stranger to jungle flicks; he played Tarzan (Johnny Weissmuller's son) in the popular Tarzan films based on novels by Edgar Rice Burroughs.

Marlin Perkins
(Page 55)
Was a zoologist and host of the famed nature show *Wild Kingdom* that aired 1963-'85.

Ted Nugent
(Page 57)
aka "Uncle Ted" and the Motor City Madman, was lead guitarist of the Amboy Dukes c. 60s before launching a solo career. He is a strong advocate of the right-to-bear-arms, has served on the Board of Directors of the National Rifle Association and is an expert bowman.

Merle Haggard
(Page 60)
is an iconic country music legend whose hits include "Okie From Muskogee" and "Workin' Man Blues."

George Wallace
(Page 60, 74)
was 45th governor of Alabama and ran for the office of president (three times as a democrat and once as an Independent).
A Southern populist he was left confined to a wheelchair following a failed assassination attempt. Towards the end of his life he renounced his earlier segregationist views.

Aunt Bea, Gomer Pyle *(The Andy Griffith Show)*
(Page 61)
The popular "boomer" show aired 1960-'68 producing 249 episodes. Characters included: Sherriff Andy Taylor and his son Opie, Deputy Barney Fife, Aunt Bea, Gomer and Goober Pyle,
Floyd the Barber, Otis the town (Mayberry) drunk, Ernst T. Bass, the Darlings.

Bonnie and Clyde
(Page 62)
Bonnie Parker and Clyde Barrow were well-known outlaws who traveled the Central United States during the Great Depression. They were gunned down in Louisiana by law officers.

Officer Krupke
(Page 63)
In the film/stage production *West Side Story,* the Jets (a New York street gang), mock Officer (police) Krupke, and the kinds of excuses authorities use to rationalize the existence of young street punks.

Tom Bombadil
(Page 67)
A character in Tolkien's *Lord of the Rings* tale who is master of wood, water and hill, eldest of all living creatures in Middle Earth. Interestingly, the one ring of power seems to wield no authority over him. He is a minor but significant character; he and his wife, Goldberry, remain shrouded in mystery.

Timothy Leary *(1920 – '96)*
(Page 67)
Harvard professor, American psychologist and writer best known for his advocacy of psychedelic drugs and popularized hippie mantra: "Turn on, tune in, drop out."

Gomer and Goober
(Pages 61, 71)
See Aunt Bea, pg. 61

Captain Bligh
(Page 78, 145)
The sadistic but capable, captain of the ship Bounty in the historical novel, *Mutiny on the Bounty.*

Jed and Granny
(Page 80)
See "Hillbillies" pg. 8

Dick the Bruiser
(Page 107)
Former NFL player, known for his gravelly-voiced tough guy persona in and out of the wrestling ring. Popular with Detroiters (Big Time Wrestling), primarily during the 60s.

Fonzie
(Page 114)
Loveable greaser biker "the Fonz" on the American sitcom *Happy Days,* a seventies show that took a light-hearted look back at the 1950s.

Ellen White
(Page 114)
Nineteenth century author whose writings are held in high esteem
by Seventh-Day Adventists and cover a wide range of topics
including education, nutrition and prophecy. Her most widely
read/published work is *Steps to Christ.*

Jack Chick
(Page 120)
American publisher, writer and comic book artist of an "extreme"
fundamentalist "christian" bent. Chick paints the Catholic Church
with a very negative and conspiratorial brush.

Keith Green (1953-'82)
(Page 120)
Contemporary Christian artist whose music was a staple on the
Nightlight Show hosted by yours truly. His South California
outreach/ministry took the name *Last Days Ministries.* Regrettably,
several of their publications like *The Catholic Chronicles,* a harsh
critique of Catholicism, lack sound scholarship and are more
divisive and overtly confrontational. Green's widow has since
withdrawn the anti-Catholic tracts her husband distributed before
his death.

Norman Bates:
(Page 121,)
Troubled, dark sinister character played by Anthony Perkins in
three *Psycho* films.

Evel Knievel *(1938-2007)*
(Page 126)
An American entertainer most remembered for his daredevil
motorcycle jumps.

Baretta
(Page 129)
An American detective television series 1975-'78 starring Robert
Blake in the title role. A streetwise pimp, Rooster, was Tony
Baretta's chief informant.

Roy Rogers *(1911-'98)*
(Page 129)
An American singer ("Happy Trails") and Cowboy actor whose wholesome image and horse – Trigger, graced many a kid's lunchbox back in the day.

Darth Vader
(Page129)
One of the main antagonists in the popular *Star Wars* saga.

Gollum aka Smeagol
(Pages 133, 158, 187)
Originally a hobbit who will become a tragic victim of the one ring (Sauron's) and who will actually possess it for 500 years until it (the precious), mysteriously comes to be found, innocently enough by Bilbo Bagins, central character of Tolkein's *The Hobbit.*
The desire to regain the ring at any cost will be Gollum's (and others) undoing, until it – the ring, is destroyed in the fires of Mt. Doom.

Red Skelton *(1913-'97)*
(Page 143)
American icon comedian (clown), noted for his clean, tasteful humor.

Goose Lake *(Page 146)*
International Music Festival (near Jackson, MI) held Aug. 7-9, 1970. Performers included Jethro Tull, Mountain, Savage Grace, SRC and more.

Vavoom
(Page 148)
A character from the *Felix the Cat* cartoon. He was small, wore a jacket with a hood, and when he yelled "Vavoom," everything (trees, mountains, etc.) in his path would be leveled.

Sea Hunt
(Page 156)
American adventure television series (1958-'61) starring Lloyd Bridges as free-lance scuba diver Mike Nelson.

Neil Sedaka
(Page 157)
An American pop/rock singer, pianist and composer. Hits included "Calendar Girl" 1961, and "Breaking Up Is Hard To Do" 1962.

Calvary Chapel
(Page 163)
An evangelical association of Christian churches born from Chuck Smith's Calvary Chapel during the late 60s and early 70s in Southern California. They currently present themselves as a "fellowship of churches" rather than as a denomination. During the 1970s they were the model for many Jesus Movement churches/ fellowships, and their encouragement of contemporary Christian music attracted many young people who'd become disenchanted with the "Peace Movement" and who now embraced the Prince of Peace – Jesus.

Adam's Apple *(Ft. Wayne, IN)* and Salt Company *(Detroit, MI)*
(Page 163)
Jesus Movement outreaches of the 70s offering contemporary Christian music as a staple.

Richard Simmons
(Page 171)
An American fitness personality who promotes weight loss programs including his *Sweatin' to the Oldies* aerobic videos.

Bob Seger
(Page 178, 317)
American rock and roll singer-songwriter, guitarist and pianist who gained national fame with his 70s/80s Silver Bullet Band. During the 60s, Seeger enjoyed Midwest and especially southwest Michigan, where he hails from, popularity. He was inducted into the Rock and Roll Hall of Fame in 2004. Biggest hit – "Old Time Rock and Roll."

Jimmy Buffet
(Page 178)
An American singer/songwriter best known for music with an "island escapism" vibe. His fans are known as "parrot-heads." His best known song – "Margaritaville."

Honeymooners
(Page 188)
An American situation comedy starring Jackie Gleason as Ralph Kramden, Art Carney, as his buddy – Ed Norton, Joyce Randolph as Trixi Norton, and Audrey Meadows as Alice Kramden. A humorous, warm, always end on a positive note episodes, detailing the day-to-day happenings surrounding two married couples, struggling to "get-by" in gritty, non-idyllic apartment housing in rundown Brooklyn.

Reggie Jackson *(aka Mr. October)*
(Page 189)
Played for four different major league baseball teams (right fielder) 1967-'87. Famed for his post season batting heroics including towering home runs (563).

James *(Jimmy)* Cagney *(1899- '86)*
(Page 190)
An American stage/screen actor best remembered for his tough guy roles such as *Angels With Dirty Faces*, which also starred Pat O'Brien as Fr. Jerry, the Dead End Kids and Humphrey Bogart. Ironically, Cagney won a Best Actor Oscar in 1946 portraying legendary Broadway musical writer, producer, dancer, George M. Cohan in the film *Yankee Doodle Dandy*.

Jack Van Impe
(Page 213)
A televangelist who hosts, along with his wife Rexella, a weekly TV program – *Jack Van Impe Presents.* Jack is known as the "Walking Bible" due to his extensive memorization of Bible passages. He is noted for his controversial End Times predictions.

Piccadilly Lane *(Page 220)*
A major street in central London running from Hyde Park Corner in the west to Piccadilly Circus in the east.

Sanford and Son
(Pages 143, 221)
An American sitcom comedy airing 1972-'77, and included in
Time magazines list of the "100 Best TV Shows of All Time."
Widower Fred Sanford, played by Redd Foxx, and his son
Lamont, are junk dealers in the Watts neighborhood of South
Central Los Angeles, CA.

Lady of Shallot
(Page 231)
A tragic young female character, based on the Arthurian legend of
Elaine of Astolat, who lives in an island castle on a river which
flows to Camelot. She suffers from a curse and may only view the
world as reflected by a mirror.

Rawhide
(Page 233)
An American Western series that aired for eight seasons (1959-
'66), and starred Clint Eastwood.

Alfred Hitchcock *(1899-1990)*
(Page 237)
An English film director and producer who enjoyed phenomenal
success in Hollywood throughout the 40s, 50s and 60s. Two of his
more memorable suspense thriller films are *Psycho* (1960) and
The Birds (1963).

Lolita
(Page 237)
A novel (film) about a middle-aged literature professor who is
obsessed with his twelve year old stepdaughter with whom he
becomes sexually involved. In pop culture, the name "Lolita"
has come to mean a sexually precocious girl.

Gomez Adams
(Page 241)
The fictional patriarch of popular "boomer" TV show –
The Addams Family.

Fay Wray *(1907-2004)*
(Page 244)
A Canadian-American actress most noted for playing the female
lead in the classic film – *King Kong* (1933).

Styme
(Page 11, 244)
A loveable *Our Gang (*aka *Little Rascals)* character often depicted
wearing a black derby (hat). His "rascal" character was replaced
by another popular Afro-American character – Buckwheat.

Margaritaville
(Page 244)
See Jimmy Buffet pg.164

Jane Hathaway
(Page 253)
The love starved, bird-watching perennial "plain Jane" spinster and
secretary to bank president Milburn Drysdale on *The Beverly
Hillbillies* (see "Hillbillies" pg. 16)

West Side Story
(Page 278, 288)
See Officer Krupke pg. 71

Chambers Brothers
(Page 287)
A soul rock group best known for their '68 hit record "Time Has
Come Today."

Perry Como *(1912-2001)*
(Page 287)
An American singer and television personality popular with World
War II and later folks who liked his smooth, easy listening vibe.
His tune "Catch a Falling Star" (1957) captures that feeling.

Rama Lama Ding Dong
(Page 287)
A popular doo-wop tune (his girl's name is Rama Lama Ding
Dong) recorded by the Edsels in 1957.

Methuselah
(Page 297)
The oldest person mentioned in the Bible (Old Testament); 969 years ... not bad!

Billy Jack
(Page 299)
A fictional "half breed" American Cherokee Indian and Green Beret Vietnam War Vet portrayed by Tom Laughlin in several late 60s early 70s films. Billy typically protects the weak (women, hippies, etc) from bikers, rednecks, and punks in general.

Recommended Readings

The following are a short list of books that I found useful in discerning my return to and subsequent understanding of the Catholic Church. In addition, I have included books on other areas of interest to which I have referred in my story, including "the Rapture," demon possession, heresy, atheism, homosexuality, relativism-natural law, Right to Life Issues, Church History, Protestantism, Reformation, and Christian/Muslim relations.

Catholicism in General

Akin, Jimmy, *A Daily Defense: 365 Days (Plus One) To Becoming a Better Apologist*, Catholic Answers Press, 2016.

Horn, Trent, *Why We're Catholic: Our Reasons for Faith, Hope, and Love*, Catholic Answers Press, 2017.

Howard, Thomas, *On Being Catholic,* San Francisco: Ignatius Press, 1997.

Howard, *The Night Is Far Spent: A Treasury of Thomas Howard,* San Francisco: Ignatius Press, 2007.

Keating, Karl, *Catholicism and Fundamentalism: The Attack on "Romanism" by "Bible Christians,"* San Francisco: Ignatius Press, 1988.

Kresta, Al, *Why Do Catholics Genuflect? And Answers to Other Puzzling Questions About the Catholic Church*, Ann Arbor: Servant Press, 2001.

Dangers to the Faith: Recognizing Catholicism's 21ˢᵗ-Century Opponents.

Huntington, IN: Our Sunday Visitor, 2013.

Newman, John H., *An Essay on the Development of Christian Doctrine*, London: Aeterna Press, 2014.

Roberts, Brian F., *Dear Brother*: Brian Forrest Roberts, 2005.

Rose, Devon, *Navigating the Tiber*, Catholic Answers Press, 2016.

Stark, Rodney, *Bearing False Witness: Debunking Centuries of Anti-Catholic History*, West Conshohocken, PA: Templeton Press, 2016.

Woods, Thomas E., *How the Catholic Church Built Western Civilization,* Washington DC: Regenery, 2005.

The Mass

Hahn, Scott, *The Lamb's Supper: The Mass as Heaven on Earth,* New York: Doubleday,

1999.

The End Times/Rapture/Parousia

Kyle, Richard, *The Last Days Are Here Again: A History of the End Times,* Grand Rapids: Baker, 1998.

Kyriakos, Mark, *As We Await the Blessed Hope: A Catholic Study of the End Times*, Bloomington, IN: iUniverse, 2015.

Thigpen, Paul, *The Rapture Trap: A Catholic Response to "End Times" Fever,* West Chester, PA: Ascension Press, 2001.

Miscellaneous

Alfred, Andrea J., and Andrew Holt, eds. *Seven Myths of the Crusades.* Indianapolis, IN: Hackett Publishing, 2015.

Ames, Christine, C. *Medieval Heresies: Christianity, Judaism, Islam*, Cambridge University Press, 2015.

Augros, Michael. *Who Designed the Designer? A Rediscovered Path to God's Existence*, San Francisco: Ignatius Press, 2015.

Baglio, Matt. *The Rite: The Making of a Modern Exorcist,* Doubleday, 2009.

Beaumont, Douglas, M. ed. *Evangelical Exodus: Evangelical Seminarians and Their Paths to Rome*, San Francisco: Ignatius Press, 2016.

Belloc, Hilaire and Ousaaani, Gabriel, *Moslems: Their Beliefs, Practices and Politics*, Roger A. McCaffrey Publishing, 2002.

Bennett, Rod. *The Apostasy That Wasn't: The Extraordinary Story of the Unbreakable Early Church*, Catholic Answers Press, 2015.

Darwish, Ninie. *Wholly Different: Why I Chose Biblical Values Over Islamic Values*, Regenery Faith, 2017.

Fanzaga, Livio, *The Deceiver: Our Daily Struggle With Satan*, Fort Collins, CO: Roman Catholic Books, 2000.

Fortea, Jose A., *Interview with an Exorcist,* West Chester, PA: Ascension Press, 2006.

Geisler, Norman L, and Abdul Saleeb, *Answering Islam: The Crescent in Light of the Cross,* Grand Rapids, MI: Baker, 2002.

Grant, George. *Grand Illusions: The Legacy of Planned Parenthood*, Brentwood, TN: Wolgemuth & Hyatt, 1988.

Gregory, Brad, S., *Rebel in the Ranks: Martin Luther, the Reformation, and the Conflicts That Continue to Shape Our World*, New York, NY, Harper Collins, 2017.

Harvey, John F., O.S.F.S.., *Homosexuality and the Catholic Church: Clear Answers to Difficult Questions*, West Chester, PA: Ascension Press, 2007.

Hoeberichts, J., *Francis and Islam,* Franciscan Press, 1997.

Howard, Thomas. *Evangelical Is Not Enough: Worship of God in Liturgy and Sacrament,* San Francisco: Ignatius Press, 1984.

Kaczor, Christopher. *The Seven Big Myths about the Catholic Church*, San Francisco: Ignatius Press, 2012.

Kreeft, Peter. *Practical Theology: Spiritual Direction from Saint Thomas Aquinas,*   San Francisco, Ignatius Press, 2014.

Kuby, Gabriele. *The Global Sexual Revolution: Destruction of Freedom in the Name of Freedom*, Kettering, OH: Angelico Press, 2015.

Qureshi, Nabeel. *Seeking Allah, Finding Jesus: A Devout Muslim Encounters Christianity*, Grand Rapids: Zondervan, 2014.

Ray, Stephen, K., *Crossing the Tiber: Evangelical Protestants Discover the Historical Church*, San Francisco: Ignatius Press, 1997.

Rice, Charles. *50 Questions on the Natural Law: What It Is & Why We Need* It, San Francisco: Ignatius Press, 1999.

Schoeman, Roy H., *Salvation Is from the Jews: The Role of Judaism in Salvation History from Abraham to the Second Coming,* San Francisco: Ignatius Press, 2003.

Sri, Edward. *Who am I to Judge: Responding to Relativism with Logic and Love*, San Francisco: Ignatius Press, 2016.

Wiker, Benjamin. *The Reformation 500 Years Later: 12 Things You Need to Know*, Washington DC, Regnery History, 2017.

Williamson, Peter S., *Revelation (Catholic Commentary on Sacred Scripture)*, Grand Rapids: Baker Academic, 2015.

Catechism of the Catholic Church: 2nd Edition, 1994.

paintings and drawings make extraordinary gifts!

to see more go to:

http://tommyroy7.wixsite.com/portfolio

or

email tom directly to discuss your project:

tommyroy@comcast.net

What's Joe up to these days? Go to
JoeShannonsBack.com

Choose LIFE

YOU made all the Delicate, INNER PARTS of **MY BODY** & knit *me together* in my Mother's **Womb.** **Thank You** for making me so wonderfully complex! Your workmanship is *Marvelous* how well I know it. You *watched me* as I was BEING FORMED in UTTER SECLUSION, as I was *Woven* Together IN THE dark of the **womb.** **YOU** saw *me* before I was born.

Psalm 139:13–16